Italian Feminist Thought

Italian Feminist Thought

A Reader

Edited by

Paola Bono and Sandra Kemp

Basil Blackwell

Introduction, editorial matter and organization
Copyright © Paola Bono and Sandra Kemp 1991

First published 1991

Basil Blackwell Ltd
108 Cowley Road, Oxford, OX4 1JF, UK

Basil Blackwell, Inc.
3 Cambridge Center
Cambridge, Masschusetts 02142, USA

British Library Cataloguing in Publication Data

A CIP catalogue record for this book is available from the British Library.

Library of Congress Cataloging in Publication Data

Italian feminist thought: a reader/edited by Paola Bono and Sandra Kemp.
    p.   cm.
Includes bibliographical references and index.
ISBN 0–631–17115–0
ISBN 0–631–17116–9 (pbk.)
1. Feminism—Italy.   2. Women's rights—Italy.   3. Women in politics–Italy.
I. Bono, Paola.   II. Kemp, Sandra.
HQ1642.176 1991
305.42′O945—dc20
                                                  90–746
                                                    CIP

Typeset in 11 on 12½ pt Plantin
by Wearside Tradespools, Fulwell, Sunderland
Printed in Great Britain by T.J. Press Ltd., Padstow, Cornwall

In memory of
Cristina Bertea
and
Gillian Skirrow

Contents

Contents

Contents

Acknowledgements

'Manifesto', 'Sessualità femminile e aborto', excerpts from 'Sputiamo su Hegel', in Carla Lonzi 1979: *Sputiamo su Hegel. La donna clitoridea e la donna vaginale, e altri scritti*. Milan, Scritti di Rivolta Femminile; 'Manifesto: io dico io', in Marta Lonzi, Anna Jaquinta and Carla Lonzi (eds) 1978: *La presenza dell'uomo nel femminismo*. Milan, Scritti Rivolta Femminile. Reprinted by permission of Rivolta Femminile.

Two *volantini* on prostitution, 'Intervento' at a meeting on prostitution, 'Intervento' at a meeting on salary for housewives, 'Sessualità maschile e perversione', in Colletivo di Via Pompeo Magno (ed.) 1976: *Donnità. Cronache del Movimento Femminista Romano*. Rome, Centro di documentazione del Movimento Femminista Romano (Via Pompeo Magno). Reprinted by permission of the Movimento Femminista Romano.

Elisabetta Rasy, 'Corteo di notte', in Rasy 1978: *La lingua della nutrice*. Rome, Edizioni delle Donne. Reprinted by permission of the author.

'Forse non so ancora lottare per la libertà ma voglio l'abolizione di un secolare diritto: quello di essere imbecille', *Differenze*, 4 (1977); 'Sessualità e denaro', 'Per un progetto', *Differenze*, 10 (1979); Roberta Tatafiore, 'Uno squardo "fuori" la lotta armata', *Differenze*, special issue on politics (1979); 'Le paure delle donne lesbiche', 'Carta dei diritti delle donne lesbiche', *Differenze*, 12 (1982). Reprinted by permission of the groups which edited these issues of *Differenze* and of the authors.

Lea Melandri, 'Dora, Freud, e la violenza', in Melandra 1977: *L'infamia originaria*. Milan, L'erba voglio. Reprinted by permission of the author and of L'erba voglio.

'Più donne che uomini', *Sottosopra* (January 1983); Lia Cigarini, 'La separazione femminile', *Sottosopra* (June 1987). Reprinted by permission of the Libreria delle Donne di Milano and the authors.

Luisa Muraro, 'Legame e Libertà', *Azimut*, 16 (1985). Reprinted by permission of the author.

'Cultura e culture nei Centri delle donne', and Adriana Cavarero, 'Diotima: la necessità del pensiero sessuato', in 1988: *Le donne al Centro. Politica e cultura delle donne negli anni '80*. Rome, Utopia; 'Progetti, progettualità', *DWF*, 2 (1986); 'Appartenenza', *DWF*, 4 (1986); 'Responsabilità politica', *DWF*, 5/6 (1988); 'Forme della politica', *DWF*, 7 (1988). Reprinted by permission of Utopia, Adriana Cavarero and *DWF*.

Alessandra Bocchetti, 'L'indecente differenza', in Bocchetti 1982: *Programma 1982–83*. Rome, Edizioni Centro Culturale V. Woolf. Reprinted by permission of the author.

Bianca Pomeranzi, 'Differenza lesbica e lesbofemminismo', *Memoria*, 13 (1985); excerpts from Ida Dominijanni, 'Radicalità e ascetismo', *Memoria*, 19/20 (1987). Reprinted by permission of *Memoria* and the authors.

'Più silenzi che bugie', in Coordinamento Lesbiche Italiane (ed.), 1983: *Il nostro mondo comune*. Rome, Felina; 'Suggestioni dalla Irigaray', in *Sono l'unica lesbica al mondo. Ricerca lesbica: realtà, etica e politica dei rapporti tra donne*. Proceedings of the Fourth Lesbian Conference held in Rome, 1–3 November 1985 (Rome, CLI, 1988). Reprinted by permission of the CLI (Coordinamento Lesbiche Italiane).

'Spunti', statement about the conference 'Per una nuova cultura della sessualità' held in Rome, 23–5 September 1983, organized by the Coordinamento Nazionale delle Donne per i Consultori. Reprinted by permission of the Coordinamento Nazionale delle Donne per i Consultori.

'Manifesto', September 1978, and 'Documento', March/April 1979, by the MLD (Movimento di Liberazione della Donna). Reprinted by permission of the MLD (Movimento di Liberazione della Donna).

Lidia Campagnano, 'Oggi un movimento di donne democratiche . . .', *il manifesto* (17 October 1979); Vania Chiurlotto, 'Assemblee di donne come ai tempi d'oro . . .', *il manifesto* (9 November 1979); Rossana Rossanda, 'Lo stupro è un reato odioso . . .', *il manifesto* (11 November 1979); Lea Melandri, 'Un'acquisizione importante . . .', and Luisa Muraro, 'Passare dall'autorità, personale . . .', *il manifesto* (18 November 1979); Collettivo COM-Nuovi, Tempi, 'Abbiamo sostenuto l'iniziativa . . .', *il manifesto* (9 December 1979); Maria Luisa Boccia, 'La non violabilità anche sessuale . . .', *il manifesto* (20 December 1979); Maria Grazia Campari et alie, 'L'affidamento raggiunge il palazzo', *il manifesto* (29 March 1985); Lidia Menapace, 'Non ci piace la leva grigio-rosa', *il manifesto* (4 November 1986); Alessandra Bocchetti, 'A chi tocca pulire il mondo?', *il manifesto* (23 May 1986); Lidia Campagnano, 'La paura di vivere del bambino senza sessi', *il manifesto* (24 May 1986); Lea Melandri, 'Il femminile uno e plurale', *il Manifesto* (25 May 1986); Piera Bosotti et alie 'Eppure le donne amano la libertà', *il manifesto* (29 May 1986). Reprinted by permission of *il manifesto* and the authors.

Anna Maria Mori, 'Premessa', in Mori 1978: *Il silenzio delle donne e il caso Moro*. Cosenza, Lerici. Reprinted by permission of the author.

'Vogliamo sapere tutto, poi valutiamo noi (comunicato di "Prima Linea")', *Quotidiano Donna* (12 February 1979); 'La mia arma è il separatismo', 'Non violenta. Ma fino a quando?', 'Ci vuole un grande amore per poter capire', 'Da sempre camminiamo su strade diverse', and 'Quel comunicato l'abbiamo letto e riletto', *Quotidiano Donna* (3 March 1979). Reprinted by permission of *Quotidiano Donna*.

'Spinte dalla violenza dei desideri . . .', in Ida Farè and Franca Spirito (eds) 1979: *Mara e le altre*. Milan, Feltrinelli. Reprinted by permission of the editors.

Edda Billi, 'Viva l'utopia', and Marlena Fabris, 'Fuori dalla preistoria violenta', *Noi Donne*, supplement (22 January 1982). Reprinted by permission of *Noi Donne*.

Elena Marinucci, 'Ma è solo il primo passo', *Avanti!* (25 October 1986). Reprinted by permission of the author.

Letizia Paolozzi, 'Un altro sabato, ma di sole donne', *L'Unità* (20 May 1986); Franca Chiaromonte, 'Perché questo 24 maggio sarà al femminile', *L'Unità* (22 May 1986). Reprinted by permission of *L'Unità* and the authors.

Excerpts from Collettivo Internazionale Femminista (ed.) 1975: *Le operarie della casa*. Venice–Padova, Marsilio. Reprinted by permission of Marsilio.

Excerpts from: 'Fuor di polemica, le ragioni di un dibattito'; Carla Casalini, 'Un ruolo impagabile', and Anna Ciaperoni, 'E se fossero tutte spine?', in *Orsa Minore*, 6 (1982). Reprinted by permission of *Orsa Minore* and the authors.

Cartoons: Eleonora Chiti, 'La Demagistris viene trasportata...', *Aspirina*, 5 (1988), and 'Sì sono sfinita...', *Aspirina*, supplement *Noi Donne*; Patrizia Carra, 'La donna non è un soggetto...', *Aspirina*, 1 (1987); 'Mamma! Il fratellino...', *Aspirina*, 2 (1988); 'Da grande sarò potente...', *Aspirina*, 3 (1988); 'Tutti i partiti sono maschi...', *Aspirina*, supplement *Noi Donne*. Reprinted by permission of the authors.

Maria Luisa Boccia, 'La ricerca della differenza', in *Il genere della rappresentanza*, supplement to *Democrazine diritto*, 1, Jan–Feb 1988. Reprinted by permission of the author.

By its very nature, this book is the result of the combined good will and effort of many people; we are grateful to everyone who has contributed:

to the Italian women's groups, the publications and publishing houses mentioned below, who have given us permission to reprint the pieces of which they hold the copyright;
to the translators, also mentioned below – and in particular to Sharon Wood, whose professional and moral support has been essential;
to Alessandra Mecozzi, who wrote her survey of women and trade unions in Italy especially for this book;
to our editor, Simon Prosser, who has been helpful and understanding throughout; to our copy-editor, Fiona Sewell, whose revisions were essential; and to Pat Devlin for her patience and administrative efficiency at the Glasgow end;

to Carla Accardi, for letting us use her 'Matter with Greys' for the cover;

to Serena Anderlini, Susan Bassnett, Drummond Bone, Rosi Braidotti, Marina Camboni, Ann Caesar, Vania Chiurlotto, Annamaria Crispino, Richard Cronin, Robert Cummings, Teresa De Lauretis, Ida Dominijanni, Rina Macrelli and Toril Moi, who have provided comments and suggestions for the introduction;

to Stefania Zambardino for her help in assembling and checking the data for the bibliographical essay on Italian feminist journals;

to Simonetta Spinelli, who researched the bibliography and prepared the chronological tables.

In the end, however, we take full responsibility for the final result, for the inevitably subjective view of Italian feminism which the selection of pieces, the headnotes and the introduction combine to give.

Brillat-Savarin affirmed in his *Physiologie du Gout*: 'Dis-moi ce que tu manges, et je te dirai ce que tu es.' We owe our final acknowledgement to the restaurant Le Grotte di Pompeo. Its fabulous food and friendly atmosphere have often helped us to relax after a hard day's work, and to plan for the next.

Paola Bono
Sandra Kemp

Translators

Our thanks to the translators as follows:

Paola Bono
'The need for a sexed thought', by Adriana Cavarero.

Rosalind Delmar
'More Women than Men.'

Giuliana De Novalis
'We are working on a different political approach.'

Giuliana Jobbi
'Culture/Cultures in the Women's Centres'; 'Female sexuality and abortion'; 'A letter to the local government of Lazio by the Coordinamento Consultori'; 'Women assembling as in the golden days', by Vania Chiurlotto; 'Statement by the Movimento Femminista Romano, at a Meeting with Lotta Femminista'; 'Documents and writings by Lotta Femminista'; 'A priceless role', by Carla Casalini; 'Without polemics, the reasons for a debate'; 'What if there were only thorns?', by Anna Ciaperoni; 'My weapon is separatism'.

Geraldine Muirhead
'A survey', by Alessandra Mecozzi.

Veronica Newman
'Manifesto' (Demau); 'Manifesto' (Rivolta Femminile); 'Let's Spit on Hegel'; 'I Say I'; 'On Prostitution: Two broadsheets and a statement'; 'Male Sexuality – Perversion'; 'Perhaps I can't fight for freedom yet';

'Sexuality and money'; 'Towards a project'; 'Dora, Freud and Violence', by Lea Melandri.

Antonella Regi
'Long live utopia'; 'Moving out of a violent prehistory'; 'Draft of a law on military service for women'; 'Call for a demonstration'; 'Another demonstration about Chernobyl – composed solely of women'; 'Why the demonstration will be women-only'; 'Whose job is it to clean the world?'; 'The "feminine": singular and plural'; 'Yet women love freedom'; 'A broadsheet from *Vivere Lesbica*; 'Slogans for the demonstration'.

Sharon Wood
'Marching in the night'; 'Practice of the Unconscious and the women's movement'; 'Bonding and freedom'; '"Entrustment" enters the palace'; 'Review of *Radicality and Asceticism*'; 'The indecent difference'; 'Lesbian difference and lesbofeminism'; 'The fears of lesbian women'; 'A charter of rights'; 'More silences than lies'; 'Suggestions – from Irigaray'; 'Belonging/pertaining'; Projects/projectuality; 'Political responsibility'; 'Forms of politics'; 'Programme of the C.R.A.C.'; 'Manifesto and document of the MLD'; 'Final statement from the conference "For a new culture of sexuality" by the Coordinamento Consultori'; 'Today, a movement of democratic women'; 'Rape is a hideous crime'; 'An important acquisition'; 'Moving on from personal authority'; 'We have supported the drafting of this law'; 'COM-Tempi Nuovi'; 'Non-violability in the sexual domain'; 'Parliamentary report on the proposal for a law of popular initiative'; 'Introduction' (Salaries); 'Preface, from *Il silenzio delle donne e i caso Moro*'; 'Broadsheet by *Prima Linea*'; 'We have read and re-read that broadsheet'; 'Non-violent, but for how long'; 'A great love is needed in order to understand'; 'We have always walked along different paths'; 'Pushed by the violence of our desires'; 'A look "outside" the armed struggle'; 'It's only the first step towards real parity'; 'We don't like rose-tinted uniforms'; 'Excerpts from the Communist women's charter'; 'Female "separateness"'; 'The gender of representation'; Chronology.

Introduction: Coming from the South

DonnaWomanFemme is the name of one of the leading feminist journals in Rome. We are now familiar with Woman and Femme, less so with Donna. This is a book about Italian feminism. It is an 'unexpected subject'.

Within the specific context of the Italian women's movement, the 'unexpected subject' is both the female subject, and a new female cogito: the rethinking of sexual difference within a dual conception of being. Dual subjectivity admits the partiality of both male and female positions (that the world must accept man's difference as well as woman's) and provides a radical starting point for the Italian feminist theory.

In the larger context of other national feminisms, however, the Italian 'subject' is 'unexpected' because it is more or less unknown. It is striking how quickly some feminist theory has been canonized, and how the rest, the Italian included, has fallen victim to a kind of cultural imperialism.

In her recent book *Subject to Change*, Nancy Miller highlights a general current recognition of the need for 'a more international geo-graphics in feminist writing' (N. Miller 1988: 17). She argues that 'as feminist critics we do ourselves in by playing the old Franco-American game of binary oppositions (theory and empiricism, indifference and identity) as though it were the only game in town . . . as though there weren't also Italians, for instance'. Her example, as she herself remarks, is arbitrary – 'Italians' because here the reference is to Teresa de Lauretis and Rosi Braidotti, influential Italian-born theorists who live and work outside Italy. But what of Canadians, Spaniards, Germans, Asians?

Our book, along with others in this series,[1] signals a change of climate, responding to the need to destabilize that binary logic which, challenged by contemporary philosophical thought and by feminist theory itself, has ironically crept in again. Deleuze's illustration of the functioning of this binary machine through a politico-geographical metaphor is particularly apt here. Taking the west and the east as the poles of the opposition, destabilizing forces will appear on the north–south axis; a Palestinian, a 'green' ecologist, a feminist. There will always be someone coming from the outside to disrupt the symmetry of polarity: there will always be 'someone coming from the south' (Deleuze and Parnet, 1977). Italian feminism, along with other feminisms, all, as it were, 'coming from the south', may help destabilize the old game of labelling feminist theory according to stereotyped dichotomies, and begin a more productive exchange.

The influence of French, British and American feminist thought can be seen at work in the shaping of a specifically 'Italian' form of feminism, but it nevertheless remains distinctively Italian.[2]

Any kind of organization of such a diversity of material is necessarily somewhat arbitrary. We have chosen to divide the book into two sections, according to what we see as two crucial characteristics of Italian 'feminism': first, the presence all over Italy of many groups (with frequently more than one group in the same city), the attempt to create nationwide networks, and the pluralism of the groups, the conflict and dialogue between them; and second, the importance of politics for Italian feminism, reflecting the strongly political character of Italian society in general.

THE CULTURES OF ITALIAN FEMINISM

By comparison with French, British and American feminism, the most surprising feature of Italian feminism is its non-institutional basis.

To look first at what we are most familiar with: all current forms of feminism grew out of the women's movements and consciousness-raising groups of the 1960s, and were initially based occupationally in publishing and journalism, and politically in Marxism.[3] In Italy, the impact of nineteenth-century socialist feminists, like Anna Maria Mozzoni, or of Communist activists in the early twentieth century, like Teresa Noce, was crucial.[4] It is also important not to neglect other earlier contributions; for example, suffragette and trade union movements. It is only recently in France, Britain and America that the universities and the institutions of psychoanalysis have become the favoured areas of debate.

Italian feminism helps bridge an uncomfortable inconsistency between feminism's theoretical refusal to countenance 'master narratives' and the political ascendancy of certain canonical texts in France, Britain and America, where the growth of feminist theory was marked by the appearance of what rapidly become classic feminist texts. (In Britain, for example, in the 1970s, writing by Millet, Greer and Mitchell).[5] One of the characteristic strengths of feminist theory remains the refusal of master narratives. What the various anthologies available today demonstrate, as Showalter points out in the case of her own, is that the single contributions 'are not pieces in a single huge critical system, but a variety of positions and strategies engaged in a vigorous internal debate' (Showalter 1986: 4). The interdisciplinary nature of feminist exchange is also characteristic. The theory crosses over the usual subject-divides (literature, history, philosophy, psychology, anthropology and so on).

In the past decade, feminist theory has also had a strong textual base in literature by women. As Jacobus notes, we have recently seen here a shift from writer to reader: 'the double question of reading woman (reading) or woman reading (woman)' (Jacobus 1986: 5). There has also been increasing exchange between the French, the British and the Americans. At the same time, however, feminists have expressed concern that the strongly institutionalized bases of feminist theorists' work have resulted in a rift between the theoretical and the personal, writing and life. This kind of feminism, so the argument goes, has no relevance or application outside the academy. In addition to this, it is predominantly western and motivated by white and/or heterosexual interests. Another related anxiety is that the urgent desire to define the precise nature of a feminist aesthetic, and to rethink systems of thought radically, has resulted in empty jargon, in new clichés and stock phrases.

Italian feminism bridges the gap between institutional, theoretical feminism and active/political feminism. Until now, there have been no 'women's studies' (in the sense of degree courses, departments, chairs or lectureships) in Italian universities. There are, of course, women in academia, many of whom have an interest in studying or teaching other women's work, or in bringing their lives as women to bear upon their subject disciplines and their modes of research. Instead of trying to institutionalize these issues, however, they manage to carve out a space in the curriculum *as it is*. In this respect they infiltrate and exploit the grey areas of academic organization.

In Italy, these women would not necessarily call themselves 'feminists' as in Britain and the States. But their links with the women's movement have in various ways informed and shaped their individual research. Conversely, their individual research has been used by the women's movement in the sociopolitical arena. In most cases, however, women have involved themselves in the feminist movement independently of their scholarly work (i.e. their involvement in, and their continuing commitment to the women's movement is as women, not as academics). Participation in the political initiatives of the women's movement has involved justifying their standing, and their involvement in 'male' culture. They have only slowly reached a stage where their competence as scholars is accepted and sought after. They have been intellectual commuters: travelling in and out of those domains of culture and politics where they mixed with men and became part of 'the system'. (This is true both for academics and for women active in political parties.) In the separatist world of feminism they were regarded with suspicion. Paradoxically, they had to struggle for legitimacy both in the women's movement and in academia. Being feminists meant questioning their whole activity as academics, questioning the importance of research and theorizing: 'How can my experience be of use for the women's movement? How should I change my skills? And how can I question the tenets of my discipline, its epistemology? Isn't participation in a male-dominated structure a kind of complicity?' And so on.

Italian academic organization may be susceptible to 'infiltration' by new themes and new methods, but it is hostile to structural change. Hence, the institutionalization of women's studies seemed, and still seems, neither likely nor feasible. Instead, there remains a pressing need for structures outside the academy in which to carry on and circulate research – 'circulate' in the senses both of making it available to other women, and of learning from and together with other women what women's culture might mean.

Hence the creation of autonomous women's cultural centres and of feminist journals and magazines, most of which are self-funded and self-distributed, and none of which is directly connected with the institutions of academia. The section on I Centri Culturale delle Donne in part I, the bibliographical essay on journals and magazines and the headnotes about the single groups all illustrate this specifically Italian phenomenon. We have also provided a chronology.

A characteristic feature of Italian feminism is its diffusion through a number of diverse groups, which operate in many cities. The whole of part I aims at presenting the varied reality of these different groups, and at giving information on experiences typical of Italy. No book of this kind could claim to represent Italian feminism in all its aspects adequately. We have chosen to concentrate on groups based in key areas (Milan/Rome) which have also been influential nationwide. It is a necessarily partial view, both in the sense of presenting only a few of the groups (and within that selection only a part of their output), and because there is obviously a strongly subjective element in our decisions. In other words, we have certainly looked for general criteria based in the 'reality' (or realities) of the Italian feminist movement, but our personal evaluation of some groups and experiences have also played a part.

Many other groups could have been selected, and we want to discuss briefly at least some of them, if only to indicate a more panoramic sketch than could be contained in this book.

In the south, the philosophers of Transizione, a cooperative based in Naples, are engaged in a lively exchange with the Diotima group and with the Milan Libreria delle Donne (see the relevant chapter in this selection), and also collaborate with the Centro Donna of Naples, financed and run by the local city council. They have organized conferences and seminars which bring together women from all over Italy to discuss theoretical issues in the areas of philosophy, ethics, history and politics.

Le Nemesiache, also a Neopolitan group, are active in the field of visual arts. They are especially interested in the cinema and in video. For several years now they have been running an annual festival of women's cinema, which includes debates on the issues of representation, self-representation and modes of expression of women's creativity.

In several southern towns – such as Caserta, Lecce and Catania – there are women's groups engaged in cultural activities. They often take the form of *Centri Culturale* (cultural centres), some of whose work is collected in the chapter on 'I Centri Culturale delle Donne'. The piece selected for inclusion was presented at the Siena national conference in 1986, and is the result of collaborative work between women from three groups in three cities: DonnaWomanFemme in Rome, the Biblioteca delle Donne in L'Aquila, and the Centro Donna in Pisa. In an attempt to outline a dynamic definition of the complex concepts of 'culture' and 'women's culture' from the centres' point of view, it drew upon material supplied by other groups as well. Collaboration and teamwork are the practice of many Italian feminists, and quite a few of the publications listed in our bibliography have collective authors.

Each centre also promotes specific projects. These projects are theoretical and political, and tend to reflect the interests of the women who run them, the local situation and traditions, and developments both in women's politics and in the larger, national and international scenario. For example, the women in Turin have always been sensitive to the problematics of work, and to the need for an international debate on these issues. In 1983 they organized a conference of women from industrialized countries to discuss the interrelations and contradictions of the activities of 'production' and 'reproduction', and to analyse the responses proffered in the different countries (see Cooperativo Manifesto Anni '80: 1984). They are now planning, in response to the great political changes in many eastern European countries, a meeting of women from western and eastern Europe, to investigate their differences and the possibility of further cooperation.

Together with the Centro di Documentazione, Ricerca e Iniziativa delle Donne of Bologna, two Turinese groups, Produrre e Riprodurre and the central cultural association Livia Laverani Donini, have been active in support of Palestinian women, while simultaneously attempting to establish a dialogue with pacifist Israeli women. They have also visited Israel and also groups in Palestinian refugee camps, in an effort to instigate communication with and between women of both nations (see Calciati et al: 1989).

The Centro in Bologna is also worth mentioning for its distinctive organization and funding. It is financed by the local city council, but it is autonomously run by an association of women, Orlando, who have signed a convention with the council.

The presence of many small feminist publishing houses is another interesting phenomenon. Some have existed for several years, others, active in the seventies, have now disappeared. New ones have been founded quite recently. Besides, many centres and groups themselves publish and circulate the proceedings of the conferences and seminars they organize, or the result of research carried out within the associations. A network has been established, comprising both the publishing houses proper and all other structures which produce printed materials of any kind, in order to discuss the problems of production, circulation and advertising. Parola di Donna, as this association is called, also takes part in national and international book fairs, by means of collective stands where all its associates are represented.

Part I of this book illustrates the work of a number of important Italian feminist groups. For each group we have provided a headnote sketching the history and character of the group. This is followed by a selection of material, either collectively produced, or signed by women influential in the group, and representative of it. We hope we have illustrated in this way the groups' different areas of interest and their positions in the movement at large, while at the same time outlining the relationships amongst them, and the changes which have taken place over the years.

The material, within the single chapters and from one chapter to another, is organized in a roughly chronological order. The recurrence and modification of certain themes (such as the issue of the autonomous production of interpretative categories; the life/theory relation; the centrality of the bond between/among women; the material and/or symbolic nature of women's oppression) give an example of the tendencies of the movement at large, as well as illustrating the position of the single group. For example, the piece by Adriana Cavarero in the section on Diotima presents the philosophical research of that particular group, but is also symptomatic of the renewed perceived need for theoretical reflection which characterized feminism in the eighties. Certainly there has always been theorizing; to a greater or lesser extent, we feel that all the writings included here are theoretical, both in their critique of the present and in their revision of the past. What is different is the explicit assumption of the need to go beyond critique and revision, towards a fully original construction, a theory of sexual difference.

Finally, it is also important to remember that right from its beginnings the feminist movement in Italy has involved women from very different areas: women in the most diverse jobs – trade unionists, schoolteachers, university students, bank clerks, airline stewardesses, nurses, civil servants, housewives, managers, etc. This is still true today.

Even the composition of women's groups engaged in theoretical research is diverse, and not in the least confined to full-time scholars. For example, the Diotima group (see the headnote to the chapter on 'Diotima') comprises six academics, two secondary schoolteachers, one primary schoolteacher and one poet, all of whom are also active in the politics of feminism. The editorial board of DonnaWomanFemme is made up of two economists (one working at the treasury, the other at the Bank of Italy), two secondary schoolteachers, one lawyer, one journalist and three academics. Alessandra Bocchetti, one of the founders of the Centro Culturale Virginia Woolf (see the chapter on this centre) was formerly a film and video director, and now works as an independent estate agent.

This larger and more varied social base does not, of course, prevent the problem of communication between women involved in the movement and those outside it. Women who are not academics sometimes complain about the obscurity and elitism of the language of feminist theorists. Thus at the national Conference of Women's Centres in Siena, attended by some 350 women from very different walks in life, Adriana Cavarero was accused of excessive obscurity, and her paper was the starting point of a lively discussion on the issues of language and communication in relation to the diffusion of feminist ideas. There are a number of questions to be considered in this respect. Perhaps a certain degree of obscurity is inevitable when one is trying to express new, unexplored concepts for which there is no existing framework within the tradition of western philosophical and political thought. The effort of formulating such a concept as 'women as subject' in a language which simply has the subject as male, the search for a language of the other, impedes certain kinds of clarity and fluency. The difficulty of understanding may be interpreted as the refusal to understand, and as symptomatic of an unarticulated (even unrecognized) disagreement with the issues being discussed.

THE LEGACY OF THE PAST AND THE TOPOGRAPHIES OF THE PRESENT

A voracious interest in foreign cultural production characterizes Italy, situated as it is at 'the periphery of Empire', to use Eco's metaphor of its marginal situation (Eco 1976). There is wide circulation of foreign books and journals, as well as a habit of quick translation of most texts which have aroused discussion abroad.[6] But this attitude, which could negatively be described as provincial, is counteracted by the continuing influence of, and pride in, a rich cultural heritage. Ideas from other countries are reformulated in the context of this living tradition, as well as in that of a distinct social and political reality.

Thus the practice of consciousness-raising groups was originally 'imported' from the USA, and, at least in Rome, it is possible to name the woman who came back from America and first proposed its adoption to her collective. In *Donnita. Cronache del Movimento Femminista Romano*, edited by the Collettivo di Via Pompeo Magno, one finds a very straightforward 'guide' to the creation of a consciousness-raising group. This includes a list of the topics to be treated in the meetings, and suggestions on the way to address them (Collettivo di Via Pompeo Magno 1976: 166–71). But the name given to this practice in Italy, '*autocoscienza*', indicates its distinctively Italian character.

It was first introduced by Carla Lonzi (of Rivolta Femminile: see the headnote to the chapter on this group) in the context of a theoretical speculation which had already moved away from the mere analysis of oppression to envisage the autonomous production of interpretative categories of reality. *Autocoscienza* meant independent, small groups of women, meeting to discuss issues of all kinds on the basis of personal experience:

> It was a simple and genial practice. Equality had not yet been achieved and, beside the weight of the continuing discrimination, women also had to bear the new burden of social integration on a par with men. It was too much; and, almost out of the blue, the prospect of reaching the same level as the other sex lost its attraction. Some, many, women turned their backs on it to cut out a totally different path, that of female separatism. Women have always met to talk together about their own affairs, safe from the male listening ear. 'Autocoscienza' grafted itself upon this social practice, which was as common as it was belittled, and gave it political dignity. (Libreria delle Donne di Milano 1987: 32–3)

Unlike the English phrase 'consciousness-raising', the term *autocoscienza* stresses the self-determined and self-directed quality of the process of achieving a new consciousness/awareness. It is a process of the discovery and (re-) construction of the self, both the self of the individual woman and a collective sense of self: the search for the subject-woman.

All this took place in a politicized context, which had its historical roots in the late formation of an Italian state, in its re-foundation after the fascist period and the resistance movement, and – last but not least – in the libertarian student movement of 1968. Partly as a consequence of the late formation of a national unified state, Italy had also experienced a late bourgeois revolution, simultaneously suffering the evils of capitalist development and those of its lack. It has been, and in many ways it still is, a land of contradictions, between the north and the south, city and country, cosmopolitanism and nationalism. Even after the Second World War, it was still a largely agricultural country, though with some highly developed industries; the only country in Western Europe where the slogan of an alliance between factory workers and peasants could actually make sense, and, unlike Britain and America, where intellectuals 'naturally' played a political role.[7]

As for women and for feminism, it is important to remember that, at the end of the nineteenth century and at the beginning of the twentieth, there had been a strong emancipationist movement in Italy, which began again in the late 1940s. In the meantime, many women had been active in the fight against fascism, and had participated in the resistance, not only working as contact and propaganda officers but also conducting guerilla warfare in the mountains. The UDI (Uniona Donne Italiane – Union of Italian Women) is a remarkably original and interesting development both of the emancipationist movement and of the active involvement of women in the anti-fascist struggle. It came into being within the framework of the political left, gradually building up its own political and organizational autonomy. Founded immediately after the Second World War to fight for better conditions for women, it tried to appeal to all women, regardless of their sociopolitical affiliation. But it was in fact made up of left-wing women. It maintained close ties with the socialist and, especially, the communist parties.

For some years this was a source of incomprehension and antagonism in the feminist movement, which stressed its autonomy from and its suspicion of all formally constituted parties, which were seen as entrenchments of male authority. Also, many of the women involved in the 'new' feminism of the 1970s came out of the experience of 1968, with its strong anti-institutional bias, and were or had been members of extraparliamentary groups (Lotta Continua, Potere Operaio, and so on) which criticized the 'traditional' left.

During the course of the struggle over the abortion law, however, this gap began to close. The feminist movement had, at least in part, accepted the need to confront the male-dominated institutions that were the true loci of state power, and the UDI had, in the daily practice of common work, come closer and closer to feminist positions. It was instrumental in bringing about changes in the Communist party's positions on abortion. This relationship of forceful opposition, gradually developing dialogue, and finally collaboration and mutual reshaping, between a strong women's organization in the tradition of the political left and of the emancipationist movement, on the one hand, and an anti-institutional, radical feminism, on the other, is a peculiar feature of the Italian situation.

The presence in Italy of a strong communist party, the largest in the western world, is also a relevant feature to bear in mind, for it has been both a point of reference and a target of criticism for all 'movements'. Thus the student protestors of 1968 attacked the PCI (Italian communist party) as itself a part of the social and political system, while also pressing it to change its positions and support their views and goals within the system. This pattern would be partially repeated by some sections of the feminist movement, which, as we have already mentioned, comprised women who had participated in that protest. A number of these women remained active in the extraparliamentary groups which subsequently grew out of it.

All through the seventies, the issue of 'double militancy' – of the simultaneous participation/involvement in the feminist movement and in the activities of an organized party or political group – was a crucial one. Even the most leftist groups proved themselves unable to understand the new consciousness women were developing in the *autocoscienza* groups, and were hostile to women's newly found determination to gain a full autonomy of expression; hostile, most of all, to any separatist activity. Feminist marches were disrupted and feminist meetings interrupted by male 'comrades', and many women moved out of these organizations to devote themselves fully to feminist politics. As for members of the PCI, not only the men but many of the women considered feminism a 'bourgeois' phenomenon, and it was only slowly that the remarkable changes briefly outlined elsewhere in this introduction and in the chapter on 'Political Representation' came into being.

The practice of *autocoscienza* was either directly or indirectly a motor for all these changes, but at the same time responded to their context; hence the need to find ways to reinvest the newly found energy and awareness in society to bring about change. At the same time, the need still held to continue that search for the subject-women, making use of (inventing) more sophisticated analytical tools than the spontaneous exchange of experiences afforded. *Autocoscienza* had signified women's difference and given it an autonomous expression. It refused any cultural mediation in order to assume the intrinsic value of women's lives, thus establishing a link between theory and practice whose importance has not been undermined in later developments (in this respect, see, for example, the editorials in the chapter on '*DonnaWomanFemme*'). Though much time was devoted to the discussion of oppression – for example, to relationships with men – this practice also suggested the possibility, the importance, the intricacy and beauty of relationships between women. Thus the experience of *autocoscienza* has continued to act within the Italian feminist movement long after it had been abandoned as an actual practice, with far more widely reaching effects than had the conscious-raising groups which had inspired it.

Both the 'practice of the unconscious' and the idea of 'entrustment' put forward by the Milan Libreria delle Donne can be looked at in this perspective. The former was an attempt to bend the tools of psychoanalysis to a deeper understanding of the dynamics of women's relationships between/among themselves. The latter insists on the need to acknowledge not simply differences, but actual disparities between women, in order to overcome a 'static separatism' – the idea of a separate women's world as a haven of peace – in favour of a 'dynamic separatism', at play in the social arena. The chapter on 'Pratica dell'Inconscio' and 'Libreria delle Donne di Milano' should clarify these concepts.

INTERCULTURALITY, INTERTEXTUALITY: ADRIENNE RICH, LUCE IRIGARAY AND ITALIAN FEMINISM

The ideas and the new forms of cultural representation and practice generated by a political movement rarely present themselves in orderly or chronological sequence. Amidst the contradictory forces which brought the various forms of contemporary feminism into being, feminists in a number of countries have consistently sought what the Italians call *'collocazione simbolica'* (symbolic placement); practices of referrence and address, even a lineage or tradition within which to situate themselves in past, present and future. The reading and re-reading of other women's writings, either in dialogue or in disagreement, has been one of the significant connections between feminists in this respect.

In surveying Italian feminist thought, it is interesting to look at two central figures – one French, one American – whose thought has been incorporated and as it were 'translated' (with the attendant risks of distortion) by a very influential group, namely the Milan Libreria delle Donne.

Influenced at first by the ideas of the French group Psychanalyse et Politique ('Psych & Po'), the women who founded the Libreria openly recognize their debt to Irigaray. Some of them had also been involved in other Milanese groups, and were among the proponents of the 'practice of the unconscious'. The relationship between Irigaray and the Libreria has not, however, been one way. Their work has helped establish Irigaray as one of the main points of reference for feminist thought in Italy, but it has also been a focus of interest for Irigaray herself. She has written explicitly about Italian feminism and Italian politics. When the whole issue of representation became crucial (see the chapter on 'Political Representation'), and collaboration seemed possible with women in the Communist party, Irigaray was a speaker in the party's summer festivals, and debated the political significance of sexual difference in the party's newspaper *L'Unita*.

Indeed, another feature of the Italian 'reading' of Irigaray is that she is not regarded as an abstract theorist at all, but as a deeply *political* thinker, whose work – often accused by British and American feminists of essentialism – is extremely concrete and attentive to the actual contexts of women's lives.[8] Her attitude is understood as it is reflected in her images of multiplication and openness, in her call for all women to give voice to their difference, and differences, in dialogue:

> For my part, I refuse to let myself be locked into a single 'group' within the women's liberation movement. Especially if such a group becomes ensnared in the exercise of power, if it purports to determine the 'truth' of the feminine, to legislate to us on what it means to 'be a woman', and to condemn women who might have immediate objectives that differ from theirs. I think the most important thing to do is to expose the exploitation common to all women and *to find the struggles that are appropriate for each woman, right where she is, depending upon her nationality, her job, her social class, her sexual experience*, that is upon the form of oppression that is for her the most immediately unbearable. (Irigaray 1985b: 166–7, emphasis added)

Less directly, Rich has also been a source of ideas for the Libreria, and more generally for Italian feminist thought. In the January 1983 issue of *Sotosopra* ('More Women than Men', included in this book) the authors talk about the need for 'a common world of women', reprinting excerpts from Rich's *On Lies, Secrets and Silence* (Rich 1979). Her intuition of the lack of a gendered network of relationships is again alluded to in the book *Non credere di avere dei diritti*, where the authors denounce 'the pain of coming into the world . . . without symbolic placement' (Libreria delle Donne di Milano 1987: 10), in a significant reshaping of the conceptual categories of post-structuralism and of distinctly British and American feminist modes of thinking. This 'mix and match' attitude, with the new insights that it produces, is a typical feature of Italian feminism.

Another way in which it has manifested itself, still in relation to Rich, is the widely diffused, though not always explicitly stated, assumption of her notion of a 'lesbian existence' and a 'lesbian continuum' (as opposed to lesbianism as a clinical concept, or as a matter of personal sexual preference: Rich 1977), within a movement which has not experienced an internal split around this issue, as our chapter on 'Lesbofemminismo' tries to demonstrate. This does not mean that there are no tensions, and in fact Italian lesbians have accused the Libreria of silently passing by, rather than confronting. Rich's own lesbianism. But in general the idea of a 'political homosexuality' is shared by most Italian feminists, so that separatism does not imply a withdrawal from and a refusal of relationships with men, including sexual relationships, but rather the existence of separate spaces of theoretical production and political action; separatism is *inside* a woman, besides taking form concretely in women-only groups.

By contrast, in Britain and America the figure of the lesbian – together with that of the Amazon – has featured in literature and in literary theory as an image of female autonomy, and an emblem for an aesthetic.[9] But from the late seventies in the UK and America, lesbians and feminists have moved into different groupings. The lesbian groups see themselves as voicing the anxieties and complaints of 'other' women, who feel excluded or essentialized through race, class, sexual preference and age.

A FEMALE COGITO: SUBJECTIVITY, POLITICS AND THE QUESTION OF DIFFERENCE

In thinking of Italian feminism, then, one returns again and again to the crucial issue of difference. A great deal of theoretical work by feminists to date has concerned itself, in particular, with the structuring and with the positive potential of 'difference' in language.

British, American and French feminist theorists have been concerned with the 'sexism' of language. The British and the Americans initially aimed at a kind of sociolinguistic modification of the surface structures: 'Ms' instead of 'Miss' and 'Mrs'; 'he and she' or 's/he' to substitute for the general use of the male pronoun, and so on.[10] By contrast, the French have been more concerned with the creation of a 'feminine' language (*l'écriture feminine*) to give voice to difference (*différénce*) and to produce the possibility of freedom from hetero-directed systems of representation.[11] But the importance of 's/he', and the resistance with which this kind of proposal has met, lies precisely in the symbolic power of language, in its capacity not just to reflect but also to create 'reality'. Italian feminism has tended to interpret and use these approaches in a way which concentrates on the links between them (their possible similarities and their complementary qualities) and suppresses their differences.[12]

It is in its particular concept of difference (and its emphasis on difference as it exists in the symbolic dimension), however, that Italian feminism remains distinct from British and American feminisms, which have often focused not on difference but on equality.

For Italian feminism, in the equality-versus-difference debate,[13] the concptual opposite of difference is not equality, but the notion of equality as it has been inscribed in the paradigms of western philosophical and political thought. As early as 1970 Carla Lonzi argued, for example, that feminism's fight for women's equality with men was misdirected, since equality is 'an ideological attempt to subject women even further' (see Lonzi's 'Manifesto' in the chapter on 'Rivolta Femminile'):

> Equality is a juridical principle . . . Difference is an existential principle which concerns the modes of being human, the peculiarity of one's own experiences, goals, possibilities, and one's sense of existence in a given situation and in the situations one wants to create for oneself. The difference between woman and man is the basic difference of humankind. . . . Equality is what is offered as legal rights to colonized people. And what is imposed on them as culture. ('Let's Spit on Hegel', included here in the chapter on 'Rivolta Femminile')

The obliteration of women through the assumption of a natural equality of all human beings can take two forms. Either the universal subject of the social contract, the equal human being, is theoretically asexual and practically male-sexed (i.e. sexual difference is cancelled along with all other accidental differences); or, alternatively, sexual difference is used to identify women with reproduction, and excludes them as women from the polis. The polis is open only to women who agree to neuter themselves. Outside the polis, sexual difference is recognized, but only in the form of a sexual role which implies inferiority. Becoming equal thus means becoming like a man. But 'being like' is never going to be as good as 'being'; and, on the other hand, being different is unacceptable if it means being inferior. According to this belief, sexual difference must become a component of the struggle for social equality. A demand for equality which sees sexual difference as a mere historical construct, and does not take it into account, risks contradicting its assumed materialist foundation (by taking the ideological framework of that foundation for granted). If, say, differences in the social position of men and women are due to the fact that women bear children and have been made responsible for them, then a more 'equal' distribution of the child-rearing responsibilities would effectively, though only partially, solve the problem. But this still does not explain why such an apparently fundamental task has been made of the bases for women's inferiority and oppression.

If one then turns to the related sex/gender argument, gender and its historical construction seem to be more closely connected with those symbolic processes addressed by French theory.[14] In this respect, Italian feminism takes sexual difference as a general cognitive and interpretative category. Sexual difference is neither only biological 'sex', nor only 'gender' as it has been culturally created; it is the inscription of both of these in the symbolic dimension. And it has to be produced and signified by woman as a subject, a subject who here and now experiences both 'sex' and 'gender'. Sexual difference is, nevertheless, an essential, originary difference, though one which may change in its phenomenological manifestations. In the words of an Italian feminist philosopher engaged in this task of signification:

> by essential and originary difference I mean that, for women, being engendered in a different sex (*l'essere sessuate nella differenza*) is something not negotiable. For each one who is born female, it is always already so and not otherwise; the difference is rooted in her being not as something superfluous or something adjunctive, but as that which she necessarily is: female. (Cavarero 1987b: 180–1)

The point is that the body itself needs to be signified and reconstructed, rather than negated. Women have to take upon themselves the task of signifying it, instead of negating its significance merely because, thus far, it has been interpreted to their disadvantage. That would be the risk of egalitarian positioning. Seeing men and women as equal in some abstract sense can easily result in identifying equality with sameness, where the model would be either the universal 'male', or a 'neutral' human being born of the combination of historically (male) created male and female characteristics. For Italian feminist theory, however, the subject would have to recognize itself in its partiality. Each subject would have to reconstitute him/herself, taking *him/herself* as a starting point. So far, this has been the case only for the male subject, who has negated women's subjectivity in the process. He has deprived her of a conceptual framework and of a language in which to give voice to, and therefore create, her own subject.

> Discourse carries in itself the sign of its subject, the speaking subject who in discourse speaks himself and speaks the world starting from himself. There is some truth in man's immortality . . . : in universalizing the finitude of his gendered being (*della sua sessuazione*), man bypasses his limited gendered being and poses himself as an essence that of necessity belongs to the 'objectivity' of discourse. (Cavarero 1987a: 45)

In place of the philosophy of the One which has characterized western thought, an 'absolute dual' is hypothesized, the rethinking of sexual difference within a dual conceptualization of being. Being-man and being-woman are both primary, originary forms, and so is sexual difference, there from the beginning in both woman and man. The world must accommodate *two* subjects. And this means not only the world of ideas, but the 'real' world of politics and economics and social relations. For a radical rethinking of the categories of western thought, and the entry onto the scene of the 'unexpected subject', the appropriation and reshaping of discourse by women, cannot be wholly without consequences in all those areas. As Rosi Braidotti puts it, paraphrasing and interpreting Cavarero's proposal, the need to establish, here and now, a philosophy of sexual difference is for feminists

> a necessary political gesture. As a collective political, social, theoretical, movement, we must found a female *cogito*. We authorise for ourselves the statement: 'I/woman/think/as/woman and therefore I am'. *What* I am, as a woman, is another matter, located at a more individual level. Let us not confuse the individual with the subject. We can all agree on the affirmation of a female subjectivity. 'We', movement of liberation of each woman's 'I', of all those women who recognise themselves in the statement 'I/woman am'. (Braidotti 1987: 190–1)

The rhetoric may sound essentialist to the Anglo-Saxon ear. But the fact is that the whole question of essentialism is not perceived in the same way within the Italian context. Cavarero draws her discourse from Plato and Hegel; Braidotti works within the framework of post-modernism. Both, in the words of the title of Teresa De Lauretis's crucial article 'The Essence of the Triangle', are 'taking the risk of essentialism seriously' (*Differences* 1989: 3–37). Much Italian feminist theory is running the risk of essentialism as it has been hitherto perceived. By taking that risk 'seriously', it may seem to speak essentialism, but enacts a new kind of empiricism.

Thus Braidotti argues against an essentialist reading of the philosophy of sexual difference. Being-woman is not interpreted in a causal, deterministic way: it is for each woman a fact, but a fact which takes place in the here and now of her birth and life, and therefore a historical fact. Woman-ness is not simply a biological factor, it is the historical experience of estrangement and separateness. It is not an immobile datum, transcending time and space; it is sexual difference thinking itself because the female living being thinks it. That is, Braidotti argues that the female living being is not an abstract essence; we are it – we who engage in politics, who work, who produce theory, who have to manage the complexity of our daily lives, and who are not willing to continue 'being like' or 'being inferior'. We want to enter and change the polis with our being-woman, reclaiming our difference and stating man's difference.

This is a highly *political* perspective, one which is likely to provoke a much harsher struggle than a simple request for equality ever would. It is not a matter of rejecting the importance of the historical struggle for equal rights, which cost many women such effort and sacrifice, and which has won us the vote, financial independence, access to education, etc. Nor should an emphasis on difference as a politically contentious issue be interpreted as a request for special spheres of activity, which would soon risk inferiorization. Difference means duality; it means man's difference, not only woman's. It has to do with the full acceptance of the partiality of both the female and the male subjects.

Man has always inhabited the world as the *only* subject, to whom woman was supposed to equate herself; reshaping the universe to accommodate duality (and therefore men's partiality) is going to entail a deep and manifold modification of all structures, at all levels – symbolic, institutional, economic. It is not by chance that in Italy – apart from their obvious recurrence in women's groups – phrases like 'sexual difference', 'bi-sexedness', 'relations between/among women', have resonated more in political meetings, such as those of the Central Committee of the Communist party (of which, by the way, Cavarero is a member), than in the university classroom.

In Italy the whole issue of essentialism is related to the French, and especially to the Irigarayan, notion of a correlation between cognition and sexual difference. Violi, for example, argues for a semantics founded in the perceptions human beings have of their bodies. She hypothesizes cognition as a quasi-biological phenomenon, seeing a difference in the mode of perception according to the materiality of the perceiving body. She thinks of sexuality as structuring the mode of perception in a significant way: that is, a difference in the point of view where the point of view has to do with the *body* of the viewer (instead of perceiving living beings as consistently neutral, or male). Rephrasing and summarizing recent theories of cognition based on neurophysiological studies, and their philosophical consequences (Violi, Maturana and Varela), Bono writes: 'Could this difference in "point of view", where the point of view is not only a metaphor, but has to do with the body of the viewer, entail a difference cognitive reality?' As she goes on to ask, if biology has a role in cognition, can the biological fact of sexual difference be ignored in discussion of cognition? Can we talk of human cognition as if the human being were 'sexually neutral'?

> What is interesting is the interplay of factors, taking the observer, nature and culture, physicality and socialised entity, as the meeting ground and productive centre: an observer, therefore, who cannot be sexually neutral, but who is marked by his/her sexuality, the significant constituent of the cognitive process and of its description/construction of reality. (Bono 1989: 437–9)

The male has conventionally been seen as the only possible model: but, as Bono shows, Violi (and others) are asking for at least two models (one female), with many internal differences.

At first sight, this characteristic so-called 'subjectivism' of Italian feminist theory could be considered essentialist. But this is clearly not the case when it is understood in context. Introducing the proceedings of a conference on women's research in Italy, the editors explore the double nature of studies where women can be both objects and subjects of inquiry:

> [in women's studies] the genitive is ambiguous: it means that women are both the subject and the object of the study. In the discussion, these two meanings have been sometimes set against each other. Luise Muraro: 'The danger is that difference may come to be seen as something which characterizes certain objects of research, instead of there being a researching subject who expresses herself in her difference'; Emma Baeri: 'It seems to me that the constitution of the sexed subject inevitably takes place in/through language; in this respect the object is almost unimportant. What really matters is the contextualisation of the subject.' (Marcuzzo and Rossi 1987: 8)

Needless to say, certain types of discipline call for subjectivism more than others: the less the object of study is women, the greater the need for dialogue with other women to create a subject. The problem of language, and of 'the constitution of the sexed subject . . . in/through language' is central from this point of view and must be taken into account. The historian Gianna Pomata comments: 'Our problem is not simply *what* to write (changing the content of history), but *how* to write: experimenting with new forms of historical narrative more adequate to the cognitive aims of women's history' (Pomata 1987). As well as the problem and signification of the female subject which is so crucial to Italian feminism, there is also a strong, related need to forge a collective female political subject in which the processes of individual subjectivity could be grounded, but not restricted.

One final point with respect to essentialism/separatism: the French and Anglo-American debate has increasingly come to be concerned with the place of men in feminism (see the 1987 collection of essays edited by Alice Jardine and Paul Smith with that title). Is feminism a politics of struggle by women, on behalf of women? Or are feminists arguing that only women can theorize their oppression because only women can experience it? *Men in Feminism* asks questions like: Should feminists use a set of perspectives whose chief proponents have been men (such as post-structuralism)? How should feminists react politically to men who write about feminist issues from a sympathetic vantage point? One way out of this impasse, according to a number of Anglo-American theorists, is to consider whether work by men on patriarchal constructions of masculinity and sexual difference can illuminate and be illuminated by feminist theory.

By contrast, in Italy, because there are really no women's studies in the universities, it does not pay to be a male feminist. Male intellectuals are often seen as patronizing, uneasy towards feminists or even resentful of them, but their interests – and careers – are elsewhere. On the other hand, because of the strongly separatist nature of Italian feminism, women are for women the point of reference in all areas; male thinkers and their theories are regarded with suspicion, though often with fascination. Italian feminists will use the structures of male theory, but only for their own purposes.

THE PERSONAL IS THE POLITICAL: INTERSECTIONS OF
THEORY AND PRACTICE

The way in which the social and economic conditions and problems of women's lives are perceived and dealt with by Italian feminists represents their own version of 'the personal is the political.' What is characteristically Italian here is the uneasy, conflictual but nevertheless sustained relationship between theoretical separatist speculation, the effort to analyse and create an autonomous subject–woman, and practical political activities.

Part II of the book is centred on the political arena, and the pieces included here demonstrate some of the ways in which the political movement which is the women's movement is related to the larger political sphere.

The piece by Lia Cigarini in chapter 15 on 'Female "separateness"', from the special edition of *Sottosopra* ('On Political Representation, and on the Art of Polemics between Women . . .'), for example, takes up the issue of the possibilities (positive and negative) of mediation between the women's movement and institutionalized politics. Can 'being a woman' be represented in classical democracy? What should women do about patriarchal language and conceptual systems? Cigarini's polemic tackles the very real problems that result from this kind of enquiry: that women are a sex, not a homogenous group: that female representation could be used to veil an otherwise legitimate desire for personal ambition, and so on.

In different ways, each of the other chapters in Part II also concern ways and means of sexualizing politics; again, there are headnotes giving some background information on the single issues, and outlining the terms of the feminist debate about them. We look at the debates within Italian feminism about two laws: the law regulating abortion and the law regulating sexual violence. We have extracted pieces which reflect Italian feminist views on key political issues: the position of women in the home (salaries for housewives); women as workers, and therefore their engagement in trade unions; political representation. And we offer some instances of Italian feminists taking or refusing to take a stand on particular problems or events: the Moro affair, terrorism, military service for women and nuclear power.

The dramatic nature of these issues would seem to bear out Susan Bassnett's thesis that 'violence' is a key concept in understanding Italian feminism (Bassnett 1989: 91–131). It is certainly true that political commitment and activities may result in violence, symbolic and/or physical. It is much more importantly true that violence is a feature of women's lives, in that they are so often its victims. We wonder, though, whether this is actually more characteristic of feminism in Italy than in other countries. The Italian feminist movement itself has indeed refused violence as a means to change, as the pieces in the chapter 'Keeping Silent/Speaking Out – Some Instances' illustrate.

The first two issues covered in Part II – abortion and sexual violence – are of course significant internationally. In Italy, as elsewhere, these issues and their links with a sexuality imprisoned in the norms of patriarchy have been central to the feminist movement, and have involved women from remarkably different social, intellectual and political backgrounds. On abortion, for example, the pieces focus on issues such as: should there be a law regulating abortion? Or should abortion be legal but unregulated? What sort of sexuality prevails and how does this influence abortion?

The social role of the Catholic church might be conceived as of some importance here, particularly because of its influence in Italian politics through the Christian Democratic party. But its intellectual role is nil. Catholic women at odds with the traditional teachings of the church and with its hierarchy have taken part in feminist activities concerned with abortion. Also, together with women from Protestant communities, they have formed groups to discuss theological issues and religious ethics, within the framework of a more general attempt, involving both men and women, to reinterpret religion in a way more open to social and economic considerations. The COM-Tempir Nuovi group, whose piece about the law on sexual violence is included in the relevant section, is just one of these.

Most Italian feminists seem more concerned to engage with the church as a political adversary than as an intellectual force. The church has saturated the cultural traditions of the country and helped to shape the prevailing images of women, but its intellectual premises are not challenging. Italian feminists are thus interested in Catholicism, as it were, only negatively; that is, as an obstacle to women's aspirations. Of course, this is our own reading of the relationship between Italian feminism and the Catholic church; it would certainly be possible to argue, as Lucia Chiavola Birnbaum does, that the Catholic church's position and influence should be central in a positive way to any interpretation of Italian feminism. But we disagree; and it is perhaps also as a reaction to what we see as excessive emphasis on the importance of Catholicism, and of the Catholic church, that we have given it so little space.

The issues of abortion and sexual violence are particularly important in Italy because of the way women have become directly involved in the legislative process. For example, the law against sexual violence was drafted, signed and submitted by women (see the headnote to chapter 11). On the other hand, it is just as significant that this legislation prompted discussions of sexuality and identity, gender and power in the women's groups who problematized it and were sometimes directly at odds with it, as the pieces in the same section illustrate. The co-existence of the two modes – one apparently more pragmatic, looking for practical solutions, and willing to become directly engaged in bringing about their realization; the other more interested in an enquiry into the psychological and symbolic aspects of the problems – and their mutual dependence, is typical of Italian feminism. The debates around sexual violence established the issues as being as much in the images men and women have of themselves as in the particular kind of violence to which men subject women, thereby also locating the problem of abuse in symbolic structures.

Changes in the scientific paradigms in the twentieth century are also reflected in the deconstruction of symbolic structures. We regret not having more space to deal with the rapidly expanding field of feminism and science.[15] But the short section on Chernobyl gives some sense of the scope of the debate. Here we see the refusal of the power of science over women's bodies; we see how the female subject brings into scientific enterprise an intentional partiality, deliberately unmasking neutrality and objectivity. More specifically, in Italy, Chernobyl triggered a sudden political awareness of the ways in which, and the reasons why, women and science are and must be related. This awareness grew out of women's having experienced, in their/our own bodies and own lives (when shopping, breastfeeding babies, and so on), the way in which the subject is immersed in the object. This brought about a sudden awareness of renewed values: a new sense of what survival means, both in the case of the individual and of the species, and of the ways in which women are always asked to guarantee survival. If 'male' science is a culture of taking risks for the sake of knowledge, then are women prepared to accept limits to knowledge? These remain key subjects of debate.

In general, for Italian feminism, a historical concern with the 'real' world cannot be separated from an investigation of the symbolic structures which both express and shape reality: 'Sexual difference . . . is neither a biological nor a sociological category, but is located at the intersection of these two levels with the symbolic dimension' (Braidotti 1988).

POST-MODERNISM?

The world does not stop just because one is writing a book, and in the interval between the completion and the publication of this book, there will have been dramatic changes on the international scene. As we write these final remarks, the whole scenario of eastern Europe has already changed. More changes in the sociopolitical and economic fields will surely occur. They will influence, as they indeed already have influenced, the Italian political situation; and Italian feminism is never socially unresponsive, as we have been stressing again and again.

The crumbling of established certainties – and the Berlin Wall is an apt metaphor in this respect – is supposed to characterize the post-modern position, always open to doubt, always willing (or compelled) to take other positions on board. We are aware of the frailty of our own stand, of the inevitable quick obsolescence of our picture of Italian feminism. Its very openness makes it vulnerable, apparently more an object than a subject of change; and yet some continuity still holds, in spite of everything. Our assessment of the Italian feminist debate, however, stops at October 1989. The chronological tables end before that; the bibliographical information goes beyond it. But our own effort to conjure up a picture of Italian feminism, through the selection of pieces as well as through this introduction, must be located there, both temporally and conceptually.

On the other hand, as Bocchetti said, women are the inevitable subjects of the twentieth century, the embodiment (carrying and signalling in their bodies) of those weaknesses, voids and pluralities of signification which are today so much the focus of post-modern enquiry:

> Women have been the inhabitants of the twentieth century since time immemorial. It is in the twentieth century that a plural, contradictory subject replaces the full and coherent subject of classical reason in the history of thought, and therefore in its itineraries of research. Women have always carried within themselves this plural subject being. (Bocchetti, included in this collection in chapter 7)

As women, we have to accept the burden of this intuition; what is also both significant and ironic here is the realization that women did not arrive at theory, they *discovered* themselves in it.

NOTES

1 *French Feminist Thought* (ed. Toril Moi) and *British Feminist Thought* (ed. Terry Lovell) have already appeared, in 1987 and 1990 respectively. Anthologies of Asian, American and Australian feminist thought are also forthcoming.
2 For an interesting and problematic account of one of the forms of Italian feminism, and of the reasons why it is still possible to talk about it in the singular, see De Lauretis (1989).
3 For a history of British feminism see Rowbotham 1989 and Lovell 1990. For French feminism see introductions to Marks and Courtivron 1981 and Moi 1987.
4 See J.A. Hellman 1987: 27–54; Birnbaum 1986: 3–31.

5 Millett 1972, Greer 1970, Mitchell 1979.
6 To take only a few examples: all of Irigaray's books have been published in Italy within one year of their appearance in France – so that *Speculum* appeared in French in 1974 and in Italian in 1975 (Milan: Feltrinelli); *Ce sex qui n'en pas un*, published in 1977, was translated into Italian in 1978 (Milan: Feltrinelli), etc.; the Boston Women's Collective's *Our Bodies Our Selves* (1974) was translated in 1974 (Milan: Feltrinelli); Rich's *Of Woman Born* (1976) appeared in Italy in 1977 (Milan: Garzanti) and so on.
7 There is no space here to illustrate this historical background and its sociopolitical and cultural aspects in any detail, either in general or with respect to women. In their studies on Italian feminism, both J.A. Hellman 1987 and Birnbaum 1986 deal with this area at some length. Bassnett 1986 is also interesting in this respect. On women in post-war Italy, see Balbo and May 1975/6. On women, Marxism, the PCI (Italian communist party) and the extraparliamentary groups, see Buttafuoco 1980, Dobbs 1982, Ergas 1982, J.A. Hellman 1984, S. Hellman 1976, Lumley 1983, Melucci 1981, Pitch 1979, Spini 1972, and Von Henneberg 1983. On the Unione Donne Italiane (UDI), see Beckwith 1985. Some general studies on Italy and on Italian politics are Allum 1973, S. Hellman 1987, and Lange and Tarrow 1980. Obviously, many more works are available in Italian.
8 A somewhat consonant reading of Irigaray is that by Meaghan Morris in 'A-mazing Grace: Notes on Mary Daly's Poetics' (in Morris 1988) where she compares Daly's elitist and truly essentialist position with Irigaray's.
9 See Showalter 1978: 7. For lesbian feminist theory see De Lauretis 1988 and Zimmerman 1985.
10 See Lakoff 1975, C. Miller and Swift 1976, Thorne and Henley 1975, Spender 1980, and Cameron 1985.
11 See Irigaray 1985a and b, Kristeva 1980 and 1986, Cixous and Clément 1986, Cixous, Clément and Gagnon 1977, and Sellers 1988.
12 See Rossi 1978, Sabatini 1986, and Violi 1987.
13 See Scott 1988, Dominjanni 1989, and Cavarero 1989.
14 For an overview and a discussion of the arguments on the sex/gender issue, see Flax 1987, where she poses a series of very interesting questions, such as: are there only two possible genders? In what way, if any, is gender related to anatomical differences? What are the connections between gender roles, sexuality and individual identity? And between heterosexuality, homosexuality and gender relations? What casuses gender relations to change over time? What is gender justice and what would be the consequences for feminism of attaining it?
15 For feminism and science, see Keller 1985, Haraway 1989 and Jacobus et al 1990.

REFERENCES

Allum P.A. 1973: *Italy – Republic without Government?*. New York, W.W. Norton.

Balbo, L. and May, M.P. 1975/6: Women's Condition: The Case of Postwar Italy. *International Journal of Sociology*, 5, 79–102.

Bassnett, S. 1986: *Feminist Experiences. The Women's Movement in Four Cultures*. London, Allen & Unwin.

Beckwith, K. 1985: Feminism and Leftist Politics in Italy: The Case of the UDI–PCI Relations. *Western European Politics*, 8(4), 20–37.

Birnbaum, L. Chiavola 1986: *La liberazione della donna: Feminism in Italy*. Middletown, Conn., Wesleyan University Press.

Bono, P. 1989: Neutrality and Cognition and the Problem of Sexual Difference. In J. Bernard et al (eds), *Semiotik der Geschlechter*, Stuttgart, Akademischer Verlag Hans-Dieter Heinz, and Vienna, Osterreische Gesellschaft fur Semiotik.

Braidotti, R. 1987: Commento alla relazione di Adriana Cavarero. In Marcuzzo and Rossi 1987: 188–202.

Braidotti, R. 1988: Feminist Epistemology: Critical Theories and a Woman-Defined Philosophy of Sexual Difference. Unpublished paper presented at the international seminar on 'Equality and Difference: Gender Dimensions in Political Thought, Justice and Morality'. Florence, Istituto Universitario Europeo, December.

Braidotti, R. 1989a: *Differenza*. Rome, Columbi.

Buttofuoco, A. 1980: Italy: the Feminist Challenge. In C. Boggs and D. Plotke (eds), *The Politics of Eurocommunism: Socialism in Transition*, Montreal: Black Rose Press, 197–219.

Calciati, G. et al (1989): *Donne e Gerusalemme*. Turin, Rosenberg and Sellier.

Cameron, D. 1985: *Feminism and Linguistic Theory*. London, Macmillan.

Cavarero, A. 1987a: Per una teoria della differenza sessuale. In Cavarero et al. 1987: 43–79.

Cavarero, A. 1987b: L'elaborazione filosofica della differenza sessuale. In Marcuzzo and Rossi 1987: 173–87.

Cavarero, A. 1989: La congiura delle differenti. *Il Bimestrale*, 1, 'Eguaglianza', supplement to *il manifesto*, 25, 79–80.

Cavarero, A., Conti, P., Maci, S. and Teandri, R. 1987: *Diotima. Il pensiero della differenza sessuale*. Milan, La Tartaruga.

Cixous, H. and Clément, C. 1986 [1975]: *The Newly Born Woman*. Manchester, Manchester University Press.

Cixous, H., Clément, C. and Gagnon, M. 1977: *La Venue à l'écriture*. Paris, Union Générale d'Editions.

Collettivo di Via Pompeo Magno (ed.) 1976: *Donnità. Gonache del Movimento Femminista Romano*. Rome, Centro di documentazione del Movimento Femminista Romano.

De Lauretis, T. 1988: Sexual Indifference and Lesbian Representation. *Theatre Journal*, 40(2), 155–77.

De Lauretis, T. 1989: The Essence of the Triangle or, Taking the Risk of Essentialism Seriously: Feminist Theory in Italy, the U.S., and Britain. *Differences*, 2, 1–37.

Deleuze, G. and Parnet, C. 1977: *Dialogues*. Paris, Flammarion.

Dobbs, D. 1982: Extra-Parliamentary Feminism and Social Change in Italy, 1971–1980. *International Journal of Women's Studies*, 5(2), 148–60.

Dominijanni, I. 1989: Donne si nasce. Differenti si diventa. *Il Bimestrale*, 1, supplement to *il manifesto*, 25, 74–8.

Eco, U. 1976: *Dalla periferia dell'Impero*. Milan, Bompiani.

Ergas, Y. 1982: 1968–79 – Feminism and the Italian Party System: Women's Politics in a Decade of Turmoil. *Comparative Politics*, 14(3), 253–79.

Flax, J. 1987: Postmodernism and Gender Relations in Feminist Theory. *Signs*, 12(4), 621–42.

Greer, G. 1970: *The Female Eunuch*. London, MacGibbon and Kee.

Haraway, D. 1989: *Primate Visions: Gender, Race and Nature in the World of Modern Science*. Ithaca, New York, Cornell.

Hellman, J.A. 1984: The Italian Communists, the Women's Question and the Challenge of Feminism. *Studies in Political Economy*, 13, 57–82.

Hellman, J.A. 1987: *Journeys Among Women. Feminism in Five Italian Cities*. Oxford, Polity.

Hellman, S. 1976: The 'New Left' in Italy. In M. Kolinsky and W.E. Paterson (eds), *Social and Political Movements in Western Europe*. London, Croom Helm, 243–72.

Hellman, S. 1987: Italy. In M. Kesselman and J. Krieger (eds), *European Politics in Transition*. Lexington, Mass., D.C. Heath, 320–450.

Irigaray, L. 1985a: [1974]: *Speculum of the Other Woman*. Ithaca, NY, Cornell University Press.

Irigaray, L. 1985b: [1977]; *This Sex Which Is Not One*. Ithaca, NY, Cornell University Press.

Jacobus, M. 1986: *Reading Woman*. London, Methuen.

Jacobus, M., Keller, E.F. and Shuttleworth, S. (eds), 1990: *Body/Politics: Women and the Discourses of Science*. New York, Routledge.

Jardine, A. and Smith, P. (eds) 1987: *Men in Feminism*. New York and London, Methuen.

Keller, E.F. 1985: *Reflections on Gender and Science*. New York, Columbia University Press.

Kristeva, J. 1980: *Desire in Language*, ed. L.S. Roudiez. Oxford, Blackwell.

Kristeva, J. 1986: *The Kristeva Reader*, ed. T. Moi. Oxford, Blackwell.

Lakoff, R. 1975: *Language and Woman's Place*. New York, Harper & Row.

28   *Introduction: Coming from the South*

Lange, P. and Tarrow S. (eds) 1980: *Italy in Transition: Conflict, and Consensus*. London, Frank Cass.

Libreria delle Donne di Milano 1987: *Non credere di avere dei diritti. La generazione della libertà femminile nell'idea e nelle vicende di un gruppo di donne*. Turin, Rosenberg & Sellier.

Lovell, T. (ed.) 1990: *British Feminist Thought*. Oxford, Blackwell.

Lumley, R. 1983: 'Social Movements in Italy, 1968–78'. Unpublished PhD dissertation, University of Birmingham.

Marcuzzo, C. and Rossi Doria, A. (eds) 1987: *La ricerca delle donne. Studi femministi in Italia*. Turin, Rosenberg & Sellier.

Marks, E. and de Courtivron, I. 1981: *New French Feminisms*. Brighton, Harvester Press.

Maturana, H.R. and Varela, F.J. 1980: *Autopoiesis and Cognition: The Realization of the Living*. Dordrecht, Holland, Reidel.

Melucci, A. 1981: New Movements, Terrorism, and the Political System: Reflections on the Italian Case. *Socialist Review*, 56 97–136.

Miller, C. and Swift, K. 1976: *Words and Women: New Languages in New Times*. New York, Anchor & Doubleday.

Miller, N.K. 1988: *Subject to Change*. New York, Columbia University Press.

Millett, K. 1972: *Sexual Politics*. London, Abacus/Sphere (rpt 1977, Virago Press).

Mitchell, J. 1979: *Women: The Longest Revolution*. New York, Pantheon.

Moi, T. (ed.) 1987: *French Feminist Thought*. Oxford, Blackwell.

Morris, M. 1988: *The Pirate's Fiancée. Feminism, Reading, Postmodernism*. London, Verso.

Pitch, T. 1979: Notes from within the Italian Women's Movement: How We Talk of Marxism and Feminism. *Contemporary Crises*, 3, 1–16.

Pomata, G. 1987: Commento alla relazione di Paola Di Cori. In Marcuzzo and Rossi 1987: 112–22.

Rich, A. 1977: Compulsory Homosexuality. In her *Of Woman Born*. London, Virago.

Rich, A. 1979: *On Lies, Secrets and Silence*. New York. W.W. Norton.

Rossi, R. 1978: *La parola delle donne*. Rome, Editori Riuniti.

Rowbotham, S. 1989: *The Past is Before Us. Feminism in Action since the 1960s*. London, Pandora.

Sabatini, A. (ed.) 1986: *Raccomandazioni per un uso non sessista della lingua*. Rome, Commissione nazionale per la realizzazione della parità tra uomo e donna.

Scott, J.W. 1988: Deconstructing Equality-Versus-Difference: Or, The Uses of Poststructuralist Theory For Feminism. *Feminist Studies*, 14, 1, 33–50.

Sellers, S. (ed.) 1988: *Writing Differences. Readings from the Seminar of Hélène Cixous*. Milton Keynes, Open University Press.

Showalter, E. (ed.) 1986: *The New Feminist Criticism. Essays on Women, Literature and Theory*. London, Virago Press.

Spender, D. 1980: *Man Made Language*. London, Routledge.

Spini, V. 1972: The New Left in Italy. *Journal of Contemporary History*, 7, 51–71.

Thorne, B. and Henley, N. (eds) 1975: *Language and Sex: Difference and Domination*. Rowley, Mass., Newbury House.

Violi, P. 1987: *L'infinito singolare. Considerazioni sulle differenze sessuali nel linguaggio*. Verona, Essedue.

Von Henneberg, K.C. 1983: 'The Italian Communist Party and the Feminist Movement'. Unpublished honours thesis, Harvard University.

Zimmerman, B. 1985: What has Never Been: An Overview of Lesbian Feminist Criticism. In G. Greene and C. Kahn (eds), *Making a Difference: Feminist Literary Criticism*. London, Methuen.

PART I

Italian Feminist Groups:
A Survey of Positions

1

Demau

The Demau (demystification of authority) group was active in Milan from 1966 to the early 1970s, when it became part of the Via Cherubini collective. This was later to be among the promoters of a *casa delle donne* (women's house) in Via Col di Lana, opened in 1976. All these groups have now disappeared. However, some women from Demau and Via Cherubini also participated in the creation of the Libreria delle Donne di Milano (Milan's Women's Bookshop: see chapter 5, p. 109) and are still actively engaged in feminist theory and practice, either in connection with the Libreria itself, or in other groups.

Questioning the ideas and the politics of the extant organizations of women who worked within the institutions for 'emancipation', Demau underlined the need to rethink the issue of women's condition in a perspective which would go beyond the concept of 'emancipation', that is, participation on an equal base in a world founded on existing values. For Demau, women's oppression is not merely the result of the economic structure of society; its specificity lies in the sexual sphere, in the subjection in relationships and in the family. Even in their first document, (the manifesto partly included in this chapter), the need for an ideological autonomy is stressed; for the autonomous production of thought free from the models imposed by male culture. The same theme is developed in their subsequent writings: 'Alcuni problemi sulla questione femminile' ('Some problems concerning the issue of women's condition' [1967]), and 'Il maschile come valore dominante' ('Maleness as the dominant value' [1968]).

MANIFESTO *DEMAU*, 1966

The Demau group (Demystification of Authority) operates outside any political or religious tendency. It believes that, at the present time and in this type of society, the participation of women and their contribution are indispensable for a renewal of human values. These are currently founded on the belonging to one or the other sex and distributed accordingly.

The group bases itself in essence on the following programmatic points:

(1) *opposition to the concept of the integration of women* into modern society. For such a concept in its current meaning:
(a) does not resolve the incompatibility of the two roles, predetermined by the division of labour between men and women, thereby allowing its enforced coexistence only for women.
(b) on the one hand intends to liberate women from ties of a practical nature stemming from traditional roles, in order to enable them to play an active part in the cultural world and in the work sphere. But on the other hand it reconfirms within society, and for women themselves, the characteristics and duties of *their* 'feminine' role in so far as it envisages a special favour only for them.

(2) *demystification of authoritarianism as a theory and a mystique of the moral, cultural and ideological values* on which the current division of labour and society as a whole are based; as a coercive element on individual values; and as a restraint upon the rights, the needs and the potentialities of all humankind in favour of privileged groups.

Demystification of such values, therefore:
(a) in the area of rights
(b) in the area of sexual relations and its related ethics
(c) in the area of conflicts of roles in family and social relationships in general
(d) in the area of education, instruction and culture
(e) in the area of work and of intellectual and scientific production
(f) in the area of scientific types of theorizing

The search, therefore, for new values concerning the whole system of relationships.

(3) *The search for a new autonomy for women*, through a conscious

evaluation of their own essential values and their own historical situation. Only in this way will women be able to participate in the elaboration of values that will inform a new society.

A search of this kind presupposes a new and wider method of enquiry into the position of women; that is to say, one that does not consider it only from the historical-evolutionary point of view of the 'women's question'.

Any study based on the conditioning of an ideologically predetermined social role which did not consider women both as autonomous objects and subjects of analysis would be insufficient grounds for a search that aims to find new directions and goals.

In fact:

(a) the study of 'conditioning' would lead to the discovery of antidotes, as pure and simple antithesis to the status quo.

(b) the inherent conclusion of antithesis is the inversion of the condition of fact.

This could only signify:

(a) a fight for supremacy over the male (an inverted dictatorship – a new matriarchy)

or

(b) masculinization of women (confirmation of the current cultural models).

2

Rivolta Femminile

Rivolta Femminile (Female Revolt) was officially born in July 1970 with the publication of its first manifesto, which the group posted up on the walls of Rome. The text expressed the identity of the group, and, by comparison, that of the women's liberation movement. Shortly after that, the group's members founded their own publishing house, Scritti di Rivolta Femminile, in order to circulate their ideas without risking misrepresentation. A few months later *Sputiamo su Hegel* was published, followed in 1971 and 1972 by other texts, which taken together fully signify the positions of the group.

In the meantime the various small groups which together constituted the whole of Rivolta Femminile came into being in different parts of Italy. Each group conducted its research autonomously, following the rhythms and needs of the women who formed it, but the groups also maintained an ongoing dialogue amongst themselves. Their research was for self-awareness: the journey into the self sought a deep internal modification. Discarding all given ideas about women, it questioned the whole cultural tradition, and analysed personal experience.

Thus, Rivolta Femminile has never been interested in political propaganda, in the sense of trying to convince other women to join in an organized movement active on the public scene for social and political change, and the groups have not directly participated in the specific struggles carried on by Italian feminists. Their writings, however, have been greatly influential, in particular those by Carla Lonzi, the founder of the group, who died in 1982; for example, 'Female sexuality and abortion' (included in chapter 11, p. 214), went straight to the crux of the matter, identifying sexuality and its imposed forms as the locus of formation/deformation of women's identity.

As the work carried out by the group was felt to be ready for publication, a new title appeared in the *Libretti Verdi* series ('green books', from the colour of the cover). Since 1980, they have published a new series, called *Prototipi* ('prototypes'), to indicate that each text presents a total reconsideration of the self, and of the issue in question, versus the established ideas in that respect; and also that such reconsideration cannot become a 'model' for subsequent works.

The activities of the publishing house have become more and more central for Rivolta, as a means of giving expression to the range of women's thought, circulating it and making it act in the world, in order to found another culture.

We have chosen to include in this section substantial extracts from *Let's spit on Hegel* and the group's two manifestos.

MANIFESTO   *RIVOLTA FEMMINILE*, 1970

Will women always be divided one from another? Will they never form a single body?

Olympe de Gouges, 1791

Woman must not be defined in relation to man. This awareness is the foundation of both our struggle and our liberty.

Man is not the model to hold up for the process of woman's self-discovery.

Woman is the other in relation to man. Man is the other in relation to woman. Equality is an ideological attempt to subject woman even further.

The identification of woman with man means annulling the ultimate means of liberation.

Liberation for woman does not mean accepting the life man leads, because it is unlivable; on the contrary, it means expressing her own sense of existence.

Woman as subject does not reject man as subject but she rejects him as an absolute role. In society she rejects him as an authoritarian role.

Up until now the myth that the one complements the other has been used by man to justify his own power.

Women are persuaded from infancy not to take decisions and to depend on a 'capable' and 'responsible' person: father, husband, brother.

The female image with which man has interpreted woman has been his own invention.

Virginity, chastity, fidelity are not virtues; but bonds on which to build and to maintain the institution of the family. Honour is its consequent repressive codification.

In marriage, the woman, deprived of her name, loses her identity, signifying the transfer of property which has taken place between her father and the husband.

She who gives birth is unable to give her name to her children: the woman's right has been coveted by others whose privilege it had become.

We are forced to reclaim as our own the issue of a natural fact.

We identify marriage as the institution that has subordinated woman to male destiny. We are against marriage.

Divorce is a welding of marriages which actually reinforces the institution.

The transmission of life, respect for life, awareness of life are intense experiences for woman and values that she claims as her own.

Woman's first reason for resentment against society lies in being forced to face maternity as a dilemma.

We denounce the unnatural nature of a maternity paid for at the cost of exclusion.

The refusal of the freedom of abortion is part of the global denial of woman's autonomy.

We do not wish to think about motherhood all our lives or to continue to be unwitting instruments of patriarchal power.

Woman is fed up with bringing up a son who will turn into a bad lover.

In freedom she is able and willing to face the son and the son is humanity.

In all forms of cohabitation, feeding, cleaning, caring and every aspect of daily routine must be reciprocal gestures.

By education and by mimesis men and women step into their roles in very early infancy.

We understand the mystifying character of all ideologies, because through the reasoned forms of power (theological, moral, philosophical, political) they have constrained humanity into an inauthentic condition, suppressed and consenting.

Behind every ideology we can see the hierarchy of the sexes.

From now on we do not wish to have any screen between ourselves and the world.

Feminism has been the first political moment of historical criticism of the family and society.

Let's unite the situations and episodes of historical feminist experience: through it woman has manifested herself, interrupting for the first time the monologue of patriarchal civilization.

We identify in unpaid domestic work the help that allows both private and state capitalism to survive.

Shall we allow that which happens again and again at the end of every popular revolution, when woman, who has fought with the others, finds herself and her problems pushed to one side?

We detest the mechanisms of competitiveness and the blackmail exercised in the world by the hegemony of efficiency. We want to put our working capacity at the disposal of a society that is immune to this.

War has always been the specific activity of the male and his model for virile behaviour.

Equality of remuneration is one of our rights but our suppression is another matter. Shall we be content with equal pay when we already carry the burden of hours of domestic work?

We must re-examine the creative contributions made by woman to society and defeat the myth of her secondary industry.

Attributing high value to 'unproductive' moments is an extension of life proposed by woman.

Whoever is in power states 'loving an inferior being is part of eroticism.' Maintaining the status quo is therefore an act of love.

We welcome free sexuality in all its forms because we have stopped considering frigidity an honourable alternative.

Continuing to regulate life between the sexes is a necessity for power, the only satisfactory choice is a free relationship.

Curiosity and sexual games are a right of children and adolescents.

We have looked for 4,000 years; now we have seen!

Behind us is the apotheosis of the age-old masculine supremacy. Institutionalized religions have been its firmest pedestal. And the concept of 'genius' has constituted its unattainable step. Woman has undergone the experience of seeing what she was doing destroyed every day.

We consider incomplete any history which is based on non-perishable traces.

Nothing, or else misconception, has been handed down about the presence of woman. It is up to us to rediscover her in order to know the truth.

Civilization had despised us as inferior, the church has called us sex, psychoanalysis has betrayed us, Marxism has sold us to hypothetical revolution.

We ask for testimonials for centuries of philosophical thought that has theorized about the inferiority of woman.

We hold systematic thinkers responsible for the great humiliation imposed on us by the patriarchal world. They have maintained the principle of woman as an adjunct for the reproduction of humanity, as bonded with divinity, or as the threshold of the animal world, a sphere of privacy and pietas. They have justified by metaphysics what was unjust and atrocious in the life of woman.

We spit on Hegel.

The servant–master dialectic is a settling of account between groups of men: it does not foresee the liberation of woman, the great oppressed by the patriarchal civilization.

Class struggle, as a revolutionary theory that developed from the servant–master dialectic, also excludes woman. We question socialism and the dictatorship of the proletariat.

By not recognizing herself in male culture woman deprives it of the illusion of universality.

Man has always spoken in the name of humanity but half the world population now accuses him of having sublimated a mutilation.

Man's strength lies in identifying with culture, ours in refuting it.

After this act of conscience man will be distinct from woman and will have to listen to her telling what concerns her.

The world will not explode just because man will no longer hold the psychological balance based on our submission.

From the bitter reality of a universe that has never revealed its secrets we take much of the credit given to the obstinacies of culture. We wish to rise to be equal to an answerless universe.

We look for the authenticity of the gesture of revolt and will sacrifice it neither to organization nor to proselytism.

We communicate only with women.

LET'S SPIT ON HEGEL   *CARLA LONZI*, 1970

The feminine problem is the relationship of any woman – deprived as she is of power, of history, of culture, of a role of her own – to any man: his power, his history, his culture, his absolute role.

This problem calls into question the whole of man's work and thought; man who has had no awareness of woman as a human being on the same level as himself.

In the eighteenth century we demanded equality, and Olympe de Gouges went to the scaffold for her 'Declaration of the Rights of Women'. The demand for equality of women with men in the matter of rights coincides historically with the assertion of the equality of men among themselves. Our presence was timely then. Today we are conscious that we ourselves are posing a question.

The oppression of woman did not begin in historical times, but is buried in the obscurity of human origins. The oppression of woman will not be overcome by annihilating man. Nor will equality cancel it; oppression will continue with equality. Revolution will not cancel it; it will continue with revolution. The concept of alternatives is a stronghold of male power, where there is no place for women.

The equality available today is not philosophical but political. But do we, after thousands of years, really wish for inclusion, on these terms, in a world planned by others? Would we indeed be gratified by participating in the great defeat of man?

What is meant by woman's equality is usually her right to share in the exercise of power within society, once it is accepted that she is possessed of the same abilities as man. But in these years women's real experience has brought about a new awareness, setting into motion a process of global devaluation of the male world. We have come to see that at the level of power there is no need for abilities but only for a particularly effective form of alienation. Existing as a woman does not imply participation in male power, but calls into question the very concept of power. It is in order to avoid this attack that we are now granted inclusion in the form of equality.

Equality is a juridical principle. To the common denominator of all human beings justice should thus be rendered. Difference is an existential principle which concerns the modes of being human, the peculiarity of one's own experiences, goals, possibilities, and one's sense of existence in a given situation and in the situation one wants to create for oneself. The difference between woman and man is the basic difference of humankind.

A black man may be equal to a white man, a black woman to a white woman.

Woman's difference is her millennial absence from history. Let us profit from this difference; for once we have achieved inclusion in society, who is to say how many more centuries will have to pass before we can throw off this new yoke? The task of subverting the order of the patriarchal structure cannot be left to others. Equality is what is offered as legal rights to colonized people. And what is imposed on them as culture. It is the principle through which those with hegemonic power continue to control those without.

The world of equality is the world of legalized oppression and one-dimensionality. In the world of difference, terrorism discards its weapons and oppression yields to the variety and multiplicity of life. Equality between the sexes is merely the mask with which woman's inferiority is disguised.

This is the stand of those who, being different, want to effect a total change in the culture that has held them prisoners.

We have realized not only the fact of our oppression, but the alienation generated in the world by our imprisonment. There is not one single reason left for woman to accept man's objectives.

At this new stage of consciousness woman rejects the levels both of equality and of difference, as a dilemma imposed upon her by male power. She claims that no human being or group should either define themselves or be defined in terms of another human being or group.

Woman's oppression is the outcome of thousands of years; capitalism has rather inherited than produced it. The development of private property expressed an imbalance between the sexes in the need of each man to hold power over each woman, while the power relationships among men were being defined. To interpret our destiny up till now on a purely economic basis is to make recourse to a mechanism whose primary cause is still ignored. We know that the instincts of human beings are typically oriented according to the satisfaction they may or may not achieve in their relationship with the other sex. Historical materialism misses the emotional element which lay behind the transition to private property. It is there that we shall look in order to identify the archetype of property, the very first object conceived by man: the sexual object. By discarding his first prey from man's unconscious, woman can unblock the origins of pathological possessiveness.

Women realize the political connection between Marxist-Leninist ideology and their sufferings, needs, aspirations. But they do not believe that women are secondary, a consequence of the revolution. They question the idea that their cause should be subordinated to the class problem. They cannot accept that the struggle be set in terms which pass over their heads. [. . .]

Subsuming the feminine problem to the classist conception of the master–slave struggle is an historical mistake. In fact, this conception comes out of a culture which dismissed the essential discrimination of humankind, i.e. man's absolute privilege over woman; it creates a new perspective only for men, as it poses the problem only in their terms.

Subordination to the classist perspective means for woman the acceptance of terms borrowed from a slavery quite different from her own; terms which actually witness to her misrepresentation. Woman is oppressed as a woman, at all social levels; not as a class, but as a sex.

This gap in Marxist theory is no accident, nor would it be filled by stretching the concept of class to make room for women as a new class. Why has it been overlooked that women play a part in the productive process through their work in reproducing labour-power within the family? And that their exploitation in the home is an essential function of the accumulation of capital? By trusting all hopes of a revolutionary future to the working class, Marxism has ignored women, both as oppressed people and as bearers of the future. Its revolutionary theory was developed within the framework of a patriarchal culture.

Let us consider the man–woman relationship in Hegel, the philosopher who saw the slave as the driving moment of history. He rationalized patriarchal control most subtly of all within the dialectics of a divine feminine principle and a human masculine principle. The former presided in the family, the latter in the community. 'While the community takes sustenance only by destroying the happiness of the family and by dissolving self-consciousness in universal self-consciousness, it produces, in that which oppresses and which is at the same time essential for it – in other words in femininity in general – its inner enemy' ('Spirit' from *Phenomenology of the Mind*). Woman never goes beyond the stage of subjectivity. She recognizes herself in her relations by blood and by marriage, and thus remains immediately universal. She lacks the necessary premises for leaving the family ethos and for achieving the self-conscious force of universality through which man becomes a citizen. Her condition, which is the consequence of her oppression, is treated by Hegel as its cause. The difference between the sexes is used to form the natural metaphysical basis both for their opposition and for their reunification. Within the feminine principle Hegel locates an a priori passivity in which the proofs of male domination disappear. Patriarchal authority has kept women in subjection, and the only value recognized as belonging to them is their being able to accept it as their own nature.

In accordance with the whole tradition of western thought, Hegel sees woman as, by nature, confined in one particular stage, which is given as much resonance as possible, but at which no man would ever choose to be born.

But the feminine, as the 'eternal irony of the community', laughs at the aging thinker who is indifferent to any pleasure and only cares for the universal. It turns to the young and finds an accomplice to share this scorn. Beyond the divine law which woman is meant to incarnate, beyond her duty to household gods, beyond the fine gestures from Greek tragedy with which she ascends from the depths of hell to the light of existence, woman reveals an attitude which would have appeared rather a threat than an oddity, had it not been for her weakness: her reaction towards mature men and her preference for the young. But because Hegel identified with the values of patriarchal culture, he treated this attitude as something purely instrumental. Women's high valuation of youth, that is of 'virility', is explained by Hegel as the stimulus for the community to focus upon the element most relevant for its action outwards, for war. Actually, we can see through her gesture and detect the patriarch's power over women and the young. Its real intention goes against the family and against society, embodied in the representative of power who dominates them both. By means of their scorn, they isolate the historical figure of the oppressor from which they wish to be liberated. But it is the oppressor who, as the head of the family and of society, is able to run the game and to turn to his own advantage any move which women or the young may make. The young man, encouraged by her attention, will indeed prove a brave defender of the community.

Wherever woman reveals herself as the 'eternal irony of the community', we can at all times recognize the presence of feminism.

Two positions coexist in Hegel: one interprets woman's destiny in terms of the principle of femininity, while the other sees in the slave not an unchanging principle of essence, but rather a human condition, the historical realization of the gospel maxim that 'the last shall be first.' Had Hegel recognized the human origin of woman's oppression, as he did in the case of the slave's, he would have had to apply the master–slave dialectic in her case as well. But in doing so he would have encountered a serious obstacle. For, while the revolutionary method can capture the movement of the social dynamics, it is clear that woman's liberation could never be included in the same historical schemes. On the level of the woman–man relationship, there is no solution which eliminates the other; thus the goal of seizing power is emptied of meaning.

Emptying of meaning the goal of seizing power is the distinctive feature of the struggle against the patriarchal system as a concurrent and successive stage to the master–slave dialectic.

The axiom according to which everything that is rational is real reflects the belief that the cunning of reason will always be in agreement with power. And the mechanism which ensures that this accommodation is in fact made is dialectic. This triadic structure of thought would lose its hold on the human mind in a way of life which was not dominated by patriarchy.

The *Phenomenology of the Mind* is a phenomenology of the patriarchal mind, the embodiment in history of the monotheistic divinity.

Woman appears there as an image whose level of significance is an hypothesis formulated by others. [. . .]

We can find within ourselves two glaring refutations of Hegel's interpretation: the woman who rejects the family, and the young man who rejects war.

The young man perceives intuitively that the father's traditional right of life and death over his sons openly realizes a wish, rather than legalizes a practice. He then sees war as an unconscious expedient to murder him, a conspiracy against him.

One should not forget that 'Family and safety' is a fascist slogan.

The anxiety which seizes a young man when he is about to take his place in adult society actually conceals his conflict with the patriarchal model. This conflict takes anarchistic forms in which a global rejection is expressed, without any compromise. Virility refuses to become paternalistic, it refuses the role of the blackmailer. But in the absence of his historical ally – woman – the young man's anarchistic experience is merely wishful thinking, and he yields to the call of organized mass struggle. Marxist-Leninist theory offers him a chance to turn his rebellion into something constructive by allying himself to the proletarian struggle (to the success of which the liberation of youth is also delegated). But by doing this the young fall again within the dialectic foreseen by patriarchal culture: a culture focused on the seizure of power. Believing that, in alliance with the proletariat, they have singled out in capitalism the common enemy, the young abandon their own ground, that of the struggle against the patriarchal system. They put all their faith in the proletariat as the bearer of the revolutionary moment. They may want to spur the workers if they seem too pacified by the successes of trade unions, or by the tactical considerations of party politics; but there is no doubt in their minds that the proletariat is the historical force of the future. By fighting someone else's battle, the young once again allow themselves to become subordinated, which is, of course, what has always been desired of them. Women, on the other hand, have the experience of two hundred years of feminism, and this gives them some advantage over the young. They tried first during the French and then during the Russian revolutions to combine their problematic with that of men at a political level, but they were simply granted the status of aggregate. Women now declare that the proletariat is revolutionary in its confrontation with capitalism, but reformist in facing the patriarchal system.

In his *Prison Notebooks*, Gramsci has a note in the section entitled 'Intellectuals and the Organization of Culture', to the effect that the young of the ruling class (in the broadest sense) may rebel and go over to the progressive class once it becomes historically capable of seizing power. But in this case, the young exchange the authority of the elder generation of one class for that of another. In either class the young are subordinated to their elders on a generational basis.

From Plato's *Republic* to More's *Utopia* to the utopian socialist theories of the eighteenth century, the ideal of a common ownership of goods had as a corollary the dissolution of the family as the nucleus of particular interests. This line of thought was continued by Marx and Engels. They, however, insisted not on the fact that the elimination of the economic element would put each woman at the disposal of each man and each man at the disposal of each woman, as Fourier wrote, but rather on the possibility of a relationship free from utilitarian considerations. The first formulation of this problem on the part of Engels appeared in *The Principles of Communism*, published in 1847:

> Under the communist order of society the relationship between the two sexes will be a simple private one which will be the concern solely of those participating in it, and with which society cannot interfere. This will be made possible because of the elimination of private property and the communal education of children, and thereby the removal of the two foundations for marriage as we have known it up till now: the dependence of women on men and of children on their parents ensuing from the system of private ownership.

A year later Marx and Engels wrote in the Communist *Manifesto*:

> Abolition of the family! Even the most radical flare up at this infamous proposal of the communists. On what foundation is the present family, the bourgeois family based? On capital, on private gain ... But you communists would introduce the community of women, screams the whole bourgeoisie in chorus. The bourgeois sees in the wife a mere instrument of production. He hears that the instruments of production are to be exploited in common, and, naturally, can come to no other conclusion than that the lot of being common to all will likewise fall to their women. He has not even a suspicion that the real point aimed at is to do away with the status of women as instruments of production.

Almost forty years later, in *The Origins of Private Property and the Family*, Engels explained the relationship between the economic structure and the family according to the principles of historical materialism, and made fully explicit his conviction that with the end of capitalism marriage would be realized in more human forms:

Once economic considerations have become secondary . . . all experience suggests that woman's equality, thus achieved, will tend much
more to make men monogamous than women polyandrous. What will
disappear from marriage are those characteristics which were impressed
in it at its origins by relations of property: firstly, male dominance, and
secondly, indissolubility. What we can predict today about the form
which sexual relations will take after capitalist production has been
swept away, which will happen very soon, is primarily negative in
character, and is limited to what will be suppressed. [. . .]

In communist countries the institution of the family has remained
untouched by the socialization of the means of production, which has
on the contrary reinforced it, since it has reinforced the prestige and
the role of the patriarchal figure. The revolutionary struggle has
actually brought to the fore personalities and values of a typically
patriarchal and repressive kind; these in their turn have created a
society organized at first as a paternalistic state, then as a truly
authoritarian and bureaucratic state. The classist conception, with its
exclusion of woman as an active force in the elaboration of the
principles of socialism, has turned a revolutionary theory into a
father-centred theory. Sexuophobia, moralism, conformism have
taken hold of the social roles, saving them from that dissolution which
had for centuries been cherished as the natural consequence of the
elimination of private property. The family is the founding stone of
patriarchal order. It is rooted not only in economic interests, but in
man's psychological make-up; in all times he has considered woman
an object of domination, and a springing board to higher deeds. Marx
himself lived as a traditional husband, devoted to his scholarly and
ideological work, with a number of children, including the one born to
his maid. The abolition of the family does not mean the communiza-
tion of women, as Marx and Engels made clear, nor any formula
which makes woman into an instrument of 'progress'. It means the
liberation of one half of humankind, which would make its voice
heard, challenging, for the first time in history, not only bourgeois
society but every society in which man is the protagonist, thus going
far beyond the struggle against that economic exploitation denounced
by Marxism. The resumption of the struggle for women's liberation is
not taking place today in the socialist countries, where the social
structure has achieved an almost medieval rigidity, with the authoritarian imposition of patriarchal myths rehabilitated by the revolution; it
happens in the bourgeois states of the capitalistic west, where the
downfall of traditional values can only be accomplished with the
intervention of women. This process involves the downfall of the

patriarchal conception, and it signifies the destruction not only of bourgeois form, but of a type of male civilization as well. Marxist thought developed within the framework of the master–slave dialectic (itself a basic conflict in the culture of a nascent bourgeoisie), giving this dialectic a concrete form by articulating it in terms of social classes. Yet the dictatorship of the proletariat has shown very clearly that it is not necessarily accompanied by a transformation of social roles. It has maintained and consolidated the family, the central institution for reproducing that human structure incompatible with any real change in values. The communist revolution took place on male-dominated cultural and political foundations, with the repression of feminism and its instrumental use. It will now have to face the revolt against masculine values that women want to extend way beyond the class struggle of the patriarchal system.

Even at the culmination of the struggle for the dictatorship of the proletariat, feminism confronted the situation with insights and methods which represented a radical break. But it was precisely in those revolutionary circumstances that communist women were forcibly reminded by their male comrades of the 'real' problems, and of the dangers of deviationism. The frustration which this caused often ended in self-sacrifice.

Lenin said to Clara Zetkin:

The list of your mistakes is not yet finished, Clara. I've heard that in your regular meetings for the discussion of literature and in your discussion with workers, you seem preoccupied with questions of sex and marriage and that this problem was the centre of your political education and your teaching activity. I couldn't believe my ears . . . I was told that sexual topics were also a favourite subject in your youth organization. They surely have plenty of material on this subject. It is particularly scandalous, particularly harmful for the youth movement, since such discussion can easily help to excite certain individuals and undermine their strength and their health. You must combat this tendency. The women's movement and the youth movement have many points of contact. Our communist women should carry out systematic work with the young. This should be to educate them, to carry them from the world of individual maternity to the world of social maternity . . . The marriage form and relationships between the sexes satisfy no one. In this area a revolution is coming which corresponds to the proletarian revolution. It is understood that this whole intricate question is as important for women as for the young . . . Many young people characterize their position as revolutionary or communist and they sincerely believe that this is so. But for us older people, there is really nothing to make us believe them. I am not altogether a melancholy old ascetic, but this new sexual life which the young lead – and often adults too – strikes me as completely bourgeois, like one of the many aspects of a bourgeois brothel ... You must know the familiar theory according to which in a communist society the satisfaction of sexual instincts or amorous impulses would be as easy and insignificant as drinking a glass of water ... but would a normal man in his right mind throw himself to the ground and drink from a puddle of filthy rain water? Would he drink from a glass already touched by ten other lips? This 'glass of water' theory has made our young people mad, quite literally mad.

And in a letter to Ines Armand, dated January 1915, Lenin wrote: 'Dear Friend, I warmly recommend that you write a more detailed version of the outline of your text ... But there is one observation that I must already make: I suggest that you suppress "the demand (by women) for freedom in love" entirely. This is not a proletarian demand at all, but a bourgeois one.' Lenin contrasts 'the baseness and vulgarity of the loveless marriage of peasants, intellectuals and petty bourgeois' with 'the civil proletarian marrage based on love'. Following her exchange of letters with Lenin, Ines Armand withdrew her text for women workers from publication.

How does the 'demand for freedom in love' differ from 'civil proletarian marriage based on love'? The difference lies in the fact that the former was made by women and taken up by the young, as one aspect of a revolutionary way of life, while the other crystallized the repressive values laid down by the party ideologists for the edification of a new man. Free love was the feminist version of the criticism of the family. Proletarian marriage was a product of the masculine order of things, the masculine interpretation of the premises of communism as they had been explained by Engels. When a communist woman from Vienna published a short work on sexual problems, Lenin wrote of it, indignantly: 'What a silly pamphlet! The few precise arguments in it have been known to women workers since the time of Bebel, and not in this arid and irritating form either. Its references to Freud's theories give it an air of being "scientific", but in fact it is a superficial muddle. Actually, Freud's theory is itself only a passing fad.'

According to Lenin, woman could develop and achieve a true equality with man, once, in a communist society, she had freed herself from unproductive labour in the home to engage in productive labour outside. [. . .]

No revolutionary ideology could persuade us any more that women and the young can or should find a solution to their problems in struggle, in sublimation or in sport. Grown men do not renounce the privilege of keeping them under control.

We see in the indifference that women have traditionally shown towards politics a spontaneous reaction to an ideological and political system in which their own problems are painfully allowed to rise to the surface only when men paternalistically appeal to women in order to manoeuvre them as a striking force.

The young are working for a social and political revolution which will exempt them from wasting their lives in the administration of a society in which they do not recognize themselves; at the same time, there is an attempt to use women's enthusiasm to solve the crisis of male society. Thus, women are allowed to fill man's roles, and this manoeuvre is made to appear a compensation for their age-old exclusion, and is passed off as a victory of the feminist movement. [. . .]

Although the nature of maternity is distorted by the conflict between the sexes, by the impersonal myth of the preservation of the species and by woman's life of forced self-sacrifice, maternity has been for us an important source of thoughts and feelings, the circumstance of a special initiation. We are not responsible for giving birth to humanity in our slavery. It is not the son that made us into slaves, but the father.

Therefore, before dismissing the relationship between mother and son as a stumbling stone for humankind, we should remember that they are held in a single bond by the authority of the father. The alliance between woman and the young is formed against this authority.

Don't ask us what we think of marriage and of its historical corrective, divorce. Any institution designed to protect man's privilege reflects a view of the relationship between the sexes which is no longer tolerable. We will blow up all the instruments of torture used to oppress women. [. . .]

The myth of maternal love will be dissolved the moment woman, at the fullest time of her life, experiences quite genuinely, in a natural exchange with the young, those feelings of joy, pleasure and playfulness which the taboos of the patriarchal system allow her to share only with her children.

The root of the Oedipus complex is not the incest taboo but the exploitation of this taboo by the father for his own protection.

A significant image of the past takes form before our eyes: on the one side, a staircase up which man proudly ascends; on the other, a staircase down which woman painfully descends. Whatever little pride she is allowed in a stage of her life is not enough to sustain her to the end.

Once the cause of women is brought into the open, it is a won cause.

Culture, ideology, institutions, rituals, codes and mores are all surrounded by male superstitions about women. This background pollutes any private situation; from this background man keeps gathering his presumption and arrogance.

The young man is also oppressed by the patriarchal system, but he is, too, a candidate for the role of the oppressor in the future. Any upsurge on the part of the young is inherently ambiguous.

The way in which the rebellion of youth is manipulated is another example of the distorting influence of the patriarchal system. By treating the hippy movement as a religious movement, politically committed students are using a politically discredited label to continue a paternalistic pattern. Secure in their ideological certainties, they claim that it is only a significant episode, but a non-dialectical moment of society. Precisely in that we recognize its peculiar value. The hippy movement represents a flight in disgust from the patriarchal system, the rejection of the politics of power and of all political patterns of predominantly male groups. Hippies no longer split the public and the private, and their lives are a mixture of the masculine and the feminine. The girl who out of frustration withdraws from the political student groups, or who in her frustration adjusts to the revolutionary behaviour of her comrades, that girl is facing a dilemma whose premises were laid down by collectives of men. They are now exploring as a specific area what in all times has been their field of action; a global view of problems is a pretence as long as men monopolize not only bourgeois but also revolutionary and socialist culture. It was the hippies, girls and boys, who first began to mock this hierarchy. On the discarded remains of aggressive and violent behaviours in which they saw the history of the belligerency of the fathers, they have tried to set up a community not based on masculine values. Ideology had always rationally explained and justified those behaviours and values as the means of changing the world. Woman's forced absence from the whole range of life in the community had magnified man's aberrant behaviour in his struggle to develop ways of living and patterns of thought. Woman's new presence has encouraged a voluntary dropping out on the part of the young; using whatever means are available, destructive, though non-violent, they express their conviction that it is necessary to start all over again from the beginning. The fact that the hippies, as many hope, will be fully reabsorbed by the establishment can in no way diminish the productive disorder which their sudden and unexpected appearance on the scene has caused. [. . .]

The whole structure of society pushes its prey, like the beaters at a shoot, towards the point at which the prey will be trapped. Marriage is the point at which captivity is made final. While governments grant divorce laws, and the Catholic church fights to prevent them, woman demonstrates her maturity by denouncing every aspect of the absurd regulation of relationship between the sexes. The extent of the male crisis can be seen in the dependence on formulae: they are the magic guarantee of his superiority.

Women have always been subjected to economic dependence, first on their fathers, then on their husbands. Their liberation, however, does not lie in achieving economic independence, but in destroying the institution which made them into slaves even after slavery had been eliminated.

Every thinker who has taken a global view of the human condition has underlined, from his own particular point of view, the basic inferiority of women. Freud himself found a theoretical basis for the curse of women: their alleged want of a penis, identified as a means to completeness. We express our incredulity at a psychoanalytical dogma which suggests that woman, at a tender age, feels herself handicapped by a metaphysical anguish at her difference.

In every family the boy's penis is treated as a sort of son to the son. It is talked about quite openly in complimentary terms. A little girl's genitals, on the other hand, are totally ignored. They are not given a name, they are not fondled like the boy's; they have no character, no literature. An advantage is taken of her body's secrecy to pass over its existence in silence. The relationship between male and female is not a relationship between two sexes but between one sex and its absence.

Freud wrote these lines in a letter to Martha Bernays, his fiancée: 'Precious darling, while you are taking such pleasure in activities and management of the household, I am at the moment tempted by the desire to solve the riddle of the structure of the brain' (letter 65, from *Letters of Sigmund Freud*).

Let us look into the private lives of great men: even the most common gestures partake of an aberration born of the daily closeness to a human being coldly defined as inferior.

There are no individuals, no geniuses, who have ever developed a correct view on all problems: no one has escaped the failures of human nature.

We live here and now, and the here and now are exceptional; as for the future, we had rather it were unexpected than exceptional.

Our greatest concern is that women retain that outburst of emotional confidence which is part of the most vital period of youth and which enables people to shape and touch the sources of creativity which will give a distinctive stamp to their lives. A girl is easily deceived into thinking that a psychic experience of which she was deprived in her youth may be recovered later. The emancipated woman is a useless model because she represents the adjustment of a personality, which failed to experience its leaps forward at the right moment.

Looking back we recognize ourselves in isolated peaks of creativity, but mostly we recognize ourselves in all the intelligence wasted in subjugation and in the endless round of daily chores through the times. We have been sacrificed and on this sacrifice idealist myths of femininity have proliferated.

We do not want to see women divided into good and bad, better and worse; for what interests us is the deepest core each of us shares with all the others, the point which is both so painful and precious.

The women's movement is not international but planetary.

The split between structure and superstructure forms the foundation for a law according to which human change always means primarily structural change. Changes in the superstructure would always reflect changes in the structure. But this is the patriarchal viewpoint and as far as we are concerned the theory of reflection has been discredited. Our chosen mode of action is deculturalization. It is not a cultural revolution which follows and integrates a structural revolution, nor one based on the validation at all levels of an ideology; it affirms the lack of any need for ideology at all. Women have countered the constructions of men simply with their own existential dimension: they have not had leaders, thinkers or scientists, but they have had energy, insight, courage, dedication, application, sense and madness. All traces of these things have been erased because they were never meant to last; but our strength lies in not having a mythic view of facts. To act is not the specialized task of some particular caste, although it becomes so when the purpose of action is the achievement and the consolidation of power. Men have mastered this mechanism to perfection; and since it is a mechanism which is justified culturally, to reject male culture is to reject the achievements of power as a basis for the assessment of actions.

With maternity a woman achieves a moment of deculturalization: she runs through the early stages of life again in an emotional symbiosis with the child. The outside world seems to her like an alien product quite foreign to the primary needs of the life she is re-living. Maternity is her 'trip'. Her consciousness turns spontaneously backwards to the origins of life, and she questions herself.

Male thought has sanctioned a mechanism which makes war, leadership, heroism and struggle between the generations all appear quite inevitable. Male subconsciousness marks a depository of violence and fear. The world is filled with his dreams of death, for which women are required to show pity; but we will no longer continue to act out this role imposed on us, and we will abandon men to the depths of their solitude.

> War preserves the moral health of a people, in their indifference to what they are accustomed to, to what is fixed. Just as the wind preserves the waters of a lake from the stagnation which would result from a long calm, so a prolonged, or worse, a perpetual peace will infect a people. For whatever is negative-or-negating in men's nature must be preserved and never allowed to become fixed-and-stable. (Hegel 1802: *Natural Rights*).

The most recent sociological and psychological studies on the origins and motives of the institution of war accept the submission of women to men as a law of nature. They analyse the behaviour of individuals and groups – primitive and modern – from within a completely patriarchal framework and fail totally to realize that in the domination of women by men they are presented with a ready-formed pathological syndrome. The father and the mother are talked about as subjects and objects of projective processes which deform what could otherwise be a normal elaboration of the given elements in reality. But the father and the mother are not two primary entities but rather the result of a prevarication between the sexes which is given formal expression in the family. Unless we start from this premise we will delude ourselves into trying to remove the psychological causes of war (the atomic threat) by advocating a return to private values and therefore a denial of the sovereignty of the state, or by promoting institutions which would prohibit war as an individual crime. Such solutions ignore the fact that private values are the values of the family, and that the family itself marks the unconditional surrender of women to male power. It is in the family that men's pathological anxiety and defences originate and it is from the family that he transfers them to the community, as its representative. Such solutions ignore, in short, the fact that this diseased condition of humankind cannot be diagnosed or cured by its own authoritarian means. [. . .]

According to Hegel, work and struggle are the two activities which define humanity, identified as men's history. The study of primitive peoples, however, can provide evidence that work is a female activity, whereas men's specific task is fighting wars. The moment a man is unable to fight, the moment he is taken prisoner and forced to work, he feels that he has lost his manhood and becomes a woman. Men used war as an external test to overcome their inner anxieties about their own virility. In its very origins, therefore, war was closely connected with men's ability to think of themselves as sexual beings. Yet what is at the roots of men's anxiety? The question is crucial because their anxiety is a constant theme of human history, reducing every conflict to the point at which it becomes insoluble and inevitably issues in the either-or of violence. The male species expresses itself in killing while the female species expresses itself in working and in protecting life. Psychoanalysis has suggested many reasons why man should treat war as a manly duty, but it says absolutely nothing about the connection between this attitude and the oppression of women. Moreover, the reasons which have led men to institutionalize war as a safety valve for their inner conflicts would make us believe that such conflicts are intrinsic to man's destiny, a given of the human condition. But woman's experience of the human condition is not marked by the same needs. She mourns when her sons are sent to the slaughter and her attitude of concern, although passive, distinguishes her role from that of men. In the destruction of the patriarchal system (through women's dismantling of the institution of the family) we can see, in outline, a far more realistic solution to the problem of war than any of those offered by the usual studies on this topic. This way we could achieve that transformation of humankind from the base which everyone invokes without having the least idea of how it could be brought about. [. . .]

We will no longer allow anyone to treat us as the bearers of the species. Our children belong to nobody; neither to their fathers nor to the state. We will give them to themselves, just as we reclaim ourselves to ourselves.

The *raison d'état* and moralism are weapons to subjugate women; sexuophobic attitudes hide the hostility and the contempt against her.

The exclusion of women is the main single assurance which priests of God possess that they belong to an army of the Father. The Catholic celibate is the most dramatic expression of man's contempt for women becoming institutionalized. Over the centuries she has been made the object of an almost inexplicable rage, sanctioned in councils, disputes, laws and violence. [. . .]

The religious and the aesthetic sensibilities have been identified by the dominant culture as two attitudes potentially antithetical to power.

Accordingly, culture has absorbed them into two major frameworks of power: the religious and the artistic institutions. We can see that the religious life is a way of living out patriarchal codes in a metaphysical region which contests and rejects worldly success; and that artistic work involves the confutation of authoritarian values through the capricious workings of one's rebellious will. While religious people and artists give cardinal importance to their own freedom of action, society applies even to them the standards of success by making use of their prestige.

The allies we choose are not those who espouse our cause but those who have avoided the worst excesses in our repression. Our character affinity to artists arises from the direct link which exists for us between what we do and its meaning, free of the anxiety which all the others feel about guarantees of cultural worth.

Let us cite another letter from Freud, in reply to Karl Abraham, who had sent him an expressionist drawing (December 1922):

> Dear friend, I have received the drawing which is supposed to represent your head. It is horrible. I know what an excellent person you are and I am all the more shocked that such a trifling flaw in your character as your tolerance for modern 'art' has to be so cruelly punished . . . People like these artists should be the last to have access to analytic circles for they are the all-too-undesirable illustration of Adler's theory that it is just the people with serious congenital defects of vision who become painters and draughtsmen. Allow me to forget this portrait while wishing you and your family everything good and pleasant for 1923.

Woman is not dialectically related to the male world. The demands she expresses do not constitute an antithesis, but a shift to another level altogether. This is the point on which we are most likely to be misunderstood and the one on which it is essential for us to insist. [. . .]

The feminist movement is full of political intruders and sympathizers. We warn male observers against making objects of study out of us. It is no concern of ours whether they agree or not. We suggest that it would be wiser and more dignified for them not to interfere.

There is no need for us to accept the demagogic suggestions offered as encouragement against representatives of their own sex. Each of us has felt enough indignation of her own, and has enough understanding and determination to find more imaginative solutions for herself.

We must insist on our being in full possession of ourselves since every time a gap opens there is always somebody ready to occupy the space and appropriate us to himself.

For a girl, the university is not the place where she will achieve her liberation by means of culture, but the place where, after having been carefully prepared by the family, her repression will be completed. Her education is a process of slow poisoning which paralyses her just as she is about to embark on more responsible gestures and enjoy experiences that will enlarge her conception of herself.

Our specific task is to search out in any event, past and present, its connection with the oppression of women. Every aspect of a culture which goes on ignoring this oppression will be denigrated by us.

It seems that, despite the atrocities of Nazism and Stalinism, and despite the present barbarities of imperialism, men still think, nevertheless, that they can redeem themselves from these terrible events. They deserve consideration, even taking account of the effort that has been made to circumscribe these phenomena. Man's real tragedy consists in the following: he is accustomed to finding the causes of his anxiety in the outside world, in the form of a hostile structure against which he must struggle, whereas now the notion that the problem of humanity is inside him, in the rigidity of a psychological structure which can no longer hold its destructive impulses, has reached the threshold of consciousness. In this way a sense of irreversible crisis is established, the only solution to which is the traditional red flag. Any self-criticism which is based in the old culture will reproduce the old conceitedness and irresponsibility. Men must break with this tradition and disrupt their historical role as protagonists. This is the change we desire.

From the beginning of the feminist movement to today we have been witnessing the exploits of the last of the patriarchs, and we do not intend to witness any more. We are living and acting in a new situation: the beginning of a new upsurge of the themes, the hopes, the struggles of the female part of humankind, for so long kept aside.

Woman is a complete individual. What must be changed is not the way she is, but the way she sees herself. We must transform the view which others, as well as ourselves, have of our place in the world. [. . .]

We will perform all the subjective gestures which will enable us to conquer a space around us. And by this we do not mean identification. Identification has a compulsive male quality. It strips the bloom from an existence and subjects it to the demand of a rationality which would control, day by day, the sense of success or failure.

Man is totally preoccupied with himself, with his own past, his own aims and his own culture. Reality strikes him as exhausted; his space flights prove it. Woman, on the other hand, insists that life must yet begin for her on our own planet. She can still see things where man no longer sees anything.

The male mind entered a final crisis the moment a mechanism was set into motion which has jeopardized the very survival of humankind. Woman comes of age by recognizing the motor force of this insane danger in the patriarch's character structure and in his culture. [. . .]

Men have been staking life for thousands of years and today they are gambling with survival. Women are still slaves because they have rejected the stakes; for this they have been made inferior, incapable, impotent. Women claim survival as a value.

Men have been looking for a meaning of life beyond and even against life itself. For women, on the other hand, their lives and their sense of life's meaning overlap. We have had to wait thousands of years for men's anxieties about our attitude towards them to stop being turned into the mark of our inferiority. Woman is an immanence and man a transcendence: in this contrast philosophy has idealized a hierarchy of destinies. To the extent that man is a transcendence, it was impossible to doubt the quality of his actions; and to the extent that woman is an immanence, then man was right to ignore her so as to be able to carry out his historical tasks. Men accordingly have abused women, but on the basis of an inevitable opposition. Woman must simply assume her own transcendence. Philosophers have said too much; on what grounds do they acknowledge man's gesture of transcendence and deny woman's? They recognize transcendence by the efficacy of actions, and while they assume it to be originary they deny transcendence where actions do not lead to an increase in power. But to measure transcendence by the efficacy of action is typical of a patriarchal outlook. Men imagine that the only alternatives are those they can see in themselves; that women must be an immanence, something inactive, rather than a different kind of transcendence which would have revealed itself had it not been suppressed by men. Women today want to assess the culture and history which take masculine transcendence for granted, and to judge that transcendence itself. As the result of countless traumas – both conscious and unconscious – even men have had slowly to realize the crisis of their role as protagonists. But man's self-criticism still holds to the assumption that what is real is rational, and he continues to propose his traditional roles, justifying this as necessary to overcome himself. Women are disgusted with the ways in which men have overcome themselves by oppressing women and at the same time blaming their immanence on them. Self-criticism must give way to imagination.

Our message to man, to the genius, to the rational visionary is this: the future of the world does not lie in moving continually forwards along a path mapped out by man's desire for overcoming difficulties.

The future of the world is open: it lies in starting along the path from the beginning again with woman as a subject.

We recognize within ourselves the capacity for effecting a complete transformation of life. Not being trapped within the master–slave dialectic, we become conscious of ourselves; we are the Unexpected Subject.

We reject as absurd the myth of the new man. The concept of power is the thread which runs throughout man's thinking, and which is the major consideration in his final choices. The subordination of women follows it around like a shadow. Any vision of the future based on these premises is accordingly false.

The feminist movement is itself the means and the end of any basic transformation of humankind. It needs no future, it makes no distinctions – bourgeoisie, proletariat, race, age, culture, clan or tribe. It comes neither from above nor from below, from the elite or from the base, it needs neither leadership nor organization, neither diffusion nor propaganda. An entirely new word is being put forward by an entirely new subject. It only has to be uttered to be heard. Acting becomes simple and elementary.

There are no goals, there is the present of our here and now. We are the world's dark past, we are giving shape to the present.

I SAY I *RIVOLTA FEMMINILE*, 1977

Who said that ideology is also my adventure? Adventure and ideology are incompatible. I am my own adventure. One day of depression one year of depression one hundred years of depression.

I discard ideology and I no longer know anything; *losing my way* is my proof.

I no longer have a glamorous moment at my disposition.

I lose attractiveness.

You will not find an anchor-point in me.

Who said that emancipation had been unmasked?

You court me now because you fear that I will be the interlocutor with the world that you could never be.

You wait for identity from me and cannot make up your own mind.

You were given an identity by man and cannot give it up.

You burden me with your conflict and are hostile to me.

You assault my integrity.

You would like to put me on a pedestal.

You would like to keep me under your guardianship.
I distance myself and you do not forgive me.
You do not know who I am and you make yourself my mediator.
What I have to say I will say on my own.

Who said that you helped my cause?
I helped your career.
But by appearing I spoilt your party.
Provocation is a gesture of attachment.
You force me to be present at painful revenges on a note of defiance.
You celebrate a myth that fell with me.

Who said that culture is a sublime goal?
It is the sublime goal of self-destruction.
In acquiring culture you have complied unreservedly with a request
that excludes you.
You have wanted to participate without existing on your own.
Ultimately you are unrecognizable.
And while this has been happening, you have suffered from a
feeling of inadequacy.

You claim solidarity because you went to the fight.
To my mind you have got yourself into a mess.
You have given your life to show that we are mediocre.
You have got stuck while climbing the phallus.
It seemed a question of time before you succeeded.
They continue to tell you that mediocrity is temporary.
I see you stuck there for ever.
You will come to envy my nothing.

Who said that you do not know power?
'To occupy oneself with' is intellectual arrogance.
The more you occupy yourself with women the more estranged you
become from me.
Do you know what exposing yourself means?
You search for error without being prepared to risk anything.

Who said that was self-awareness?
That would be a pantomime for fools.
It would be over before it had even started.
It has become swamped in misunderstandings.
It has vanished into stale air.

Don't talk to me if you have 'experienced self-awareness'.
Self-awareness is the other one.

Have you heard the one about 'double militancy'?
And the one about 'the private is political'?
And the one about 'you are not doing enough'?
I have found my source of humour.

3

Movimento Femminista Romano

This group began in 1971 with the name of Collettivo di Lotta Femminista (Feminist Struggle Collective), bringing together women with different backgrounds. Some had moved away from Rivolta Femminile, because they felt that they also wanted to engage in active feminist politics. Others had taken part in the Students' Movement and had a basically Marxist outlook. A number were not politically engaged in the common sense of the term, but felt the need to understand their unease as women. They all wanted to try to blend together theoretical reflection and daily life, the search for self-awareness and political action. The group was separatist, that is, it did not allow men to participate in its activities, and, in all fields, it privileged the relationship between women.

In 1973 some feminists from the Movimento di Liberazione della Donna (Women's Liberation Movement), a group affiliated to the Radical Party, decided to move out of it. They felt political engagement in a mixed group as a contradiction. When they also joined the Collettivo, it was decided to change its name in order to signal both the coming together of so many different experiences and the group's identification with the feminist movement in other countries. Thus the Movimento Femminista Romano (Roman Feminist Movement) was born, 'Roman' being merely a geographical qualifier. It met in a rented flat in Via Pompeo Magno in Rome; for this reason, it is also known as the Pompeo Magno group.

The group has been active in all the feminist struggles in Italy. Because it has no rigid organizational structure it has witnessed the comings and goings of many women among its members, as well as the simultaneous participation of some of them in other groups. It is now part of a collective body, called Movimento Femminista Separatista

Romano (Roman Separatist Feminist Movement). This comprises various groups who negotiated with Rome's city council to be assigned part of an old building in the centre of town for their separate and joint activities, after being evicted from a council-owned property which they had occupied.

The Movimento Femminista Romano has not produced fully articulated theoretical reflections, but rather short, to-the-point analyses of single issues, often in relation to its political action. Its practice centred on the discussion of personal experience, and on the attempt to theorize, in the discussion, the question of sexuality, both as a foundation of female subjectivity and in its sociopolitical aspects. Therefore the Movimento was in the forefront of the battles about abortion and against sexual violence (see chapter 11). We have chosen to include here some short texts which consider the issues of sexuality from various points of view, together with a more literary piece by a writer, not herself a member of the Movimento, who reinterprets a significant moment of the Movimento's activity: a night march against sexual violence after a particularly brutal episode of rape and murder.

'Marching in the night' is part of a book published in 1978 with an introduction by Julia Kristeva, *La lingua della nutrice* (The Nurse's Tongue) by Elizabetta Rasy. The book is an exploration of language and writing, a mixture of genres which does not belong to any of them – neither fiction nor journalism, neither essay nor diary, at times neither prose nor poetry, and yet all of them.

As the book's blurb puts it:

> Autobiography, diary, gossip, love stories – women have more often inhabited the margins and the peripheries of language, its interstices, minor and oblique discourses. Outside the signs and the time of the Father, before Oedipus, *the nurse's tongue* appears, rather than a system, a subterranean archipelago of signals or symptoms which points to the 'black continent' of femininity, women's dark world, history of phantasms behind the frail history of facts and certifications, built on its own repression, fed of its own censure.

Elisabetta Rasy lives in Rome, where she was born in 1947; she has been active in the feminist movement and is now a journalist for one of Italy's most important news-weeklies. She has published a book on women and literature, and is also the author of two novels.

ON PROSTITUTION: TWO BROADSHEETS AND A
STATEMENT   *MOVIMENTO FEMMINISTA ROMANO*, 1973

The following is the text of the leaflet that Turin's Feminist Alternative group has tried to distribute outside the daily La Stampa *where, in recent days, the newspaper has been trying to collect 50,000 signatures for the proposal by popular initiative to reform the Merlin law, alongside the similar proposed bill put forward by 29 Christian Democratic deputies:*

Prostitution exists.

It's not a matter of hiding the prostitutes.

It's a matter of eliminating prostitution.

As women, we are against a society where any man can buy a woman. As women we have never been disturbed by prostitutes. Instead it is their clients who, in public places, accost us 'intentionally', 'continually' and 'unequivocally', offering us their sexual services and preventing us from walking through the streets in peace. Will 50,000 signatures really be enough to ensure that women are no longer bothered when they go out at night? Is it not perhaps the first step towards reopening brothels? Let us not forget that in Turin prostitution brings in 150 billion lire a year. Will you sign? Then you agree that prostitution should continue to exist but behind closed doors. Your signature would be better used supporting a campaign for courses of sex education in all schools, for the establishment of family planning clinics in all quarters of the city, for making abortion available and free to all women.

The Roman Feminist Movement shares the Feminist Alternative group's initiative and invites women to meet at 9 p.m. on Wednesday 3rd January 1973 at the movement's base in Via Pompeo Magno no. 94 (Prati), tel. 386503, in order to discuss the possibility of opposing the proposals for the reform of the Merlin law.

(Only women are invited to attend)

Let's save morality. Let's preserve children from scandal. Let's protect public health and women's dignity. Under these banners Christian Democratic deputies, supported by a campaign led by the Turin newspaper *La Stampa* to collect 50,000 signatures for an analogous bill by popular initiative, have presented a bill to the chamber. This bill, with the pretext of attacking prostitution, actually leads to the limitation of personal freedom and freedom of movement for all us women. In fact every woman who finds herself on the street, especially at night, will be subjected to a personal evaluation by those (that is, the police) in charge of enforcing its norms. They will be able to decide at their own discretion whether or not they are dealing with a prostitute. And this suspicion, with a police warrant, could lead to an arrest of up to ninety-six hours with no means of defence.

As regards prostitution itself, it is significant the way yet again an attempt is being made to lay all the weight and moral blame on the woman rather than on the clients who allow themselves to pay a human being to gratify their own sexual pleasures.

Prostitution is a product of the patriarchal society, which invented the double standard, and in particular of the patriarchal-capitalist society that excludes women from the work market, pushes them into consumerism and forces them to various forms of prostitution in order to survive.

Prostitution is a male problem. If the 'sad spectacle of accosting', the invitation to 'sexual intercourse, and to illicit trading of the body' exists, then it is offered by men who attempt to accost, invite and offend any woman who happens to be passing by in the street. And for the umpteenth time we women are forced to hide in the ghettos of our houses.

Do they wish to apply repressive laws? In that case let them start by stopping men who molest and hassle women. They want sanitary control on venereal diseases? Every car that slows down near a woman is a threat. Enough false moralism!

This letter has been sent to various newspapers; if they choose to publish it, they should do so in its entirety.

What follows was read out on 25.2.73 during the meeting convened by the Roman Feminist Movement in the Sala Belloch on 'feminine prostitution in Italy'.

The Roman Feminist Movement, following the presentation:

1 of the proposal of law for the revision of the present Merlin law by 29 Christian Democrat deputies
2 of the proposal of law by popular initiative promoted by the Turin daily *La Stampa*

believes it is important to attempt to bring together all the women's groups interested in the problem in order to discuss not only the negative implications of the eventual approval of the above laws, but the problems of prostitution in general. As feminists we believe the Merlin law is positive in as much as it does not regulate and therefore does not punish prostitution, but tends to eliminate the exploitation of those who actually practise prostitution. It is because of this law that since 1958 prostitution has no longer been an offence in Italy even if, as we will see, prostitutes do not enjoy the same rights as other citizens.

The Merlin law, therefore, does not regulate prostitution but sanctions the abolition of brothels, punishes the instigation of or profit from prostitution, and prohibits the compilation of lists either by the police or by the health authorities.

The only offence that can at present be committed by anyone practising prostitution, according to the Merlin law, is the offence of 'inviting anyone to libertinism in a scandalous or molesting manner'. For this offence not only can the woman be punished but also whoever follows her in a car in a troublesome way, whoever importunes another person and offers sexual services in a molesting manner: in other words a large part of the male population could be punished.

We believe that it is important that a law should exist which, in principle, serves to catch indiscriminately whoever, man or woman, invites anyone to libertinism with harassment, and that it should not place the responsibility solely on whoever practises prostitution. For this offence the present law provides, however, not for preventative arrest but for denouncement to a judge who can inflict detention or enforce a fine. It is precisely the 'liberality' of this article that has drawn the fury of the counter-reforming crusaders of the Christian Democrats and the daily *La Stampa*.

In both proposals of law the penalties are made harder and can be applied only to whoever practises prostitution, even if not in a scandalous or troublesome manner.

In the projected laws neither the accoster nor the client can be punished, because they say the act of accosting must be continuous and unequivocal. In order to be able to talk of a continuous offence it is obvious that the persons in question should be under control; in other words, the existence of lists drawn up by the police, which we believe were never destroyed, would be legalized.

The repression of prostitution on the streets is not, however, to be considered an aim in itself, the idea of only a few puritans: it is part of a much wider plan for the control of the whole population, even if as usual women will be the first to suffer.

With the ominous provision of the establishment of a police warrant that would enable any policeman to arrest for up to ninety-six hours any person he suspected of intending to commit an offence (and in our case of intending to accost) one can say without exaggerating that it would become dangerous for any one of us women to go out at night without a man.

In contrast to the Merlin law, which provides for detention only in cases of the re-establishment of brothels and not in cases of prostitution by one person in their own house, the new proposals for law would lead, because of the possibility of denouncement by others within the building, to the creation of ghetto areas reserved for prostitution, such as already exist in other countries.

Both proposals would furthermore re-enforce the sanitary listing of persons practising prostitution: this would be justified by the alarming increase in venereal diseases. We believe that the spread of venereal diseases in Italy is favoured not by prostitution but by the aura of shame and ignorance that has always accompanied such diseases: a situation aggravated by article 554 of the fascist penal code to defend the health of the Italian race. This article, which no parliament, in 27 years of 'democracy', has proposed annulling, allows for penalties of imprisonment for up to three years for anyone who, aware of being a carrier, spreads a venereal disease. The fear of such a penalty inflicts on anyone, but especially the young, psychological conditions that lead to hiding a disease that the law believes is an offence, thereby making medical intervention more difficult. It is discriminating to impose only on women prostitutes certain health passes when this disease is contracted by men as well as by women. It is clear that in Italy it is the clients of prostitution, that is to say a majority of the male population, who spread venereal disease.

It is otherwise impossible to understand how women in brothels could be infected, if not by those visiting from outside, considering that the women were found to be healthy on entering the houses. Therefore if a health pass is to be issued let it be issued for the whole population. But this will certainly never be proposed!

For these reasons we consider as positive the Merlin law, which in 1958 represented an attempt to overcome the patriarchal law which deprives women of the possibility of managing their own bodies. We do, however, denounce the lack of correct application of the law, because it is never interpreted in the spirit with which Senator Merlin proposed it; that is, trying to make it easier for anyone who wanted to abandon prostitution to do so.

From the little evidence collected, it seems that this very law is used to perpetuate prostitution as it serves this society. The cases brought against keepers of brothels and profiteers are very few. Even when a woman denounces an exploiter the case is bogged down or proceeds very slowly. Every time a brothel is discovered the press carries only the names and surnames of the women involved, but never those of the clients caught in the act. Most women prostitutes tell us they cannot obtain a driving licence because they do not have a certificate of 'good conduct'. They cannot set up any business venture for five years after giving up prostitution. This necessitates accumulating millions of lire on which they must live for five years, which is almost impossible, as the violence these women suffer from their clients imposes on many the necessity of having a protector, who then appropriates a large part of their takings.

These women are, however, 'known' by the police, and their reinstatement into business is extremely difficult if not impossible in a society which virtually precludes these women from external work and which needs prostitution as a release valve for violence.

Anna, Matilde, Giuseppina, Paola

MALE SEXUALITY — PERVERSION *MOVIMENTO FEMMINISTA ROMANO*, 1976

Patriarchal society is based on authoritarian-exploitative relationships, and its sexuality is sadomasochistic. The values of power, of the domination of man over the other, are reflected in sexuality, where historically woman is given to man for his use. Sexual language also incorporated this concept: it is not by chance that one says that man 'takes' woman and that she 'gives herself' to him, or that man 'possesses' woman.

The idea of woman as man's property is fundamental to her oppression and she is often the only possession that dominant men allow exploited men to keep.

The very expression 'proletarian class' means 'he who possesses issue', and it goes without saying that it also means 'he who possesses the means, namely the woman, to produce issue'.

In other words woman is given to the (exploited) man as compensation for his lack of possessions.

Furthermore, man's frustrations as subordinate in a power-relationship is eased by the possibility of turning himself from oppressed into oppressor.

The transformation of sexuality into a sadomasochistic model of power and submission means that effectively what in the male world is defined as sexuality is none other than perversion.

Male frigidity, that is to say the impossibility of expressing true sexuality, is fundamental to this perversion. Man tries to conceal this frigidity behind a behaviour that is defined as 'virile' and 'active' and which in reality is an ideological concept for mystifying violence.

In patriarchal society virility is the same as violence.

The symbol of virility, *the erect phallus*, is therefore the symbol of violence.

But to the extent that virility equals violence it is not a vital force but only a cover for the real frigidity. The erection of the penis is not a sign of sexual vitality, but only a conditional reflex.

Man, while he seeks to hide his own frigidity, tries to force onto the woman an open and accepted frigidity. Woman must be the inert and passive object that, when moulded and manipulated by violence, will give the frigid man an illusion of vigour.

This leads to the total oppression of woman's sexuality and of her own identity.

Overwhelming woman's sexuality means crushing her vitality, her creativity, creating in her a masochism that makes her an object to be exploited more easily.

True sexuality is the spontaneous reaction to stimuli, whether psychological or physiological, that come together to obtain sexual pleasure, and it is also the awareness of the whole body as a source of sexual creativity. Spontaneity and the ability to control pleasure, which are indispensable for this creativity, cannot exist in patriarchal society, where they are repressed so that the sexual urge can be channelled into a perversion based on violence, fear and frigidity.

We denounce as the latest form of woman's oppression the idea of a 'sexual revolution' where woman is forced to go from being one man's object to being everybody's object, and where sadomasochistic pornography in films, in magazines, in all the forms of mass media that brutalize and violate woman, is bandied about as a triumph of sexual liberty.

This is freedom for the woman in the same way as the Nazis interpreted freedom when they wrote on the doors of Auschwitz 'work is freedom'.

The discovery that sexual oppression is the mainstay of male power, thus one which renders women different from any other oppressed group, was only possible when we began to free ourselves from all present structures and ideologies.

PERHAPS I CAN'T FIGHT FOR FREEDOM YET
ELENA, MOVIMENTO FEMMINISTA ROMANO, 1977

Perhaps I can't fight for freedom yet but I want the abolition of an age-old right: the right to be stupid.

One of the greatest difficulties facing me lies in confronting tradition, as a sense of reality, with the deepseated need to eradicate it. For me this means dislocating meanings – in language, behaviours and their links. To my advantage, or at any rate as an aid to my clarity in breaking these mechanisms, is my distance from history, which even so has involved me deeply and still involves me. I do not therefore identify myself with any avant-garde politics or culture or with the new structure of dissent, when I am only the displacement of a problem, a sort of second-rate culture.

I welcome the crisis in the precise sense that my life is ideological existence, that my identity surpasses itself as it affirms itself. In fact the radical fault lies in the transmission of a knowledge which is based on the automatic inevitability of repetition, the privilege of exactness rather than the truth of relationships.

Thus for me words must be used with the utmost vigour, in the sense that this use should also border on the unutterable. The border is non-authoritarian, non-institutional language. It escapes therefore the compensation offered to ignorance by formalized languages, rituals of a pretended exactness, obsessive repetition, a priori containers for objects and not meanings.

Within this kind of communication problems are given a solution, one might say, on the basis of a lack of understanding of the origins.

Always negating me as a woman, as the incommunicability of motives stands firm, they integrate me, perhaps better historically, into my position of new function and new symbol.

Thus one cannot take one step further than conventional language that expresses everything around me and only includes me in its own terms. The maximum gain then becomes the achievement by the male of a new partial understanding of a reorganization of a misunderstanding; the mirage of the word faces the defeat of silence, its emptiness of experience. Thus, once again the attempt is to establish some order, but never a balance; to establish, with honour as well, the new statute of the alienation of the emancipated woman.

Woman is always excluded from life and from the language that expresses this life, because all her psycho-physiological factors are excluded, and in their place is the attribute-attribution that according to male preconception expresses woman. It is one of the ways of ensuring the inertia of woman and of organizing even her modifications.

The male 'mad conjecture' has been the only reference to reality, the principle for men's survival. The madness lies in the common morality, because alienation and identification are the norm. Man has sought the universal and has only succeeded in being generic; his ridicule verges on the sublime and sinks into tragedy, which is his true dimension.

Feminism erodes all this; their words, the reality that they offer us, is no longer courted but rather is overturned. I wish to be lucid, to be aware and not to please. I have always paid by pleasing for that small portion of peace and quiet that they have given me. I am fed up with having to repress myself for being intelligent. I want to expand, to express myself, I who have suffered to gain merit have no cult of values, of right, of sex.

Besides, the certainty of sex is not sexuality. It is, however, on these certainties that power and perversion are based, the utilitarianism of relationships, the politics and economics of affection, the functionalization of inexistence and identification, which feeds the man–woman barter: you sacrifice yourself and produce (it is your affection and your sexuality), I use you because I recognize only myself.

But how can such a stupid mystification have been accepted for so long? It is the triumph of vulgarity, noises and masks in place of the quality of life.

Who will ever understand that *I am*, except someone on my side (and how much time will the best of males need to free himself from his age-old fantasy)?

My dimension lies neither in power nor in my reproductive ability but in consensus and sexuality.

In fact I do not give precedence to one part of my spirit or one part of my body, I do not produce always and anyhow, I do not divide myself into pieces or categories according to the occasion. I try to live in moments of 'sympathy' where I wish to express myself as a whole, I experience my own sexuality as one that is 'consensual', experienced and lived, not spoken – organized – prefabricated – publicized – orgamized.

Elena

SEXUALITY AND MONEY   *MOVIMENTO FEMMINISTA*
ROMANO, 1979

I found the suggestion that I might be happy on the market stalls
where the vendor and the buyer were not different but only dressed
differently. On sale besides were only an infinity of needs of the
highest quality (desire for) and of the worst production (need for).
The cost was lifelong instalments of the obligation to speak, my
signature was not sufficient, it had to be guaranteed by the role of
being a woman. A game of request and offer whose answer is always
missing because it has grown up amid offers 'born' of questions that
were not mine, that were consciously wrong, in which one always
looks for the proof in favour, and this proof is history. It is the market
of logic where reason never enters, where sadomasochism is a
substitute for an impossible intensity, because the subjects are points
of flight for anxiety, possession and power, the eroticism of diversity
that declines the repetitiveness of estrangement.

This market is the only reality that can be paid. Its currency is the
coin and the symbol of inexistence that become the exemplary gesture,
the adjustment to the market's rate of exchange by abstraction, where
my thought has no currency.

The buying and selling of my unreality; the connotations of
representation, where I am always invited to pretend myself in love or
convinced of the need to marry power or dissent, culture or counter-
culture, while being forced as a schizophrenic subject into the
hierarchy of identification. I condemn capital while they force me to
capitalize on myself, but today I know that economy is never neutral,
that time and the economic relationship are other from me, but are
imposed on me as reference points to organize my defence.

Economy therefore becomes all unerasable memory, because I have
to defend myself continually and affirm that I exist with recognizable
gestures and thoughts that can be given a price. I am therefore forced
into a humiliating battle, because the market does not sell feminism
and I have to impose it; yet I don't want the word of history; rather I
want to be subtracted from history; except that this subtraction must
find a means of expression, because otherwise it is based only on the
other version that, having always been defined and used as my
absence, is filled by the greed of order.

I can still make recourse to pathology to criticize the norm, and I
have to be careful that it is understood as sanity and not as a product of
folly. I am forced into, but not converted to, emancipation, yet I must

be careful that it is not a new kind of inclusion where I become a subject only because I can be assimilated.

I want to be myself but I also have to be a 'movement' which expresses the political nature of a conscience that helps one to discover and manage the right to happiness and knowledge as real faculties; not as the duty to be a place recognizable for the absence of desire on the part of the dominant castration, that has no rights but only codes and procedures against which I 'must' fight because I have a right to myself, and the ignorance of the male removal offends me with the categorical imperative of having to impose it on him.

The 'movement' therefore becomes the 'currency' of a displacement which is outside economic logic, the number and suffocated mentality that finally starts to act, an open number, not so much because it accumulates but because it is 'fluid'.

I feel no morality about this necessary currency unless it is in making sure that it is not for us or amongst us that it must circulate for ever.

Nowadays I am so unromantic that I can begin to live. I am now so unromantic that the 'becoming woman' talked about by the male who runs after the money of 'his' female part does not seduce me on the black market of alternatives. I am seduced by the gestures we do not make, the language we do not use, the fact that you and I both know so well the measures that we submit to and that we frequently offer in return, although not loving it, and that every time you present yourself with a 'category', my declaration of love and my political proposal is in succeeding in conjugating the verb of refusal to recognize ourselves and make us alike in that way.

The gold market has no tables for us, but it is not because of this that I do not wish to be rich with you.

I hope you do not need me to sign my name.

TOWARDS A PROJECT   *MOVIMENTO FEMMINISTA ROMANO*, 1979

Why is it difficult for a feminist with a few years of militancy behind her to accept the idea of women assuming power?

1   Until today a few women have been given the 'privilege' to eat, under the master's table, the crumbs that are so condescendingly and arrogantly dropped. So this dreadful situation was accepted by

virtue of a feeling of inferiority. What else can one do if they are superior to us?

2   One deduces from this that assuming power in these conditions (we being inferior because they are superior) can only provoke a new type of domination in which she who is a servant and *really believes it* creates herself 'in the image and likeness' of the master, leaving intact the vertical structures and substituting herself only physically.

In short, without making anything happen.

3   It is instead true that the road to be followed is overcoming the concept of inferiority. How?

(a) – with a gaining of conscience
(b) – with separatism
(c) – with intransigence

As regards the gaining of conscience we know enough today to say that we are only at the beginning, but at least we are on the right road.

As regards separatism we have used the most showy, exposed part. Meetings, groups, street demonstrations. For the rest, many mechanisms, especially in private, have been set into motion that were mainly tied to affections that have reduced the concept to pure ideology.

It is the fact of not having been able to break the thread that we believe ties us to existence, the fear of reappropriating our essence outside the definitions wished on us by the other, that has stopped our wish to separate ourselves in order to exist, from making that great leap that would have freed ourselves from those who, instead, as can be seen, continue to manage their own separatism unperturbed.

When we described as 'womanity' this desire to be apart from them, we did this with our hearts rather than with our heads. Our heads kept us firmly bogged down in humanity.

It is almost impossible for us to accept and really take for our own a world made to our measure, almost as if the idea of escaping from the rules of the male world would make us orphans.

Thus the debate, that began with the beginnings of feminism, has continued to base itself on the man–woman contradiction, while now should be the time to declare that the main knot is to be found in the man–man contradiction.

That he is demolishing the world, attacking all the states, all the economies regardless of their political colour; self-destruction alone is the goal offered, while we unfortunately are also dragged along tied as we are to this great carriage of death.

It is because of this that the intellectual and political stagnation in the male world is so large, given that if stagnation exists it can only be ascribed to them, though it also involves many of us, especially those more tied to their culture.

Our analysis was right. We understood at once where to find the knot which, once untied, would bring liberation in sight. It needed courage, and lots of it, to break the umbilical cord radically and not to stay and dither over it, unsure whether or not to cut it, retying it at once after looking anxiously at the effect it had; liberation was only one step further, but the ancient subjection was there to hold us.

One definitive wrench from their culture, which makes us dependent on their caravanserai of living dead, losing players in the challenge they are forced to create for themselves every time they destroy what we women create. And all of us, some more than others, chained and imprisoned according to class status, according to the small slice of power managed by male methods. 'Separating ourselves from' has wide implications that do not allow for revision according to the needs of the moment. Not being intransigent on this point takes us back to archaic times. Where one talks but does not act. In the company of sister witches, of sister suffragists.

In this way we undo that small bit of cloth that we had started to weave. In the meantime he sits laughing on his prick, which becomes ever more invasive because he has no intention of putting into question privileges and 'rights', and obtusely and grotesquely he reproposes the roles, considering 'his' own impotence a punishment for women.

Let us recover our own way of making politics, privileging the relationships between ourselves, putting our trust in one another, without now useless ideologies of the 'woman is beautiful' sort, but deepening love where it exists, recognizing ourselves as similar, giving ourselves space in life in order to find life in this cemetery that calls itself male society. Let us act out our separatism without letting ourselves be ensnared by our own need for security, still believing that it can be satisfied by someone who has managed love only in relation to ideas and things, never in relation to women.

We must look right into this need (or desire?) for recognition by the male which is translated into dependence. We must see how deep it runs within ourselves in order to eradicate it. This is where our liberation stems from. Since now the climate in which we women live is becoming pure survival, we will have to make up our minds and take our money away from the hands of these bankrupts.

In order to do this I have a proposal to put to all women; we must open a debate on how to manage public affairs and we must each begin by asking 'What happens to all the money that is taken from my pay packet each month? And a lot is taken, too much in relation to how much I earn.'

I demand that of this sum, which belongs to me, not a single lira should be spent on contrivances of war, on means of death. Instead it should be directed to building houses for women, nursery schools, canteens, gardens, objects intended for life.

Since the use it is put to by the male economy also destroys me, I say enough is enough. And what if all the women in the world were to say the same?

AN INTERPRETATION: MARCHING IN THE
NIGHT   *ELISABETTA RASY*, 1978

At night feminists in Rome march against violence. Many of them are heavily made up, heavily masked as women. The procession goes through the area round Termini station, shrine of the poorest, meanest prostitution, place of the most public and radical remission. The nightly *misé en scène* is a trap. In miming prostitution, the ventral, nocturnal feminine repressed by its own exhibition, the women of the Movement in Rome act out, behind the alibi of a reversed sign, both in their own eyes, and in the eyes of the men lying ready to ambush them along the sides of the streets, the ceremony of offering themselves. They experience prostitution, rediscover the condition of the seraglio.

> ('We could tell each other apart only by physical differences. When a woman said "I" she meant the whole of herself, from top to toe. We felt our I in our legs and our feet almost more than in our eyes or fingers. I can't remember how any of the girls spoke. But I still know how each of them walked.')

The growth of the feminist movement in Italy, in the years from 1968 to 1977, takes the form of the discovery of a 'female position'. Splitting off from, or moving away from, the luminous certainties of the New Left, but also from the obscurer ones of the Historic Left, from the start neo-feminists pretend a political ingenuity which they do not feel, behind the figure of the 'refusal'. In this way they decree a 'degree zero of politics', which to start with is more a schematized desire than a real condition of their political activity. There is the hope, and the utopia, that 'feminist militancy' means fighting for one's own condition as a woman.

('To consider woman as worker seems to us particularly unreal and reductivist. We would also point out that that in talking about working conditions which are not lived in the first person one risks seeing some situation from above, and "objectifying" the people who are being talked about. Some of the statements by women seemed to us particularly significant and interesting, when women talked about their own position as housewives, unmarried mothers and working women; at least we managed to be "with" people and not talk "about" people and problems.')

During the occupation of the universities, from February 1977, 'feminists' met 'students'. The 'eccentricity' of the student proposition highlighted the non-eccentricity of the female position for the feminists themselves as well. Women are marginalized, isolated 'in the centre'. Starting with its supposed externality, feminism discovers itself to be a movement 'within' other movements or institutionalized situations in the social sphere. Feminism is not 'external' to politics and society, as the New Left has suggested, thus placing it alongside the mentally ill, drug addicts and homosexuals in the peripheries of the consciousness of male-Marxist discourse. Nor is it internal, in that it does not belong to that omnivorous totality, the class struggle, as the Historic Left would like to see it. Rather, it is a movement 'within' these other groupings, their hidden and repressed double. Just as 'woman' is the condition of alienation which society carries within itself, so feminism – grouping or organization of all that is hidden, covered, shrouded, silent and secret – is the condition of internal alienation which every revolutionary movement carries and conceals within itself. It is this 'insideness' with regard to the social and political which marks the passage from the feminist movement to the women's movement.

('Male comrades have the right to see women's problems, since they too live in a family where they have a mother, sisters, a wife, and so they have the right to accept these problems and not to deny them, because they are everybody's problems. When they refuse to listen to the problems of their women comrades, in reality they are denigrating themselves, because they too live this same reality and it is not right to deny these things. This is why women refuse to stay with them, not because they don't want to.')

In its early stages feminism reproduces and exhibits the forbidden relationship of women with the social sphere, with the symbolic order. The 'society of women' forms itself through the 'small group' which takes apart and reformulates a maternal context. In the 'small group' women tell their 'personal' histories, put them side by side, lay one over the other; they sketch out the invariables of 'private' histories, an 'inner' history, which runs parallel to and subtends the History of the records. This is very often a history of forgetting, of failed acts, lateral messages which make up the obscure double of the other. Through these throbbing whispers, feminism opens up a magnetic crack in the categoric universe of the male-Marxist vision of the world, painfully exhibiting a history of ghosts behind the slippery facade of facts and certainties. The absolute materiality of the ghosts who embody need and desire stands in contrast and opposition to the phobic philologies of the existent and the existed.

('I'm not afraid of mysteries, I'm worried by more concrete things.
– But for women indeterminate things are worrying too.
– Perhaps that's what men like to believe.
– And perhaps they're right – said Rosebery, who liked the idea and found it totally convincing. – It's easy to imagine footsteps behind you, when all you are hearing is the echo of your own.')

A misunderstanding and a threat are weighing on the Movement. The lack of a bourgeois revolution, the absence of historical movements and groups for bourgeois freedoms and civil rights which would make the social more humane and the private more comfortable, means that the women's struggle is read institutionally as claiming these rights (some say that abortion is a civil right).

The threat: the fear of recognizing in the female the condition of alienation within society means that when women get together and organize they are considered the ultimate, disposable 'other': country of utopia (women's 'sickness' is their truth, their exclusion from the social body is 'health'), or territory to be conquered. All parties in Italy are attempting a new colonization, based no longer on implicit contempt but on proclaimed esteem. From being 'invisible', women become 'better'. In 1975 the court in Pisa refuses a request for damages from a girl who was 'seduced and abandoned', in the name of emancipation and female dignity. The institutions are assuming an abstract feminist morality, opposed to the real, 'base' needs of women, in order to exorcise the fear of the 'base' which is in the 'feminine'.

('I was in hospital to have a baby, and they left me alone with a bell in my hand so I could call them when the moment came. I was terrified I was going to give birth there and would have to make sure my child didn't fall on the floor.')

The women's movement mustn't give in to the calls to move upwards, to the illuminated places of the institutions; it must cut a strategic path downwards. In the small groups, 'gossip' – the flow of words which interrupts the historic aphasia and dumbness of women, useless with regard to the progressive economy of the world of production and its representations – enacts its own epic, that of autobiography. It's with autobiography that the women of Lotta Continua can crack open the smooth 'political discourse' of their comrades at their second national congress in November 1976.

('You see, I found the courage to say this not only because I'm here with all my friends, but because I got totally pissed off about something I've only just understood and which has really knocked me sideways, that after all this, for these reasons, because I didn't know what part I had to play, and I tried to make a part for myself by having a child . . .')

The language of autobiography is also 'inner' language, a shifting and shadowy discourse of feeling – as opposed to the productive male language of reason which organizes and counterorganizes reality in self-contained systems – in which what counts is only the series of words, language lost in itself, pure occupation of space, without economies (gossip as exact symmetry, and antidote, to domestic penny-pinching), exhibition – as in asking for love – of the waste of words, words-noise which give shape not just to a ratio, abnormal as it may be, but to a psychic landscape.

('It would have been nice if as well as granting me ample opportunity to describe my prayers and what the Lord has done for me, they'd also given me the freedom to speak out at least a bit about my miserable life and my terrible sins. It would have been a great comfort to me. But they didn't want to, and they really curtailed what I could say.')

The women's movement is a new type of political formulation, not only because it is marginalized 'in the centre' and not on the edges of the social body, but because it is 'naturally' without a project and 'historically' without a destiny. Because of the structural female impossibility of symbolic elaboration, the front of expression is a priori impracticable; that very front along which plays the internal contradiction which paralyses and exorcises any political avant garde, which in order to enounce the prevarication of the existing order gives way to what structures and coordinates it: its language.

After a long period of dumbness, the child loses its own idiom, the full and special language he shares with the woman who nurses him (a language characterized by psychosis, according to Jakobson), and is born to the symbolic order. The child loses his idiom and is born to language but the woman, who still nourishes him, retains it. This language, the language of the nourisher, is peculiar to her. A psychotic language then, a language of non-communication which assures, beyond ideology and every new positive norm which the Movement thinks it is elaborating, inner contacts, but makes contacts with the outer world unlikely.

('She who is called mother of her children does not generate them, but only nourishes the seminal fluid; it is the male who generates.')

The political and economic crisis is trying to use feminism as a political avant garde, is pushing for the emergence of a leadership, and is transforming diversity into currents. At the same time it pushes women back again, takes away their space. This transforms the feminist movement more decidedly into the women's movement, a political formation which springs from the awareness of a radical alienation which has its origins not in the factories but in the sheltered places of reproduction, the production line of sexual assembling and most of all of the more or less admitted, the more or less recognized elaboration and conservation of love. The Movement's vitality depends on its capacity to maintain its own characteristics of 'rearguard politics', to develop no policies which are not a strategy of the unforeseen with regard to institutional politics. Over the past year many women's collectives have formed spontaneously in work places, on the railways, in banks, ministry offices, unions, and factories.

('I want to talk about what the avant garde is. I started getting involved in politics when I was at school, at training college, and I was what they call the avant garde of the masses. When I said so we went on strike, everybody always agreed with everything I said. But I think it's worth considering that I wasn't at all in the avant garde of the masses, for two important reasons. Because I was in a women's school, and couldn't talk to these women, they were looking for boyfriends, I felt "better" than them, I didn't understand, I couldn't find a way of talking to women like me, who lived the same contradictions as I did. The result of all this was that there were no comrades in that school, no other avant garde, no other militant.')

Night-time procession. Their mouths modulate sounds echoing primitive modes of communication, they stick tight together, they hold on to each other, they lift up their torches. Dress is again used to give out a message, as a sexual signal, negatively for the men who stand on the side of the road and watching the procession march, positively for women. Reappropriating ourselves, re-claiming prostitution, traversing our own condition as sign, standing up to the provocation from the roadside, from 'outside', means going collectively and politically towards the tunnel of regression. Being with other women and experiencing again the condition of seclusion, the intimacy which blinds and divides, the impossible communication of contact. Surmounting historical ritualism, oblique expression (Achilles' slaves weep 'with the pretext of Patroclus / each her own woe'), penetrating by an act of will the aphasia which tries to seek compensation with the language of the body. It means to experience and consciously acknowledge the inevitable, non-programmatic solidarity of our regressive condition. Regression, as a positive value, is what the women's movement is introducing into the political universe.

('Strange that I should choose you for the confidant of all this, young lady: passing strange that you should listen to me quietly, as if it were the most usual thing in the world for a man like me to tell stories of his opera-mistresses to a quaint, inexperienced girl like you! But the last singularity explains the first, as I intimated once before: you, with your gravity, considerateness, and caution were made to be the recipient of secrets.')

4

Pratica dell'Inconscio

In the small groups of women which had sprung up all over Italy and who met regularly to analyse their experiences in order to gain a deeper understanding of themselves – the so-called *gruppi di autocoscienza* (self-awareness groups), partly inspired by the consciousness-raising practice of the USA feminist movement – the focus of attention slowly shifted from the mechanics of oppression (and therefore the relationships with men) to an investigation of the relationship between/among women.

This meant on the one hand a great feeling of freedom, the discovery of a different sociality, centred on the mutual recognition of value. It was possible and satisfactory to be among women, to talk, to dine, to travel, without feeling 'alone', as women had been made to feel when there were no men around to lend them status and visibility in society. On the other hand, it soon became apparent that a number of difficulties, already experienced in relationships with men, and connected with mechanisms of envy, aggressiveness, power, re-emerged also among women.

Psychoanalysis seemed to offer valuable tools for the understanding of these issues. But individual recourse to therapy also dislocated the problem, restricting its analysis to the area of the self, without taking into account the political dimension of relationships among women. With reference to the experiences of the French group Psychanalyse et Politique (Psych & Po), some women tried to overcome this difficulty by using a psychoanalytical approach within women's groups. The 'practice of the unconscious' focused on the contradictions between feelings and words, on what was left unsaid in relationships for fear of a rejection or of a confrontation. The piece reproduced here sets forth the reasons, aims and features of this practice, as it was understood by the groups (two in Milan, one in Turin and one in Rome) which adopted it in 1974–5. Although it has not become widely diffused, the practice was at the centre of many discussions, and it has indirectly influenced later theoretical and political developments. Lea Melandri was one of its proponents, and her essay on 'Dora, Freud and violence' further investigates the ambiguous issues posed by psychoanalysis for women.

PRACTICE OF THE UNCONSCIOUS AND THE WOMEN'S MOVEMENT *PRACTICE OF THE UNCONSCIOUS GROUP, MILAN*, 1986

Analytic relationship and institution

These are the first arguments in favour of the project:

The analytic institution is a hierarchical institution of power and prestige, in which the construction of knowledge passes through the stages typical of power and prestige. Some who are outside the institution are unaware of its existence, they do not realize that the institution exists, that it is as important in the construction of knowledge as it is in the analytic situation. It is all the more easy for these people to fall into the passive acceptance of the element of power, submitting themselves to the law and the person who makes the law – unless, of course, they can pass over to the other side, the side of those who are 'qualified', and so unconsciously acknowledge what in their ingenuity they seem to ignore.

The analytic relationship also bears the mark of the institution, with all the features described above.

In the analytic relationship the analyst appropriates what the patient produces. In general it is understood that the advantage for the patient is in the possibility held out to him of freeing himself from a particular form of suffering. Fine, but there are still two things to be considered:

(a) removing a suffering which is immediate and strongly felt can mean damage or threat in another area. For example, a woman who undergoes analysis because she is frigid might find that this problem is resolved, but at the cost of being chained more forcibly and forever to the institutions of marriage-family-children, and so she loses even what chance she had of perceiving how her own self was reduced within these institutions;

(b) what the analysand brings to analysis has more value than what is given in return. The analysand brings not only suffering, but a particular knowledge of that suffering. The story of Breuer in the case of Anna O. makes this clear.

The conditions of the analytic relationship are now so changed that this fact of appropriation is not even seen clearly any more. This is certainly because, right from the start, analytic knowledge was subsumed into capitalism.

There is an unconscious production which is collective. The dual, private relationship set up in psychoanalysis does not take account of this fact. So it ends up in the private sphere. In our movement, in the practice of relationships between women, we are developing a specific unconscious discourse whose reconstruction cannot occur within the individual private biography.

The circulation of analytic knowledge

How would the transfer of the analytic relationship into the movement modify this situation of appropriation and privatization? I don't think the answer to such a question can deal with concrete forms to be adopted, since these can be established only during the course of a practice which does not yet exist. What we can do is see how the fact of shifting the site of the analytic relationship has certain initial effects, and what such a move would mean.

We can appreciate the positive element of being outside the psychoanalytic institution. This doesn't mean being outside of all institutions. The women's movement is an institutional site where, however, the development, acquisition and formation of knowledge are not interwoven into a structure of power. We can't exclude the possibility that the existence of an analytic relationship will produce something like an embryonic power structure, but I don't think that the relationship in itself would bring such a thing about, if there is no accumulation and capitalization of knowledge.

This can be avoided with *the circulation of knowledge*, a practice we have already begun. This circulation also has to do with analytic capacity. Amongst the things to be put into circulation will be the non-desire to be an analyst and the non-desire to be analysed. This is important because it helps to maintain the position of partiality, and the partial value of this relationship. As there is no reciprocity, so there is no transitivity in the analytic relationship. Fantasies of transitivity and reciprocity (doing to the analyst what he does to me; or, doing to someone else what the analyst has done to me) occur when the relationship is institutionally ordered in such a way as to prohibit the possibility of a reciprocal (if dissimilar) change, or shift it to the level of pure hypothesis. When the so-called patient cannot see that the analyst too is changed by their relationship, in the end she finds herself dependent as children are on adults.

Transferring the relationship into the movement also means giving it a context in which the change wrought in the analyst as well as the analysand can occur visibly. There would be no more reason to fantasize reciprocity. Reciprocity is open to criticism for another reason; if the same position that is mine (and hers) were attributed to the other, no empty space, no distance could open up to permit the discourse of the unconscious this side of rationalizations and representations. The attribution to the other of me, the game of mirrors, and reciprocal identification are the modes of communication. This is what is missing in the analytic relationship. The lack of reciprocity is its structural condition. In order to avoid infantile dependence becoming fixed and eternal as soon as it appears, we cannot have recourse to reciprocity; we need something else [. . .]

Common practice: analyst/analysed

Transfer of the analytic relationship to a position within relationships between women would have the traumatizing effect of removing analysis of the unconscious and the body from the hands of the law.

Up to now there has been, as well as the power of the analysts, the crushing weight of knowing that Freud's discovery signposted the liberation and subversion of sexist society, a discovery which we have not yet been able to take advantage of.

The proletariat has the same relationship with Marxism. Our political practice has led us to understand the importance of the unconscious in our oppression.

I don't want to speculate too long on what the set-up of the analytic relationship might be like. A dual relationship: reciprocity would be struggle, aggression, who argues better, who understands more; all modes of communication in this society would be set into play; exchange, and exchange of roles. It is monologizing delirium, the imprisoned body.

Deep down it's the absence of communication which we like in the analytic relationship. Having a person who appears to be interested only in your liberation, who has to keep hidden her aggressivity, and so on, I might know that it is a relationship between two unconsciousnesses, but I don't want to focus on that, the predominant desire is not to know who he is, but who I am [. . .] The important thing is that he should speak the truth.

We know, outside of analysis, that we have shifted our position within the power system, that there is a specific power structure which oppresses us: that the unconscious exists.

That the analytic relationship develops at the level of language which has defined what we are, that the discourse of the unconscious in psychoanalysis is what defines what we are at a deeper level, but still censures the body of the woman.

That the symptom is the negation of language, the silent resistance of the body. That transference, reliving infantile relationships of dependence and of love of parents, is a reductive structure which cuts out the social (the political practice of relationships between women), site of transgression and shift.

For women, dependence on the father and the mother is eternalized by their dependence as women. For us women, the level of the symbolic is precluded.

A knowledge which shows us how psychoanalytic knowledge about women is ideology. Knowledge and practice *common* to analyst and the woman being analysed. This is the modification which works on both of them.

Symptoms: hysteria, frigidity, refusal of maternity, traces of trans-gression in infancy and after, non-acceptance of the united parental couple. How does psychoanalysis see these symptoms? How do women see them?

It is this disturbing shift which I would like to take as starting point.

Some doubts

I don't agree with an interpretation of the 'project' such as that given at the beginning ('bringing the analytic relationship into the move-ment'), because it leaves subjects and modes so vague that in the end it does not mean very much. It can allow positions such as mine, a person who wants to start her own analysis in a way which will not go to enrich another person who is contrary to my struggle, or perhaps curious and even in favour of it but quick to capitalize elsewhere – in 'analytical knowledge' – on my contradictions and my neuroses; or even that they should enrich a person who is at my side in the struggle, but who would be enriched in an uncontrolled way, in a way which might, for example, lead to an increase in the power of the person I ask to listen to me and whom I trust, not only on my own behalf (this I can anticipate in some way) but also on behalf of other women who are outside this dual relationship.

But it can raise hopes of adventurist subversion, which I felt hinted at in the discussions on 'reciprocity'; we analyse each other, or do a group analysis, or some such thing. I don't believe in this and reject it as fanciful [. . .]

The project allows us to express in any old way the desire to listen to someone; discussion over the first evenings showed me that in some women it is not possible to distinguish – beneath the very understandable desire to do something strongly affirmative – how far a relationship of this kind is desired and fantasized as repetition 'from the other side' of an experience perceived from this side, how far it has to do with the capacity of the other to understand and his pleasure in doing so, the power you have over him, the position you come to occupy with regard to others, the desire to have someone who loves you, and so on. None of this has been clarified, and a project which permits all these ambiguities is still unacceptable as such. Which is why I want us to go on discussing it.

'Bringing analysis into the movement' does not, finally, say enough about analysis: is it what we are doing now, with its theoretical and practical corpus, that we are trying to bring into the movement? If, as many women have said, analysis has been of immense help to them, why do we fear a change which will hinder it and diminish the benefits to be gained from it by inserting it among the things we do and discuss? Or do we suspect that there is something 'incompatible' with our struggle, such that an analyst and the woman being analysed can't do it together? If this is what we feel, I would say that it's the contradiction between public and private that is re-emerging, and that this time it is analysis which is having to pick up the bill. If this incompatibility exists, we feel it and act on it more, even if we don't speak about it – like work or time for anything which is necessary to us, but ownership and judgement of which is taken away from us. Just as we have done so far, we can seek out motives and determining factors in order to turn them to our advantage, without trying to destroy them there and then, without having to proclaim the new world tomorrow morning, without feeling 'guilty' because we feel old needs, because we feel an even clearer and more heartfelt sense of urgency.

The relationship with the mother

It's not only men who are frightened by feminism.

For many women, participation in feminist groups is strongly opposed. And not only by objective matters such as housework or looking after children.

The dreams and unconscious fantasies which lie hidden behind women's widespread resistance to feminism deserve greater political recognition. This has not so far been possible; probably for the same reasons that every political movement tends to deny or remain silent about what could cause internal differences or splits.

The search for *identity* as search for *the identical*: in political 'geometry', which every activist dreams about, everything must overlap smoothly: ragged edges are seen as threatening or unhelpful.

Resistance to feminism hides the feeling and fear of something that might happen in the normal run of women's relationships. Today, after several years of feminist practice, we can see that something really has happened which could throw the unity of the movement into crisis. The search for solidarity between women has seen the simultaneous growth of a store of experiences, often unspoken and not analysed, which now come up again in a much more clearly conflicting way as the 'private/personal', cut off once more from politics. The embarrassment of this discovery and the confusion we always feel when faced with the tortuous meanderings of personal casuistry could lead us to try for a new composition of the movement through external expedients: a unitary organization, unifying objectives, and so on.

Behind this ephemeral political identity, however, there would still be the problem of how to construct relationships between women which would not repeat, without our realizing it, dependency and alienation.

The new familiarity created in a group between the women who are part of it reactivates and sets into play the *relationship of the little girl with the mother*. This complex situation of love-hate, desire-aggression, is pointed to by the hesitation which accompanies the approach of many women to feminism. Later, one of the two terms, the more disturbing one, seems to disappear in order to permit the search for common interests.

The destructive impulses which every woman can easily trace in the history of her relationship with her mother and with other women are unconsciously pushed to one side, given the need to stay together, the desire for warmth, and so on.

So aggression, the inner enemy most resistant to the unifying efforts of women, if it is denied or reduced exclusively to the violence which *others* do to women, completely escapes the process of political analysis.

But it does not then disappear. It returns as the presence of a dissonant personal history, reluctant to inscribe itself within the schemes of feminist ideology.

The practice of consciousness-raising is in crisis: the wall of solitude between the individual and the group rises up again: unexpected and apparently inexplicable tensions provoke separations and splits.

At this point it seems only two choices are possible: those who don't feel they can cope with the problems which have arisen by digging around in their personal lives look for a psychoanalyst; those who believe that militancy 'heals' even what seems most irreducible in the individual's experience redouble their efforts within the organizing drive of the movement.

The will to construct a theory which seeks in sexuality the material conditions for making women inferior, which also keeps in mind the historical-cultural conditioning which has affected the very development of sexuality, compels us, on the contrary, to look for other solutions, avoiding the flight into the 'political'; to reconsider facts which otherwise risk being passed over as unfortunate incidents; to revalue fantasies and unconscious processes, not only because they threaten group unity but because they constitute a significant aspect of reality which both the repetition of the identical and the possibility of modification pass through.

There is a lot said about the need for women to reappropriate medicine as care and knowledge of their bodies. It's all the more important to take control of analysis of the unconscious, which marks the history of the body and its illnesses. It would be naive to reject something which is useful to us simply because up to now it has always been used to justify the existing laws of patriarchal culture.

It's not a question of founding a new feminist psychoanalytic school, but of rereading, outside of sexist ideology, material which comes out of the psychoanalytic tradition. It's especially important to find new approaches to theoretical research, which today is politically essential to the women's movement.

The separation of this need from the destructive impulses which threaten it is to be found in the history of feminist groups as in the history of almost all groups. But whereas in political groups this rejected aggression finds other concrete, institutional outlets (cult of the leader, authoritarianism and so on), in the feminist movement the persistence of this separation jeopardizes the principal political goal, which is to set up relationships between women which are not marked by dependency and oppression.

Attachment to the group and the effort to keep it 'harmonious' can in fact conceal a powerful filial regressive desire, while not exhausting the charge of aggression which the woman–child made in her turn against her mother.

As always, but here particularly clearly, the present is loaded with previous history, which we must try to reconstruct in order not to be stuck with it.

In analytic writings, *masochism* has been widely termed a common attitude in women, to the extent of confusing it with the 'female position', with the social destiny of women. Ideological preoccupations have often twisted analysts' interpretations to make appear separated what, in other writings of theirs, is seen as closely connected. Melanie Klein, for example, acknowledges that the destructive impulses of the young girl against the mother's body are more powerful and long term than those of the boy, and so all relationships which she later enters into are inevitably affected by the persistence of her sadistic fantasies. The obsessive repetition of the sexual act, and also frigidity, express the search in the outer world for reassurance against the dangerous fantasies of the inner; the woman shifts outwards impulses otherwise directed against her own body. 'In extreme cases only serious punishment, or unhappy experiences which the individual perceives as punishment, can substitute the imaginery punishment which he fears' (Klein, *The Psychoanalysis of Children*).

In the woman, then, even if this seems to be a contradiction, powerful aggressive impulses go hand in hand with strong ties of dependency, the scarce possibility of sexual gratification and equally scarce possibility of sublimation. Only if the self-destructive impulse diminishes can the woman turn her aggression to something more useful and leave more freedom for the body's pleasure.

And yet, even the absence of pleasure does not discourage women from seeking out male company, as if sexual gratification were, necessarily, secondary to other advantages. Klein insists on the Oedipal impulses which 'naturally' push the little girl towards the father, but she cannot explain why the father is then frequently interiorized as the sadistic father, other than by returning to the frustrating relationship with the mother.

Homosexuality, in a wide sense, as relationship with the mother, is, then, the fundamental, primary relation of all women. Rivalry with male sex is the consequence of this and not the cause, as Klein thought. The mother disappoints the little girl not because she 'incorporates the paternal penis' but because she is *possessed* by the law of the father. Through the desire of the mother, the 'penis' acquires great prestige in the eyes of the little girl; it becomes the object of admiration and desire. In this sense Freud seems to have got closer to the truth. Only possession of the 'penis' guarantees omnipotence and therefore power over the mother (the power to possess her and to destroy her). *Identification/assimilation to the male*, set into motion by penis envy, *precedes* love for the male.

In the little girl, sadistic impulses are soon associated with the fantasy of possessing a destructive 'penis', while the object of desire and aggression, however, *remains the mother*. With the man, on the other hand, she establishes a sort of 'pederastic complicity', which means that she either takes on male characteristics herself, or, through seduction and the sexual act, repeats the symbolic introjection of the penis. Heterosexual love for women, then, is generally the reassertion of the masculine position. At this point we should modify the standard claim that in the man the woman is looking for the mother, and say that through love of a man – the repeated appropriation of the penis – what the woman is really aiming for is possession of the mother.

In this way we can explain situations which would otherwise remain incomprehensible:

the case of women who have suffered a lack of maternal love and nurture powerful aggressive fantasies, who then seek out sadistic companions in which they find not the love they never had, but a convincing incarnation of their negative inner impulses. A 'maternal' man who does not encourage this externalizing of aggression would in this case be intolerable and would only make the woman's anguished state worse rather than better.

jealousy; the appearance of another woman shatters the unconscious complicity with the man and traumatically opens up again the whole business of her 'first love', in other words the insecurity and frustration experienced by the little girl in her relationship with her mother. Hence the sense of exclusion, the fantasy of possessing the other woman, the awakening of sadistic impulses towards her.

Fantasies such as these lead many women to orgasm, either in masturbation or in coitus.

The objection that could be made to a discourse of this kind, and more generally to every research in analysis, is that the discovery of interiorized violence risks passing over objective violence in silence.

The 'almighty penis' is not, unfortunately, a fantastic invention by women, or at least not as long as woman's body does not have a name, its own existence and attributes.

Nonetheless, if we agree that the relationship between women can only be a point of arrival, it's worthwhile anticipating all the obstacles it might meet on its way.

When a women's group needs to say, in order to reassure itself about the joy of being together, 'there are no men here', this is the moment we should most worry about the reappearance of a possessive and authoritarian masculinity.

Mother, group, aggression

The group has heard two dreams women have had since the women's conference at Pinarella di Cervia:

> I'm on the beach at Cervia with some other women, I go into the water saying it's calm and clean, not polluted, some of them follow me in, when I see coming up on the left an enormous wave which covers the whole line of the horizon, I think I won't be able to escape it, the only way is to hold my breath and wait for it to pass. E., who is near me, says we should move along to where there is a peaceful spot which will not be swamped, I look, I don't see any part of the sea which can escape the wave, so I hold my breath, the wave goes over me, I feel as though I'm suffocating, I think I was wrong, I might drown.

The second dream, another woman's:

> I'm along a very steep cliff, below me there is a creek with calm, clear water, the creek is bound by a strip of land with medieval houses on it, beyond the strip of land the sea is stormy with waves thousands of feet high, so high they reach the roofs of the houses, and I think, it's impossible to live in those houses, it's dangerous.

The image of calm, clear and unpolluted water had brought to mind to the two dreamers the ideal, the good mother, the breast which gives unpolluted milk. The enormous wave: something threatening, bad, aggressive. Other associations: feeling good with other women, fearing their aggression . . . The feminist encounter, although this had not been spoken about, had brought the ghost out again. The group had to face up to the impossible relationship with the mother. After the first claims made against the man-father, the women's movement has straightaway addressed itself to the mother. We have tried to see how much of the mother is inscribed in the male symbolic order; she has children, and how much this is censured; her woman's body, her sexuality, her aggression, her desire.

It still seems to me, however, that censorship is at work in our political practice. We think of the relationship with the mother in the sense of symbolic order, mother–daughter, the relationship of the mother with the little boy or little girl, and we come to the conclusion one way or the other that the desires of the mother and the little girl are organized round the penis/phallus. And so we cling on to the 'feeling good with women', 'there are no men here', 'return to the mother', as if these fortresses will protect us and defend us from the disintegration of the body that for others has already happened.

So the women's movement too becomes an institutional site, on the defensive, as if the desire to know and change ourselves was split and alienated and we could accept only the relationship with the idealized mother.

The unpolluted sea, a dazzling metaphor for the ideal, good mother, must be clearly separated from the threatening wave. Ideal tension on one side, aggression on the other. On the contrary, if we were to look into the abyss of our own aggression and violence (might we find erotic impulses imprisoned there, tangled up with them?), we might be able to see the pleasure and desire of the woman-mother, *on the sidelines* of all that has been said and that we can say (the mother's desire is the penis-baby, to possess the mother the daughter must possess the father's penis . . .). We must break out of the temporal sequence, think of the woman-mother apart from the filial relationship. Beginning with the materiality of our body, which is censored and blocked but in which we perceive sexual impulses and desires, we can lift the ideological weight placed on the mother. Not the other way round, not beginning with the mother, idealized figure and producer of ideology even within the movement, as we have seen.

If we cut out aggression we can keep everything superficially pure, even if inside us, deep down, there is something which becomes more and more threatening; are we not leaving out something which has always been repressed and forbidden to women? Women are gentle, everybody says so; should we pay attention to what everybody tells us or to the new, strange things that are happening between us? Besides, any definition of the modes of female sexuality, even if given by the movement, inhibits once again the play between me and my body.

The two dreams about the wave which threatens and overwhelms the clear, calm waters – the clear separation between the good and the bad mother which comes out of this – have shown me that for us the mother *is beginning* to exist in autonomous fashion; she is no longer just the mother introjected within us.

And we can reconstruct the reasons for this and how it happens, which is what happened at Cervia, and gave rise to the image in the dreams. In other words, something which referred to the body's pleasure and the extraordinary collective dimension of that meeting (five hundred women), which brought us out of the dimension familiar to all women, even in small consciousness-raising groups.

ON THE USES OF PSYCHOANALYSIS: DORA, FREUD AND VIOLENCE *LEA MELANDRI*, 1974

Dora's dreams

Sigmund Freud: Case Histories 1. 'Dora' and 'Little Hans', The Pelican Freud Library, vol. 8, Penguin 1977. Translated from the German by Alix and James Strachey.

The 'case': Dora, an eighteen year old girl under analysis with Freud for three months. Dora's father and mother.

Mr and Mrs K. An amorous relationship between Dora's father and Mrs K. Attention paid by Mr K to Dora: an episode on the lake at L, a visit by Mr and Mrs K, the repetition of a similar approach in which Mr K had tried to kiss her that happened when Dora was fourteen.

'We were on the point of clarifying, using material gained in analysis, an obscure episode from her infancy, when Dora told me of having had a dream a few nights previously.' This refers to Dora's incontinence, which continued until she was eight. Behind this illness is hidden what Dora did not want to remember, and this, Freud is about to make her admit, was masturbation in infancy.

The first dream:

> 'A house was on fire. My father was standing beside my bed and woke me up. I dressed quickly. Mother wanted to stop and save her jewel-case; but Father said: "I refuse to let myself and my two children be burnt for the sake of your jewel-case." We hurried downstairs, and as soon as I was outside I woke up.'
> ... the dream was a recurrent one ... she remembered having had the dream three nights in succession at L— (the place on the lake where the scene with Herr K. had taken place), and it had now come back again a few nights earlier, here [in Vienna]. (p. 99)

The repetition of the dream is obviously related to the analytical situation. Freud likened the episode of Dora's meeting with K at the lake at L with the transference the patient makes to him. His preoccupation with making everything fit into the scheme of the father/daughter Oedipus relationship leads him, however, to a reading of the transference only in a horizontal key; the analyst/K/Dora's father; the mother is present as a rival and as an object of jealousy.

The transference instead reveals itself to be strictly tied to that 'obscure episode of infancy' which is going to be *discovered* when Dora relates her first dream.

> 'Something occurs to me,' she said, 'but it cannot belong to the dream, for it is quite recent, whereas I have certainly had the dream before . . . Father has been having a dispute with Mother in the last few days, because she locks the dining-room door at night. My brother's room, you see, has no separate entrance, but can only be reached through the dining-room. Father does not want my brother to be locked in like that at night. He says it will not do: something might happen in the night so that it might be necessary to leave the room.' (p. 100)

Dora's first association is the most illuminating. It is not by chance that she tends to diminish the meaning, a sign that it involves something more closely related to the removed subject. The mother wants to close the door to the room in which the brother sleeps at night (there are many corroborations for the Dora/brother substitution), while the father thinks something might happen to necessitate a hurried exit (fire/incontinence/masturbation). Therefore the mother is seen as though she wants to *keep a secret hidden* (the jewel case), to stop something coming out which she is in a hurry to hide. This is the most interesting association data linked to the situation by the lake at L. There it is Dora who, having received the key from Mrs K, wants to lock herself in in order not to be found by K when she gets dressed.

The central motive is always the *key*, the *locking oneself in*, the hiding a secret that is linked to the sexuality awakened by the episode on the lake. K excites Dora's sexuality. But which sexuality? The one directed towards him or towards her masturbatory desires?

The link between K/Dora's father/Freud is clear enough: the father is responsible for having left her with K, responsible for her first sexual excitement and for the consequent illness (as is K). K appears suddenly in her room while Dora sleeps.

Dora's fear is of being found while getting dressed. Freud is doing the same thing: he insinuates himself into the deepest secrets of her infancy, he again raises the desire for and fear of masturbation (episode of the purse and the letter). Dora both fears and desires that her secret be found out. Freud had made her believe that to hide it is harmful (in the dream the mother puts her children's lives at risk for the sake of her jewel case). But to let it come to light (to renounce the key to the case) could provoke fire/the outlawing of sexuality.

This leads to another possible link between Freud and the father: Freud, by revealing removed subjects, again excites her sexuality (as did K, as originally did her father) – in this sense he is an object of hostility (Dora's desire to break the analysis, Dora's accusations against her father, the source of her illnesses) – but it is also he who can save her from the fire, just as in infancy her father woke her to prevent incontinence (manifestation of the desire that Freud, just as her father in infancy, should free her from the anguish that originated in her sexual impulses).

> 'In the afternoon after our trip on the lake, from which we (Herr K. and I) returned at midday, I had gone to lie down as usual on the sofa in the bedroom to have a short sleep. I suddenly awoke and saw Herr K. standing beside me . . .
>
> 'This episode put me on my guard, and I asked Frau K. whether there was not a key to the bedroom door. The next morning I locked myself in while I was dressing. That afternoon, when I wanted to lock myself in so as to lie down again on the sofa, the key was gone. I was convinced that Herr K. had removed it.' (pp. 101–2)

Dora stayed at L for four days. The dream occurred three times. Dora admits that it happened after the incident but doesn't know whether it was in the first three days or in the last three. Instead of answering Freud's question she talked about the afternoon sleep and K's entry into the room.

This would seem to be the most important event for understanding the dream. The comment on the situation confirms it: the father stands close to Dora's bed as K did on that afternoon.

Another confirmation is added by Dora (Freud instead underlines the scene at the lake):

> 'It was then that I made up my mind not to stop on with the K.s without Father. On the subsequent mornings I could not help feeling afraid that Herr K. would surprise me while I was dressing: *so I always dressed very quickly*. You see, Father lived at the hotel, and Frau K. used always to go out early so as to go on expeditions with him.' (p. 102)

The greatest anxiety derives from the fear of being found, a fear of freeing the removed subject of sexuality (the fire).

It must be noted: in the dream there is a reversal of Dora's feelings towards her father: hostility, jealousy of him, the reproof of being the original cause of her sexual desires/ilness, are all transformed into the opposite: from the father can come salvation.

In the sittings immediately preceding this dream her father instead appeared as the cause of illness both for her and for her mother.

Besides, even in Dora's references to the relationship between her father and Mrs K, Dora always blames her father ('I cannot forgive him'): it is he who *induces* sexuality in the woman (sexuality = illness) and therefore takes from Dora the love of the woman/mother/Mrs K.

We are facing an overturned Oedipus: the object of love is the woman/mother. As regards her father, Dora now opposes him in a hostile manner, now identifies with him, assuming his own disturbances, either from a sense of blame (self-accusation) or in order to attribute the attentions to and love for Mrs K.

Dora's wish to think him important, to relegate him to the role of one who offers a tender help against sexual temptations, also becomes part of the same circle of hostility, jealousy/love-identification.

'Mother is very fond of jewellery and had a lot given her by Father.' . . .
'Perhaps you do not know that "jewel-case" is a favourite expression for the same thing that you alluded to not long ago by means of the reticule you were wearing – for the female genitals, I mean.' (pp. 104–5)

The jewel case, like the purse, can allude to the female genitalia, but it also immediately brings to mind the idea of something used to contain precious and secret objects.

In the first case it is easy for Freud to deduce that what Dora wants to extract from it by means of a trap is her virginity; in the second case we are led rather to the sexual subject which is linked to masturbation, the secret that Freud is about to wrest from her.

This is the real danger from which Freud or her father ought to save her. In order to be faithful to his Oedipal interpretation, Freud is forced to reduce and trivialize the mother's role in the dream, while the associations with the sittings preceding the dream ought to have made him give this a far more important role.

'. . . the mystery turns upon your mother. You ask how she comes into the dream? She is, as you know, your former rival in your father's affections . . . So you are ready to give Herr K. what his wife withholds from him. That is the thought which has had to be repressed with so

much energy . . . But what do all these efforts show?
. . . these efforts prove once more how deeply you loved him.'
(pp. 105–6)

A facile and unsatisfactory explanation that could not have pleased Dora.

It is at this point that Freud, perhaps not by chance, feels the need to deepen the analysis by recovering, alongside the recent hint, also the infantile roots of the dream. (This is where he inserts the account of the sittings preceding the account of the dream, but Freud does not, however, manage to link the transference to the ,analytical situation, which has become 'alarming' for Dora. He thinks that Dora has transferred to him the love removed from K.) The 'disaster' that might occur at night and that might make one 'run outside' is brought back to the nocturnal incontinence without Dora's objection.

'. . . my brother used to wet his bed up till his sixth or seventh year . . . Yes. I used to do it too, for some time, but not until my seventh or eighth year. It must have been serious, because I remember now that the doctor was called in. It lasted till a short time before my nervous asthma.' (p. 108)

The most likely cause of this kind of bed-wetting, Freud reveals to his patient, is masturbation. Only at this point does Freud seem to remember that at the moment in which the dream was referred to *the enquiry was leading directly to a confession of masturbation in infancy.* Dora tenaciously resists admitting this.

I added that she was now on the way to finding an answer to her own question of why it was precisely she had fallen ill – by confessing that she had masturbated, probably in childhood. (p. 112)

The illness referred to is not only the bed-wetting but also a form of catarrh that Dora traces back to her father's being affected by venereal disease.

Her mother had also suffered from the same disease for the same reasons.

Her father is therefore the source of the illness, but also of the sexual excitement (venereal disease, licentiousness). There comes to mind here a picture painted by Dora of her mother to the analyst: estrangement from her husband, obsessive dedication to housework. In Dora's dream and in their associations she is the one who is preoccupied with *closing*: closing the room, saving the case. In the infantile memories she undergoes and carries the consequences of the dissolute life (sexuality) of her husband.

The incentive towards the sexual impulse therefore seems to be tied to the man, to the person who in coitus usually has the initiative and the active role.

But what can be the object of desire for Dora as a girl and for the female in general in an age in which, as Freud recognizes in his writings, there are no great differences between the erotic manifestation of the two sexes? The bed-wetting, and therefore the masturbation, continue in Dora's story until the appearance of the first *hysterical symptoms* that show themselves as a substitute for the onanistic satisfaction. The first difficulties with breathing and asthma are tied to a precise event, from which Freud cannot draw all the considerations that might throw light on the definition of the female sexual development.

> Dora's symptomatic acts and certain other signs gave me good reasons for supposing that the child, whose bedroom had been next door to her parents', had overheard her father in his wife's room at night and had heard him (for he was always short of breath) breathing hard while they had intercourse.
> ... A little while later, when her father was away ... she must have reproduced in the form of an attack of asthma the impression she had received. (pp. 116–17)

The crisis is apparently provoked by external causes: a trip in the mountains that had tired her. But the associations, however much masked, reveal the true nature of the symptom: her father's difficulty when climbing, his effort during coitus with her mother, the worry that *this might have hurt him.*

Does Dora really fear or desire her father's illness?

In the trauma that the girl undergoes when being aware of her parents' coitus, who is the true object of love and who the rival? Assuming onto herself her father's illness (difficulty in breathing, asthma) Dora seems to respond reactively to a deep sense of blame that stems from the hostility-jealousy felt towards him.

There exists a note by Freud that would seem to confirm this interpretation.

> She had in truth been a wild creature; but after the 'asthma' she became quiet and well-behaved. That illness formed the boundary between two phases of her sexual life, of which the first was masculine in character, and the second feminine. (p. 119)

But what in fact does this second female phase consist of?

Is it the acquisition of her own sexuality when faced with man and his difference? Or is it rather the removal, with the consequent appearance of hysterical symptoms, of a pregenital sexuality, directed towards the primary object tied to masturbatory fantasies that are no different from those of the male, and that enter into conflict with the male position when this becomes, as in her parents' coitus or in the relationship between her little brother and her mother, the position of the conniving rival?

The phase 'of a female character' in which the girl should take on the role that *society* has assigned to her, with procreation as its end, is therefore often, and not only in extreme cases like Dora's, the renunciation of sexuality, the traumatic abandonment of the first object of love (while for men there is no solution of continuity) and finally the beginning of the complex event of dependence-hostility/love-identification with the man for a nostalgic and impossible search for the lost mother. Freud indirectly confirms this:

> For if Dora felt unable to yield to her love for the man . . . there was no factor upon which her decision depended more directly than upon her premature sexual enjoyment and its consequence – her bed-wetting, her catarrh, and her disgust. An early history of this kind can afford a basis for two kinds of behaviour in response to the demands of love in maturity – . . . an abandonment to sexuality which is entirely without resistances and borders upon perversity; or there will be a reaction – he will repudiate sexuality, and will at the same time fall ill of a neurosis. (pp. 125–6)

I do not think it is difficult to see in Dora's prehistory, one that is common to many other women, in its hysterical symptoms the 'normal' disturbances of solitude and waiting, in its secret and refuted desire for masturbation one of the causes of 'normal' female frigidity.

The second dream:

'I saw streets and squares which were strange to me. Then I came into a house where I lived, went to my room, and found a letter from my Mother lying there. She wrote saying that as I had left home without my parents' knowledge she had not wished to write to me to say that Father was ill. "Now he is dead and if you like you can come." I then went to the station and asked about a hundred times: "Where is the station?" I always got the answer: "Five minutes." I then saw a thick wood before me which I went into and there I asked a man whom I met.

He said to me: "Two and a half hours more." He offered to accompany me. But I refused and went alone. I saw the station in front of me and could not reach it. At the same time I had the usual feeling of anxiety that one has in dreams when one cannot move forward. Then I was at home. I must have been travelling in the meantime, but I knew nothing about that. I walked into the porter's lodge, and enquired for our flat. The maidservant opened the door to me and replied that Mother and the others were already at the cemetery.' (pp. 133–4)

When Dora tells Freud this second dream that follows a few weeks after the first one she has already decided to stop analysis: the oneiric fantasy of her father's death is too obvious a sign.

Freud interprets: the possibility of a vendetta with her father who does not pay enough attention to her, hostility towards K, who had turned to her with the same amorous offers previously reserved for the governess.

The putting into practice of the transference that equates them (Freud = K) surprised him. But the surprise stimulates a search for the truth and accustoms him to it.

> The longer the interval of time that separates me from the end of this analysis, the more probable it seems to me that the fault in my technique lay in this omission: I failed to discover in time and to inform the patient that her homosexual (gynaecophilic) love for Frau K. was the strongest unconscious current in her mental life. I ought to have guessed that the main source of her knowledge of sexual matters could have been no one but Frau K. . . . Her knowing all about such things, and at the same time, her always pretending not to know where her knowledge came from was really too remarkable. (p. 162)

These are interpretative acrobats by Freud in order to lead this second dream as well back to Dora's amorous hopes when faced with K.

This is a curious transference turned upside down, from which certainties stem that are immediately contradicted:

> 'Had not the K.'s often talked of getting a divorce?
> . . . I know now – and this is what you do not want to be reminded of – that you *did* fancy that Herr K.'s proposals were serious, and that he would not leave off until you had married him . . .'
> . . . because of the unknown quantity in me which reminded Dora of Herr K., she took her revenge on me . . . I suspect that it had to do with money, or with jealousy of another patient. (pp. 149–50, 161)

The Oedipal fantasy that the analyst projects onto Dora subconsciously

('I could not make myself master of the transfer at the right moment') stops him from recognizing in this second oneiric episode the sequel to a story that now finds its epilogue together with his most important interpretative misunderstanding.

The analogies with the first dream are all there. One above all: the pre-eminent position of the parent figure of the same sex (Dora's mother/Mrs K).

In order to have the album that is referred to by the city of Dora's dream she had the day before asked her mother where the box was that contained it.

> *She asked quite a hundred times* . . . On the previous evening they had had company, and afterwards her father had asked her to fetch him the brandy . . . She had asked her mother for the key to the sideboard . . . 'I've asked you *a hundred times* already where the key is . . .'
>
> 'Where is the *key*?' seems to me to be a masculine counterpart to the question:
>
> 'Where is the *box*?' They are therefore questions referring to – the genitals. (p. 136)

Taking into account that, at least in the first part of the patient's dream, as Freud observes, she identifies with a young man, it follows that the object she turns to so anxiously (the station) is the possession of another woman.

Freud's astonishment:

> If in all this she had been thinking of the engineer, it would have been appropriate for the goal to have been the possession of a woman, of herself. But instead of this it was – a station. (p. 136)

And 'station' = 'box' – box and woman. The question is clearly directed towards the female genitalia.

Another detail can be added: in the letter of the dream is written: 'if you wish', with a strange question mark. The same expression was to be found in the letter in which Mrs K had invited her to stay at L, by the lake.

All the figurative elements that are associated with the dream also lead to the woman/mother/virgin: the Madonna of the picture gallery of X, the thick forest with the nymphs against the background of the exhibition of the secessionists (a reference to female genitals).

Lastly: the two points added by Dora in the following session, that unequivocally clarify how the abandoning/leavetaking of the man coincides for Dora with the desire to conserve childish intimacy with a person of the same sex.

> 'I saw myself particularly distinctly going up the stairs . . . I went to my room, but not the least sadly, and began reading a big book that lay on my writing-table.' (p. 134)

The large book that Dora refers to is the dictionary, where children read prohibited things *in secret* for fear of being found.

But it was in secret that Dora held her intimate conversations with Mrs K.

> I then found that the young woman and the scarcely grown girl had lived for years on a footing of the closest intimacy. When Dora stayed with the K.'s she used to share a bedroom with Frau K., and the husband used to be quartered elsewhere. She had been the wife's confidante and adviser in all the difficulties of her married life. (p. 96)

Having 'displaced' for ever the father (and therefore also Mr K and Freud, who would have put her 'secret' in jeopardy), Dora can 'calmly' give vent to her sexual curiosity. She no longer even needs a key to lock herself into her room because 'her father has died and all the others are at the cemetery'.

Dora's vendetta against man therefore has roots that are more complex than those to which Freud is trying to lead. It cannot only be jealousy for her father's betrayal, offended pride for K's betrayal, who treats her as he treated her governess, and even less the pure and simple transference to the analyst of the love she felt for K.

The train of thought most deeply hidden within Dora concerns her love for Mrs K, which imposes itself as the dominant thought in the last dream. It is in the desire to preserve her childhood secret, the sexual intimacy linked to her mother, on which, among other things, rest the strongest feelings of blame (self-accusation, illnesses), that can probably be found the explanation for that 'unknown factor', which makes the patient, once she has identified in Freud a danger similar to the one represented by K, revenge herself on him by abandoning the analysis, just as she had wanted to revenge herself on the other man.

Freud's astonishments

(S. Freud, *Sexual life*, Boringhieri)

Lost happiness: 'The retrieval of the object is really a rediscovery.'
Freud's tenderness in describing maternal love:

> The suckling baby attached to the mother's breast has become the model for every loving relationship.

> The mother reserves for the child feelings that stem from her sexual life, she caresses him, kisses him, rocks him, and quite clearly takes him as a substitute for a sexual object of the normal order.

The patriarchal culture can assume detestable tones in its classification of the 'properties' of the two sexes:

> The male encompasses the subject, the activity, the possession of the penis; for the female is reserved the object and passivity.

But he does not always succeed in hiding the innocence of desire:

> The vagina is now considered the lodging-place for the penis and takes over as heir to the mother's stomach.

With the appropriation of the woman/mother the cycle of male sexual development opens and closes.

Need and pleasure, self-preservation and desire of the object of love, are not obliged to separate, because the aim and the source of satisfaction remain the same. Where the man finds continuity and rediscovery, the woman finds rupture and loss.

Freud's astonishment:

> How does the corresponding development occur in the little girl? Our material here becomes *incomprehensible* – much more obscure and full of gaps.

> We thought that in little girls everything unfolded in a fairly similar way . . .

> The mother was at first the object for both; we were not surprised that the male should conserve her in the Oedipus complex; but how does the

little girl come to renounce her and instead take on the father as object?

Dora does not want to renounce possession of her mother: she gives her governess notice when she discovers that she is closer to her father than to herself; she distances herself from her cousin after she has accepted the post of companion to her father; she is fascinated by talking about Mrs K's body, and shows jealousy of her 'that could have been felt by a man'.

And yet Freud is astonished that his patient so tenaciously resists Mr K's amorous offers.

'Perversion' and 'normality' become for the woman the historical-cultural limits against which her sexual and intellectual development clash precociously.

> The sexual activity, *which is so surprising*, of the female against the mother, expresses itself with the passage of time in tendencies that are first oral, then sadistic and finally even phallic, but all directed against the mother.

> In order to become a woman a further distancing is necessary, which removes an element of infantile masculinity and prepares the woman for the change in the leading genital role . . . while the man has always preserved the same one from infancy.

> . . . transference of the erogenous excitability from the clitoris to the entrance to the vagina . . .

An entrance to the 'normality'/distancing of the libido that is tenaciously linked to objects of childhood – conversion of the desire into illness.

For a moment Freud comes near to the truth:

> One must therefore consider the possibility that a certain number of females stay firmly tied by the primitive maternal bond and never complete the required change in the direction of men.

What if the number of these women were quite large, if frigidity were to be the norm and not the exception?

What if women were to refute the sexual suggestion 'indispensable for the maintenance of marriage in a civilized society'? Man could impose . . . This is a hypothesis that Freud, strangely, does not take into consideration. The reason for this appears elsewhere:

Freud remembers that primitive men feared woman as a fountain of dangers. He who dares have the first coitus with her can expect her hostility, which she shows 'by insulting him, raising her hands against him or even by actually striking him'.

Anthropology or ghosts? The outcome does not alter: nature is more reassuring. This is how, after all his astonishment, his doubts, his happy intuition, Freud falls into one of those interpretations that would have made Dora exclaim: and where could these great results be?

Paraphrasing Napoleon's words, we can say that anatomy is our destiny.

The awareness of the anatomical difference pushes the little girl away from virility and male onanism towards new paths that lead to the explanation of femininity.

Tenderness

A eulogy on tenderness as an exquisitely feminine endowment: the tenderness that woman seeks in man, the tenderness she can give man, the tenderness of maternal love. Women can renounce sexuality for a tender and affectionate man.

Only psychoanalytic investigation can show that behind this tenderness, this veneration and respect are hiding the ancient sexual aspirations of the partial childish impulses.

Tenderness and sensuality: the two currents, according to Freud, are indispensable, in order for the 'normal' sexual development of men and women to be guaranteed.

The first important differentiation: on the women's sexuality he imposes a heavy prohibition (a sense of blame, enforced shift of the object of love).

The libido is forced to hide itself behind tenderness, which thus becomes the predominant component in the loving relationship.

The current of tenderness is the most ancient one. It derives from the very first years of infancy, it is formed on the basis of the interests of the impulse to self-preservation and directs itself towards people in the family . . . it corresponds to the primary infantile choice of object.

The tenderness hides a sexual search that does not manage to free itself from the *need for survival*. Hence its central role in women's relationship with man. Sexual and intellectual subjection are a consequence; the possessiveness and exclusiveness that most women demand in their relationship with men are only the distorted face of need: the insecurity about woman's existence and her illusory turning back to vindication of possession.

Up to here Freud's contribution against the sentimental-illusory myth of 'eternal femininity' is illuminating.

What remains to be clarified is why sexuality and prohibition are so closely linked in the development of woman, and when the involution that fixes the libido to its infantile subject is born.

The assumption of the feminine role appears fairly late, when the displacement has already taken place. The prohibition can only therefore return one to the relationship with the woman/mother.

Freud's astonishment is again revealing about his theoretical discoveries:

> Another reproof is *astounding*, one that is directed towards a closer reality: her mother had given her too little milk . . . this would appear from the affirmations made in analysis.

> The mother does not satisfy the amorous expectations of the girl.

> Unwitting hostility (of the mother) that the girl guesses at.

This underground hostility on the part of the mother for the person of the same sex, mirror-like negation of her own body, feeds the spectres of prohibition in the girl.

Dora discovers with great turbulence that women betray her: her cousin, her governess, and even Mrs K, who does not hesitate to sacrifice their intimate friendship in order to conserve the friendship of the father.

Woman is made for man.

From the suffering for the betrayal to the envy of male power/ incentive and at the same time an obstacle for the liberation of women.

Invisible violence

Solitude of women enfeebled by waiting
Emotional beggary and the resentment for the absence of men

The difficulty of extracting oneself from the times and ways imposed on the relationship by men

The incapacity for physical and psychic perception of self outside men's eyes

The inability to elaborate a means of intellectual/sexual/emotional existence *of her own* outside the norms imposed by men

The primary desire for a relationship with the body of the woman/ mother, and therefore with her own body, violently altered by the intervention of phallic modalities: the mother belongs to the father and the girl cannot love her and make herself loved by her without going via the father and assuming the father's sexual role towards the mother

The obstinate attachment to men as a desperate search for the material/impossible love, a search that constrains submission to the male wish

The genital sexuality of the man/exclusion-repression of progenital eroticism of woman

Liberation understood as effort to *convert* man, as well as facing him with changed relationships

The argument against man's everyday violence as well as the analysis of the violence women have been subjected to in their growing up. The mother with her eye intent on man can remember the image only in the male. The girl remains excluded from this relationship of mother/woman–man/son. She has no choice but to make herself loved: either she must submit to or try to assume the masculine role; that is, in every case, the negation of her own body and of her own sexuality

The emptiness of motherly love, the interruption of the relationship with the person of the same sex, that continually pushes the woman to appropriate male power, to identify with man in the sexual rela- tionship, to preoccupy herself with the man's body and not with her own, to use her own body to procure pleasure, to renunciate her own desires for the desires of the other

To guarantee love by possessing man

But the possession of the other is alienation from oneself, renunciation of self. A double set-back: the emptiness of maternal love is not overcome and one loses possession of oneself and of one's own body.

5

Libreria delle Donne di Milano

The Women's Bookshop opened in Milan in 1975, after about a year spent in planning, finding the necessary money, locating a site, solving the legal questions, etc. It was founded by a group of women active in the feminist movement in Milan, either in the Demau group, or in the Collettivo di Via di Cherubini, or later in the 'practice of the unconscious' and in the Via Col di Lana groups (see chapters 1, pp. 33–5 and 4, pp. 82–108). The Libreria is on the one hand – obviously – a bookshop, that is a 'public' space and an enterprise subject to economic laws; on the other hand, as a 'women's' bookshop, it inevitably has a political dimension, as do all the other women's bookshops in other Italian cities (Rome, Florence, Bologna, Cagliari). Any enterprise by and for women is a 'deviation of female energy' away from socially accepted channels for the purpose of gender-marked activities.

But in the case of Milan, this political dimension is particularly important; in fact, the women of the Libreria have been and are a significant point of reference for any political and theoretical debate in the feminist movement. Their writings have been very influential in shaping this debate, and the issues of their irregular publication, *Sottosopra*, have always aroused great interest and provoked discussion. They have also edited two *Cataloghi*, and later a few issues of a journal, *Via Dogana*, devoted to a commentary about books by women, often grouped around a theme, such as the search for a symbolic mother or women's attitude towards war. Their work bears the mark of their interest in French feminist theory, especially in the ideas of Psychanalyse et Politique, and later, more cogently, in the thought of Irigaray, with whom they entertain a relationship of reciprocal esteem and of collaboration.

In 1983, 'More women than men' (included here) set going a lively discussion on the nature of women's social difficulties. They proposed 'entrustment' as a means of overcoming this paralysing situation; that is, sexualizing social relations by always choosing another woman as one's point of reference with whom to establish a privileged relationship even in the work place, and accepting, even supporting another woman's social superiority and wish for affirmation in view of a symbolic (and eventually a practical) gain for oneself and for other women. A proposal which, either enthusiastically endorsed, or rejected as an authoritarian demand for hierarchies and a betrayal of sisterhood, has anyway become central to later discussion; for example, those about the relationships between/among women, or about the possibility of gendered representation in the institutions (see chapter 15, pp. 339–67).

Included here are two more pieces which further develop the ideas of 'More women than men': 'Bonding and freedom', by Luisa Muraro, a leading figure of Italian feminism, who is also a member of the Diotima group (see chapter 9, pp. 181–5) and 'Entrustment enters the palace', by a group of women lawyers and magistrates – among them Lia Cigarini, whose writing about the issue of representation is also included in this collection. (Other pieces by women of the Libreria, either collectively or individually signed, can be found in the chapters on abortion, on sexual violence and on Chernobyl.)

In 1987 the Libreria authored *Non credere di avere dei diritti* (*'Don't think you have any rights'*, a quotation from Simone Weil), a highly subjective, idiosyncratic and therefore fascinating reconstruction of the history of the group and of Italian feminism. Parts of Ida Dominijanni's review, highlighting the main issues of the book, and discussing them in relation to events and themes central to the movement in Italy, are also included here.

MORE WOMEN THAN MEN   *LIBRERIA DELLE DONNE DI MILANO*, 1983

A group of women, involved together in political and emotional relationships, record here what they have gained from the last few years of movement and struggle, and, on that basis, assess what they still lack.

We have fought, effectively, against the social poverty of women's condition. We have discovered the originality which goes with the fact of being women. Through the political practice of relations between women, by spending time with other women, by loving other women, we have come to value ourselves. But at the moment we have no way of translating the experience, the knowledge and the value of being women into social reality. In social relations, outside our groups, we feel uncomfortable, as if in a world where the best part of ourselves is unknown and counts for nothing. This is something which weighs more heavily on us now than it did a few years ago, when we were uncertain about what our own desires, our own wants, could be.

We have experienced this sense of inadequacy even in our groups, when we have been with other women: perhaps this is because the sense of discomfort and blockage of which we are conscious in the social world is associated with every desire and every wish to be active. Our strongest and deepest desires risk becoming the wellsprings of paralysing fantasies so as not to remain unexpressed. But in a women's group there is at least the chance to question this experience and, even more important, to estimate its proper weight, so that we lose nothing of what any of us can become conscious of and desire. We enter social relationships for various reasons – some of us to earn a living, some to satisfy their own ambitions, some simply because it can't be avoided – and in these social relationships our unease has remained completely unspoken. *There*, the fact of being a woman has proved meaningless, an embarrassing peculiarity which we have to justify or which we forget and want others to forget. To a greater or lesser extent this uses up a part of our intelligence and diminishes our enjoyment. And it reacts back on the project of women's struggle as well, impoverishing it. We lack any positive experience of self-affirmation in social life, and this is, by reflex, missing in our groups. Instead we act like beginners and copycats.

It is no longer a matter of discrimination

We want to start from our present condition and talk and ask questions about our failure to achieve in social life. This failure reverberates in a diffuse sense of discomfort, a feeling of inadequacy, of mediocrity. As failure it needn't be anything special: on the contrary, in general it doesn't present itself as extraordinary failure but more as inhibition, as a block on capacity, a source of anxiety and withdrawal.

In the face of this experience it is an advance to acknowledge openly that we try hard but that our results are generally mediocre and that for the most part we are unequal to the performance demanded in social transactions. We focus on the feeling of being blocked because it reveals more intensely than does our vague sense of discomfort that we want to do something, we want to achieve, and that perhaps something inside ourselves stops us, says 'no'.

We are not dealing with an external obstacle. To think of ourselves and present ourselves as victims of discrimination against women by now no longer signifies what is essential about our condition. It runs the risk of being a cover. We know that discrimination exists and can return, especially when material conditions are hard. But this is an easily recognized difficulty which we know how to fight and which has no power to inferiorize a woman or make her feel inadequate. On the other hand, a sense of inadequacy contributes not a little to reinforcing the residues or the return of discrimination.

This sense of inadequacy must therefore be brought into the open and questioned on its own account as a more profound stumbling block than any which derives from an unjust social order. We are therefore discussing the failure of our social performance in terms which do not attribute it to discrimination. We are relating our sense of blockage to what we want for ourselves, not to what others want of us against our own interests. To discuss this just in terms of discrimination is to remain silent about something which is a part of our experience – which is that our difficulty does not only come (does not essentially come) from external obstacles, but from our own wish for social recognition which clashes with its own excess. It is enormous, abnormal, not because it is itself greater than it should be, but simply because it finds no means of satisfaction.

The wish to win through

There is within us a wish to live in the grand manner, to have a secure familiarity with things, to find every now and then the gestures, the words, the behaviour, which correspond to our own feelings and are appropriate to the external situation, to follow our thoughts, our desires, our projects, through to their end. We call this 'the wish to win through'. We wish to be victorious over everything which makes us insecure, unstable, dependent, imitative. And yet at the same time we do not want to betray anything of what we are, not even that part of ourselves which at the moment speaks only hesitantly.

To begin with we have to overcome our fear of our own wish to win. When this wish presents itself it does so as something abnormal, almost without an object and without any relation to our own resources. At the moment of a 'block' we recognize our wish as hesitant but insuppressible.

We can speak of our 'block' and attempt to understand what we mean by it, to follow it through, because in these years of struggle we have shifted the emphasis of our work on to our own desires. The women's movement has revived in us the sense of fearlessness we had in childhood and thought we had lost. We find in this a point of reference for becoming what we are and wanting what we want.

We have inside us a wish to win which paralyses us rather than carrying us forward because, separately from any form of discrimination, the possibilities offered by this society do not correspond to it. Because of this clash society will perhaps have to change.

Estrangement

When we place the sense of blockage we experience in our attempts at social existence alongside our persistent wish to win, a resistance or an estrangement is revealed; something within resists an entry into social games, doesn't want to be there, isn't there.

What can it be, this something which says 'no', this stumbling block? It can't be named, because it hasn't a name. Our estrangement consists precisely in this, that something inside has no means of expression or self-realization but still exists, making its presence felt the more the wish to win presses its claims. Its way of making itself heard is as a mute presence which hinders us, provokes paralysing fantasies, robs us of words. What we are in the social lives we lead – mothers, housewives, professional workers, political activists, those who make a living where they can – inspires criticisms of this society; but no criticism is as radical as this objection, raised by something which doesn't want and can't stand what society offers as the possibility of a life.

The wish to win and the sense of estrangement are components of the problem, not reasons for it. What creates the obstacle, the refusal to have anything to do with social games, whether experienced as a block or as diffuse discomfort, is definitely the fact of being and having a woman's body. If we want to name what it is in which a sense of estrangement resides, all that can be said is that it is being and having a woman's body, something in itself quite common, as common as having a man's body. And yet they are not comparable and never have been. To be sure, with each day that passes fewer obstacles are put before women who want to realize themselves in social life and our eyes become accustomed to seeing women in men's places. But meanwhile, within each woman, where the eye cannot go, there is a constant labour unwinding to make her keep her body, a woman's body, in a place where those who are given pride of place have a man's body.

This constant internal work will never cease because there is something inside which will never get used to it; every now and then the work is interrupted by an almost physical refusal of the effort involved.

The sense of blockage is produced because this society is fashioned by male desire, by being and having a man's body. To be a woman, with a woman's experience and desires, has no place in it. This is the only way to explain why it is that when the wish to win is not intimidating it becomes inevitably an aspiration to virility. By following this line of thought, much more than by using the idea of discrimination, we have realized how much society is imprinted with male prevalence; the imprint of the male is clear within us, in the desire to exist, to act, to count for something, which in fact takes the form of a desire for virility – the only form of victorious desire, one can say. But a woman's stake in this game is her body: this is what she can lose.

When a woman enters the social world, even in the simplest way, for example, by speaking at a neighbourhood meeting, there is always an *extra* effort to be made so that she can explain herself according to procedures which do not harmonize with either her feelings or her thoughts and which result in her feelings and thoughts emerging more or less distorted. Each time there is a void to be filled, a sense of having to climb a little higher. In this way a fantasy of perfection can be born, which paralyses because it doesn't foresee, doesn't admit of, mistakes. The feeling of real estrangement is also given by this: one cannot live comfortably in a world in which everyone is bound to make mistakes but *you* are not allowed to make them.

There are those who will say, 'But I manage, I can do it.' Perhaps. There are certainly women who, in given circumstances, manage to establish their equality with men, even their superiority. But this is at the cost of a disablement which is often shadowed by personal suffering and eventually manifests itself as isolation from those like you, an inability to understand them and, underneath, a contempt for your own sex. This disavowal of the loser, in yourself and others, is the reason why many of the few socially successful women are conservatives or reactionaries.

It is undoubtedly the case that some men feel themselves inadequate to the virile model and to the social performance which corresponds to it. But a man has always his body, his being and having a male body, which can be displayed to his fellows and made something of, even if in a manner marginal to or opposed to their models and values. In a man the experience of inadequacy can be and often is the occasion for raising the stakes in the social-sexual game and renewing, for example, the terms of the dialectic between sexuality in its literal sense and its sublimation (or displacement) into areas like careers, the arts, finance, politics and so on. Female sexuality, in *its* literal sense, does not enter into any of this. In social life its display of virility is not attached to the body and therefore has no real stake, to such an extent that it often ends up rigid, imitative or conformist. The fantasy of perfection which paralyses so many women or makes them insecure comes from this inability to put their body into what they do – to those who put their body into the social game is given the right to make mistakes, to transgress, but this right is given by a body which is never completely bounded by the norms. Our paralysing fantasies derive from an asexual model, interposed between body and language.

In this society the profound feelings of a woman, an intelligence true to her emotions and desires, are not allowed free rein. In one way or another they end up either distorted or forced into silence. As a rule we use our sense of estrangement as a corrective to our wish to win, and our wish to win as a corrective to our sense of estrangement. And we divide in this alternation into those who support (or exhibit) what is foreign about us and those who support (or exhibit) ways of enjoying inclusion in the social world.

The loneliness of the emancipated woman

Social existence is won in a sexual competition between men. When discrimination disappears a woman can enter the competition, but it remains a men's event. She finds herself alone even if there are other women around, alone in the midst of male self-assertion, which is men loving themselves by making careers and money, creating knowledge and political parties, attempting revolutions and so on. Female emancipation equals letting women enter a social competition which confirms virility. Emancipation, of necessity, places an emphasis on individual talent. The most women can achieve is solidarity with their own kind as a defence. In other words, emancipation puts us into a social game with words and desires which are not our own. And it induces us to play down our feelings of inadequacy and blockage as things to be ashamed of, when in fact they contain an objection and a force for change which is usually not effectively exercised because women exhaust their energies in efforts to adapt.

Bring sexual differences into social relations

The massive entry of women into social life does not automatically modify this situation. What automatically happens is that women tend to assimilate themselves to the male model.

We need a moment of reflection and a specific political practice which can make our sense of unease and inadequacy in social transactions into the principle of a knowledge and a resolve in relation to society. As a result we will be able to say: society is made like this, functions like this, demands this kind of performance, but I am a part of society and am not made like this, and because of this society will perhaps have to change so as to give expression to my existence within it as well; through an understanding of this contradiction we can become aware of what we wish to be.

Social relations must be sexualized. If it is true that social and cultural reality is not neuter, that within it human sexuality is expressed in a displaced form, then our search for social existence cannot but clash with the domination of men over women in the fabric of social and cultural life. To sexualize social relations means to tear away their apparent neutrality and show that a woman cannot be fully herself if she adopts the socially current ways of relating to one's peers, either with regard to her pleasure or with regard to her abilities. In fact the stimuli to become involved in social games, to treat their rules and rewards as everything, are directly or indirectly addressed to masculinity, fashioned so as to bring it out or to gratify it. It is difficult to become involved in a situation in which your own pleasure is always in suspense.

From this it can be understood why many women, even given the choice, prefer to keep themselves apart from social life and do not follow the path of emancipation through to its end. They are defending their own integrity. What must be taken up from their attitude is their knowledge (the knowledge that men prevail in social relations) and their implicit resolve (resistance to assimilation into the male).

It therefore seems to us mistaken to continue to insist on discrimination and beside the point to issue demands for more social and cultural space for women. The concession of greater space is a response to a flagrant injustice, that of a society half made up of women but almost entirely run by men; but it doesn't touch the substance of the problem, which is that in this society as it is, women find neither strong incentives to become involved nor real opportunities to develop to the best of their ability.

The struggle for a sense of ease

For at least a century the politics of emancipation has developed amongst socially underprivileged groups, aiming to achieve equal acceptance in the social world. As far as material conditions are concerned we are approaching the finishing line, but nothing has yet been done about a perhaps more serious disadvantage: that of finding oneself inducted into a social life which provides no pleasure, no sphere of competence, no sense of ease. These are also material elements. The emancipatory struggle passes, unseeing, over energies which are blocked by a sense of real irreducible estrangement, and does not touch those energies which are exhausted in the effort to adjust.

Some writers from socialist Germany, one of the most advanced countries from the point of view of the struggle against discrimination against women, tell of this deep sense of estrangement, this not being able to stand it, which comes from a woman's body. Read, for example, *Mutation* by Christa Wolf. The process of emancipation has a limit which may emerge later but which is there at the start, in its demand to women that they push forward, enter a condition which is in many respects desirable but where it is not possible to take with you the integrity of your own most elementary experiences, those associated with the body and with sexuality. And yet the integrity of your own experiences is a fundamental condition for entry into society in the best way. Without that, mediocrity and a sense of blockage are almost inevitable.

From the moment that this becomes clear the struggle against discrimination appears secondary. What comes to the fore is the struggle to have a sense of ease in social life: to stay in the world whilst being faithful to one's womanhood, having emotions, desires, motivation, behaviour, criteria of judgement, different from those which are aligned to masculinity and which therefore still prevail in society, governing it even in its freest expressions.

It is because we do not wish to give up our social existence that we are now concentrating on our sense of unease. First of all we wish to emerge with an explanation of its roots. Our difficulties in social transactions are caused by the prevalence of the male, a maleness which translates itself into money, careers, culture, politics, art, and which arrogantly demands admiration and imitation. We are saying nothing new. These are all things which are known in the abstract, yet in practice are negated. To sexualize social relations means to oppose this act of erasure. In practice it means constituting separate women's groups even when and where we are in search of a social existence, in order to interrogate this 'block', to recognize our wish to win, to start a struggle to be at ease with the world.

Against static separatism

After ten years and more of political movement the experience of discomfort and 'block' in the struggle for social existence remains an individual fact which everyone perceives on their own or with a special friend or therapist. It is difficult to talk in our groups about the conflict between our wish to win and our sense of estrangement, although the outcome of this conflict is fundamental to all the choices we make (or do not make) and not just to those about work. The women's movement has neither studied this point enough, nor has it developed a political practice around it.

Within our groups there circulate in abundance accounts of our experiences in relation to men, women, children, even animals and nature in general. Anything regarding wider social transactions is passed over in silence, or labelled as soon as it is mentioned as an aspect of discrimination of which we are the victims and the male world the author. This glosses over one part of the situation: our own wish to achieve and the checks that this encounters. As a wish it endures through various adaptations and disguises and operates even in choices which appear by their very nature to be purely sentimental. One can also have a child because of the wish to succeed or the fear of failure. We tend to present ourselves as human beings dominated by emotional needs.

The insufficiency of analysis is reflected in the fact that the movement, whilst arousing in many the wish to change their own lives and the wish to win, has at the same time served as a cover for the small change of marginality and emancipation. Women's groups risk becoming the site of female authenticity, cut off from social intercourse and involvement in social exchanges. The proclaimed marginality of women, like the emancipatory process, does not prevent women from meanwhile being subject to male initiatives in social life, whether as chatty collaborators or as paralysed mutes. Feminist separatism, understood as women with their specificity on this side, society with its specificity on that, merely prolongs the silence of desire and of women's knowledge: it does not end it.

We draw to one side in relation to groups dominated by men (dominated, that is, by projects thought by men in language appropriate to the male) in order to find an existence by reference to those like us, and in order to articulate our own desires and knowledge of ourselves, how we are in the world, what the world is like. We draw aside in order to exist in the world and to participate in it, not in order to celebrate a marginality which is either bogus or despairing and hopeless. In other words separation is an instrument of struggle, not a way of regulating relations between women and men. If we respond to our desires as was done in the past, by choosing between emancipation and evasion, between making it through our individual abilities or giving up, our relationships with men, which we have been able to modify in part, will also regress.

Our profound estrangement from society and culture must be interrogated at the moment at which we become involved in society, when it is felt alongside the wish to win through, to exist, to count for something in the world. These two, estrangement and will, working together rather than negating each other, demonstrate that society will not be the same when women's desire and knowledge run free within it. At that point man will be able to discover his own incompleteness and free himself from his oppressive universality.

A common world of women

The main difficulty we face is that we lack 'a common world of women'. This insight comes from Adrienne Rich. A woman who in some way tries to live socially, whether to make her living or for her own satisfaction, enters the common world of men, a world where the things which to her seem basic and essential fall into the void, count for nothing; they have never existed there. And where, conversely, she has to confront things in which she cannot recognize herself although certainly she knows they exist: masculinity has no difficulty in getting itself recognized. With the political movement of these last years, personal relations between men and women have changed, and so have our ways of talking about them between ourselves. This is not the case in social relations, where we still lack any criteria rooted in our own interests and therefore lack freedom of judgement.

An analogy can be made between sexual frigidity and blocks on achievement in social life. The frigidity of some women revealed to us the mute resistance of the female body as well as the violence that male sexuality exercises on women, and this pushed us to a struggle to change personal relationships with men. In a similar way, to feel blocked in social life, unable to speak, anxious, uncomfortable, 'speaks' of an estrangement and a resistance.

Up to now resistance has only been silent. In the social world we are still isolated and uncommunicative except about matters that are marginal to the situation. Even when moved to criticism we are silent or repetitive about essentials. Conformists or subversives, we act and think according to criteria into which our womanhood does not enter. Society does not deny us position and even success just because we are women. But this is really because in terms of social acceptance the fact of being a woman is irrelevant. What a strange existence we have, creatures who are not men but who cannot come out as women.

Only by reference to those like us will we be able to rediscover and therefore support those contents of our experience which social reality ignores or tends to cancel out as scarcely relevant. This is also perhaps the only way in which women can give to man the measure of his incompleteness, letting him perceive the existence of relationships and interests which do not put him first. So long as the incompleteness of men/women remains without substance in social and cultural life, society is maimed and, for us, maiming.

It is almost unthinkable that women can manage alone in a world in which, from the factory to the laboratory, from the nursery to the football stadium, from law to poetry, what circulates and is willingly endorsed is the excellence of having and being a male body. Once a tissue of preferential relations are woven between women, within which the experiences associated with womanhood are strengthened by reciprocal recognition, and once ways have been invented of translating this into social reality, then women can manage. This is what we call the common world of women, a web of relationships and references to others like yourself which is able to register and make consistent and effective our experience in its integrity, recovering and developing the practical knowledge which many women in difficult circumstances have already intuitively acquired. In other words, we must develop ways of being in the world whilst at the same time holding on to relationships with others like us. Through this, substance can be given to what male predominance negates, the basic fact of our being women rather than men. There is only one world, inhabited by women as well as by men, children, animals and various living and non-living things, and it is in this world which is one alone that we wish to stay, at our ease.

Create a strong precedent

Solidarity is precious but it is not enough. What we need are diversified and strong relations in which, once minimum common interests are safeguarded, what links us is not just the defence of our interests; relations into which differences enter into play as enrichment and no longer as threat.

Differences between women sometimes take the form of real and proper divergencies and with the recognition of difference goes an attribution of value. Such an attribution of value can have its place amongst women: on it depends the feeling that it is valuable to be a woman. Not in a general and abstract sense, but in a context in which everyone lives with their own wish to achieve and their own sense of estrangement. To attribute value in this context means to put one of your own kind first, to privilege her wish to win through, her sense of inadequacy, and to do this in your own interest. In this way a material link can be established which can allow the communication of things which have been forced into silence or distorted in individual confrontations with male society.

Our objective is to weave a world in which the interests associated with being a woman circulate, and in which a woman can exist without having to justify her existence. To this end we are using our political practice of relations between women to make a contribution to the issue of disparities between women, the need to engage with them and the need to practice a confidence in and reliance on one of your own kind.

Generally we do not admit of difference and disparity in our groups, in the name of an egalitarianism inherited from the youth movement. But this refusal is also and perhaps fundamentally a reaction to the obliteration of the mother in our society. The relationship between mother and daughter has no form in patriarchal society; it is therefore conflictual and mother and daughters are both the losers. We have come to understand that we can engage with disparities between women in our political practice and that this is precious. To recognize that someone like us has 'something extra' breaks the rule of male society according to which, once the mother is removed, all women are definitely equal. At the same time it liberates us, intimidated or inferiorized as we are in relation with men, from a reactive need to feel on a par with our own kind at least. Women were also brought into the world by a mother. In order to struggle against patriarchal society we must give real strength within our relationships to that ancient relationship in which there could be, fused together, love and esteem for another woman. Every woman had, in her mother, her first love and her first model.

Are we then proposing to reproduce in our relationships that hierarchy of 'better than'/'worse than' which rightly we detest because in our society we find ourselves the losers? The answer cannot be other than 'yes' and 'no'. 'Yes', because there is a need to break with the regime of sameness between women which is based on an undervaluation of womanhood – parity between us has its roots in the deep insecurity each one of us feels. To that extent it does not impede submission to the hierarchies current in society. But 'no' as well, because the 'better than' which determines a disparity between women is being given space in a relationship in which love and esteem circulate together.

The recognition of disparities between women is therefore not an end in itself. It is the practice of a contradiction, a practice which is needed to allow freedom from the fear of being less than other women and through which each woman can arrive at a sense of her own value because she can rely on what is valuable in others, and treat it as an element of strength.

That this recognition of value and mutual trust takes place between women who spend time with each other and work together creates a strong precedent. It means we have a point to refer to where the integrity of womanhood is confirmed and the 'something extra' which is being looked for can be found.

To the extent that we can engage in the recognition of disparity, we will be able to find an order, a dynamic, the fertility of the primary emotions linked to the ancient relationship with the mother. With the recognition of the 'something extra' that another woman can be, these old emotions will find a means of positive expression – freeing themselves from ambiguities and us from recriminations.

In the light of a living desire

The articulation of emotions is part of our journey towards a sense of ease, the diminution of anxiety. Ease is in fact the third term between a savage wish to win and submission, between fantasies of omnipotence and failure. Ease is a sense of connection between our own emotions and what we think and do in a given situation. This is not a psychological matter. The search for a sense of ease is a political practice which continually says: 'The effort to masculinize our mind and our emotions is oppressive and, what is more, useless'; 'We wish to translate women's experience and desire within a society which doesn't want to know, and to change things that way'; 'A sense of ease is a most material need along with other material needs, and a struggle for a sense of ease is subversive in a world in which desire is petrified.' This wish to stay comfortably in the world brings things back into a living relationship with the desire for them to be examined. In the light of that desire they can be changed (a lot or a little, probably a lot) to the degree that it is necessary.

BONDING AND FREEDOM *LUISA MURARO*, 1985

Before talking about the relationship of entrustment between women, perhaps we should clarify that 'relationship of entrustment' is a new expression indicating something which already exists in relationships between men, as in the relationships many women have with men. To put it simply, this relationship occurs when you tie yourself to a person who can help you achieve something which you think you are capable of but which you have not yet achieved.

In our society relationships of entrustment between women are rare. Why this should be so is a complex question. Here I would prefer to go round it and approach it from the other side, explaining why I have tied myself to a woman in the way I have just been describing.

I work in philosophy. My training has been in philosophy, at the expense of the community, and philosophy is what I am now paid for, still at the expense of the community. I don't know what need society has of philosophers, or how many. But I do know that up to now society has expressed no need for philosophers to be women rather than men. I've been able to study philosophy and now I teach it and write about it, because I have shown my abilities to be no less than those of others, of men, who have the same aspirations as me. This society acknowledges that my right is no less than theirs. But this is only a right. By which I mean that it has not been accompanied by expectations and requirements with regard to my sex.

I will not linger on the mental confusion which this absence of specific requests has produced in me. In effect I couldn't translate my abilities and inclinations into a project to which I felt bound. Not long ago I read the biography of a Milanese woman, Gaetana Agnesi (*Le scienziate sante del Settecento* [*The Holy Scientist of the Eighteenth Century*], Giovanna Tilche, Rizzoli, 1984). Up to the age of thirty she was a mathematician of great renown, but with the death of her father, who was enormously proud of her, she abandoned the mathematical sciences and devoted herself to looking after poor and sick women. It seems to me that in this story we can see the parabola of superfluous female thought.

All programmers of female emancipation break down at this point: sexual difference has no meaning outside the family. Women's presence in society satisfies the need for justice towards women but it is not a response to an intrinsic social need. This has two major effects, which have become clear to me over the years as I have tried to sort out my own mental confusion. There is an inner effect of uncertainty about what one is to do in life. As far as society is concerned, if we do not take on children and a family one female project is the same as the next, and the only support for it comes from yourself, from the fact that you, on your own, wish to achieve it. Nothing and nobody will help when you run into difficulties and you are tempted to forget all about it. The second effect is an external one but corresponds to the other. This is that a woman's words and actions carry very little social weight, no matter what their intrinsic value is. There is a general lack of attention which neglects to acknowledge value just as it easily forgets mistakes and lapses.

In these conditions we can't do philosophy; perhaps we can't do anything with a keen sense of personal involvement. It's depressing to know that you are useless. Old people know it, orphans in institutions know it, the unemployed know it. And when we get to that point, if we have the strength we have to draw a conclusion about this, and do something about it. What I did about it was to tie myself in a relationship of female entrustment, at the moment when this idea of entrustment took shape in a woman's mind and was communicated to me.

In the idea of female entrustment, which is actually far richer and more complex than my description of it here implies, I suddenly saw the possibility of tying myself, of emerging from superfluity and having the support of precise requirements to put forward or to satisfy.

I feel very strongly this need for a social tie which gives me answers, which tells me when I am wrong, which agrees with me. This possibly has something to do with the fact that I work in philosophy. However, the question of sexual difference, which has no recognized reason to exist outside the family, doesn't affect me alone. It is a general fact that whatever a woman does outside the family is seen as something she does through choice or personal need, except in those cases where women are called on to substitute for absent men. And in all cases, including this last one, society does not signify a need for a female social presence; neither, therefore, does it have expectations and criteria which would give sense to what a woman does as well as to what she is, a human subject of the female sex.

I think it's because of this that a woman often feels her aspiration to a free social existence to be almost a denial of her sex, and that so do other women. Society's interpretation of this aspiration as virile might faithfully reflect the experience of some women, but it certainly betrays the way many others feel about it. In her diary, Virginia Woolf tells us that when a book of hers was due out, she was mortally shaken by terrifying fears of humiliation. Other women, especially those with family ties, are tormented by a sense of guilt. My own experience tells me that these phenomena arise from a conflict between what we want to achieve and the fact that sex is excluded from this something: excluded in two senses, which are interdependent: both as a part of the individual woman's human identity and as that part of humanity which is like her.

It would be a mistake to turn this conflict into a problem which women should resolve within themselves. The problem has very definite personal aspects, but its solution affects the whole of society. Indeed, society is structured in such a way that in realizing her desires a woman almost inevitably finds herself split between her aspiration to a free existence and the privacy of her sexed body.

But it would be equally wrong to make of it a question of social justice, because society does not have the means to establish the ties which woman really needs, between body and word, between herself and her peers. Society can only register it when it happens, and this it does.

The relationship of entrustment between one woman and another constitutes this tie, which is simultaneously intimate and external, personal and social, which makes a coherent whole of being a woman and having a social existence; which makes sexual difference visible and significant in social relationships, in that the female aspiration to something more is reconciled with fidelity to her own sex.

In the feminist movement much has been said against emancipation. Here I would like to add my strongest argument against emancipation. It was available to me, and it attracted me, because of my human need for an autonomous existence. But every step I took was like taking something away from another woman or from all women. When I finished school, with a lot of female friends, women began to seem to me generically wretched, and I felt within myself that I had impoverished them. It's not difficult to work out what was actually happening: faced with the social pre-eminence of the male sex I was denying my own sex its wealth; denying first myself and as a result all others whom I saw as similar to me. In this sense the relationship of entrustment is also, for me, a restitution.

ENTRUSTMENT ENTERS THE PALACE   *M. GRAZIA CAMPARI, ROSARIA CANZANO, LIA CIGARINI, SCIANA LOALDI, LAURA ROSEO AND CLAUDIA SHANMAH*, 1985

In general women steer clear of taking on the law. These days, however, there are a number of women lawyers and magistrates. Because we feel compelled to place ourselves in the most telling situations, perhaps. We've given a name to this compulsion: the wish to win through. Yet we know that in these places there is no leading role for us, and we hesitate to make one for ourselves because we realize that the rules of the game have been worked out by the other sex and not ours. And so we are happy with a kind of reflected glory, staying on the stage and sticking as closely as possible to the spotlight.

When a group of women lawyers and magistrates met in Milan, after *Sottosopra* came out in 1983, we took these contradictions as our point of departure, knowing that in our experience it was a hard nut to crack.

So hard that straightaway we ran into the problem of recording coherently and developing in any detail the contradiction between our wish to win through and our estrangement. A gap inevitably opened up: on one side we carried on our professional role in the world with its reflected, individual glory, and on the other side we used the women's group as a source of comfort and consolation. In the group we took our time, we relaxed, all judgement apparently suspended, with an every-ready justification for our every failing. Relaxed, indeed. We treated ourselves as men do, according to their image of women.

There, with our likenesses, everything which in any other place was a failure or a source of anxiety just disappeared. After that interlude, comforted by the group experience we had gone through together, we would return to our work which – in spite of everything – gave us the sense of something of value.

Some of us defend this manner of relating between women and maintain that in this way 'we reclaim our bodies'. We don't agree, because the body recovered in this way remains separate from the word, and the pleasure of relating with other women from the production of value. And so it is that when we speak, be it in the field of law, science or politics, our words have no sex, they are the words of a neutralized body with no substance of its own.

Precisely to stop this split repeating itself we chose to take the 'failure' as the privileged moment of our analysis, our point of departure in changing the world. It's quite clear that that women's group, comforting and consoling, was useless for us. Indeed, it avoided the suffering of failure, and relationships within the group tended to reproduce the split between female pleasure on the one hand, professional seriousness (value word) on the other. So much so that within the group we couldn't even accept with any equanimity the disparity that there certainly was among us, while every contribution had to be given the same value. As if we didn't trust ourselves enough to imagine that someone like us could contribute something valuable and worth taking seriously. And so, paradoxically, that 'something extra' which women have won circulates in and nourishes the world as it is, and doesn't nourish the women themselves.

In the end we realized that not recognizing the disparity among us, standing in the way of the strongest proposals and desires, actually annihilated the value of each and every one of us, insinuating a sort of desperation as to the possibility of our sex creating anything original or modifying the existing situation.

At this point some of us separated ourselves off, putting ourselves in a situation of disparity which we accepted, and which was made practicable and positive within relationships of mutual entrustment. Which is to say that we acknowledge the oldest and most experienced among us, the one who is intellectually gifted, the one who carries authority within the group. We have a common desire for change, a common refusal to content ourselves with what we have, an awareness of the limits of emancipation, the will to be recognized in society as we are, with our sex.

Our fundamental stimulus is the desire for change, which must be shared by the women who place themselves in a relationship of mutual entrustment; the refusal to accept our lot, overcoming the tendency to live in society as it is – marked by the male's imprint; so that women are ashamed of the lowly status of other women and therefore of their own sexed being. Cutting out for themselves a tiny space, a niche which is never totally secure.

As it happens, we are all lawyers; the magistrates have not taken this step. Together we've set out a plan of work in the field of law. We've chosen a limited area but one which we think is particularly telling, that is, family law.

In family law (law, jurisprudence and court trials) different and sometimes contradictory interests of the two sexes come into play. It is the case that the interests of the woman often give way because of the very difficulty experienced by women in knowing exactly what they are and being able to stand up for them when confronted with the other party. A power situation is recreated which the law, leaving to one side its intrinsic justice, only encourages.

We've noticed that this happens repeatedly, even though there are many women lawyers and judges in the section of our tribunal which deals with this area. This is a matter of circumstance which has no effect on the administration of justice because the person who administers it either is a man and speaks as a man, or is a 'neutral' being, in other words a woman who wants to be impartial because of her insecurity as a woman.

We are working to bring this conflict out into the open, to shed some light on it, to act it out in the first person, so that both men and women can measure themselves against it.

Talking amongst ourselves we decided not to take the path of legislative intervention because it seems to us that it passes over the reality of the conflict, and reduces the fractures of the situation to abstractions.

If women hesitate to defend their interests and rights because of their own inner censorship and their aversion to confront the law, it will certainly not be the laws which recognize these rights (see the law on parity, on sexual violence, on family rights) that will help them to fight, to be involved as 'different' subjects, with their own specific interests. A relationship of entrustment serves to make the female sex visible in society, to give it presence and a voice, and the social visibility of the female sex is fundamental for our project, as it is for the whole women's movement.

Sexual difference in society as we saw it functioned only at the level of physiology and the family, not in a social context where the man remains a man and the woman becomes a neuter. We thought that this is because women do not have a network of significant and pleasurable relationships, a circularity of reciprocal desire such as men have amongst themselves, and women have with men.

That's why we choose to begin with ourselves and our own contradictions, just as the women's movement has done over these past few years. In other words thinking of women not as objects of intervention, in this case legislative intervention, but as subjects.

In practice, then, we put the politics of jurisprudence at the centre of our work. The politics of jurisprudence means taking on the whole area of conflict between the sexes at the moment in which it comes up against the reality of the law, that is to say the moment of conflict in the courts.

It should be said that in this very field and at this very level women have an intimate knowledge and an intimate competence, because of their involvement in personal relationships and because of their very conception of the world, seen not as an abstract entity but always through ties lived in the first person.

The relationship on entrustment constitutes a new kind of social relationship which takes us out of our isolation, and puts into circulation that something extra that a woman can be, to the advantage and gain of those who produced it.

RADICALITY AND ASCETICISM   *IDA DOMINIJANNI*, 1987

'Language is the social dress. In other words it is the symbolic apparatus which makes sayable what is, so giving sense to what a human being lives inside him/herself, and which can be the death of him/her if he/she can't externalize it by signifying it to others.' I begin with this quotation because it sums up perfectly the sense of the political proposal of *Don't Think You Have Any Rights* and the *raison d'être* of the book itself. The sense of the political proposal: what a woman suffers from is being put into the world without a symbolic placement, deprived precisely of that social dress which is language and of all the successive mediations that can 'signify' her in the world; that is, speak her sexual difference and give it a social existence. It is this suffering which calls for a revolution, and so the revolution of feminism will be of a symbolic order, just as the nature of that suffering is of a symbolic order. The *raison d'être* of this book is to give a name to that which didn't have a name; to put into words a political practice, so turning it into theory; to reconstruct and circulate its language, thus giving it a 'social dress'. So that it might finally be sayable, signifiable to others, transmittable.

It seems to me that this is precisely where the first merit of the book lies, in managing to communicate a political experience which in its turn – just like the existential experience of the subjects who constructed it – could have stayed within the realm of things lived but not signifiable to others – to other women – not translatable into the explicit and settled heritage of memory. And in managing to do this while giving that political experience an interpretation. Anybody who spends any time within the spaces of women's politics knows that one of the hindrances to communication, one of the obstacles in our way is exactly the lack of a consensus on an interpretation – or to be more exact of several interpretations which might not always agree with each other but which are consequent – of our political past. This obstacle not only makes women fall back on the interpretation and politics of the present, it removes power from the memory, makes it difficult for things to take root in the mind, removes security from the subjects themselves, the very women who have constructed that political past and who should have it at heart to transmit it.

The authors say of this interpretation they make of the facts of the past that it is partial and selective – just as for the present, they add, there is in the book 'the partiality of taking up a position'. The rereading of the past does not present itself in the form of a story, but as the subjective journey of the group who lived through it, a signed accumulation of moments of experience and thought. Will all feminists recognize themselves in this interpretation? Perhaps not, certainly not. We know that the very writing of the book was not without conflicts on the reconstruction of the past, and it is likely that other women readers will not agree with it. They will say that things didn't happen exactly as they are written down here. [. . .] They will criticize the lack of context – political, social, cultural – in which these twenty years of feminism are gone over again. One way or another they will defend themselves from the radicality of this book, which is in fact its greatest merit.

Yet for one thing I believe that everybody will have to recognize themselves in *Don't Think*: the way the book and its language can restore experience to us. This obviously can't be put down just to a good piece of writing (and all recognition for this should go to Luisa Muraro, who was largely responsible for the final version of the book), but is bound up with the political and cultural choices made about the book's field of observation. It's a crucial point, which explains the almost total absence of 'context' I was speaking of just now. The context of the twenty years between 1966 and 1986 in which the book moves only appears as occasional background hints: the society of emancipation in which feminism matures, the politics in action in mobilizing on abortion, the sociological interpretations which tried to reduce feminism to a 'cultural movement'.

But the context chosen here is in reality another, and only that: the political practice of the relationships between women; that is to say, the very core of feminism, the original nucleus of its theorizing and its politics, what brought together the feminists of the seventies aside from the incidence of external facts and loyalties. This is a context, we might say, which becomes a text, because that practice is the site where female experience shows itself at its root level, and searches for a solution at that level – a root level which could not show itself in previous women's movements which did not consider this practice. This also helps us to understand the organization of the book, in which the rereading of the political past, the analysis of the 'female condition' (I will give it this provocative term to underline the colossal distance from figures which traditionally go under this name) and the theoretical and political proposal of entrustment are tied together. In the practice of relationships between women the female condition becomes legible, and the practice of relationships between women suggests the way to change it.

We will come back to the rereading of the political past which the book performs. For the moment let us stay with the 'female condition' as it is here described and assumed. What the woman suffers from, we were saying, is 'being put into the world without a symbolic placement', with no sense-horizon that would connect her being of female sex with her living in society. It's an age-old state which goes back to the original constitution of the symbolic order and of sexual roles in western civilization, but more importantly it is a condition which has been not eased but worsened by the society of emancipation. Indeed, a woman's existence in the world has sense only if it is tied to her anatomical destiny and to corresponding social roles; if she wants to move outside these roles, then she must forget about being a woman. Outside of these roles, societies which want the emancipation of the woman will give her many other possibilities but will not value these female activities, will give them no reason, necessity or responsibility: 'freed from the slavery of her anatomical destiny, a woman becomes not automatically free but superfluous.' To the extent that in emancipated societies the great majority of women 'restlessly move backwards and forwards between emancipation and female roles, they try to do the most disparate tasks at the same time, they go from one project to the next, they try one thing, then another, like somebody pursuing something which exists only in her mind and is nowhere.'

Hands up who doesn't feel described or jolted by this description . . .

And yet women, a lot of women, have great designs on the world, they have desires and projects, they want to be in the world and leave their trace in it. But this binomial, being a woman and making claims on society, is a combination which our societies cannot tolerate, unforeseen and therefore unvalued in their symbolic order. From a binomial common to every human being, it is destined to become for women a split: between body and language, between female sexual difference and the symbolic order. This split reveals the absence of a symbolic mediation between women and the world, it explains the defect of liberty in which woman finds herself acting. So it is at the root, at the literally radical level, that the problem of woman should be tackled.

The connection with the reading of past political practices is now clear. It is in the political practices based on relationships between women that this split has been made visible, in the form of a repeated split between 'inside' and 'outside' (you will remember this as the jargon of *autocoscienze* groups), between the search for the self and the search for social existence, and has shown itself in its effects, in blocking projects or in political impotence. Revealing itself in this way it has also become dealable with, subject in its turn to theorization. The rereading of successive practices of feminism in this book is rich in many elements of analytic density, but in substance it is the story of this 'repeating split' and of the many attempts to resolve and overcome it, up to the idea and theorizing of the proposal of sexed mediation: this will be, philosophically as well as factually, the mediation introduced to knit back together those two split terms.

Let us look at the main moments of this history. It is with the exhaustion of *autocoscienze* – 'simple and genial practice', but naive in believing in the authenticity of the lived experience and of the word which expresses it, and therefore unable to go beyond the recognition of each woman in her fellow-women – that we see the 'double and opposite movement of the female mind, turning inwards to her own darker side and turning out towards society'. The meeting with the Frenchwoman of Psychanalyse et Politique steers the second side of this double movement into the social practice of relationships between women, thus beginning a 'period of female association which continues to the present day', the separate and transgressive channelling of female energies which in itself transforms social relationships. The practice of the unconscious on the other hand nourishes the search for the self, the analysis of that denied part of female experience which it will turn into a political issue; it brings to the surface the lack of connection in woman's behaviour between the word and her real motives, it analyses her dependence on man, her anxiety for approval, the invasive role of fantasy which compensates for women's difficulty in interpreting themselves and imposing their own desires, as men are able to do; it brings into focus what blocks women's access to the symbolic and, tied in with this, the problem of an unresolved relationship with the mother.

But as the first Pinarella national feminist conference (1979) was to show, that 'double opposed movement' finds neither agreement nor mediation, and furthermore women's groups tend to reproduce within themselves the split between body and language, deep female experience and its social tranlatability. The following 'practice of doing', which over the years was to give rise to a number of initiatives still going, is created precisely to get round the solid block of the word, to give female desire the opportunity to address objects and projects directly (which nonetheless, as the text acutely observes, themselves also express desire and mastery of the word: they are most of the time bookshops, libraries, publishing houses, information centres . . .). It links this 'doing' in separate female spaces to the transformation of the social body, but it soon reveals, in the effect of self-moderation which it produces, that female desire remains reticent, it does not come out into the open. Not only this, but the 'collective space not regulated by male interests' seems to have no relationship with the world; female experience remains without social existence. We had to wait for the two 'memorable disasters' of Col di Lana (feminst groups' common premises in Milan, 1975) and Paestum (third national feminist conference, 1976) before abandoning what had to be abandoned and going down a new road. But in the meantime, and this is also extremely important for the analysis, there was the impact of the whole issue of abortion and sexual violence.

This is the point where the story becomes more unilateral, where we can and should say to the authors that things could have been told differently; for example by those in *autocoscienze* groups (the taking of sides by women in favour of demonstrations and by those in collectives was not as clearcut as the book makes out), who decided, once it was clear that there would never be a straight decriminalization of abortion, to participate in the battle over the law, even while being aware of all the contradictions between the poverty of legislative tools and the complexity of female experience (sexuality, conflict with men) which came into play over abortion. They decided this not so much to 'give substance' to what would otherwise have been an impoverished battle, but because they are aware that through the contamination of diverse practices – for example, through the severe clash of those years with much older organizations such as the UDI, through throwing into question and breaking up any 'double militancies' and 'double allegiances' – they could spread the practice and content of the *autocoscienze* – based kind of feminism. The difference of interpretation of this struggle has to do not so much with the final judgement about the choice to take to the law: today – in the current climate of increasing male initiative over abortion, and a context such as that of the 'right to life' campaign, which have little in common with our reasons for acting then – there are, I believe, very few women who would not subscribe to the thesis developed by the book; that 'when women turn their attention to the law and ask Parliament to resolve some of the social conflicts which affect them, and when sexual difference and the man–woman conflict are involved, they damage their own sex and put it into a position of lacerating contradictions.' The difference of judgement has more to do with the effects of that battle *within* the women's movement; they were not without influence, for example, in the relative lack of support for the law by popular initiative on sexual violence, which was soon to follow.

But the Libreria's strongest point of interpretation of both 'legislative' ventures during those years is another, and has to do with the representing-representation nexus of the female sex. Both struggles, the authors write, were based on a lowest common denominator representation (image) of women as the oppressed sex, and did not take account of the differences with which the female sex is marked. The struggles frustrated and made irrelevant the 'extra' of those women who did not identify with that kind of narrow image. Moreover, whoever carried this battle forward did so as a 'representative' of the whole female sex, in the name of that mistaken representation. There are two consequences. One leads directly to a problem which we see today; whether and how it is possible to work out forms of political representation which do not simply reinforce that 'common-denominator representation', and which would be authorized by women in their complexity as a sex and not as a presumed oppressed social group. [. . .]

The second consequence, the slow divorce from the collective representation and self-representation of common oppression, takes us back to the main strand of the book; it will become a matter of urgency to free ourselves from that representation when we understand that it is a main reason for the impotence of female desire, for that 'repeating split' between female experience and self-awareness on the one hand, and on the other estrangement from society and subordination to prescribed roles.

Critique of the ideology of oppression, and of the related politics of vindication of rights, is one of the cardinal points of the book, going right through it, from the rereading of the first documents of Demau and Carla Lonzi right up to today's questions. But it is important to point out that it remains firmly tied to the analysis of female subjectivity, of that part of it which is denied, and brought to the surface by the practice of the unconscious. The moment of crystallization, the abandoning of the acknowledgment of a common oppression, is placed by the authors during the Col di Lana episode, an emblematic example of the vicious circle which occurred in groups because of the passivity of so many women in the face of the power of a few women – a power which was both unrecognized and blamed. This was in 1976: we all have memories of similar situations. In this setting of collective impotence to go forward, we can see down to the bottom of the weakness of female desire, the difficulty it has in expressing itself in both the 'passive' women and the 'authoritative' ones, those who are seen but not said to be as such, and who are blamed for being so.

A figure intervenes to break this vicious circle who, even on a linguistic level, is one of the most effective in the book: 'the objection of the silent woman.' Not the woman who never speaks, the oppressed woman, but 'that part of every woman which refuses to be described, illustrated or defended by anybody', and certainly not by those women who would like to describe her by grouping her together with others living in conditions of oppression: 'If that part were to speak it might say, for example, that she couldn't care less about those for whom abortion is a problem.' The 'silent woman', then, is the figure of a female experience which had found neither place nor words in the victim-oppressor scheme which feminist language had followed up to that point; the figure of the experience of those who could not express active claims and desires in that scheme of things, who were a priori censured by that scheme. So it is the figure of the 'loss which is the fault of no-one, but is the desire for something.' The way is open to an analysis of the female 'extra', the desire of the woman who wants existence but who cannot come out into the open from the shadow of this lowly representation of women, free female thought which in the scheme of oppression was a contradiction in terms.

So the way is open for the passage from the 'subordinate female symbolic', in which to speak of oppression suffered was all but in which female freedom could not be said, to an 'autonomous female symbolic' capable of representing female freedom in its female origin. This is the beginning of 'political work on the symbolic', which will consist of 'dividing into two the unity with which the functioning of the social body is represented, showing its sexed nature. And in giving legitimacy to the presence of female sexuality in the social, to female desire which seeks satisfaction in taking part in government and knowledge of the world.'

For those who have followed from the green *Sottosopra* ['More women than men', reprinted in this chapter] onwards the proposals of the Milan Libreria delle Donne, the rest is recent history, and in fact the book talks about it in the present tense, as of 'what we think and want today'. In the meantime, however, it is the case that in giving a name to things past, things of the present take on the density of history. So that the theoretical-political proposal of sexed mediation takes on a body and reasons which it did not have in the Libreria's previous, more abstract theorizations; it sweeps aside a series of objections made to it over the past three years (disparity as synonymous with hierarchy, authority as synonymous with domination, the coupling of ethical issues which aim for a 'better' society to the practice of sexual difference) and opens the way to new passages – it draws conclusions, as the authors prefer to put it, which are very demanding when they touch on the sacred territories of freedom, of social responsibility, of justice, of sexed thinking and acting in and on the world. [. . .]

'Liberty' is the noblest word in this book, and is the word which inspires it. I notice while reading it that it is a word which has disappeared from feminist political vocabulary, as well as that which is not feminist. When we used to speak of liberation we did so with reference to oppression; and, as we read in these pages, that politics of liberation lacked the originating power, the foundation of female freedom. Here this foundation is located in a conscious and binding belonging of woman to her sex: 'A woman is free when signifying her belonging to the female sex is what she chooses to do, knowing that it is not really an object of choice.' It is a necessary foundation, not abstract: if the cause of female lack of freedom lies in being woman, in the tie with an anatomical destiny, we must turn this cause of non-freedom – which we cannot eliminate, as we cannot eliminate the fact we are born women – into a principle of liberty.

But freedom, as always, has a price, and feminism in the seventies was mistaken in thinking that it did not, or that women could obtain freedom just by claiming it from society as a denied right: society is founded on female non-freedom and therefore constitutionally has no need of female freedom and will not grant it. The price which every woman has to pay for her own freedom has to be paid not to society but to other women, first of all the mother. The price of female freedom is the 'payment of the symbolic debt' towards the mother: to put it another way, the recognition of the relationship between women. This simple gesture – visible, public, made through relationships of entrustment which in this sense reveal themselves as social relationships – removes female transmission from the invisible and the insignificant, frees woman from the over-powerful image of the mother, authorizes her to feed on the mother without betraying her, establishes a symbolic economy of exchange between women. It is the founding gesture of a female social pact: 'freedom gained in the relationships between women is for a woman her own freedom, and the social pact with which she ties herself in her freedom to other women ties her to the whole world.' So this gesture is the foundation of a new social pact: women being excluded from the constitutive and originary act of the current social pact.

This social pact is presented, in *Don't Believe You Have Any Rights*, as a social pact clearly divided into two: sexed: that is, one for men – what we are used to seeing as the universal pact – and one for women – the one which puts an end to the 'wild state of relationships between women'. It interrupts the register of female survival based on relationships between them of simple solidarity and mutual help, and inaugurates the register of female freedom. That we have here a real social pact can be seen by the consequences the authors see in terms of justice and social responsibility.

On responsibility, for example: 'A woman is responsible for the world insofar as she has to account for herself to her peers, and she has no social obligations which cannot be derived from her obligations towards her peers.' It is true, the authors add, that these affirmations are 'unjust' with regard to justice as we know it; but it could not be otherwise, because they come from something – the social value of relationships between women, and female freedom – which that justice has not considered. So for women, thinking justly cannot come first, but only after fidelity to themselves and their experiences, interests and desires:

the value of female difference is not inscribed in the system of social relationships, and nothing of what needs to be done to bring it about appears with the guarantee of justice. We, in flesh and blood, must put ourselves in the place of the missing guarantee, of the justice which is yet to be done, of the truth which is yet to be known. It is an inevitable step.

But is what is constituted thanks to a 'flesh and blood presence', to a willed and reasoned 'putting oneself in the place of' that symbolic order which does not exist, a *strong* symbolic? Is it not a gesture which is still too closely tied to the day-to-day business of politics, the temporality of women's politics and the physical persons of those who engage in it, here and now? It seems to me that here this book does not resolve fully that continual movement from the register of the symbolic to the factual register, which is the point of friction, the other face of the richness and originality of this thought and in a way of all the thinking about sexual difference.

One more point about the question of a sexed social pact. The Libreria of Milan is often accused, and from many directions, of wanting finally a society which is divided and non-communicating between men and women. The book gives an answer which is paradoxically soothing:

> It is clear that things will no longer be the same, neither for women nor for the whole of society, if the help we gave each other in order to survive becomes an alliance which guarantees our social existence. But it will not be the end of the world. Dividing into two a social pact which already functioned of its own account in a divided manner – the bargaining between men, the solidarity between women – will not give rise to chaos.

6

I Centri Culturali delle Donne

The second half of the 1970s marked the birth of a new type of feminist association, one which had its roots in the experience of the *autocoscienza*, but also moved away from it in search of a more definite structure. For about a decade small groups of women all over Italy had got together to investigate their lives. In the process they had acquired a clearer awareness of themselves as women and of the need for change; they had also created an informal network of political action; a 'movement' with a nationwide identity in spite of its fragmentation and its inner differences. The stress on togetherness, and on the similarities of women's experience, a dislike for hierarchies and an extreme diffidence towards all forms of organization had characterized this phase; also a diffidence towards the traditional forms of politics and a reluctance to engage in any transaction with the institutions. There was, finally, also a mistrust of 'culture', of the so-called objectivity of research, of the misrepresentations handed down by the cultural tradition.

Obviously, these were tendencies, not dogmas, and they often resulted in the invention of new forms of political action and of new ways of cultural production. The Centri are an instance of such a process of continuity and modification. Since the first was founded in 1976, there has been a dramatic increase in the number of groups which have constituted themselves as separate and autonomous sites of sexually connotated research, in order to preserve, transmit, produce culture as/for women. In 1986, when their first nationwide conference took place in Siena, there were about a hundred of them spread all over Italy. More than a third had also assumed a formalized legal structure, and these are listed in the 'Table of Women's Centres', with the geographical location and the date of foundation.

These groups usually take the form of cultural associations with purposes of research; 'centres' to which women can refer for information and where the members can meet to discuss issues and carry out research on projects they have elaborated. They are for the most part self-financed through the contributions of their members, though a small amount of money is available from local and state institutions. A few are directly connected with the council of the city where they are located and are financed by it – with the obvious difficulty of having to engage in a constant battle to retain their autonomy in terms of cultural choices. Though different in outlook, and in their specific activities, the centres are all characterized by the awareness of the need to give roots to women's culture; hence the creation of libraries and the organization of seminars and debates to circulate and stimulate theoretical reflection.

We have included here part of a paper written by a group of women from three Centri for the 1986 National Conference in Siena. It is a reflection on the meaning/s of culture and on the changes this concept has undergone in the experience of the women involved in the feminist movement, and more specifically in the Centri.

CULTURE/CULTURES IN THE WOMEN'S
CENTRES   *WOMEN FROM THREE* CENTRI *AT THE
NATIONAL CONFERENCE OF WOMEN IN SIENA*,
1986

It seems to us that, as the first Centres were created, there was an unresolved contrast between 'feminist culture' (value of the body, of subjectivity, of daily life, and so on) and codified culture. At the origin of the Centres, therefore, is a sort of challenge, a transgressive vein which is directed not only at the existing cultural order, but also at the feminist movement itself, as well as at its rules, informal yet strong, unsaid but very effective in the individual consciousness. Mediation and composition were much needed: this was a proposed meeting point, after having been a battlefield between contrasting tendencies and needs.

This appears evident if – even before looking at the Centres as collective institutions and juridical forms – we consider those women who ideated and created them.

Ten years ago we could perceive an uneasiness, a void between the new consciousness and freedom – originating from the feminist practice – and the ambiguities this situation revealed without, however, proposing a solution. Emancipated women, endowed with an average–high degree of culture (we speak here of formal education), with jobs involving intellectual activity, had discovered the importance of their own common experience as women, as well as the fallacy of emancipation and the deceit of male culture. But it was hard to be rid of it at all.

For the women who in those years – roughly before 1980 – ideated and established the Centres, this was meant as an attempt at healing the fracture between their own feminist commitment and that part of themselves and of their life which had found a – though conflictual – space in the world of codified culture. They wanted to be able to criticize and revisit that culture; they felt the need to invest, in *every* part of their life, intelligence and passion at the same time. They intended to transfer into the analysis of the world, the study and the research, those possibilities of relationship which had been discovered and built by the movement. At the same time, they wanted to make their competences and knowledge act in a positive fashion in the relationships among women.

This need was tied up with the dissatisfaction with rich but changeable and short-lived relationships, with a production of culture which left its mark in the individual consciousness – and this is not a matter of little importance – and managed to spread with a hidden, extraordinary strength, but which always appeared threatened by that same subjectivity which sustained it. Closeness, conversation and immediate, merging identification with the present interlocutor appeared – at a certain point – insufficient in order to create an identity. Who knows whether the Centres have also been an intentional detachment from the excessive emotional demand on the part of self-consciousness groups and – sometimes – of collectives. It might have been a desire to overcome the potentially destructive immediacy of experience in favour of an intellectual reflection which would protect the value of experience itself while transforming it into an element of knowledge.

We think that – although in different ways – that need of reunion between 'feminism' and 'emancipation' has been fundamental in the foundation of all Centres, even though it is certainly important to distinguish the various stages and the peculiar characteristics of each single Centre, as well as the geographical and political elements. We have the general impression that the composition has gradually begun, and that the mediation too does no longer appear so unbecoming. Therefore, we think that – for the more recently established Centres – the fact of belonging to the movement and the legitimacy of cultural activity have not been reasons for excessive doubt.

The invention of places where – beyond individual and specific activities which are carried on – it is legitimate to exercise one's own mind *among women* for the sake of knowledge, is also a sign of a new social custom centred on female intellectuality. In the Centres, some women have taken up as a political project the idea of transforming their own personal competences in collective female culture; on the other hand, women of differing cultural levels have decided – on their own – to meet to make projects and produce occasions for and objects of culture. In doing this, they have been looking for discipline and instruments, in order to redefine the proceedings of knowledge, to make culture be a moment of self-organization and therefore of creation.

However, it turned out from the meetings of the coordinating committee while organizing this conference, as well as from cards describing the Centres and even more from their 'autobiographies', that, when one tries to define what is meant by 'culture', and in particular by 'women's culture', there is often no clarity of ideas. In fact, there are still many unresolved points in this regard.

In some Centres, the attitudes on 'women's producing culture' are intentionally left vague, while one recognizes as equally important and valuable both the material and the theoretical aspects of this activity. In other Centres, the lack of homogeneous orientation is underlined, the fact of privileging pragmatism and empiricism, as if to ward off heavily ideological or utopian tendencies. In other Centres, finally, they consider as premature any definition of 'women's producing culture' if an 'existence' has not been built beforehand through 'thinking of ourselves'. Other ideas come from those Centres – actually very few – in which they have tried to define their own conception of culture: these ideas must be taken back again to be examined and studied in depth. For example: women's culture conceived as the expression not only of rationality, but also of emotions and body, in order to reconstruct in harmonic unity that female entity which ages of male power have crushed and made dumb: culture, therefore, as a process of deconstruction of patriarchy, as a search for a language of sexual difference.

Still more: culture conceived as formulation of the theoretical thought necessary in order to demand the alteration of what exists now; as a moment of formation for the consciousness. Women's culture, in other words, as a sexualized approach to reality, in order to build up the consciousness of one's own difference against any homologization.

But are the Centres actually doing all this? At first glance, it seemed to us that we could reach the following interpretation: that the Centres, more than developing a theoretical activity, are spreading data often achieved somewhere else. We recognize, however, the value of cultural *production* to this work, since it sets into motion the cognitive processes and authorizes individuals – so to speak not 'qualified' – to exercise knowledge and criticism. (In this sense, the experience of the Virginia Woolf cultural centre in Rome is the most well known, but we could quote other experiences, such as that of the Filo d'Arienne in Verona: in any case, this happens, in different ways, in all Centres.)

In this regard, we participate in a phenomenon which has not yet been analysed in all its manifestations, namely the exchange which the Centres have actually provoked and encouraged – with the passing of time – between women working in the Centres themselves (as managers or users) and the so-called 'academic' women. The reciprocal, progressive and sometimes visible influence, with its connected process of modification (on one side, a greater need for scientific rigour, on the other, a braver use of personal professional means), have represented, in our opinion, one of the most interesting political and cultural results in recent years, and certainly constitute a specific peculiarity of the Centres.

This is only an example of how the very existence of the Centres has made possible the development of different ways of approaching culture and knowledge, through the validation of acquired certainties as a political sphere of thought, as, for example, sexual difference as fundamental category of interpretation.

Disciplines: the season of our discontent

The whole cultural policy of the Centres has been influenced by the analyses and the political questions made by the movement. From this point of view, therefore, we think one has to interpret the choice of particular themes, the prevalence of subject areas on which women's researches have been concentrated, as well as the programmes and the initiatives of the Centres.

We are therefore proposing for this phenomenon an interpretation which, though necessarily schematic, is general enough to allow an understanding of the Centres' experience, without having to compete – for the moment – with the various stories and typologies.

One could also say that our cultural-political analyses have always hinged on two central pivots, two 'generating nuclei' from which any other question about ourselves and the world came and still comes: namely, the denunciation of the present condition of women and the search for a new collective and individual identity.

Both questions have given rise to a third one (on which a considerable amount of study and thought has been spent), namely the problem of the origins of the oppression and therefore of the *process of formation of the present gender identity*.

If we exclude the practice of self-help, which is more specifically bound up with the criticism of a sexist health service and with medical research, there is no doubt that our cultural work (in the form of seminars, debates, launches of books, research and so on) has been mainly directed towards humanistic subjects, with a prevalence – at first – of the so-called social sciences, and – afterwards – of literature and history.

Extradomestic work, motherhood, familiar and social roles, juridical inferiority and all that was included in the definition 'female condition' had to be described, in the form – for example – of enquiries. We thought that the act of showing and measuring would be enough in itself to point out contradiction and injustice. This attitude partly came from the tradition of the so-called 'woman's question' (with its neopositivistic tendency towards social sciences) and from the movement for emancipation and 'equality'. At the same time, the instruments for such description were identified precisely in sociological disciplines, which were in fashion at the beginning of the seventies and which, however, had been put into practice in the study of work and family roles even before feminism.

Sociology was after all entitled by its own nature to analyse social movements and was therefore the discipline *of* social movements. Even recently, the feminist movement has appeared to many women sociologists to be *one* of many contemporary movements which could be analysed through categories which were not different from those used for the analysis of the movements of students, the unemployed, the young and so on.

Beyond the 'vulgar' use which has not rarely been made of it, sociology has, however, represented, thanks also to its 'weak' disciplinary statute, a huge reservoir from which much has been taken for remarkable researches on the family, on domestic roles, on factory work, on education and so on. We can also ascribe to feminist sociologists valuable elaborations on categories such as that of female intellectuality and double presence.

The first question, which we defined earlier on as the criticism of the woman's condition, has attracted attention not only in sociology: various groups of women engaged in the juridical field also gathered around this theme. Amongst other things, at least two laws concerning us closely were being discussed in parliament in the middle of the seventies. Namely, the law on equality, which was passed in December 1977, and the law on abortion, which was approved in the spring of 1978, while the Collective of Via Pompeo Magno in Rome, the MLD and the UDI were elaborating the text of the law – by popular initiative – against sexual violence. Later on, in 1979, they launched a campaign by collecting signatures.

At the DWF Centre of Studies, for example, various initiatives took place between 1977 and 1979, with the intervention of some women jurists on the theme of the relationship between women and the law, or even between 'women and institutions'; a project was begun, and then abandoned, for an 'encyclopaedia of the law from the women's point of view', in which the historical, religious and philosophical roots of some Italian laws would be explored in comparison with other European law systems. After the agreements with a publisher had been made and most contributions were ready for print, the project was dropped: an 'extreme' case which is however indicative of the sense of saturation – on one side – and dissatisfaction – on the other – which took hold of us when faced with our own products.

The dissatisfaction came from the consciousness of the fact that working within a discipline (in that case, law) – no matter how much we try to enrich and articulate its statutes and the ways of approaching it – never really succeeds in expressing the modes of our condition and our own view of it, in our individual differences and the experiences we have been 'living through'. This consciousness, already present on the political level, had not been yet 'attempted' on the scientific level, where professionalism was a predominant value, and was still mainly intended as conformity to the standards of so-called objectivity.

We do not think, therefore, that the fundamental problem consisted in going beyond single disciplines to an interdisciplinary method: we were actually willing to undertake this method of analysis, but the problem concerned rather the relationship between subject and object of the research, and our own identity as 'agents of culture': in other words, as the upholders, popularizers and promoters of an accumulation of women's thought on themselves and on the world, with a political aim.

It is therefore for the second question, which we defined as the *search for a new identity*, that the role of disciplines has lost some of its importance, and prevailing themes have emerged.

Psychology and psychoanalysis have doubtless still enjoyed a large space in this area. But the question of identity has been treated in the Centres from other, different points of view.

The question of identity has – for example – been the origin of a wide-spread interest in female writing (with consequent analyses of language and communication among women) and in creativity in general, so that there was a huge production – sometimes in a group – of poetic works, videos, films and the most various interventions in the field of visual arts and applied arts in general.

Thus, new contents were joining 'old' contents in our consciousness and desire for knowledge: relationships among women, with the theme of solidarity and difference even before the theme of love (which emerged explicitly only a short time ago and is perhaps still not fully present and authoritative in the debates of the Centres); relationships between mother and daughter; motherhood; relationship with work as a self-recognition of one's own skills and competences; political separatism, cultural separatism and many more.

At the same time, we had a greater and greater need to place some phenomena in a historical perspective, and to identify their spread in different civilizations. But the incentive towards fields of analysis such as cultural anthropology, history, literary history was always linked to a need of *history* – a historical platform – more than of historiography. Once more, it was not a question of adapting ourselves to a *single* discipline, unless in the sense of recognizing in that discipline the means and the methods with which we could satisfy that need.

The Centres shared the demand – largely felt by women – to feel part of a history of the female gender. A history which has been seen at first as a violent oppression on the part of male culture, and then as the building up of a female identity which is never passive, never completely defeated, but rather capable of reaction and of 'rebel thought'.

Thence the attention given to the historical 'roots' of the contemporary movement with the – just starting – study of the emancipation movements. This is a field of study which, in many aspects, implies a search for legitimation and self-legitimation and which, however – for this precise reason – is not nowadays explored in a dimension of the history of ideas: what we want to find are lives, female individuals and groups, 'paths of female identity between memory and amnesia' (this is the title of a long seminar organized in the spring of 1985 by the Casa delle Donne in Ancona).

Another paper has clearly discussed the need for a larger and firmer conservation and transmission, which has been one of the basic principles at the origin of the Centres and of the coordinating committee, and, all things considered, of this conference itself. The recurrence of particular words in the name of the Centres themselves – documentation, studies, library, research – is an evident sign of this.

More recently, we assisted to the spreading of an interest – on the part of specialists – in the theme of sexual difference, or, better still, for the 'thought of sexual difference', but we refer in this regard to Adriana Cavarero's paper [see chapter 9].

Very recently, there have been associations of women scientists for, and specific attention by women in general to, the use of science and the possible definition of a 'female' science (a phenomenon which was noticed at once by publishing houses: we may think of the recent translation of Evelyn Fox Keller's works and of an anthology about women, technology and science, edited – for the Italian edition – by Elisabetta Donini).

It is an attention which has become more lively and urgent, especially – as everyone knows – after the Chernobyl tragedy.

7

Il Centro Culturale Virginia Woolf di Roma

The 'Virginia Woolf', also known as 'the Women's University', is one of the most important feminist cultural associations in Italy. Founded in Rome in 1979, it has annually organized courses, seminars and conferences on a wide range of subjects. It includes among its teachers some of Italy's most noted thinkers and intellectuals, academic and otherwise. More than 300 women a year have attended the Centre, women from very different walks of life, many of them not otherwise involved in the politics of feminism. In fact, one of the problems of the Virginia Woolf, as well as of the other Centres, has been how to bridge the gap between the organizers and the teachers on the one hand, and the 'pupils' on the other – that is, how to transform a pedagogical enterprise into a more deeply political one.

Since 1981 most of the courses have been organized around a single theme chosen by the organizers and set forth by one or more of them in a paper prefaced to the year's programme. They are all fascinating and of remarkable theoretical standing; we have chosen Alessandra Bocchetti's 'The indecent difference' (1982), which has come to be regarded as one of the seminal texts of Italian feminism. But Anna Rossi Doria's analysis of 'Feminine excess' (1984), Bia Sarasini's 'On borders' (1985), as well as the many-voiced elaborations on the issues of power by/among women (1987), must be at least mentioned.

THE INDECENT DIFFERENCE   *ALESSANDRA BOCCHETTI*, 1982

Women have been the inhabitants of the twentieth century since time immemorial.

It is in the twentieth century that a plural, contradictory subject replaces the full and coherent subject of classical reason in the history of thought, and therefore in its itineraries of research.

Women have always carried within themselves this plural subject being: they have always experienced the impossibility of the split between affective life and social and cultural reason, between body and thought, an impossible one for them. Between passion and ethics, they have always lived this multiplicity, always embodied the crisis of a reason which was supposed to be singular and bodiless; with their silence, their historical silence, they have always represented an implicit radical criticism of the foundations of this thought, which resolved all difficulties by suppressing its own contradictions.

We have become used to living without God, without the concept of God, and as Foucault says it seemed a crazy, impossible undertaking: in the same way we will have to get used to living without the concept of man, that man whose gaze consecrates reality, the man who lays claim to being the only measure of the real. The crisis of this man and his luminous reason brings with it silence, the silence of the 'key words' in which his thought was grounded.

The silence of words

Silence is a theme which is very evident in the culture of the early twentieth century, and much talked about. In 1902 Hugo von Hofmannsthal wrote 'Lord Chandos's Letter', which is an emblematic work of this kind.

Chandos highlights a *'sickness of the soul'* which impoverishes words, sucking any certainty of meaning from them.

'I felt deeply uneasy even just saying the words "spirit", "soul", "body"! I found it deeply impossible to express any judgment.'

But it is precisely the silence of words, their crisis, which is beginning to reveal a fertile space with new possible interpretations, new figures and shapes.

As the unifying and approving gaze of man as bearer of unique reason fades, new possible reasons begin to appear. From this situation of apparent wretchedness, the theoretical richness of our century is born.

The result of this process is that today we can think of the child other than as an incomplete man, of the primitive other than as a savage, an uncultured unethical man; and it's possible for woman to see herself and be seen in her difference, no longer and not simply 'reduced' to her difference.

In order to think in this way we have had to abandon our old image of the world as an extension of man, just as in order to discover America we had to abandon our image of the world as a flat carpet. From this different perspective, it has been possible to bring into being new languages, new words, new practices of knowledge.

So modern pedagogy, anthropology and especially psychoanalysis are born; these things come about only after we go beyond the simplifying gaze and assert a desire for knowledge which confirms the existence of the other in her or his difference and which does not set out to reduce or deny it.

Psychoanalysis, too, is born from the silence of classical reason, and takes shape precisely because of the need to overcome this silence, this crisis.

Overcoming the crisis doesn't mean finding the strength to reassert old values, but finding new ones, finding new words. Psychoanalysis displaces the word man, the concept of a full, coherent, singular I, with an I that is divided, plural, poliform; that very I which has always been the experience of women.

We don't need to remind ourselves that psychoanalysis is born from listening to women's bodies. If Nietzsche brought the body violently into philosophy, it was only with Freud that the body's knowing, its reasons, begin to be unravelled; and with it a process was begun to fill exactly the gap, the silence which the death of 'classical reason' had left. It's from the reappearance of what had been removed by history and culture that psychoanalytic language and practice begin to take shape.

Freud discovered the unconscious through the bodies of women. If we think about it clearly, the unconscious is the first great discovery of the female body. All women know how much the female body has been neglected, ignored, unseen by what we have learnt to call the sciences which for centuries have produced nothing but superstitions about it.

But we don't want to tie the 'discovery' of woman so much to psychoanalysis as to the whole process of our century with its crises and its overcoming of crises, its silences, its words and its invention of new words. Paradoxically it's the silence of words, and the need to overcome this silence, which brings to an end the silence of women. How could woman recognize herself, think herself, produce thought through a full, complete, bodiless I, she who is a bearer par excellence of a multiple I, bearer simultaneously of body and soul, of passion and reason.

Only now, within this process which affects everyone, both men and women, does her subject being '*spurt*' out of the mute folds of history. Only today, through the affirmation of a multiple, contradictory subject, do women find themselves within a theoretical space, with the possibility of producing a discourse.

A crisis was necessary for this space to open up; the silence of men and their full words. Only through this process of loss of sense and acquisition of new senses does woman find herself the subject, and not just the object of knowledge. This passage from silence to discourse doesn't belong to women's history, but to history full stop; no apprenticeship, no evolution, no gradual journey was necessary. Women did not arrive at theory, but discovered themselves in theory.

The silence of women

We have spoken much about women's silence, the absence of their words in history. It's a discourse which frightens us: we live this silence, this absence, as a profound and secret sign of our wretched state. This is why some women have stubbornly dedicated themselves to discovering women poets, composers, painters and architects who were forgotten or hidden. And so we try today to deny a past which is mute and awkward, or simply feel sorry for ourselves. But it is always the idea of women's wretchedness which inspires these efforts.

We believe that women's silence will keep coming up, and will be the phantasm that will continue to haunt our actions and thoughts, until we manage to make some sense of it, insert it into a historical perspective of thought, fill it with knowing; until we change the perspective in which to look at it; that is, at woman's implicit wretchedness. Our hypothesis is that we should take women's silence not as a sign of their poverty of language, but of the poverty of language.

People often say to us that the silence of women should be avenged, but it's only by reclaiming it that we can open up discourse for ourselves, make a discourse open up. To do this we need to look at women's silence as a sign not of incapacity, but of the impossibility of 'resistance'.

The few examples of women who managed to leave some trace of themselves behind, the few examples of a 'full past' which we have, should be searched through to find the sense of this 'mute past', because only here will we find the deposit of meanings which can inform our word today.

When we speak of women's silence people object, often reasonably, that we don't consider how many men have remained mute on the stage of history, and in this way the modestly unspoken discourse of male 'genius', and of the few women who are 'geniuses', raises its head. But true silence takes place when something is silenced, when we are not included in discourse and so it is impossible for any one to hear us, when there are no words to say it with. The most anonymous mute man has been neither silent nor absent, because the values which informed his actions and his thoughts were recognized by a discourse which included him, even if it went beyond him.

For a long time reason queened it over this discourse; she guaranteed a clear, shining view on the world, and the innocent and crystal-clear nature of actions separating true from false, right from wrong, mad from wise, rich from poor, life from death. This reason could not but dismiss the uncertain and contradictory terrain of feelings; there discourse got confused, and it became impossible to define what was true, what was good, what was wise.

The representation of this chaotic territory was entrusted almost exclusively to women. Woman's body was the resting place after wars, after the effort of thought, and was also the place to be fled, a terrifying mirror of a darker world. So women found themselves almost sole inhabitants of the territory which is beginning to flower only in our century. Only today can we begin to separate (if this still means anything) women who will remain mute from those who will speak. Too many sacrifices were necessary for women's words, too many denials, and little or nothing is produced by denying ourselves.

The suppressed

Working on women's silence, their few words, to understand better the silence which surrounded them, and searching out their private muteness in those few words (not so much what was said as what remained unsaid), means working on what is dismissed, suppressed, on material which reason has long pushed aside, seeing it as opaque, deaf, meaningless. We shouldn't think of this as our own private task, our own difficult path as women; it's the only work possible in these times, the path taken by culture today. Freud discovered the unconscious when he looked for and found meaning in what had been dismissed. Such was women's hysteria: without sense and opaque to almighty reason. Today we study the language of delirium, history in the lives of people.

We study what has been dismissed, cast off, failings, silences, non-answers; this path is rocky and uncertain for us all. The road to wisdom is no longer clear, straight, continuous. Often it's hidden, goes underground, falls away; there are no longer tracks or signs to guide the traveller. The material shows a poverty which befits its status as rejected. It's in this sense that someone who is involved in cultural studies today is a 'hard labourer' rather than a 'worker'.

But what does it mean for us, to work on what has been rejected, and more particularly what exactly *has* been rejected?

We have been speaking for a long time now of our oppressed condition, we have denounced our own misery and the injustice which burdened us with a wearisome 'destiny' just because we were women. We know the issues involved in these protests, in that they form part of our everyday lives. But all this represents only a part of our experience. It is not suppressed, not by us, not by culture, not by social organization: society knows of this injustice precisely because it practises it through the law, morality and tradition. The suppressed is never that which is practised according to reason, it's what reason doesn't know and doesn't want to know. The suppressed is often dumb: whether hidden or evident, it is still meaningless. It can push us in the direction of new meanings only if it is filled by them in its turn; it's a space still empty of knowledge.

Pleasure

One domain that has been dismissed is for us, and not only for us, that of pleasure. Indeed, women's pleasure cannot be anything but transgression within a value system which labels woman as '*mater dolorosa*'. Women don't talk about it, nobody talks about it, or else they talk about it just enough to place it in the metaphysical domain of the ineffable.

What does it mean to talk about our own pleasures? And what is women's pleasure? What is the imaginary which contains it?

Don't believe that searching out our own pleasures, attempting to trace a genealogy of pleasure, means a reconquest of female territory by those who want to see women serene and 'happy'. On the contrary: we believe that by doing this we are setting out on a harsh road where it is possible to touch the depths of our own misery and experience the greatest sadness.

Pleasure is the portion of a woman's life which 'power-wisdom' doesn't know and which simultaneously allows this 'power-wisdom' to perpetuate itself: it's what exceeds it and at the same time keeps it alive.

We women have never opened up this debate because it had to do with that part of our lives which would have us be losers, the part of us which connived at our own oppression, our reactionary part. We have ourselves dismissed it, often undervaluing it, reading it as a small secret folly or hiding it as one hides a theft, an illegal act. We have never considered it a worthy subject of analysis; when there have been analyses of this kind they have been cautious, hesitant or fearful; coming from the masculine imaginery they found themselves enclosed in the trap of masochism, the interpretative key which opened all doors of the feminine. And yet it seems to us that precisely this ground is most fertile for an analysis of the feminine as difference, in the effort to bring out values which have been submerged, different, other meanings which it suggests.

Telling, analysing our 'pleasures' generates not denunciation but discourse. This is an analysis which only feminine subjects can undertake; if denouncing injustice is a discourse which all 'just' people can partake in, women's pleasure is so unacceptable institutionally, so transgressive in their own eyes, so secret, that only women can talk about it.

Women often respond uneasily to this kind of discourse, as if the kernel of feminist discourse were being taken away: oppression, men's power. Focusing our attention on male power has been an important part of our journey. But if we are to open ourselves up to the idea of construction, going beyond the phase of denunciation, we need to tell and analyse what escapes this power, what exceeds it, what is hidden from it. We need to get rid of the mythological aspect both of male power and of women's oppression. And in doing so we are not denying that they exist.

The mute past of women, the paucity of their words, cannot be wiped out with a denunciation. They must be understood, as we must understand our uncertainties, our anxieties, our sense of shame, our 'resistances' to the cultural and the social.

We need to give an account not of how women have been oppressed, but of why they have not rebelled, and what conditions prevailed in the instances when they did rebel. Whatever historical period we consider, this kind of research will give us not historical information but current knowledge. And vice versa; a new awareness of ourselves will give meaning to what was apparently flat to the 'simplifying gaze of habit'.

Resistance

To read women's silence as a sign of 'resistance' to a discourse which does not take them into account is not to tie up a problem with a solution; if anything it is to open it up by introducing new factors.

It is still necessary to search out the roots of this 'resistance', and the imaginary which generates it.

One site of resistance for women is creativity. We know how agitated women get when they talk about their creative problems in seminars, especially literature seminars.

In one such seminar, a woman told us how inadequate her own writing seemed to her, how meagre and false her attempt seemed compared to the fullness of sensation which she had wanted to communicate.

'If art', she asked, 'art and artistic creation are the feminine side of men, their procreativity, why is it so difficult for women? What is it that stops us doing it, that makes it such a big deal for us?' She went on, 'Even at its best the consequences terrify me. I'm frightened by Virginia Woolf's suicide, Sylvia Plath's head in the oven, Emily Dickinson shut up in her room for twenty years, not wanting to come out of it any more until she was dead.'

Before this question was put, another woman had said that perhaps we had to learn to 'bring books into the world as we bring children into it'. A rare example of the maternal as metaphor; women are not very good at accepting and using this over-diffused metaphor. We steer ourselves well clear of it, as if this distance guaranteed us some private salvation.

This woman, then, had said: 'To bring a book into the world we have to lose it, accept its difference from us, be there at its birth, look at it living its own life, share it with others. My son is there, he is different from me even if I'm not different from him; I know he'll betray me, he'll leave me, his path won't be mine, but this is the only way to give him existence.'

This woman theorized writing and creativity as an exercise in abandonment. That's what writing is: an inevitably partial product of an inexhaustible personal totality, the fruit of faithlessness to the fullness of one's own imaginary, the sign of an abandoning, a renouncing of this fullness.

That's what real maternity is like too, an inevitable confrontation between our flesh-and-blood child and our imaginary child, the 'child of the night' as Silvia Vegetti Finzi calls it, the child which all women carry inside themselves, which they stubbornly cling on to and which often leads them to reject real maternity. The real child is only infidelity to the complete, indivisible child of our imaginary.

This is the same point of view that the other woman was wondering about, why it was that if creativity has the same economy as the maternal, women's access to it is so difficult and traumatic.

Starting from these observations and questions the seminar tried to analyse in economic terms of loss the fundamental experiences of women's lives.

Leaving the mother's body at birth is an experience shared by both sexes, as is the abandoning of the 'figure' of the mother and of her world to enter the world of the law of the father. But this second severance is quite a bit harder for women, and the abandonment of the mother inevitably means a negation of the self.

The sexuality which ties us to the mother is another area of abandonment. Women will only find the mother's body again by transgressing the law which takes female sexuality as complementary to the male and tied to reproduction. And, anyway, transgression is itself marked by loss, since transgression alienates one from the social context, makes one 'different'.

In sexuality, women are allowed to practise the male imaginary which sees them as mothers. But their own maternal imaginary is as a matter of course denied, buried. From this angle our own maternity becomes an 'involuntary shock of memory': the woman is the only one to experience total fusion with another body, and the end of this experience is always separation. This is the moment when the loved-hated figure of the mother reappears with all the violence of a long denial.

We still don't know the consequences of all this for a woman's body and for her imaginary. But it's probably in the chemistry of these events that we can investigate what we call 'women's time', with its tenacious dynamic between past and present and difficulty in imagining the future.

One woman said, 'Women don't imagine the future, they make it. They don't think time, they make it. When I'm on my own at home, cooking, I feel that I'm keeping my children alive, that I'm giving them the strength to come home. It must be that, because I've been cooking for twenty years, and I hate cooking.'

But the paths of abandonment for women don't stop with the body of the mother or the body of the child. There are other levels they can operate on too.

To gain access to thought, woman is asked to forget her sexed body.

The words 'being', 'individual', 'person', 'subject', fundamental to western thought, are only apparently neuter.

With time woman loses her youth and beauty, that great symbolic territory in an economy of representation which has placed women in the role of the hunted.

And more . . .

The seminar spent a long time working on these reflections, listing the sites of loss, and female economy appeared profoundly marked by abandonment. But in the midst of all this we discovered the imaginary as a site of iron resistance, a secret hiding place where woman jealously preserves her entirety, her 'child of the night', where she resists creativity, the last possible site of loss of the self; it's not written into her destiny, so the choice of creativity is a particularly dramatic one.

To speak of 'resistance' is to speak not of activity but of passivity. When faced with the prospect of creativity, yet another site of loss, woman, creature of losses, puts up a sort of resistance and refusal which marks her experience in this field with enormous suffering and struggle.

The result of this seminar was certainly no comfort to that woman whose writing appeared to her so inadequate. We're not out to console, and the practice of knowing isn't consoling; but it certainly gave her a clue as to why Emily Dickinson decided to stay shut up in her room for twenty years, in a dramatic effort to represent at least in space a closure which would screen/shelter, keep her wholeness/ entirety, to counterbalance her loss, her bodily being opened up in writing.

The imaginary

Women's imaginary is a deposit of fullness, the root of pleasure. The more the being it belongs to is tried by abandonment and loss, the more closed and secret it is.

This is a whole area which we have yet to investigate. We know the male imaginary which inhabits us: the maternal which is 'giving', constantly called on to give; but the other one, more jealously hidden, the 'taking' maternal imaginary, the female imaginary, can be known only by entering a new phase of telling of ourselves.

The woman who hated cooking and had been cooking for twenty years showed us what could lie behind women's 'habits'. 'Habit': a body which is time, peace, repetition, resting place for men, dear place of homecoming after his adventures. Only women, organizers of habits, know what abysses, terrors, obsessions, mad pleasures are hidden for them in the word. This woman's 'mania' is doubtless what has been secretly suppressed in her good sense as mother; it belongs to the imaginary which takes rather than the imaginary which gives. Reflecting on this 'suppression', what had escaped the flatness of evidence revealed itself. But to do this we had to assume a point of view from which 'the familiar appears unknown and the known strange'.

This woman's reflection seems emblematic to us. The material we investigate in its difference is only the other, secret, indecent face of our experiences and our lives: our contentments, our resistances, our secret pleasures, our visionary ability, the real reasons for all of which lie in the darkest corners of our imaginary.

Difference

We've already said that opening up this new phase of talking about ourselves doesn't uncover new areas to be avenged, but it can lead to the discovery of a new self-knowing by women: knowing difference.

Behind the avenging discourse of women has always been the idea of the equality of the sexes. This may be a right and necessary claim on a social level, but it is not exhaustive, not satisfying, nor does it bring knowledge for subjects who are different or who have been made so. Paradoxically it's the discourse of equality between the sexes which reveals 'women's oppression' and which simultaneously creates an awareness of this oppression.

This discourse came into being with the need for feminine labour in the factories. Indeed, it was reasonable for women not to think of themselves as different, so they could take up equal roles which would take them out of the home. The site of difference shrank, reduced itself to unequal salaries, to the double burden of job and housework, to not having the vote. These were the sites entrusted with the task of representing differences, where difference became simply inequality, inequality, inequality, against which women have rightly struggled, and against which they continue to struggle.

Before the necessary discourse of equality between the sexes, the discourse of difference was wider and was conducted by men whose wisdom explained women either as animals, and so a part of nature, or as incompetent or inferior.

It's legitimate to wonder why in the face of this kind of thinking, which imposed rigid rules which women had to obey, living conditions which were often very harsh indeed, women didn't rebel.

One possible answer is that thinking of women as other to yourself, animals or inferiors or whatever, meant at least speaking and practising a difference; it meant guaranteeing the separation of two worlds each with its own laws and regulations, two different spaces, two domains.

Today we can still find traces of this separate female world. For the peasants in the south, the figure of the mother is 'other', different, but she also has her own laws, her own spaces.

If we think of our own generation, our 'luckless' marriages, our paltry and often precarious emotional equanimity, we see that our generation is perhaps the first to try really living with men: school, university, politics, travel, free time, debates, worries.

Perhaps it's gone wrong because the discourse of difference has been silenced; we ourselves have tried to deny it.

The discourse of difference seemed to us to be reactionary and in fact it had always been so, but this needn't be the case if it's used not as an instrument of denial of the other but as a path of self-knowledge by women.

The feminist movement's claim of political separatism already contained this discourse. If the old separatism–denial closed the door in the face of knowledge of the other, the separatism of political sites of today's women suggests more than anything a possible knowledge of the self in difference, but opening up the discourse of difference as affirmation.

The idea of difference leading not to denial but to knowledge inevitably comes about by looking at what escapes normal evidence, at the secret corners of our experience, at what exceeds the norm.

The old discourse of difference asserted maternity as its focal point: 'Since the woman is mother she can't ... she mustn't ...', and so became prescriptive and negative, grounded in what was evident. But what a mother is, only a mother can say.

Maternity has been situated in, prescribed as one of the 'good deeds', sacred even. But what is indecent in maternity, only a woman can say.

'The ambiguous maternal', the only theme we put forward a couple of years ago, which hypothesized the maternal in the realm of passion, was an attempt to analyse the secret indecency of this experience.

Indecency

By 'indecency' we mean what isn't spoken about, what we are not supposed to speak about. We attempted to reach a point where we could speak about what exceeds the maternal role prescribed by law, by good sense, by tradition, exploring the pleasures and damnations of this experience or of the possibility of this experience.

From the eighteenth century onwards, passion has been banished by philosophy. Reason admitted its representations only in novels and drama. Passion was exiled. And even today the theme of passion is not in fashion. Our time, the time in which we think the future, can only push aside this excessive sentiment since it belongs only to the present.

Indeed, passion is an indecent feeling *par excellence*. It takes us out of the 'project time', it constructs and destroys only itself, it represents only an experience which is irredeemably private, its appearance indicates a frightening relativization of the real.

By assigning all these implications to the maternal we might seem to be approaching the theses of the cultural right in the early twentieth century, and in particular of Weininger. In *Sex and Character*, Weininger talks about women, about the mother as amoral being, and maternal love as immoral. He asserts that maternity 'represents not a relationship with another I, but from the very beginning a kind of symbiosis'. So Weininger too speaks of the indecency of maternity, of the maternal; but since his thought was directed to the desperate affirmation of values which were crumbling away under his very eyes (he wrote *Sex and Character* in 1902) he can only conclude that 'woman is nothing, she is only matter'; he can only dismiss her out of hand as subject.

But what were those values that were crumbling, which had dried up as a source of knowledge and were fit only to be abandoned, left behind?

What was being abandoned was the concept of an I full of unity and the real. Freud was already affirming a plural subject, a divided, plural and polymorphous I was taking shape, an I which was exquisitely female, as Weininger very well saw.

But today it is precisely this plural I which is posing the question Weininger didn't want to ask: what other 'morality' does woman's amorality suggest? What values are implied in her secret indecency? What other image of the world is formulated by the needs of this different subject?

Freud too drew his life and work to a close asking the question, 'What does a woman want?', a final and honest question from a man who had spent so much time working on and studying women's bodies. This question suggests the existence of a point of view which Freud himself hadn't managed to find.

'What does a woman want?' is, then, the question we ask ourselves, not so much to find an answer as to find a different way of asking the question. An enigma is a suggestive phrase, which suggests an object without disclosing it. The matter which forms it is what has been suppressed, memory, assonances, similarities, all those things which the hidden object evokes in the eyes and experience of the person who poses it.

Working on this difference for us means beginning to bring into this enigma other things previously suppressed, other memories, other assonances and similarities which our eyes and our experience have found.

As a child Benjamin used to embroider the edges of pieces of paper, and in his 'Childhood in Berlin' he tells of how he often stopped what he was doing, his attention caught by the underside of the embroidery where all the threads were tangled up together; the indecency of embroidery.

This seems to us an extraordinary parable of the work we plan to carry on. We have to look at the underside of the embroidery to know something of who we are and what we want. To go on with the embroidery or to unpick it would mean in the first instance remaining in a state of obedient unawareness and in the second denying our history in the name of a utopia which, honestly, we haven't got.

This year too, we hand this theme over to the reflection of the women at the Centre, this work which anywhere else is improbable, inadmissible or simply unallowed because it has so little of the orthodox about it: a continual confrontation between imaginary and knowing.

8

Lesbofemminismo

Bianca Pomeranzi's paper gives a clear and succinct account of Italian lesbian feminism and of its position within the feminist movement, and it also provides some useful bibliographical information. The other pieces in the section are from journals and books quoted in her article, and further illustrate the themes and the development of lesbofeminism in Italy.

A couple of points she touches upon might be worth stressing again: the virtual absence in Italy of a lesbian movement separate from the feminist movement as a whole; the meaning of 'separatism' in Italy, which does not imply a lesbian preference in terms of sexual life, but signifies the existence of only-women groups for purposes of theoretical elaboration and political action, and stresses their adherence to a sort of 'political homosexuality', that is, the privileging of women as the point of reference in all areas.

A SURVEY: LESBIAN DIFFERENCE AND LESBIAN
FEMINISM   *BIANCA POMERANZI*, 1985

Introduction

In the following brief notes it is not my intention to give an exhaustive picture of the lesbian movement in Italy over the last twenty years, only to point out the characteristics of a new formation which has been taking shape in the eighties.

It is not easy to read these events, since they are bound up with the history of feminist separatism and the practice of a number of collectives.

The difficulty of getting hold of the most interesting texts, together with the general lack of interest expressed so far by some of the more 'academic' studies of and on feminism, has hindered the development of a real and proper debate on the origins of lesbian formations in Italy, and in many cases make a national picture impossible. In my outline I have used not only 'chronologies' but also my own personal 'memories' as a militant, having been present at many of the 'events' which marked the rise of lesbian groups. All this will perhaps give my work a greater subjectivity than I would have wished, and I can already foresee that I will not be able to cast the right light on the work of many individual women as well as groups who have worked over the past years to raise the visibility of lesbianism.

I think I should mention some work and some chronologies which have appeared in the form of cyclostyled sheets in an attempt to make some order out of the most recent events in the history of lesbianism in Italy:

Rina Macrelli, an article in *Quotidiano Donna*, July 1981.
Rosetta Froncillo, cyclostyle of the CLI (Italian Lesbian Union) for 8 March 1982.
Rina Macrelli and Giovanna Pala, cyclostyled pamphlet entitled *Lesbianism and feminism*, January 1983, which reconstructs the birth of political lesbianism within the Roman feminist collective Pompeo Magno, in the years from 1971 to 1981.
Rina Macrelli, *Towards a short calendar of lesbian feminism in Italy*, cyclostyle for the 4th National Lesbian Conference, Rome 1985.

Although all these documents, which I would recommend to anyone interested in getting a more detailed panoramic view, date from around 1971 onwards. I prefer to locate my analysis between the end of the seventies and the first years of the eighties; new forms of aggregation take shape during these years, the qualitative and quantitative results of which have been evident in the recent conference held on 1, 2 and 3 November at the Feminist Separatist Centre in Rome.

The appearance of the lesbian association, 1979–1981

The first 'visible' manifestation of the lesbian association within the women's movement was the appearance of two lesbian placards at the 8 March demonstration in Rome in 1979: 'Artemis – group of lesbian women in revolt' and 'Zanzibar, only for women, only with women'.

This episode was the point of arrival of a tortuous route begun within feminist collectives, where throughout the seventies a number of lesbians had been active in the objectives and analyses of feminism.

The process of diversification began in 1977, undoubtedly assisted by the political climate of those years, in which the transformations within the (more or less informal) structures of the women's movement reached their peak.

It is important to emphasize that although the birth of the first lesbian groups led to a process of scission from feminism, the term 'separatist' is assumed by these groups to distinguish them from the operations of Fuori [the Italian front for homosexual revolution]. It is not by chance that a lesbian group was formed in Turin: the Sappho Brigade split off from Lamda [an organization parallel to Fuori] precisely because of this need to be distinguished from normal homosexual politics.

The debate on separatism in those years involved diverse subjects from feminist militants and began a process of aggregation which we can define as 'intermediary' between the women's movement and the homosexual movement.

It was the characteristics of mediation between two very different types of political action that provoked a tormented debate between these new groups and the feminist collectives still operating. It is likely that lesbian feminists had the impression that these processes constituted not a new aggregation but a form of disintegration of the issues and heritage of feminism.

We must remember that it was during these years that translations on the birth of the lesbian movement in the United States, and the consequences within the feminist movement, appeared in Italy.

In the same period there had been some changes in political activism which lent a sharper edge to this sense of disintegration, and which lay behind the fear that the women's movement would dissolve into a thousand tiny offshoots. There is still need for an analysis of the way in which widespread terrorism modified the forms of feminism, and how far it influenced the acceleration of theoretical work on the analysis of differences.

Certainly that process together with theorizing on separatism, formed the connective tissue of this new lesbian aggregation, which in its early stages differentiated itself into two main strands. On the one hand there were those who attacked the feminist movement for concealing the social conditions of lesbians, while on the other, mostly within feminism, there was an effort to analyse the constitutive difference of feminist practice within collectives in which heterosexual women were also present. We can schematize this by saying that the first years of lesbian aggregation were marked by two strands: one, external and immediately visible, exclusively lesbian; the other, internal and analytically theoretical, lesbian feminist in character. The characteristic of this second thread makes it difficult to quantify the aggregations of those years which still have for the most part a metropolitan character and are distinguished by the birth of 'closed' groups.

We have to go to the end of 1979 for some 'external' manifestations, for example a concert of German and American lesbian singers in the Women's House in Rome in October 1979, or from September 1979 onwards the beginning of a lesbian page in *Quotidiano Donna*, with articles by both groups and individuals.

In 1980 there are no episodes of direct interest to the lesbian aggregation, unless we count the publication by the Felina publishing house of *E la madre tra l'altro è una pittrice* (*And the mother amongst other things is a painter*) by Matilde Finocchi, Rosetta Froncillo and Alice Valentini. The book, which is a collection of interviews with lesbian women, marks an opening up in the national press of the question of lesbianism as opposed to generic homosexuality, and it was reviewed by Ida Magli in the widely circulated daily *La Repubblica*. That year also saw the unfolding of meetings and debates on the question of lesbianism, between feminists and women of Fuori, between city-based groups who begin to talk of the possibility of a lesbian national conference.

With regard to the year 1980–1, it seems to me of much more interest to mention an episode of recent feminist history which had indirect consequences for the modalities of lesbian aggregation; the presentation by the UDI and some feminist collectives of the law by popular initiative on crimes of sexual violence. The meeting with other women's realities, on the part of collectives in which the debate on lesbian feminism was this far advanced, modified the way the groups themselves, and especially Pompeo Magno, acted around this problem. The most obvious result of the change was, in the first half of 1981, the convocation at the Women's House in Rome, by the whole of the Pompeo Magno collective, of the first national meeting on lesbianism.

On that occasion we began to see the outlines of lesbian geography in Italy, since of the almost 400 women who attended, only some belonged to groups or lived in the big cities.

The form taken by the meeting, which is now remembered as the first national lesbian conference, was that of personal statements and not elaboration; something very similar to what happened in the first feminist meetings except that, in this case, the sense of fear in breaking silence on some aspects of one's own life, which many women perceive as dangerous, makes the whole thing much more complicated, painful and visceral.

The image of these lesbian lives emerges sometimes through a negative attitude towards feminism itself. Perhaps it is for this reason that the next conference held in Rome in December 1981 was organized not by the Pompeo Magno collective as a whole but only by a part of it, the lesbian group which takes the name Vivere Lesbica (Lesbian Living), working to organize the conference together with women coming from different types of experience.

The importance of conferences in the first phase of lesbian aggregation cannot be doubted. They were able to put in touch isolated women, coming from different backgrounds and experiences, who were interested in a type of political practice tied more to everyday life than to militancy.

It's no accident that in the six-month period between the two conferences in Rome the CLI [Italian lesbian union] was born, the structure which best synthesizes the characteristics of this new aggregation, since it addresses itself not to groups but to individual women. The founders seem to me to have clearly expressed the substance of this diversity in a brief announcement which appeared in *Quotidiano Donna*, 20 November 1981:

> Three of us, Giovanna, Leila and Tonia, have decided to form the CLI, all of us having spent more or less time in feminist collectives and consciousness-raising groups. We wanted an organizing structure which would also be a meeting point to be with other lesbians in a way which made space for initiatives, which was enjoyable and which made for the deepening of our lesbian identity.
>
> The most important thing was to unite together with all other lesbians whom we knew to be isolated.
>
> A number of different groups have been formed (Phoenix in Milan, Tiaso in Bologna, Lesbian line in Florence), a number of women's initiatives – lesbian and otherwise – are taking shape and more and more news is coming from abroad. It seemed to us that the point of departure was to distribute this information, thus spreading our energy around, to give useful information to whoever wanted to go outside Italy, exchange journals, pamphlets, videos and ideas. Everything remains to be done: the CLI will develop and act in ways that are so far unforeseeable, in response to the needs and suggestions of those who join us. This bulletin, which from next January will appear every month, is the first moment of union and contact; then we will see.

In this declaration of intentions by the founders we begin to see the thread of the lesbian line, not the lesbian feminist one. Above all the formula of the 'service' structure recalls the flux of analogous structures within the international gay movements, and the reference to lesbian identity is a polemical one if we think that the feminist elaborations of those years had never accepted, even when debating on differences, the split between women and lesbians at a theoretical level.

I think that the no longer simply polemical debate between the lesbian line and the lesbian feminist one began only in the December 1981 conference, when the first elaborations written by lesbian groups began to appear alongside individual statements. The way the conference was organized into days on various pre-prepared and discussed themes made it possible to articulate a discourse tied to the existential problems of lesbian women: their fears, sexuality, identity and identities.

The twelfth issue of *Differenze* in May 1982, edited by Vivere Lesbica, reported the debate that went on in those days, and it remains one of the first direct statements about the way this new aggregation was taking shape. Indeed, apart from the effort at chronological reconstruction, very little has been produced between the years 1981 and 1985. The CLI bulletin itself, the only element of continuity in the life of this association, has often found itself reflecting the reality of a large number of small groups interested in promoting collective initiatives such as camp-sites, meetings, information sheets and editorial initiatives rather than raising consciousness. Over the last few years the most productive theoretical moments have been conferences or seminars, while in political practice the new lesbian aggregations have become more and more integrated into the new regional networks of feminist associations.

From lesbian difference to the growth of lesbian feminism, 1982–1985

It's the last three years that are the most difficult to analyse for the qualitative and quantitative dimension of this new way of being together. There's no doubt that the contraction of women's spaces, the negotiations within local bodies, in Rome and the rest of the country as well, have all gone to create new forms of solidarity between lesbians and feminists, all experienced within the logic of separatism. Polemics have subsided and given way to a succession of debates on the most notable cultural productions of feminism. This has also been made possible by the fact that in all these years no separate political objectives or specifically lesbian struggles have been put forward. If we do not count the October 1981 demonstration in Rome for the release of two women in Agrigento (imprisoned for insulting a public official and for acts of indecency in a public place, since they had been caught kissing in a park), there have been no other organized protest demonstrations in the panorama of Italian lesbianism.

From the 1981 National Conference in Rome onwards it was possible to predict this tendency. Suggestions put forward there for political objectives were rejected by the groups as a whole, who thought that a long period of consciousness preparation and analysis of specific topics was needed in order to bring about a struggle which might marginalize women who still felt themselves at the mercy of society. Indeed, in their dealings with institutions they have preferred to give themselves objectives other than claiming civil rights, making instead specific requests for space and money for cultural activities. The third national lesbian conference, held in January 1983 in Bologna, was in fact partly financed by the local council, and in the same year the Le Papesse of Catania began to work together with local authorities in Syracuse for the financing of exhibitions and seminars.

The reason behind these choices are linked with the growth of the lesbian feminist strand and with the particular historical circumstances Italy has been going through over the past few years. We could perhaps add that in some institutions outside big cities, an individual or group declaration of lesbianism can seriously affect the work prospects of the women involved. In many cases militant lesbians belong to the middle classes, who have something to lose socially by declaring themselves to be different. Another fundamental reason is that, unlike their results in other European countries or the States, the practice of political separatism and its theorization within the feminist movement have increased the distance from other political formations and from those parties which might otherwise have guaranteed the necessary 'cover' for an institutional struggle. Given this separatism it's easy to explain the lack of lesbian candidates in the most recent elections, while there were on the other hand a number of homosexuals standing for the left.

It is easy to see the separatist tendency within the CLI itself over the last few years. In fact, this association has participated in the struggle to get the Separatist Feminist Centre, of which it is a part. But it can be seen even more clearly in the association's bulletin reports.

Especially from 1983 onwards, analyses have remained within the spheres of feminist debates. One specific publication entitled *Our common world*, published by Felina in 1983, is presented as CLI's contribution to the debate opened within the feminist community by the Milan document 'More women than men' (see chapter 5), and it was written for a seminar organized by the Virginia Woolf Centre in May 1983 in order to discuss the document in question with its authors, Group 4 of the Libreria delle Donne in Milan. The book's preface still shows some trace of polemic with regard to the unspeakable nature of lesbian experience within feminism and, as always in the life of CLI, there is a refusal to adopt collective forms because the authors define themselves as a 'thought group'. They reprove the Milan document for abetting the ambiguity of heterosexual society, 'not mentioning the fact that Adrienne Rich is a lesbian woman and yet affirming that a common world of women does not exist, which would implicitly sanction the absence of any chance of withdrawing from the "common world of men" and their values'. After this, however, polemics of this type have tended to disappear. Indeed, in the debate preceding the fourth lesbian conference in November 1985, discussions on the question of entrustment took the form not so much of claiming lesbian difference but of contributing to the general line of argument, quoting from writers such as Irigaray, who constitute a cultural heritage common to both feminism and lesbianism.

The very title of the conference, 'Ethics and politics of women's relationships', suggests a language typical of feminism and a desire to insert differentiation from feminism not in theoretical terms but through analysis of practice.

Once again the conference gave a picture of the state of lesbian aggregation in Italy. Of around 300 women present, a good 30 per cent were young women under thirty. Only about a half of those there had been connected to some other experience of feminism in the past, and a good part of them came from centres outside the big cities.

For the first time in the history of lesbian conferences, personal statements gave way to elaborations and written interventions, polemics to analyses. The term lesbian feminism, repeated a number of times in the course of the debate, didn't provoke any reactions in the meeting but gained consent. The new lesbian aggregation seems to have assumed a precise shape, which is transmitted through channels which are not exclusively those typical of feminism, but which are closely bound to them.

THE FEARS OF LESBIAN WOMEN   *ANNA*, 1982

A list of fears

We have put together a list of lesbians' fears in the hope that they will help other women think about their own. First we would like to make clear that this list of fears is born from our need and desire to live out our love for women in a way which is psychologically healthy, in other words in the social context.

Fear of loneliness

The lesbian woman who is alone socially risks carrying that loneliness over into a loving relationship with another woman.

Overcoming our own loneliness is an act of personal consciousness quite apart from the woman with whom we have a love relationship, but with whom one can build an authentic love, free of oppressive elements, free of fear, one which allows a relationship with other women as well.

Fear of losing our identity

The love relationship between women is one of growth if we can consciously try to rid ourselves of role models. The lesbian woman who still lives out masculine or feminine roles must try to go beyond them and live them as if they were steps on the way to the appropriation of her own identity.

Historical fear of male dependency

This is the classic fear perpetuated on women through an infinite series of repressions which aim to intimidate us, but which in the case of lesbian women becomes a form of retaliation.

Fear of losing civil rights

Loss of job.

Loss of custody of children.
Sexual violence.

Fear of losing our humanity

The male models of struggle are full of images of overwhelming hate. Losing sight of humanitarian feelings in a struggle can transform the desire to live into hatred towards men or towards some particular women. Hatred is a useless sentiment which can only take much from us.

A CHARTER OF RIGHTS *GIOVANNA*, 1982

How to emerge from our fear

The primary need to come out of our meetings has been to make our condition visible to the outside world, rejecting the clandestinity which we have been forced into and which we have forced ourselves to adopt, driven by fears induced in us by a hetero/patriarchal world which uses the subtlest of means to suppress the liberating and subversive charge of lesbianism.

We believe that a practice based on raising our own consciousness is indispensable to bringing our own fears out into the open so that we can begin to overcome them, but we believe that we also need to seek other tools which will allow us to impose our existence on the world.

After analysing (if only summarily, given the short amount of time we have been together) the fears and needs expressed by each woman, our group chose to propose to the movement the debate as it developed among us, and the (sometimes contradictory) suggestions which came out of it.

The possibilities we have established are these:

1 Choosing to follow the 'lesbian utopia', which means refusing any dealings with the patriarchal system, and thereby total revolution of the values and non-values of contemporary society without coming to any compromise with it.

2 Or else demanding equality of rights as people, extending the laws which govern heterosexuality to cover lesbians too, asking for the possibility of creating social nuclei comparable in terms of rights to families formed by marriage between people of different sex. This means proclaiming a general equality and parity without

taking into account one's own choices, refusing our label of 'difference' and appealing instead to article 3 of the constitution which states that 'All citizens have equal social dignity and are equal before the law, with no distinction of sex, race, language, religion, public opinion, personal or social circumstances. It is the duty of the republic to remove social and economic obstacles which by limiting the liberty and equality of our citizens hinder the full development of the human individual.'

3 Or else again, impose specific rights connected to our own particular circumstances, rights which we have elucidated at various points and which take into account some of the needs we face. We are talking about a 'Charter for the rights of lesbian women', even though few are aware of the fact that such a charter will offer only a partial guarantee when compared with the second possibility.

Charter of the rights of lesbian women

1 Daughters and sons can bear the name of the mother when she so desires.
2 Like all citizens in a state of need or otherwise, the lesbian woman can have a council house even if she is not married, not living with a common-law husband, and without dependent children or relatives.
3 When working she can ask for family allowance and free medical treatment for the person or people she has chosen to live with if they are unemployed, bereft of means or under age.
4 After her working life her matured pension can be passed on to the person or people who in her judgement would benefit from it, bearing in mind the requirements of the law and the rights of legitimate heirs, if she has any.
5 In her will she can dispose of her own goods and assets in favour of whomever she wishes, except for a certain sum to be set aside for older relatives or younger dependants who are either under age or in real need.
6 Lesbianism cannot be classified as an 'offence against our common sense of shame', and as such cannot be a negative factor in the case of matrimonial separation or the awarding of custody of children to the mother when she wishes it.
7 If a lesbian woman is open about her sexuality at work, this should not become cause or motive for discrimination.

Personally I believe in the possibility of carrying on a struggle on the basis of this charter of rights, using it as an instrument through which to affirm our diversity, and hence the incompatibility of our choices and praxis with institutions functioning as a norm which is alien to us.

To move on from this alienation to identify our specific needs is the beginning of a search for our collective and individual identity, the only way to resist being made 'invisible' by patriarchy.

MORE SILENCES THAN LIES   *RAFAELLA*, 1983

Feminist research and feminist theory which contribute to the invisibility of lesbians or their marginalization work against the liberation and strengthening of women as a group.
Adrienne Rich, 'Compulsory Heterosexuality and Lesbian Existence'

The compulsion towards exclusively heterosexual sexuality has resulted over time in the total, or almost total, cancellation of lesbian existence. Based exclusively on the needs of male sexuality, heterosexuality as the norm has been imposed, often brutally and violently, or else by making subtle generalizations about women, as the only possible choice for women's consciousness. In a universe constructed on heterosexual values and models, from the example of our parents to the models of happiness offered to us as women from our childhood (from fables to love songs, from comics to bestsellers, from films to TV scripts), we have been inoculated with heterosexual behaviour by a thousand daily pointers which sanction our complementarity to the male, and our completeness as women only in emotional and sexual synthesis with the 'other sex'. But as well as this subliminal persuasion to heterosexuality, acceptance of the heterosexual norm has also been profoundly conditioned by a continual intimidation, or rather a real form of terrorism organized at the social level against the very possibility of a woman's recognizing her own desire for another woman: from emotional to social blackmail, from verbal to physical violence.

The decision to resist masculine claims of access to our bodies has always been severely punished and cancelled out. The fear of punishment has been so strong that it has prevented many of us from recognizing ourselves, from choosing. How many of us on realizing our lesbianism haven't felt that we were alone, the only ones in the world? The very prohibition imposed on a lesbian memory has also prevented the construction of a lesbian imaginary (not heterosexual or

patriarchal) and has further conditioned and impoverished the consciousness of many women, forcing them into heterosexuality, as if
this were the only path open to them.

Even the research into women's past and the studies of feminist
groups, from cultural associations to self-help collectives, are characterized by the predominance of heterosexual values and views. Even
studies on lesbian writers, such as Gertrude Stein or Virginia Woolf,
ignore their real identity or refer to it as an 'adjective', a qualifying
element, not as a 'noun', carrying an existential substance. This is also
a way to 'encourage' implicitly the acceptance of heterosexual compulsion and to 'discourage' a lesbian choice.

The exaltation and literary codification of love as loss of the self and
unavoidable negation, with the implicit message of (self-)destruction,
reflects the absolute dominion of male eroticism, which is nourished
and fed on disparity, inequality and difference.

The heterosexual norm has been imposed on the minds and bodies
of women to the point where, despite the violence, the failures and the
disappointments, most women (but not *all*, and it's important to
remember that) have accepted and often supported the male's right to
his own privilege and his own supremacy, accepting without criticism
these sexual values. This codification is rooted so deeply that in the
social context it as an a priori fact, taken for granted, that each women
has a heterosexual identity.

Every woman who freely demands her own right to a lesbian
existence breaks the barrier of heterosexual solidarity, and is therefore
a threat. She is and always has been in a contradictory and irreducible
relationship to patriarchy, in that she constitutes for other women a
clear message of liberation and of reappropriation of our own bodies
and our own autonomous existence. The scandal of denying one's own
body to historical demands is intolerable for the heterosexual world.
For this reason every image and possible allusion to similar denials in
the past has been wiped out, or at least twisted into unhappy images of
female solitude, 'cloistered affections' and sorrow. As for today, while
we are generally rejected as lesbians who have 'come out' and are
visible, we enjoy a great deal of esteem in our jobs as invisible and
hidden lesbians: clerks, shop assistants, researchers, psychoanalysts,
mothers.

Provided of course that we don't make people hear or see, as long,
that is, as we lack the courage to live out our lives properly, and so
undermine patriarchal rule with our own pleasure. In this sense the
Milan document only repeats the same ambiguity, not mentioning the
fact that Adrienne Rich is a lesbian woman and yet affirming that a

'common world of women' does not exist, which would implicitly sanction the absence of any chance of withdrawing from the 'common world of men' and their values.

The invisibility and silence of lesbianism reign in the document, impoverishing its analyses, which are anchored in a generic, fantasy female condition that, while it leaves heterosexual women ample space for interpretation and subjectivity, does not deal with lesbian women at all. Or perhaps we are to be mentioned only when we are speaking specifically and exclusively about sex?

One of the first manifestations of the way our existence has been cancelled from history is in the very inability to use the terms 'lesbianism' and 'lesbian'. This silence facilitates the wide range of ghosts, desires and ambiguities with which the male heterosexual fills these words.

Unfortunately many lesbians accept this censorhip too: from the woman who feels a certain unease and, masking her own difficulties, regards it as nothing but a label, to the woman who succeeds in rejecting it firmly and so suffers to the full the negation of her own existence and desires operated by a sexuality, language and culture which reflect exclusively the needs of the male. Lesbians frequently act as their own censors, saying that they voluntarily choose their own invisibility, clearly unable to face up to the serious self-mutilation that a false heterosexual identity inflicts on them.

The visibility of their emotional and erotic life can cause them severe difficulties in the common world of men; accepting the position of real opposition to society which being a lesbian implies, or giving up the 'privileges' of ambiguity, can be very difficult, but it is also extremely liberating.

If naming a thing is the essential act of attributing existence to it, reluctance to use the term itself constitutes a serious threat to understanding the possibility or concreteness of what it defines. This is perhaps another reason why the imperative survival of the heterosexual order and the imperialism of male sexuality make people blind with regard to lesbianism. When faced with the words or the concrete reality of visible lesbian existence, heterosexual men and women manage not to see it. A sort of 'celibacy' or 'spinsterhood' is imposed on lesbian women by the heterosexual imagination. Where I work even the women who know that I have loved and love women, that I'm a lesbian, that I have a woman lover, that I live with her, that there are a number of women with whom I share my social life and affections, that my life is a full one, relate to me as if I were totally alone, with no affections, in other words as if I was as many of them are when they are without a man or solid, lasting friendships. It's as if they wanted to push us back at all costs into 'the well of loneliness'. Perhaps in order to feel less acutely the poverty of a prefabricated life, the wretchedness of being unable to imagine, live or see the narrowness of their own margins of choice.

We have to shout out, go too far, provoke, to get our existence recognized: we have to impose ourselves. This way we become excessive, petulant, egocentric, 'imperialist and neocolonialist' if not 'neofascist', according to those women who feel threatened in their exhausting and daily balancing act. It's difficult to recognize freedom in others if we cannot recognize it for ourselves, just as it's difficult to love and respect the bodies of other women if we do not acknowledge full liberty for ourselves, for our own woman's body.

For years my parents saw me living the life of a lesbian, they found me in bed making love with another woman . . . nothing was ever said. The day I said to my father 'I'm a lesbian' everything changed, he began to find me 'peculiar', and we couldn't communicate any more. My insolence had become intolerable, I was even proud of it all! I had spoken that dreadful word, breaking the rule of silence and secrecy.

Even more functional for patriarchy is the 'unhappy lesbian', a stereotype you can always find in the cinema, for example: lesbians who collaborate with Nazis, lesbians who hang themselves, who kill each other, hysterical lesbians who do nothing but throw up and are consumed with jealousy: the 'real' (that is, bad) lesbian always discovers that the 'pretend' (that is, good) lesbian is having an affair with a man, and it's the good one who returns to the heterosexual fold and survives. It's plain from just these few examples that silence serves not only the survival and advancement of compulsory heterosexuality, but also the stimulation and gratification of the male imagination.

In Devoto and Oli's *Dictionary of the Italian Language* (latest edition) we read: '*lesbianism*: anomaly of sexual behaviour in a woman (also called sapphism and tribadism) consisting in the search for and satisfaction of erotic pleasure with persons of her own sex'. So with no right to exist, spoken only quickly, under one's breath, the word 'lesbian', in that it defines a sexual anomaly, loses significance, becomes other and in the end can be filled with anything that the egotism of heterosexuality wants to attribute to it; after all, there is an enormous consumption of more or less explicit images of 'lesbian love' in art history, literature and pornography.

The heterosexual imagination, the basis of our whole culture, reflects, in the image it has of the 'lesbian' for its own use and consumption, the inadequacy and narcissism of male sexuality, which is often so conditioning for many women too in their understanding of the real lesbian existence. In Italy, in the feminist movement, lesbianism has for years been compressed, silenced, made invisible or at best tolerated by heterosexual women, who often had the consistent support of a number of lesbians. From seduction to insufferability, the life of many lesbians has been barely acknowledged in the golden age of the feminist movement by other women, who were clearly unable to see in lesbianism its real significance of resistance to patriarchy and a stimulus to think clearly about the origins of their own heterosexuality, the equivocal nature of their own sexual 'choice'. In this way they have contributed both to their own private and social oppression and to the marginalization and isolation of lesbian women. And all this when at the same time a lot of lesbians devoted their ability, time and energy to feminist endeavours and to the building of the common world of women.

SUGGESTIONS FROM IRIGARAY *SANDRA*, 1986

There is a woman's body: a project as well as a starting point. There is a body which tries to move out of the gaze of power in order to articulate its own pleasure. There is a body which seeks a 'house of its own'. We seek a place where we can look at each other, 'touch' each other. We seek words to tell the story of our body: tell each other so we can fall in love, seduce each other, lose ourselves in each other. To learn to 'be', to live in the world 'in the grand manner' within a sexed body. Our lives are inscribed in the lives of all women but there is 'something more' which urges us, which wants to be spoken.

'Woman is historically separated from love of herself, from being able to surround herself with something which will speak her pleasure' (Irigaray). This is what we need: to separate ourselves from images of women secreted by history, images which are so powerful they can determine behaviour and feelings and become the empty shell of our identity. Our sexuality is detaching itself from models, it is taking shape outside of permitted rhythms and forms. We presume to experience pleasure, separating ourselves off from the values of the world. Love of self is the dynamic element which creates a new attraction between women's bodies, which creates new images. It happens that we experience pleasure together and this is what we want to reflect on, but there's the risk of being petrified by ideologies, of consuming our desire without recognizing it as a force which produces 'mutation'.

It is difficult to unmask the work of ideology on the body. We often proceed by error and suffering. The body suffers from being organized and at the same time fears transgressing. We are between the gendered woman and the neuter women, we are between the impossibility of flight and the possibility of flight by means of a mask: the individual, the 'person'. We have difficulty in living between ever more advanced forms of emancipation and the mother/housewife model: between fear and rigidity, between unawareness of and complicity with the values of the world. We are between a sexuality understood as an emptying of the self and a sexuality channelled into imaginary spaces; deviated from bodies to mute objects.

The sexual act between women is still 'separate'. We need to begin to reflect collectively on the fecund nature of the act. We need to be 'adopted' by the fantasy of other women: there is a desire for wealth, to emerge from our marginalized position. We need to learn to look at each other with desire, to develop a dimension of seduction which can fuel passion. We need a 'silence' which will allow us to listen to and transmit images of bodies, a silence which is the dimension where precious messages pass between women. To silence the gossip around us, the vague need to express ourselves, to create the background that will encourage women's sexual speech. To know how to listen to each other is to silence judgement, prejudice, schemes, between us . . . to learn how to give each other space.

There is a body which continually shifts the level of difference; there is a scandalous body which experiments with intense states of life. From this point we can try to question ourselves about the sense of our difference within differences: 'as if the parting sea / revealed another sea, this another and then a third / and these three were only the presage / of an infinity of seas / and the sea itself a shore' (Emily Dickinson).

We are wretched when we conform to ways of life which are unable to speak the complexity of our emotions, when we give in to the temptation to lose ourselves in equality, annulling the differences between women. It is as if we lent ourselves to this cancellation, this concealment of the traces of the lesbian body.

Women's places where we feel comfortable are those where we can given each other strength, where a deep and tender relationship with ourselves can slowly, and ironically, emerge. The capacity to root ourselves in a space and not to imagine it is politics. This desire to exchange amongst ourselves values which emerge from our difference, and which speak it, is politics.

There is a body which shouts, which breathes, in the din of the city; there is a body which is forced to function against itself and watches itself living, obeying the rules. There is a woman who goes in and out of the body she inhabits. There is a woman entangled, imprisoned in the order of things; there is a body which resists, which opposes the need to be perfect and which begins to listen to the waving rhythm of excitement. Pleasure is continually learnt and again forgotten.

We live waiting for a woman: at times we seem to have touched her, at times a whole life seems too short to get close to her. Then, suddenly, it happens. The other appears almost as if by chance, and knowing that she is something more creates a moment of joy: life which overflows its bounds. Then the body becomes our greatest security. Our capacity for passion is made up of this desire to perceive female beauty in all its different shades, this feeling ourselves united to women in the 'memory of the touch'. It requires a certain intelligence of the passion. Storing a pleasure we can later refer to to recall the memory of the body, to fuel passion further. Constructing a place which modifies itself with every modification of the body. It's necessary to maintain a certain distance from the other, to recognize her as irreducible difference. It is impossible to possess her. We can try to seduce her, but we must 'let her exist, let her go' (Irigaray), not desire to be like her, more than her, within her, but by her side inhabit together the places of passion.

What must hold us is a very strong tie with ourselves, being rooted in ourselves, otherwise we create an 'umbilical cord' with the other woman or with the group which we are then afraid to break for fear of dying. Each of us is learning to push aside a whole bit of the world in order to make space for her body. We are women of this time, this fragment of history and at the same time we are out of step. There has been a shift of feeling. Enormous physical changes have taken place. Imbalances, great innovations with regard to gender have been created. The absolute evidence, our being here now, this woman's body has become a new, unforeseeable reality, to be sought out, a complexity to be articulated. There is a body which is only ours and which experiences pleasure with us, and which for the world has become awkward, embarrassing, a provocation. By rooting ourselves in our bodies we have opened up a space of desire, and politics itself measures this capacity to keep the space open and to develop a language which belongs to the body. In gaining materiality the body has become a perturbing guest in the social. We are seeing a bombardment of images, a propaganda of the physical, of alternative practices of the body, just at the moment when this new 'figure' has registered itself in the space of the metroplois. Powerful means are used to dispel us, to make us normal, predictable, to recuperate our knowledge within the logic of production. There exists very strongly within us the daily conflict between the rhythms of production and the spaces of passion, between a woman's strength recuperated and inserted into social mechanisms, and a strength which is constructed and maintained through sudden fractures, fusions, distances, re-births, metamorphoses, passages of matter between us. Politics is not the art of disguise aimed at seducing power, but the collectively acquired power to transmit a sexual force beyond ourselves, towards other women: the force to maintain ourselves within a sexed body even in social spaces.

9

Diotima

Diotima is an only-women philosophical research group, or, as its members would prefer, a philosophical 'community' of women. It was formed in Verona at the end of 1983 by women already engaged in the field of philosophy, professionally and/or because of a true, passionate interest in theoretical thought. They have since published a number of articles and essays, and a book of collected papers, *Il pensiero della differenza sessuale* (Milan: La Tartaruga, 1987), and *Mettere al mondo il mondo. Oggetto e oggettività alla luce della differenza sessuale* (Milan: La Tartaruga, 1990).

The short paper by Adriana Cavarero included here was originally read at the first nationwide conference of Women's Cultural Centres, held in 1986 in Siena.

THE NEED FOR A SEXED THOUGHT   *ADRIANA CAVARERO, 1986*

I belong to the group Diotima, a group of women philosophers which was founded in 1983 at Verona University. Since Diotima has achieved a precise theoretical configuration, namely 'the thought of sexual difference', it would please me a great deal to identify the theory we have been developing as the consequent result, or, if you will, the mature elaboration, of the theoretical speculations carried on in past years by the feminist movement in Italy. In other words, I'd like to be able to put it this way: feminist theorizing has developed over the years to the point where it demanded a philosophical 'systematization' of its concepts and categories. Diotima has then responded to this need by engaging in the production of a 'sexed thought' (pensiero sessuato).

When I was invited to participate in this Conference, I was asked a question. Is it possible to trace the stages of women's journey of critical revision through culture, in which different areas have in turn been privileged terrains of investigation (literature, history, anthropology etc.), until the idea of giving a theoretical foundation to the thought of sexual difference emerged? Or is this philosophical enquiry on difference not the result of a collective process, but rather expresses the interests of a number of women engaged in that field?

In order to answer I must become somewhat autobiographical and tell you my own subjective truth. I have not experienced my engagement in thinking philosophically about sexual difference as the logical conclusion of a collective cultural process. This autobiographical notation might draw attention to an accident of little interest for you; on the other hand, it allows me to introduce a discourse which I believe is relevant and significant – the discourse of the internal self-founding need of the thought of sexual difference. I shall therefore look at the question on two levels: one having to do with my subjective truth and my own personal experience; the other concerned with a historical-collective truth, which in some way also concerns me, both for its conditioning nature and for an inescapable need for comparison.

Before Diotima I did not participate in the feminist enterprise of theoretical production. I occasionally attended meetings, and I obviously had access to and made use of the information on feminist culture. My feminism, or rather my stubborn feeling of rebellion, grew out of the daily experience and passion of sexual difference. This is to say that I came to wish for a theory which would conceptually represent my being a woman, knowing very little of the already existing reflection in the field, except for a few books by Luce Irigaray.

On the other hand, I had even too much culture and knowledge as a result of my profession: a burden of sophisticated conceptual apparatuses – for I am a sophisticated scholar – which forced my thought to travel through a field dominated by strange asexual subjects: 'the self', 'the one', 'the being', 'the cogito', 'the idea' etc. But most frequently 'man': 'man is a rational animal', 'man is a fragile reed' etc. A monstrous 'man', one which was unrepresentable, neutral, universal and, at the same time, of the male sex.

Being the discipline which, more than any other, transcends the accidents of individuality and therefore the 'accident' of sexual difference, philosophy forced me into a neutral-objective theoretical cage where my being a woman underwent a double neutralization. On the one hand, man, the subject who reigned over discourse, universalizing and making absolute the partiality of his sex, also included and assimilated me. Man spoke and thought also for my sex, an absent and unrepresented sex, yet included in that male-neutral subject. On the other hand, practising and cherishing philosophy, I produced the self-denial of my sex, actively contributing to keeping it 'unthought'. The unease stemming from this double neutralization was once very clearly and forcibly expressed by a woman philosopher at a meeting in Naples: '*When I am a philosopher I am not a woman.*' This paradoxical statement reflects a sad experiential truth: since philosophical thought (actually *all* thought) cancels out female sexual difference, a woman who engages in philosophy cannot but reproduce this cancellation. Self annulment in action. Because the pretended neutrality of thought, which should guarantee its objectivity, forces a woman who gains access to it to transform herself into a neutral thinker, cancelling just that sexual difference which is yet hers as a 'real' subject.

Both for me and for my friends, women philosophers who had different theoretical backgrounds, often influenced by their involvement in the feminist movement, this realization was a fundamental turning point. From it came the need for a sexed thought. Such a thought could not simply unmask the false neutrality of philosophy. It would have to become the representative potency of and for a female subject able to name and think herself, having as her starting point her originary and irreducible sexual difference: sexual difference as the foundation of thought for the female subject, neither absorbable in and by the other sex, nor mere accident.

We have had to deal with the problem of breaking into thought with the tools of thought; breaking out of neutralizing conceptual systems using those same conceptual systems. We have had to measure up to the dangers of abstraction, in order to find here and now, not at the dawn of history, that sexed subject who wants to think herself in order to recognize herself. We have had to worry lest sexual difference, being/becoming thought, incorporate all women as undifferentiated and equal. But I won't go into that now. Rather I want to make a very simple point, but very important for us: the *need* for a thought of sexual difference, a need not only born of desire, but founded in theory, and ready to bear the strain of conceptualization.

In other words, the need for a sexed thought can certainly proceed from a historical analysis of women's marginalization, or from the cultural reflection carried on over the years by the feminist movement

– but it can also be founded in a clear subjective awareness of the relationship woman–thought, a relationship which in western history has thus far appeared as a contradiction. The fact that woman, for thousands of years excluded by the realm of thought, has now gained access to it, does not in itself solve the contradiction. But the contradiction can now take roots in the subject who has for thousands of years suffered it. The awareness of this 'taking roots' of the contradiction within ourselves has turned for the women of Diotima into a decision to think philosophically about sexual difference. Into a decision to be without contradiction both women and philosophers, to be and to think of ourselves as we are.

I can now move to the other level of analysis, that of a historical-collective truth, leaving aside my own history.

I have a feeling that often, in the so-called journey of critical re-vision through culture, sexual difference has simply consisted in the sex of the women who did the journey; that it has not become a reality capable of asserting and representing itself conceptually. It was a difference materially present in the separatism of the groups, but it hardly gave birth, on the theoretical level, to the potency of a symbolic representation. The same idea of a 'journey of re-vision' signals the weakness of the subject who makes the journey. A subject until then absent from culture, who begins a journey through it in order to master its conceptual tools (I am thinking especially of psychoanalysis and Marxism) and to bend them to her own point of view. In this perspective sexual difference runs the risk of being reduced to just a 'point of view'; sexual difference and knowledge are two elements which meet but do not inform each other.

The greatest danger lies in not acknowledging the *need* for a sexed thought, of acknowledging instead its superfluity. If western culture is not put into question, not in its specific features, but in its deep and founding male essence; if on the contrary its neutral-objective value is recognized, culture produced from women's point of view becomes an adjunct, a production alongside the other. Thus women's culture denounces its superfluous character, recognizing the non-necessity of a theoretical foundation of its own, the non-necessity of a thought of the female self which has in the self the origin and the goal of its thinking.

In philosophical terms, the fundamental point is that sexual difference must come to master ideas beginning from its own thinking of itself. Engaging in an enterprise which does not preliminarily centre on the meaning of sexual difference, women risk differing infinitely in the need for its assertion.

The female subject does not emerge from history simply because one investigates her existence, almost driving her out of silent crevices where she has kept herself safe, far from the word of the other. Rather, the female subject can emerge when she decides to be her own subject, to think about her subject taking herself as her starting point, here and now. The assertion of sexual difference through symbolic self-representation is needed, in order that she who seeks herself may know her image, and thus find and recognize herself. One finds what one looks for, and one must already know what one is looking for. Thus the female symbolic, content and form of this knowledge, reveals itself as the transcendental essence of any enquiry about woman.

I have only partially answered the question I was asked. I can only offer a tentative solution. Apart from my autobiography, the theory of sexual difference which Diotima is developing does certainly not stem out of nothingness, as though feminist culture were a meaningless void. This much is obvious, self-evident and sensible. Neither is it the casual result of a professional interest. It is both a theory which gathers and re-elaborates the problems investigated by a collective process in other cultural fields, and a theory which finds its foundation in the radical acceptance of the need to think the self by ourselves.

10

DonnaWomanFemme – *DWF*

Founded in 1976 by women engaged in various fields of research inside and outside academia, *DWF* (in that phase a sort of Italian *Signs*) was the first journal in Italy to try to bridge the gap between the culture of the feminist movement (with its emphasis on personal experience, spontaneity, the oral mode of communication) and 'traditional' culture (the need for rigorous research, the stress on objectivity) in order to envisage a different relationship between the subject and the object of knowledge. The themes of the monographic issues (twenty-two until 1982 plus two more in 1984–5) were often similar to the ones being debated in the movement, such as feminism and institutional politics, friendship and love between/among women, the issue of a feminist epistemology, etc; but reformulated in a historical perspective, at a more theoretical level, and with a view to making available in Italy the research on those questions carried on in other countries.

The year 1986 marks the beginning of *DWF* new series: a different formula, a new graphic layout, a new editorial board (though with some continuity) for a more openly politico-theoretical journal, actively engaged in the evaluation of the feminist experience, and of the knowledge it has produced, as a means for the foundation of a 'politics' of sexual difference. The writings included in this section belong to this new phase in the journal's history. The topic of each issue is now decided through discussion in the editorial board, focusing on a theme they identify as relevant to themselves and of interest for the movement. The pieces are then commissioned as answers to and reflections on the line of discourse proposed by the editors. The editorial of each issue is a part of this discourse, referring to the previous one and pointing to the next: an exploration of questions of both individual and collective importance for women, a dialogue with the other groups engaged in the theoretical and political enterprise of feminism. This section includes four of these editorials.

BELONGING/PERTAINING   DWF *EDITORIAL BOARD*,
1986

Over a year ago, we began the new *DWF* series *with a presumption*: that the need to resume a discussion on ourselves as collective subject was real and widespread; *with an observation*: that, in representing themselves, women often leave unsaid the cultural and political hypotheses which are being implicitly proposed; *with an intention*: that our journal should be the site of expression of individualities who yet do not elude the fact of belonging to their own sex, to the history of their gender, to a political history.

The continuous effort to adhere to the (always male-produced) models of maleness and femaleness, the continuous withdrawal from them because of an unrestrainable perception of their lack of authenticity, have both been read as permanent elements in the history of our gender. Between the effort and the withdrawal there lies a space which must be interpreted because it is the space of our lives; which can be interpreted because our political history makes us aware of the sexed nature of this oscillation, and of the perversion of a mechanism which condemns us to be alien either to our sex or to the world. Both kinds of alienation are easier to declare than to live through, and often lead to alienation from ourselves.

But if our lives are contained in that space – as we know they are – in that same space is also a subjectivity which makes choices, measures coherences and evaluates its interests. In the editorial of our first issue, 'I like it, I don't like it' was proposed, not as a well-wishing attempt at self-legitimation, but rather as a cognitive category which would allow us to name the meanings of what we already do and want. That is to say, the meaning of our projects, the relationship between their construction and outcome and the sense of belonging to a political female gender: for this reason our second issue was entitled 'Projects/projectuality'.

Neither site of two geometrically related lacks, nor condemnation of the gender's accepting its being itself a sign, nor metaphor of a femaleness posited as an ethical petition/reservation: the space between adhesion and reserve is for us the dimension of a woman's life, a dimension significant for its implicit sexed connotation and for the idea of oneself and of one's own sex to which such a space lends existence.

Our third issue, 'Biographies. The feedback effect', identified in the relationship between female subjects the possibility of making explicit – finally – the wish for an advantage. In the case of biographies, this lay in uncovering and signifying all aspects of a life; we said that 'When it is not presented and perceived as misery and meaningless-ness, the hidden side of another woman's exceptional life becomes knowledge of the self and of one's own sex.'

The intention to reflect on the concept of 'belonging' tends to explicate the problem of the connection between individual life and collective thought on the issue of sexual difference. Those who identify themselves in a political practice which is more an area of thought and an experience of research than a given institutional structure, such as a political party or a union, usually find it particularly difficult to define the *form* of their participation and collocation. In fact, it is not always enough to say that one belongs to a woman's group or that one is engaged in political work with other women. It is not enough especially if one wants to account for the experience shaped by the relationship between the individual and the collective, for the intertwinings of personal and social history, even when by 'social' one refers to the small group of women who are one's ideal and concrete reference. Talking of belonging in these terms is an enterprise fraught with obstacles; it may actually appear impossible.

We have identified at least three types of impossibility (1) the impossibility of defining a clear and assertive form which would translate into life the statement that claiming one's belonging to the female sex is the will to draw an advantage from the fact of being a woman; (2) the impossibility of renouncing, to take into account those parts of the self which resist belonging as a political line-up, those 'nomadic' and obstinate parts which cannot be fully represented by the fact of belonging to a group; (3) the impossibility of ignoring the phantasms of belonging as a 'being part of', a being possessed, a dispossessment of the self. With some degree of simplification, it could be said that these three difficulties concern respectively the issues of women's subjectivity, individuality and identity. Knowing that these three areas of discourse are tightly interrelated has often turned out to be a further obstacle. Not by chance, analyses focused on only one of these three perspectives are countered by emphasizing the needs descending from the others. Mediating the problems connected to these discursive areas is a task which still needs much discussion.

With regard to belonging as a relationship between the individual and the collective in the shape of the problem of individual emancipation, the fact of having met with serious difficulties has not prevented an analysis of the way in which this problem works for most of us. For my part, I can contribute an example from my recent experience. For those women who, like myself, have begun their process of emancipation after feminist criticism of emancipation had already taken place and become established, entering the labour market has implied a series of difficult questions. How should I face in a sexed fashion the mediations with society required of those who have to cut their own path to emancipation starting from now? Here the problem of claiming one's belonging to the female sex as an advantage clashes with most empirical evidence, which still confirms that it is an obstacle or at best an inconvenience. Here, however, the usefulness of a *political* gesture of recognition becomes clearer; here a form of belonging as relationship between the individual and the collective can be realized. Let us go back to my personal example. In the strict system of rules commanding socialization in the work place and defining professionalism, it would have been very alienating to put up with the strain of fitting in and finding a collocation there, if I had not had the *desire* to give expression to the advantage of being a woman. In some way I took upon myself a 'political mandate' as a *motivation*: namely, the responsibility of the social representation of a female human being who expresses her desire to work and live freely. Claiming my belonging to feminist political practice has therefore two functions: it reveals oppression and it is a drive to change. This simple mechanism has different implications for the kind of relationships which I establish with my female and male colleagues, and with the object itself of my profession. But its most interesting effects are in the relationships with the women who are my political and affective interlocutors, and who are not necessarily my colleagues. I demand from them a critical ability and a research on themselves which should be similar to mine and open to continuous verification. I demand from them a verification – or is it a supervision? – of the proceedings and the outcomes of my 'political mandate'. In our relationship it is essential that we accept the risk of losing one another; that is, that we do not prefer affective reassurance to intelligence, the meta-world of consolation to the ability to express curiosity about the world and the self. This *risk* is the main guarantee to prevent belonging – as the symbolic and real tie to other women – from becoming a 'family' tie, which is not chosen, but rather compulsory and indulgent: the sort of tie which the recognition and uncritical acceptance of individual needs and shortcomings tend to produce. The forced and dull intimacy which often results from and in spite of the new habits of socialization among women is not an advantage for any of them.

The research for a structure which would no longer be only the expression of a unity among the oppressed is nowadays shared by many women and many groups. The presence of so many formations in itself bears witness to the will to escape the alienation of not-belonging and the solitary effort of giving political status to one's own autonomy as a subject, that is, of being each time and time after time the living proof of a sexed existence. However, the unwillingness of many women and groups to name their political practices (as well as their tendency to avoid the exemplary assumption of authority of groups with a great emphasis on political proposals) invites us to question the nature of the bond on which common projects are founded, and which underlies the painful and conscious loyalty to one's own individual life story.

This has been a starting point. We could not consider belonging a 'category', either of a cognitive or of an ethical nature. Yet investigating the concept of belonging meant for us proposing an itinerary of knowledge, at the same time pointing out some needs which we defined as ethical. For they imply the necessity of renovating our politics and its procedures, in order to reassess our goals, which cannot nowadays be completely identical with the proposals supported in the past by the women's movement.

Thence the hypothesis – to be verified – that belonging might be read as a 'measure', a measure of ourselves in relation to everything else; therefore a measure of the presence of the subject in any process which she enacts. It is also a measure of the individuality of the self, which can be a stage preceding the constitution of the subject; not an inevitable stage, but one which – in certain moments of women's history – is the premise or the alternative for the subjectivity under discussion here.

It seemed to us that belonging was also a measure of the degree of adherence posited – and perhaps experienced – by the subject with regard to her presence in the social sphere and in all the aspects of private life; the latter being a sphere connotated as the domain of emotions, where the possible failure in the passage from individual to subject in social life (with all the sufferings it entails) is more clearly recorded. If these premises were accepted, belonging would then become also the measure of the relationship which the women's movement may have, choose or endure with the spheres of culture and politics, both when belonging is defined in terms external to the movement itself, and when its properties are part of a research within the movement.

But once again, this is a hypothesis, a starting point.

A hypothesis and a starting point which defer the possibility of a definition, even though they uncover grounds for intervention: factors, elements, areas which on the contrary can be defined, if they are seen and measured in terms of belonging.

It is a 'negative' approach, which neglects the main object of the analysis and turns it into a tool. It can, however, be a valid approach, since a definition may still come from the results which, as a tool, it uncovers or causes.

Belonging, as a measure of the degree of intimacy which the subject has with the representation of herself, in the relationships she establishes within women's society, in the confrontations she sets up with the social structure, has a historical precedent in 'belonging to the movement', to a feminist culture which is not only knowledge and writing, but also models, forms of behaviour, neuroses. The oscillation between memory and nostalgia characterizes many present political actions. It is the memory of a symbolical structure which has created a sense of belonging in the comparative reading of our lives, and has produced intelligence through conflict. When it is not simply nostalgia for a dream, it is nostalgia for that intelligence.

As is the case for all political structures, and actually more, the movement has been, before and besides a political structure, a symbolical one.

The recognition which each woman offered and demanded, the being and the belonging, took different forms, which were all marked by the *knowledge* of that recognition and of that belonging. These forms were implicit for many women, who experienced them, as it were, in the corners of their lives, without a statement or a continuous presence. But these corners became the cipher of life, they were the meaning of existence.

For all women, belonging was a choice but also a necessity, and it could therefore take over a nuance of imposition. Loyalty to the movement – be it loyalty to a specific group, to a person, or to an uncertain feeling of inner collocation – demanded betrayal. The strength of unsaid commands marked the adhesion and provoked the refusal. The strength of a bond woven of words and persons fed the rebellion also to that discovery of the self and of other women which had nurtured rebellion. Especially for those women who had overcome the more evident forms of oppression, for the emancipated or half-emancipated women who already took part in cultural and political activities, for women who were no longer constrained to only a domestic role, who studied, worked, sometimes held posts involving responsibility, for women who had achieved an identity as 'persons'; especially for them *seeing the oppression*, accepting its existence, claiming it as their own together with all women, meant the separation from those rules which had dictated – transgression is recognition – their process of growth and their assertion of their right to exist. Suffering this separation, not only individually but as a gender, has been our first entry into the symbolic.

An insufficient entry – perhaps we must face other separations.

Every hypothesis of political structure suffers an excess – of dependence, sublimation, voluntarism, imitation – because it mimes, even before investigating it, the sense of belonging. It assumes, without interpreting the evasions, the differences and the divisions among women, that a *unity* of interests is possible, before evaluating what sense of belonging can determine for each woman that *strategy* of interests which signifies a life. Faced with a life which imposes its daily routine, the inevitable banality of existence, each woman – in the impossibility of choosing both a total belonging to her sex/gender and a total alienation – mediates according to her untenability. The phantasm of loneliness – the reverse of the assumption of authority by the female subject when she moves in the world as an individual – shows that the sense of belonging demands its visibility, its history, its political forms.

When the self becomes passionate for self-knowledge, longs for its image and therefore chooses to identify its own intensity – its inner sense – then this bond to the self is a sign of belonging.

This bond, so painful for the female being, has involved in the dimension of experience the impossibility to do without a singular identity, while always submitting it to a process of subjectivation in order to trace its style, to outline and name its forms.

Between the thought of a feeling of the self, and an organization of life, this investigation finds in the sense of self-belonging a measure of reality and of the relationships with what is other than the self.

The need to belong to a political female gender has introduced in history this relationship with the self, it has given it form, placed it within a production and circulation of knowledge, within power relations.

One cannot be the solitary witness of oneself, unless as a melancholy desire to exist. Belonging to a gender relieves the solitary witness of the unconsolable pain of having to repropose a story and an image in order to fill the lack she experiences in being the only proof of her own existence. Taking risks, and belonging to one's own chosen risk, means moving out of what is recognizable and reassuring because it changes existing relationships and reveals their degree of alienation.

Escaping alienation – not-belonging – also implies considering one's own social self, therefore striving to win what one can name.

Separatism is a form of belonging; it is the social visible aspect of our unshakable resistance to a 'moral' code against which the feminist movement opened a conflict in the field of politics. In fact, the movement began a reflection about power, hence about that knowledge which decrees the statutory inexistence of a female subjective truth and the impossibility for a woman of being the agent of her own actions.

An idea of the self as conception of one's own sex/gender creates nets of relationships which not only involve persons – that is, female subjects – but also concern the sexed events belonging to those subjects.

The female subject–event bond outlines a dimension of belonging.

Imagining and trying to enact the idea and the practice of one's own belonging means learning to recognize the peculiar and specific signs of the self, without considering them ex-centric with regard to the given code; nor with regard to the political female gender, for it can be named and it can name its internal differences.

The emotion of self-belonging, of belonging to one's own sex/gender, can also be fear and loneliness; but they are a form of wonder, not the pain of a missed happiness.

'Necessarily having to' face and represent oneself finds in the necessity itself the silent part of belonging, as the sexed pleasure of existence.

Perhaps even the irony of 'having to be' a subject belongs to the will to win through.

PROJECTS/PROJECTUALITY   *DWF EDITORIAL BOARD,*
1986

We have identified a space: a space as though suspended – we said – within the age-old dynamic of adhesion and reserve. We have set out to investigate it, its relationship to life and knowledge, because it seems to us that it is there that our precarious sense of self is located; and it is there that the attempt to construct meaning by and for oneself should be measured. To sustain this proposal (at the same time exposing it to risk), this issue attempts a thematic analysis, a preliminary, partial exploration, to give word and voice to what is articulated and organized around the construction of this meaning.

It was in and through the women's movement that we first sought and found the stimulus to give ourselves meaning, and that we came to feel that we could do it. The story of this search begins with the assumption of similarity, a pre-existing identity which had simply to be revealed. Although perhaps inevitable, this solution turned out to be suffocating. While similarity offered us identity, it also made us aware of the inadequacy of that collective subject, and of a common history totally based on the equality of oppression, its exposure and the re-evaluation of our fellow-women past and present, who were to be rescued from the hostile world which spurned them. Not that this subject has become alien to us; it has at least offered us proof of our existence in the social sphere and has stood against the epic form of emancipation suggested to us in that sphere. We have expressed our dissatisfaction not by drowning alone and afar, but by distancing ourselves. The choice made by many of us to differentiate ourselves, and to value those differences, has not cancelled out our will to listen; rather it has turned listening into a mode of relating. Even when we go out into the world and measure there our differences, just as we want to measure them in women's spaces, the choice of listening allows us to find new similarities which do not simply raise us all to the same level but offer us mutual support.

For us this is a discipline of relationships, which sometimes delimits the terrain in order to make it easier to pass over. So to talk of projects and projectuality has led us to cast another look over our own lives, with a gaze which is inclusive yet focused, locating meaning in our singularity and, simultaneously, in the relationship which unites our lives both one to the other and to other women's lives. It has led us to seek the tension which sustains our lives, to trace its signs and reconstruct its subtext.

Since this is an exploration, we went at it cautiously, trying different paths, doubling back on ourselves, changing direction. We have no conclusions to offer, nor even perhaps a coherently organized discussion; our reflections often turned on questions which each of us interpreted, reformulated, amplified and emphasized differently. Looking at ourselves and our own experience, and to as much of other women's experience as it is given to us to know or imagine, we asked ourselves first of all if there is, and what would be the nature of, a female modality of relating both to the act of forming projects and to their products. We spoke of a sense of loss, of a desire to succeed undermined by the inability to value that success, of a lacking symbolic foundation. We asked what was the link between these problems, our individual histories and our history as a gender; between them and the metaphorical structure which sustains social organization and is sustained by it. How does our sexual structure unfold in the area of projects? Is difference embodied in that area?

We have often made projects without positing a relationship between such an act of construction and the process of self-identification; without recognizing the mechanisms of projection and introjection which we were activating. It has now become indispensable for us to focus on the relationship between the self and what one does, to come to speak of projectuality, overcoming the tendency which we have noticed in ourselves and in other women to remain cautious about what happens in our lives when we are the agents of our lives. We refer particularly (but not only) to our professional lives, in which we have frequently achieved high levels of knowledge and competence, investing considerable energy and intelligence but – we feel – without fully recognizing ourselves, always remaining aware of the partiality and the impossibility of representing ourselves fully in our work. The way we have explained this to ourselves points to the fact that the sign system and the order of the world are alien to us – and here then is an example of relating by difference. On the other hand, we feel that the residual part which these choices leave behind them weigh us down and stop us.

We need to go beyond a reflection on women's actions as process and as product in order to get right to the heart of the matter, to the relationship between subject and action; to try and work out ways of calculating investments and returns, facing up to the problem of outcome and its laws. We are referring here to the final stage of that complex if limited experience involved in making and carrying out a project; the question becomes interesting particularly if we are able, as women, to recognize how necessary projects and the act of making projects are. We need to make projects because by doing so we place ourselves in situations of social confrontation, we become familiar with hierarchies of value and with a precise critical activity. Making projects we have to deal with concrete events, and are forced to move away from an unproductive emphasis on the emotions; we become aware of the finite nature of our own experience, and so the illusory nature of omnipotent justification is revealed to us. What is never put to the test knows no failure; the passion for wholeness which avoids realizing itself in actions – for actions can only ever be partial – is closely tied to the culture of the female subject as mystery. We can benefit by moving from this area, in which complexity becomes the trap of an immobile compensatory experience, to the more limited arena of a trial, or a trying out.

This confrontation, however, the active investment of the self in actions and existential patterns not (always) separate, inevitably contains the risk of being emancipatory and nothing else. The finished project, the act straining for completion, 'success', risk returning us to an identity of plenitude, where all demands must have been met; what remains outside and excluded is relegated into the category of the useless, retranscribed as the residue of infantile omnipotence, sign of an inability to evaluate ourselves.

Discovering, perhaps inventing, modelling like a memory of the future a transitional terrain; a space which would go beyond that infantile thought which is alternately free from any need of proof and in absolute need of absolute proof; but which wouldn't become the domain of the dreadful thought of existing 'at the expense of' inflicting or enduring a constant negation of the self. Transforming the transitional into a state of being, accepting its unstable condition, the oscillation between partial definitions, which are no less true for being acknowledged as temporary, and moments of recurrent questioning.

From the territory *in between*, finding a way out which would lead elsewhere, the site of projectuality.

The project, structured on a social metaphor, seems to situate itself more easily in the world of dreadful thought. Projects make visible themselves and their makers, but they are intertwined with exclusions. Projectuality is dynamic, it keeps open the possibility of change and conflict with regard to our self-knowledge. Projects are and must be a priori speakable; in speaking themselves they trace borders, which are necessary in order for them to have some meaning, for meaning is always produced partly at least by this game of opposition. In what way can a process of identifying and putting into action a strategy of interests consonant with projectuality as a whole join together with the time and space of individual projects?

If we want to give voice also to the mobile principle of contradiction, projects are not enough; they gain sense as projectuality only in an a posteriori reading, unfolded over the course of a whole life. The outcome is the measure of how much of the original investment is satisfied, the exercise of its reading, a greater identity for our needs. But while social verification of the outcome necessarily concerns the project, which has no existence outside collective relationships, the verification of the self with the self is the ambit of projectuality, which does not exclude the collective subject, but which founds it rather than being founded in it.

For this reason we need both to affirm the self and to make it problematic; we seek the proof of success, but we want to question its final validity in order not to find ourselves caught between unproductive hierarchies on the one hand and absence of value on the other. Self-affirmation, in itself, is an authoritarian discourse; making the self problematic, by itself, has no legitimation and does not legitimate. The inner sense of self, our own sense of being women, cannot be put to the test in the social sphere; that is not the way of turning it into a factor of change. For this reason, analysing our actions in their external realizations is not enough; we feel that it is important for us today to recuperate and formalize the *intention* which today makes us act; each of us as individuals but without forgetting our (actual and virtual) collective subject.

To verify an outcome, in this sense, we need to move from a passive to an active position in the management of our lives; even more importantly, we need to reach the point where we can represent for ourselves this active living and our own being in this action, circumscribed as it is by chance and necessity. The intention underlying all this, however, is not presupposed right from the start; the ambiguity which exists for all women, when they want to break with the vanishing act which social rules and the world order tend to enact, should be consciously named and dissolved. The laws governing the outcome are not sufficient to define us if we do not juxtapose them with the force of our intention; on the other hand, intention itself is measured and serves as a measure only in relation to separate, single outcomes. Being there by intention, then, means recognizing in every segment of the self the destiny of being there totally.

The need for projects, like every other need, presents limiting elements. So that we don't emerge mutilated and deformed from this social confrontation, this knowledge of hierarchies of value etc., which we have considered positive to insert as factors in our journey to meaning, we must also bring into play what we call the force of intention. Intention and not just will. For us intention is different from will in that it is not a statutory component of our doing, it is not an almost obvious attribute of action. The will to be and to do is shaped by the same necessity which – by consent or by opposition – is its correlative; for women it has often been the will/need to escape the threat of being cancelled out by society. Intention is more tied to the subject, more grounded in the interior recognition of one's own existence and one's own sense of self; with intention one names the self for the self, thus allowing oneself an external verification in which the risks of deformation are reduced.

The wholeness of self-affirmation must be critically analysed. The sense of loss which goes with a project cannot be simply sublimated in its fulfilment; the statute itself of the project should be subjected to revision. We are certainly not suggesting the acceptance of this loss, or resignation to the state of victims and the treasuring of pain; rather, we want to argue for an unprejudiced investigation of the possible dymamics of these processes, for the compilation of a provisory balance sheet where profits and losses would be carefully noted down, and exchanges between the columns could swiftly take place.

The field of enquiry defines itself between self-affirmation and the residues which make it problematic; we think that the work of recognizing sexual difference can concentrate around the sense of intention. Women's communication of their own lives, and the communication we have attempted in discussing and writing this editorial, appears unsatisfying. We have become aware that our doing, the projects we make for and of ourselves, are entangled with elements of fantasy, unspoken emotions, conflicts of knowing and discarded hypotheses. From our memory of our politics we can see there a destructive connotation which might interrupt the work of signifying the self. We would like to understand the reasons for this, get to grips with the interior aphasia which prohibits the retranslation of an entire self into what we do. The projectuality which we would like to trace and read as a history of the female gender is the unresolved tension which cannot speak itself without being made explicit, partially or falteringly as this may be. However, this tension *is*, and when decided it can guarantee existence a mobile plenitude which would not be grounded in the fiction of what is rejected; a fullness in movement, capable of a complexity which would relieve the female subject from the fear of considering herself inexistent every time she is denied visibility in the social sphere. If thinking and knowing take place largely through metaphoric and metonymic processes, the production of sexed 'figures' and the identification of the sexuality of those already existing is a vital act. The critical activity of unmasking a phallocentric symbolic order already has a history. The passage to invention is much less obvious and easy, because here our differences must more clearly come into play. Here too the equality of oppression, the simple reversal of given categories, which still owes them its existence, are easier concepts.

We know that recognizing a sexed projectuality is a political gesture which transforms the biological given, already socially defined by the word of the other, into an awareness of difference and of its intrinsic value. This makes us individuals of a gender, and can lend force to a re-reading of existence which will acknowledge but also go beyond the dynamic of adhesion and reserve. Complexity as a possible sexual metaphor becomes also a structure of interpretation and a measure of the real; thus it makes room also for the ambition of an excess, in a projectuality rendered active by the interest in and of one's self.

POLITICAL RESPONSIBILITY   *DWF EDITORIAL BOARD*,
1988

The feeling of belonging to a political female gender is – by nature of the bond – a 'political' feeling. It is founded on, and founds, significant relationships among women who are the political subjects of that feeling. 'Some' women, who are in a way separated from the rest of the women's world; and yet they cannot but also be part of it. The interval between 'some' women and 'all' women is the site of the examination and verification of political conceptions and strategies, of the bond between life, theoretical production, political practice.

Using life as a reference to measure the relationships between theory and the political practice this theory means to realize has been – and still can be, in our opinion – the 'scientific' criterion which has sustained an immoderate use of hypotheses. The continuous anchorage to the materiality of daily life allowed us in the past to elaborate apparently utopian hypotheses, and to impose them as political. The separation between life and politics, on the contrary, creates criteria which imply the moderation both of theory and of behaviour. This procedure becomes a betrayal of the bond between self and gender; a bond depending on the intertwining of public and private, personal and political, individual and collective. The fact that this betrayal may pass for a radical position, with claims moving between a call for the millennium and immediately satisfiable ambitions of change, can only momentarily displace the problem, which still remains unsolved.

Neither changes in the context, nor a more sophisticated research on and a more articulated realization of the female subject, seem to us to justify the elimination of this reference to life, affective and political locus of feminism, object of the women's movement culture; since the link affectivity/politics is for us the link between inner modification and social expression.

Nowadays the link life/politics seems to be less relevant to feminist theoretical production, which therefore seems less interested in investigating this link in the shape of the relation between theory and political practice. As a consequence, in the space of politics (and

theory and practice are spaces as well) a divergence between affectivity
and politics is established, whereas in the past we have chosen to unite
them. Radicalism, which should still be the time and space of inner
modification and of its representations, is thus reduced. If the link
between political theory and practice, between affectivity and politics,
is no more considered indispensable, or at least is less important than
it used to be, this means that we are not interested in the analysis of
inner modification, but rather in its worldly forms.

The choice of divergence can be a form of discipline within a
strategy of interests; but if the investigation of women's lives (desires,
needs, aspirations, including those to a higher sense of self) is not
posited as a principle of our action, if the analysis of what kind of
relationship a practice establishes among women is abandoned, then
the consequence is a moderate use of hypotheses regarding the female
subject both in life and in politics.

Certainly, the pursuit of an aim requires that some rules be
observed; it cannot allow the times of emotions to slow it down. The
rhythms of life and the rhythms of thought do not coincide mechani-
cally, nor can thought always find its proof in life, or life in thought.

If the aim is the foundation of a thought of female subjective truth,
and of the conditions for its circulation, the link affectivity/politics
might appear to delay it; but only if it privileges a dimension of
waiting for inner modification, instead of establishing a circular
relation between such a modification and politics.

For us that link is still inescapable; it is the watershed between
'some' women and the rest of the women's world, it embodies the
nature/culture of the political female subject. The conception of
political responsibility which we want to discuss has to do with that
link. To reflect upon this conception, our starting point will be a
definition according to which political responsibility implies a bond to
a theoretical foundation which cannot but investigate it – as the link
affectivity/politics and as the link theory/political practice.

This means that the measure of such a link is given by the
relationships among women which are established by founding a
theory or by living a political practice. The need for a theoretical
elaboration of that particular relationship which is lesbianism stems
from the fact that the link between affectivity and politics appears in
this case a structural element. In all relationships among women,
however, the weaker the link becomes, or the more irrelevant it is
considered, the more one moves away from women's politics to social
transaction or to imitation. Moreover, the female figures we can create
in the community of women and in the social sphere are reduced.

Political responsibility, then, signifies itself in the awareness of a need; that of realizing conditions which, hypothetically, would allow all women to move from belonging to the female gender to belonging to a 'political' female gender. It is important that this passage be guaranteed not only by the foundation of a theory, but by the practice which informs action. There are no settlers of a political belonging; it is never given once and for all.

We said that this sense of belonging is founded on and founds significant relationships among women; hence, we think it is important to try to identify which relationships we consider significant and therefore necessary. It is also important to know what female figures are created by these relationships, and what investments of life-energy they produce.

For us the existence of significant and therefore necessary relationships is both the object of women's politics, and the *guarantee* for a survival of such politics. Significant and necessary are those relationships which allow an attribution of value to women's political intention. This is why political action can also be based on relationships mainly informed by its specific modes of being, which are not necessarily affective, in the sense of having to do with the private sphere. They are nevertheless affective, if this term can be applied to the sense and the feeling of an intention aiming to change life for a 'female subject'.

Besides, it is to those who are willing to name their doing as 'politics' – thus implying a thought and an action which require collective meaning – that political responsibility should in the main be ascribed; not to those solitary journeys of the self which nevertheless aim at one's becoming the agent of one's own existence. At this point, the question arises of the historical necessity of political responsibility, and of the awareness of such necessity.

In order to call oneself responsible and to transmit the sense and the necessity of this responsibility, an explication of the bond which today ties 'some' women to women's politics is required. Unless we identify the nature of this bond, there can be no passage from the *community* to the *society* of women.

The political and cultural activity undertaken by the women's movement in the course of time, most notably in the seventies, and the reflection on sexual difference which connotes the eighties, have founded the value of a female subjective truth on ourselves and on the world, thus creating the necessary conditions for belonging to a political female gender. The sense of belonging already establishes its responsibility.

But perhaps the bond to politics implies for each woman something more 'individual', that is, that self-recognition which is interrelated to the destiny of this historically defined *community* of women. A necessary bond which is not located in the area of homologation, or of mediation or of a weak self-legitimation (which are all situations characterized by a lack of respect for one's sense of self); this bond is to do with 'value', that is with expression.

Establishing the conditions for the attribution of value to the female subject – adventurous journey of the mind to a subjective truth of life – entails political responsibility. It means that it is indispensable to hold on to one's own sense of self; but this sense is not in itself sufficient, if the inner I is not related to the political I.

The investigation of the self and the pursuit of one's own coherence demand a verification first of all in the existing collective relations among women.

It does not seem that new 'contexts', more significant than the community of women which we have experienced, have been identified by the reality principle, that unveiling which allows one to read the present because the reading of memory has changed, and to imagine one's future, thus giving a future to one's interests. Without this community, the single adventure of each woman in the world is still destined to neutrality. This is the case also for the adventure of the 'winning' woman; not only because of the imitative modes she is forced to adopt, but because the word of that 'victory' does not speak her *difference*, unless there is a community of women to support her. A community where the memory, the ease, the pain and the interest for the circulation of that word can exist, in order to measure the social figure produced in this community; or better still the *plural* social figures which can/must be produced there. Even though female misery has not yet disappeared, this does not mean a dichotomic oscillation between woman as oppressed and woman as winner. Such a dichotomy reduces precisely those figures it is our interest to multiply.

The multiplication of female figures permits the passage from gender to political gender; it entails a strong bond with the community and with a conception of society where discipline does not stem from the assertion of an individual's greater value, but from the interplay of values. We do not mean to deny disparity; but it should be experienced according to non-disciplinary modes, striving for a self-expression which 'stands up' to the other woman, while recognizing her greater value. This would establish not a hierarchy, but a vertical *movement*: the growth of each subject in holding on to her own sense of self.

FORMS OF POLITICS   *DWF EDITORIAL BOARD*, 1988

We have come as it were naturally to a reflection on the forms of politics; in fact, our preceding editorials have laid the premises for it by highlighting two key concepts of such a reflection, that is, belonging to one's sex/gender as a source of value, and political responsibility as a consequence of this conscious choice of belonging. We are convinced that the sense of belonging is the foundation of significant relationships among women, and that only this sort of relationship can, in turn, generate the bond to one's own sex/gender as principle and guarantee of female freedom.

However, there are other reasons as well. Our participation in what is happening, and our attention to what is not happening, in women's politics, have also motivated the investigation of this problem. Which means do we consider, in the present juncture, to be most effective for establishing our freedom? Which lacks do we experience as most painful? We wondered whether the link between life and politics, which marked feminism in the seventies, is still strong. In those years, stories and behaviours were analysed and judged by female groups for whom the words 'identity', 'personal/political', 'self-determination', 'lesbianism', 'separatism', 'battle of the sexes', already articulated female disobedience to the law of the one, which sanctioned the naturality of roles, and the consecration of inferiority.

We think that the history of female freedom has progressed for each woman who has come to value herself and/with her likes.

Today, there are a number of women's groups, and there is dialogue and confrontation; there are diverse views of the world and of our political conceptions. And yet, a sort of uncertainty seems to be in the air, concerning what can today be defined as political activity, and which forms of politics we acknowledge as effective in creating the conditions of female freedom. Different political histories, different conceptions and experiences come here into play; they can create conflict among women in an enriching challenge, if we dare do away with reticences and declare our interests. This is already a political action, when the assumption of difference means apprehending the necessity/responsibility of a point of view and of its project. In contrast, it seems to us that sometimes theory becomes a *jargon*, that is, an abstraction separate from its substantive project, or even lacking a project. This is the case when an allegiance to the political criteria connected to the theory of sexual difference is declared, expressing consensus for that theory, but without giving it substance and

meaning in terms of choices and practices. Or it can happen that
objections are heard to the theory of sexual difference, with the idea
that it produces a repression of the still existing situation of female
non-freedom; for this theory would lessen the perspective of women's
conflictual position against power, by dismissing the necessity of a
political action which concretely engages women, making them visible
in society. These two attitudes – jargon and hostility – have not
succeeded in founding significant relationships among women, nor in
making the conflict of ideas and projects visible and political, nor even
in positioning women in the world's scenarios.

Taking difference as the starting point in politics means choosing
the sort of political action which marks intentions and practices with
the awareness of a belonging to one's own sex/gender and to one's own
partial truth; that is to say, which marks with such an awareness both
the overall projectuality and the single projects. No mediations are
possible here, because they would inevitably end up by playing
someone else's game, and with someone else's rules. The responsibility of belonging implies the adherence to the rules that the community
of women create for themselves, if one wants to claim that one's
actions are inspired by those rules. The conflicts one can choose to
raise in the institutions in order to achieve a specific advantage for
women, and also to fulfil one's own ambitions and put to the test one's
own competence, cannot make allowances about sex-belonging in
favour of other belongings. Rather, the latter should be measured in
terms of the former.

Political action in institutions, or having to do with a relationship
with institutions, that is to say, that form of politics which we call
negotiation, is not in itself a loss for/of female subjectivity. In fact, such
an action may create conditions favourable to the elimination of
objective social inequalities at the expense of a sex which has now
started to value its own difference, but which still sees this difference
translated into inferiority, according to hetero-set rules. Equal opportunities committees, legislative instruments, positive actions, female-
oriented choices in some trade union policies – to take some examples
– can lead to the achievement of favourable social terms, but only if
they do not imply a mediation about the belonging to one's self and to
one's sex/gender, only if they do not imply a delegation of power to
other procedures, thus weakening that bond among women which is
the foundation and the guarantee that women can create by and for
themselves. The opposite of *negotiation* seems to be that form of
political action which is entirely concentrated on *inner modification* and
which becomes a subduction, not so much to someone else's rules, as

to the visibility of the female political subject. It is the political form of an itinerary and of a consolation insufficient even for those who act and think within this kind of relationship; because it pays the price of a modification which remains within the confines of intimacy, without finding a sexed social expression for this intimacy, or which does not measure its intention in relation to an openly declared political proposal.

In the editorial on political responsibility, we expressed our conviction that *significant relationships among women* are a form of politics because they produce a plurality of female models, and bind a woman to the politics of her sex/gender in founding its authority and its autonomous rules. The political sign of a significant relationship consists in making visible a shifting of forces and energies, which are transferred from the world of the one to that of the female sex. It is therefore a relationship presupposing a relevant investment of the self, which cannot leave out of consideration the will to obtain advantages for the self. We think that this form of politics, that is, the *relationship among women*, should express and enact speculations and projects, in order to put into practice the strategy of one's own interests and the assertion of one's will for advantages; the relationship among women should also appropriate and transform the modes of negotiation, so as to avoid the defeat of a negotiation 'about' women and to mark it with women's point of view. The relationship among women should be the projectuality and the social voice of inner modification.

There are needs which still limit women's lives and desires; lives which experience the fragmentation of complexity. Faced with this complexity, we must think about what is *today* necessary for our freedom, what conditions we should impose in order to avoid politics being only sublimation, assumption of 'neutral' behaviours, separation of our inner experiences from our worldly expertise. Turning our competence into political action, for example, can mean exchanging advantages and strengthening the sense of belonging, instead of the impoverishment to which role-play forces us.

The form *relationship*, politically established by women among themselves, must act as an obstacle against the inequalities due to economic problems, the neutralization in working places, that cultural transmission responding to rules of sexist deformation which renders the political female gender invisible, the deceits of formal democracy.

Women must be the rightful owners of the instruments and of the procedures which they think useful for their advantage.

Unless our chosen instruments and procedures bear the mark of female will and freedom, they become useless adjustments granted to us, the different sex, difference being the *vocation* (promoted to dignity in the last papal encyclical) to a separation from one's own freedom. In our opinion of the world, and in the evaluation we make of female political theories and practices, we must bear in mind the link with the realization of conditions likely to bring other women to invest energy in their own sex/gender; these theories and practices cannot remain relevant points of reference only for a small number of women. Paradoxically – for our heritage of meaning, history and projects is not small – there is today a sort of passive *political fruition*, which fixes political action in an audience of supporting, dissenting, or silent women, and therefore reduces the link between life and politics and consequently the reality principle of the bond to one's own sex/gender. Certainly, this cannot be called conflict among women, in the sense of a confrontation and a measurement of wills, investments and aims, where each woman is responsible to herself for her project, and then seeks an alliance.

It is not a form of politics that the (often unspoken) relationship which marks the knowledge and the responsibility of 'some' women – almost a political elite – should confine other women elsewhere, to find in the existence of this political elite either consolation or pain, but always to end up in a space either too empty or too full. There can be challenge or alliance between women, but female mediation between women and the world requires a responsibility of the self and one's political dimension, hence recognition of the other and a measure of reciprocity. It is absolutely vital to reason and act in terms of effectiveness with regard to the identification and affirmation of our advantages and control of our own significance.

To be motivated by a strong investment in the self and tied by sexual allegiance means seeking political forms which do not oblige this investment to minimize itself, conflict between the sexes to remain hidden, desire between women to be repressed, pleasure to remain outside life and politics. Conflict between women is not a question of *hostility* and the solution does not lie in a network of *solidarity* – neutralization of the relations between women – or the rules of hierarchical functions. It is according to the measure of *advantage of sex* that we should deliberate on women's power and the power between women that is inscribed in thinking on political forms. Women's power relationship in the world is the affirmation of a truth which is advantageous to them because it is their own. It is a political approach which can take many forms, but all forms generated from within female relationships. These relations are not founded on nor sustained by the relationship of power between women for at least one apparently fundamental reason; they compel us to see the other, while the power relationship compels a ritual which repeats itself, leaving women isolated from the relation.

We maintain that the multiplicity of female models set into motion by the multiplying of form-relation between women hinders this very ritual and breaks it down.

Power relationships between women which might occur in the form-relation do not demand simply that we think about power as the regulation and organization of disparity, but that attention should be focused on the nexus that we hold to be indispensable between theory and life. An investigation and examination, therefore, of the disparity which lies between *relations between women as symbolic and political foundation, and the concrete practice through which relations exist and order themselves*. Rather different is the identity of an engendered power of *freedom* which comes to rule the responsibility of the female political I and legitimizes it.

Every woman who has a stronger sense than another of her own liberty, and so invests more in her own sex, has more power than the other.

Every woman who has this 'more', but does not defend it from the other who has less, has no political responsibility.

Every woman who does not give political shape to this 'more', turning it into a condition of advantage for the other woman too, makes power of women and between women the impolitic form of allegiance to one's own sex.

PART II

Changing the Context: Ways and Means of Sexualizing Politics

PART II

11

History of Two Laws

ABORTION

In Italy as elsewhere the issue of abortion has been central to the feminist movement, and has 'naturally' involved women from remarkably different social, intellectual and political backgrounds.

Its (questionable and questioned) links with sexuality – a sexuality imprisoned in the norms of patriarchy – made it an inevitable area of analysis both of one's personal condition, and of the social structure in which such a view of sexuality was prevalent. The repressive nature of the legislation which considered abortion a crime, thereby forcing women to face the dangers and humiliations of illegality, elicited solidarity between women and prompted them to fight against the existing conditions.

They did this on the one hand by organizing a network of information about the ways of aborting safely, and on the other by bringing the issue into the open, so that it become impossible for the political parties and for parliament to continue to ignore it. The Movimento di Liberazione della Donna (Women's Liberation Movement) was from the very beginning in the forefront of the battle, with the support of the Radical party, to which it was affiliated.

Since the early seventies a series of laws were proposed by most of the parties, mitigating the harshness of the extant law; but there were still remarkable limitations on having an abortion, and – what is more – the final decision still rested in the doctor's hands. The feminist movement was not united in its attitude towards the regulation of abortion, as the writings included in this section demonstrate. But freedom of choice for women was a tenet of all, and internal differences did not prevent united action in demonstrating against all attempts to deny women's right to self-determination. Until 1978, when a new abortion law was passed, the movement acted as an informal pressure group on all the parties, and most effectively on the parties of the left. Also, women *in* the parties could not be indifferent or wholly inimical to feminism (though there was diffidence and some resentment on both sides). Thus the Communist party, for example, changed its position to support a law which, though taking the doctor's advice into account, left it to the woman to take the final decision. In this respect, the role of the UDI in support of self-determination was fundamental; it influenced many communist women, and it helped them in their effort to bring pressure on the party to modify its policy.

Law 194 was in many ways a compromise, but in its general lines it accorded to the wishes of a large part of the feminist movement, who defended it again a few years later when a referendum to abolish it was organized and defeated, and who have insisted on its correct and full application.

Sexual violence: the 1979–1980 debate

Parliament has been debating a new law against sexual violence since 1979. At the moment, in 1990, rape and sexual harassment do not come under the rubric of crimes against personal integrity (such as murder, assault and the like), but are considered crimes 'against morality'. This is a clear indication of the lack of recognition of women as subjects and as full human beings. Besides, the way in which trials are managed, and this is certainly not only the case in Italy, turns the victim into the accused, putting the burden of proof on to her shoulders, and questioning *her* conduct, her life, her good faith; the underlying idea being that she must have asked for it.

The history of the new law, which has had to be rediscussed more than once, due to the instability of Italian governments, has been troubled from the first. In Italy it is possible for a law drafted by individuals or groups outside the parliament to be debated in Parliament, provided that the draft is endorsed by 50,000 signatures; it is a *legge di iniziativa popolare*, a law by popular intitiative. In 1979 the UDI, the MLD and the Movimento Femminista Romano decided to follow this procedure; the MLD procured a draft of the law, asking some women lawyers for advice, and then they set about collecting the necessary signatures.

The MLD was one of the groups in federation with the Radical party; not necessarily women's groups, but rather groups engaged in the area of civil rights, such as the gay movement or associations in favour of free contraception or sterilization on demand. The MLD itself was separatist, and had constantly been active within the feminist movement, although some of its members had moved out of it, regarding as contradictory its allegiance to a mixed body.

The UDI, the MLD and the Movimento Femminista Romano were joined by other feminist collectives in their efforts to assemble signatures, reaching the number of 300,000, and the law soon came to be regarded as 'women's law'. Actually, right from the beginning it provoked a very lively debate within the movement at large; a debate which has been resumed through the years every time the law was discussed again in one or the other branch of parliament.

Things have certainly changed since 1979, both in the movement, and more generally in Italian society. Yet, with some degree of simplification, it could be said that the basic terms of the debate as it took place then still hold. And since it would be nearly impossible to account for its developments without on the one hand going into the details of Italian politics, and on the other including many more texts than space allows us, we have chosen to select for this section a number of writings which appeared in the press at the time when the law was first drafted.

The chronological tables (and in some measure the bibliographical indications) will, we hope, provide information on the later stages of the history of this tormented law, which will probably be taken up by parliament once again by the end of 1990.

But we want to mention here a notable development which emerged when the law was discussed in parliament in 1988; that many women MPs made explicit reference in their speeches in the House to the debate in the feminist movement, stressing their belonging and their allegiance to the female gender – and this regardless of their particular party politics. Women were still divided on the law, but not on the basis of already determined political groupings; and their point of reference was the other women. So that although, as we have said, the basic terms of the dispute are still the same, and in this sense the pieces included here are truly representative of the various positions, the subjective mode of positioning oneself has changed. The reflection carried on in the movement about the issue of representation (see chapter 15, pp. 339–67) and the ways in which, also through the women in the parties, feminism has 'infected' Italian politics, have indeed left their mark.

ABORTION

Female sexuality and abortion   *Rivolta Femminile*, 1971

We of Rivolta Femminile maintain that the estimated one to three million clandestine abortions each year in Italy are a high enough figure to nullify the anti-abortion law. The female community have risked their lives, and the civil and religious ostracism of a patriarchal state, by illegally practising abortion; last resort for an unwanted pregnancy. Today we refuse to suffer the affront of a few thousand male and female signatures becoming a pretext to demand from the men, those in power, the legislators, what has actually been the meaning of millions of women's lives, slaughtered by back-street abortions. We shall achieve free abortion, rather than new legislation on it, together with those millions of women who constitute the history of female revolt. In fact, only in this way will we turn this fundamental chapter of our oppression into the first chapter of the long process of self-awareness by which we shall undermine the structure of male domination.

A forced and repetitive procreation handed over the female species to man, thus forming the initial basis of his power. But today what liberating meaning can even a freely chosen procreation have in a world where culture exclusively embodies only the male point of view on existence, therefore conditioning at its roots any free choice on the part of women? Are free sexuality and free motherhood – in other words, the premises of woman as a person – still passing through the affirmation of free abortion after thousands of years? Free motherhood and free sexuality must find their meaning within our consciousness: only in this way shall we be sure that the freedom we are talking about is really ours and not that of the male who fulfils himself through us, through our most hidden oppression.

Women abort because they get pregnant. But why do they get pregnant? Is it because of their sexual necessity that they have intercourse with their partner in such a way as to risk conception? Patriarchal culture does not question this, because it does not admit of doubts on 'natural' laws. It is actually only avoiding the question of whether – in this matter – what is 'natural' for man is so for woman as well: it takes it for granted and defends with all means the sexuality of patriarchal man as a 'natural' sexuality for both men and women.

But we know very well that when a woman gets pregnant, and has not wanted to, this has not happened because she expressed herself sexually, but rather because she has adapted herself to the sexual act and pattern which are certainly favoured by the patriarchal male, even if this could mean for her getting pregnant and having to face an abortion. In the patriarchal world – that is, in the world where women are tied to an inferior and servile condition through a mythicizing of man and a self-depreciation which are systematically and continually requested by social and private life – men have imposed their pleasure. The pleasure imposed by man on women leads to procreation, and it is on the basis of procreation that male culture drew the line between natural and unnatural sexuality, between the forbidden and the accessory, preliminary sexuality. But when will the procreative aim be officially denied by the whole of society? In a world forced to have contraceptives and anti-procreation, we must absolutely intervene with the consciousness that nature endowed us with a sexual organ which is distinct from procreation. On these premises, we shall find our autonomy from man as our master and bestower of pleasure to the species made inferior, and we shall develop a sexuality starting from our physiological centre of pleasure, namely, the clitoris.

Man left woman alone in front of a law which forbids her to have an abortion: alone, denigrated and unworthy of society. One day, man will end up by leaving woman alone in front of a law which will not forbid her to have an abortion: alone, gratified and worthy of society. But women are asking themselves: 'For whose pleasure did I get pregnant? For whose pleasure am I having an abortion?' This question contains the germ of our liberation: by formulating it, women abandon their identification with men and find the strength to break a conspiracy of silence which is the culmination of colonization.

Women are now wondering: if they have been risking conception in adherence to a sexual model imposed by men, then men have been risking conception at the expense of women's bodies. Conception is therefore a fruit of the violence of male sexual culture at the expense of women, who are then made responsible for a situation they have actually endured. By denying the freedom to have an abortion, men transform their abuse into a female guilt. By conceding women this freedom men lift them from their condemnation, and draw them into a new bond of solidarity. A solidarity which would refer to an undetermined time the moment in which women will wonder whether the fact of getting pregnant goes back to culture – that is, to male domination – or to anatomy – that is, to natural destiny.

Men have created the cultural conditions according to which women resort to abortion as a solution which is connected to their own reproductive nature. Women actually enjoy – they have this possibility due to the biological mechanisms of their species – a sexuality which is external to the vagina, and therefore liable to be asserted without risks of conception. Men know that women receive with varying degrees of emotional and physical involvement their orgasm in the vagina. They know that this orgasm is theirs, rather than the women's, and consequently know that women may get pregnant against their own will, and may therefore be forced to have an abortion. Notwithstanding all this, men make love like a ritual of virility, and women happen to get fertilized in the same moment in which they are robbed of their specific sexual enjoyment, in the moment in which the act which makes them sexually colonized takes place. Once they are pregnant, women discover the other side of male power, which makes of conception a problem of those who have a uterus, rather than of those who hold the culture of the penis.

In this light, asking the male for legalized abortion has a sinister aspect, since both legalization of abortion and free abortion will be used to codify the pleasure of passivity as an expression of female sex, thus reinforcing the myth of the genital act, which is concluded by male orgasm in the vagina. Through an undramatic practice of their utilization women will confirm for ever the sexual 'phallocratic' culture.

To try to protect our lives through a demand for legalized abortion leads – on allegedly philanthropic and humanitarian pretexts – to our suicide, the predominance of one sex over the other is ratified, while the 'weak' sex seems to be moving towards liberation.

As spokeswomen for an immense number of women who have had and are still having clandestine abortions, we consider the anti-abortion law no longer valid, but, above all, we consider as no longer valid that culture of the penis according to which this concession made to women, that of facing motherhood as a free choice, is presented as a feminist victory. In reality the patriarchy is reinforcing and renovating its management of the world.

The patriarchy reaffirms the prestige of a sexual culture which gets women pregnant and denies them the right to express themselves sexually by emphasizing their ability to agree with, and favour the pleasure of, the other, the patriarchal man. Through the diffusion of abortion and contraceptives, he makes sure that this pleasure is not disturbed by the vision of a crazy overpopulation of the globe. The liberalization of abortion has become – over thousands of years – the condition through which patriarchy foresees the solution of its contradictions by keeping the terms of its own domination unchanged. What meaning does male orgasm have – to our eyes – in a vagina which is covered with spermicides and condoms? Does our colonization actually lead us to overlook the deceit of a sexual culture which finds its own justification in the procreative structure and then, though denying the procreative aim, forbids access to the clitoris? On what scientific premises can male culture still afford to consider as immature the clitoral orgasm, and push women to the strenuous and unlikely achivement of vaginal pleasure, thus dignifying a process of acculturation if ever there was one as a spontaneous process of female uninhibition and normalization? Does a girl perhaps aspire to become the dull and submissive grown-up woman, the physical and psychological appendix of man who is his companion in the patriarchal world and is only proud of redeeming her passivity by mythical and voluptuous agreement? Is this not the goal a girl would reject heart and soul? And when she eventually achieves it, has she not actually realized the final stage of a conditioning rather than of a development of her own autonomy? She must know that the psychophysical relationship to which male culture still drags her, unwilling and upset, is the same one in which the Turkish slave or the favourite concubine of an Indian harem found intense pleasure. A moderately erogenous zone like the vagina has become, in virtue of male prestige, women's sex. We are horrified when reading of African tribes who remove the clitoris from young women, but what else have Freud and Reich done? What else have men enjoyed in women unless a substitute sexuality which women have developed after the cultural mutilation of their own sexuality?

This is a refusal of a thousand-year-old history, which – on the one hand – has oppressed the great number of women who questioned the union with man in an effective state of slavery and humiliated themselves in frigidity, without managing to adapt themselves to this union in a state of slavery. On the other hand, when there was an agreement with the man during the manifestation of his virility, what was the pleasure of the woman expressing if not that of an individual brought up in a state of complete, passive adoration for another being? Clearly, it was a pleasure connected with an historical situation which no longer existed, because this kind of female erotism was supported by her gratification from a person superior to herself, and this can no longer take place in a condition which excludes the mythicizing of man.

The abortion admitted by society aims at prolonging and giving a new artificial force to a female erotism which has paralysed and destroyed women for 4,000 years. We are claiming the right to a part of our body which gives us pleasure without condemning us to

procreation and which will release us from the emotional condition of
an inferior being who gives herself to a superior one. This is why
vaginal pleasure has been emphasized by both eastern and western
male cultures, and found in the theories of Freud and Reich a support
to prolong its glory for another thousand years. We feminists are going
to stop this conspiracy and save ourselves from complete ruin.

Let us try and think of a civilization in which free sexuality does not
appear as the apotheosis of free abortion and the contraceptives
adopted by women: it will show itself as the development of a
sexuality which is not specifically procreative, but polymorphous; that
is, free from vaginal finalization. It will no longer be a question of
preparing a meeting between the sex of a leader and his instrument,
but rather between two human beings, woman and man, and their
sexes (with any foreseeable and unforeseeable fluctuation in the
heterosexual attitude of mankind). From site of violence and volup-
tuousness, the vagina would become just one of the possible sites for
sexual games. In this kind of civilization, it would be clear that
contraceptives are only for those who want to have procreative sex,
and that abortion is not a solution for free women, but rather for
women colonized by a patriarchal system.

Programme of the CRAC   *Comitato Romano per l'Aborto e la Contraccezione*, 1975/1976

This Committee intends to become promoter in Rome of the campaign for the liberalization of abortion, a campaign which originates in
the struggle of the feminist movement over the past few years.

It's not by chance that the people in the front line of this struggle
today are the militants in the feminist movement, women comrades in
political organizations and women who, though outside any organization, fight this dramatic aspect of their oppression. Ranged with them
are the political organizations most aware of the importance of battling
against one of the elements which characterize the whole female
condition.

Abortion is always an act of violence, and women are compelled to
turn to it in the absence of any real alternative. For this reason the
Committee is engaged in the campaign for the liberalization of
abortion, but cannot split off this issue from the more general struggle
waged around all the problems of free choice of motherhood.

Abortion reveals particularly harshly coercive material and ideological factors:

material because women are forced to have backstreet abortions in appalling conditions, risking both health and life.

ideological because the clandestine nature of the abortion and the risk involved, like every other factor which characterizes the female condition, are seen as the price to be paid for individual choices and experiences, which are almost never seen to be the result of a particular social situation.

Yet abortion is a social fact, a mass reality: in the current situation, which is characterized by a lack of alternatives, abortion and the violence which goes with it are the price which women are still forced to pay for refusing a sexuality which aims solely at reproduction.

Backstreet abortion is a class of violence, and working-class women, once again, are the ones who pay the consequences most dramatically. The political forces which want to maintain abortion as a 'crime', an illegal and hidden act, are the same forces which protect the squalid black market of abortion, which grows and develops by exploiting women, getting about a million lire from them each year.

Women are rebelling against a society which imposes on them the whole responsibility for maternity and bringing up children, yet doesn't offer the conditions for motherhood to become a free and informed choice.

Women are fighting for the right to motherhood against:

those who speculate in their lives, forcing them to backstreet abortions.

those who force millions of women to abort spontaneously because of intolerable work conditions.

the reactionary ideology of power with regard to women, family and sexuality.

The committee has been formed to:

win the right to free abortion on demand for all women, including minors, within public health structures, and for the woman to make the decision without censorious interventions by so-called experts.

develop a policy of prevention with a network of clinics controlled by women, who will give information and distribute free, effective and safe contraceptives.

The committee will:

practice self-management of abortion as a moment of struggle, in centres where abortion will be carried out free in hygienic, safe conditions; this will relate to the growth of the women's movement, which will encourage the widest possible mass mobilization.

hand out information on contraceptives and sexuality in clinics controlled by women and recognized by the state; procreation will not be seen as the only goal of sexuality, and motherhood and bringing up children will no longer be imposed on women at the expense of other social and political activities.

involve medical and paramedical staff in the discussions on abortion and contraception until they adopt a clear position on the matter, fight the issue within the health sector and push for scientific research to be orientated towards simple, harmless contraceptives for both men and women.

explore all the areas currently permitted by legislation until a practice of abortion within the public health sector is established, and, in particular, fight for therapeutic abortion, granted by the Constitutional Court for both psychological and physical reasons, to become a real possibility for all women who need it.

promote a law by popular initiative which guarantees that all the above objectives will be reached, withdrawing the support initially given to the proposals of the Socialist party, seeing that this party doesn't seem to have any intention of presenting and defending the amendments announced in January.

fight against all changes, trials and attempts at repression, making them political deadlines and the focus of mobilization, and denounce those who are responsible for spontaneous abortions, fighting for better and more hygienic working conditions, which will not produce them.

Platform for clinics, 1976 The coordinating body in Rome for self-managed clinics came about through the initiative of feminist collectives present in many districts in and around Rome. This structure of coordination has now become part of CRAC, which is making its own the proposed platform for clinics. In San Lorenzo, Ostia, Romanina, Centocelle and Monteverde these collectives are creating structures of movement and struggle, self-managed clinics, where women meet, get together, discuss and compare notes in order to reach a greater common awareness on problems of motherhood, contraception, abortion, control of their own bodies and sexuality, and to develop an organization which will struggle against all forms of their oppression. This political initiative of ours has faced many difficulties in locating suitable buildings, in getting established in a district, and because doctors are not prepared to collaborate.

Each situation has its own distinct experience. In some 'clinics' women meet to develop moments of a wider awareness of themselves, to compare and discuss, to the point where they form a collective self-help group.

By self-help we mean the moment when women tackle problems normally considered to be of an exclusively medical nature, but which involve a woman's whole emotional and psychological relationship with the social, economic and political structures which have oppressed us for centuries. With the practice of self-help we want not to replace the doctor, but to enable women who have acquired an awareness of their own bodies to have a new, active relationship with health structures.

The clinic must make sure that the woman recovers a positive relationship with her own body. It was the lack of this kind of relationship which led to women's ignorance about their own state of health, making it impossible for them to prevent illnesses and rendering them incapable of actively organizing contraception, pregnancy and birth.

In other clinics, starting with the reappropriation of the body, sexuality and health, abortion is organized and practised using the suction method, by small cooperative units organized by women. These units represent a first level of experience of self-management for women's health, using the instrument of self-help and collective support to tackle autonomously, and in a different way, the problems of our bodies, contraception, abortion.

It's because this practice has become more widespread, as a moment of struggle, that we are succeeding in breaking the shameful business of medical speculation.

In February the national law on public clinics comes into effect: we want them like the ones we are experimenting with now. We don't want the clinics to be surgeries limited to gynaecological examinations, an authoritarian public service once again borne by women, who are then sent off to deal with all their other problems within the four walls of home.

The clinic, then, should be a political site for a real meeting between women, for meetings on women's health, knowing our bodies, reappropriating our sexuality and organizing on these and other aspects of our oppression which are objectives for the common struggle. We believe that clinics for the problems faced by couples, as envisaged by current projected bills, are a political choice which once more sanctions the couple–family identity, at the centre of which is perpetuated the primary exploitation of women, the sexual one, which covers the most global oppression.

This is why we want the clinics to be by and for women.

We would like to suggest that the following points be discussed by all women and women's collectives:

1   Our clinics must be financed out of public funds: self-management does not mean self-sacrifice. Control and revocation of the doctor must be our right, because in the clinic we want to make sure that the 'knowledge' and 'science' of the doctor are socialized, at the service of women.

2   The clinics should be established straight away, in sufficient numbers in every district, and evenly distributed within each district.

3   Since the clinic is more than a health service, a room set aside for meetings and debates is absolutely essential, where we can organize the political activity of the clinic in the area where the woman lives and works.

4   The clinic cannot be what is envisaged by current proposals, an island of contraception, separated from the dramatic reality lived by women today, that of abortion. So the clinics should be equipped to:

(a)   deal with the termination of pregnancy before ten weeks using the suction method. Since for us abortion depends on the self-determination of the woman, the rights of minors should be safeguarded here too.

(b)   ensure medical, social, psychological assistance after the abortion, and any psychotherapy.

(c)   put up a struggle when the abortion law is passed to make sure that the right to abort is guaranteed, and so take the wind out of the sails of doctors who claim to be conscientious objectors.

(d)   widen and make more easily available information on contraceptives, and fight for contraception to be not only for women, as the marketing of the drugs industry would have it. We will here have to overcome not only the atavistic male resistance to women's contraception, but the even stronger resistance against using their own. It's no accident that the minute amount of work already done on male contraceptives is looked at with ideological prejudices, envisaging the possibility of side-effects.

(e)   The clinics must also function as centres of legal and psychological aid to women who are raped (rape centres).

5   The clinic must be a reference point and meeting place for women
    for the construction of a unified, autonomous movement based on
    a redefinition of our identity, the reappropriation of our bodies and
    a sexuality understood as something more than 'sexual pleasure',
    to be seen rather as a relationship of knowledge with ourselves and
    others, as relational.

Only on this basis, by beginning with ourselves, can we create a
collective will to struggle against a 'political' power which feeds on our
oppression.

We are working on a different political approach   *A group of women from the feminist collective of Via Cherubini, Milan,* **1975**

We have not supported nor participated in the demonstration for free
abortion on demand: we are working on a different political approach
to the problem of abortion.
   Free abortion on demand means that we will spend less money and
be spared some physical pain: for this reason none of us is against a
medical and legal reform which is concerned with the prevention of
pregnancy, and its interruption. But between this and going on
marches in general, and what is more with men, there is a big
difference; because such demonstrations are in *direct contrast* to the
political practice and to the consciousness which women engaged in
the struggle have expressed in recent years.
   Meanwhile, let us say at once that for us, abortion for the masses in
hospitals does not represent a conquest for civilization, because it is a
violent and death-dealing answer to the problems of pregnancy which,
moreover, further culpabilizes the woman's body: it is her body which
commits an error because it makes children which capitalism cannot
support and educate. So we arrive at the American obsession, 'There
are too many of us; we won't be able to breathe, we won't be able to
eat, etc.' And the problem to be solved becomes that of controlling
births and not that of changing the sexist and capitalist structure of
society. We cannot be complicit with this false consciousness.
   The political approach is directed towards, and the solution sought
in, the affirmation of the female body, which is: *a sexuality distinguished* by conception, the capacity to procreate, the perception of an
internal, cavitary sexuality: uterus, ovaries, menstruation. And the
relationship with our resources, with nature, with the production and
reproduction of the species, is focused on socialization, rather than on

the attempts to rationalize, whilst maintaining, the family structure, private property and waste.

In any case, legal abortion is not 'the end of a shameful thing'. The majority of women who have abortions in secret are not ashamed of being secretive. If there is shame, it is for other things and other reasons.

Even women who have every means at their disposal and have access to interuterine and chemical contraception, who have the means to think about and organize their sex lives (in terms of choices, times, modes, forms and partners), repeat the phenomenon of conception and, more often than not, of abortion: they repeat, that is, the negation and affirmation of pregnancy, they themselves repeat the violence which women are subjected to, and which they perpetrate against themselves. Women's 'invincible archaism' – as bourgeois rationalism says – or, for us, vital information for political thought and work. Here, the contradiction between feminine sexuality and masculine sexuality emerges; the reality of masculine *domination* over women, revealing how far the problem of abortion implicates women – consciously and unconsciously – in their relationships with their sexuality, with motherhood and with men.

The secrecy of abortion is a shameful thing for men, who by packing us off to hospital to have official abortions will put their consciences at rest once and for all. We will continue as before, and better than before, to make love in ways which satisfy the physical, psychological and mental requirements of men. We are still forbidden to situate ourselves in another sexuality, one not oriented entirely towards fecundation.

A woman's body, her sexuality, her pleasure do not necessarily require those means and forms of intimacy (coitus) which leave her pregnant.

On the contrary, we women prefer either to be left in peace (the statistics on frigidity are quite clear) or to seek pleasure and happiness by other means.

So what should we desire and seek in the first place? Our own well-being, pleasure and happiness or a (violent) remedy for the pleasure and preferences of others – that is, of men?

There is a profound division and contradiction between man and woman, between male sexuality and our sexuality. This contradiction is not resolved by removing the significance of women's separate struggle (that is tantamount to privileging once again the interests of men and to confirming the subordination of women).

If need be we could demonstrate with men on other emancipatory issues (for social services, for the right to work) but not on this one, on abortion, where, as we have explained, the contradiction between masculine and feminine sexuality explodes: where surgical violence on women's bodies is nothing other than the dramatization of sexual violence.

To ask for free abortion on demand together with men is to recognize concretely the violence which is done to us in these relationships of power with masculine sexuality, by making ourselves complicit with it, and consenting to it, at a political level too.

Among other things, men are marching today for free abortion on demand instead of putting their sexual behaviour, and their fecundatory powers, into question.

Our political practice does not allow us to split up and pervert the nature of our interests. From now on we wish to begin with the materiality of the body, to analyse the censure which has been visited upon it and which has become part of our own psychology. We wish to take action for the recuperation of our body, for a different knowledge and practice which would start from this materialistic analysis; without which it is ridiculous to talk about 'the freedom to manage one's body'. The attainment of the reforms will serve to suffocate our struggle instead of developing it.

Furthermore, we should not reduce the significance that the women's movement has in our practice by privatizing it, in a dynamics of 'the traditional political group': all women represent it in the first person.

Manifesto and document of the MLD *Movimento di Liberazione della Donna*, 1978/1979

Manifesto, 1978 It's become more and more clear to all women recently how the parties are using the whole issue of abortion. The feminist movement used to jump into the ring shouting 'No to the compromise which kicks us in the teeth'; now part of it is contradicting itself, joining with the UDI in asking for a compromise, a good law which will regulate abortion.

We don't want there to be any misunderstandings on the matter which would be to the advantage of those who are trying to divide the feminist movement in order to bring about a state feminism.

This manifesto aims at making our position clear, and we hope that it will help to encourage debate among women.

We're more convinced than ever that we don't want laws on our bodies.

We maintain that any law on abortion will give the state the power to decide for us.

We want the repeal of the fascist law which defines abortion as a crime, and this can be achieved only by a referendum. We've already collected 800,000 signatures towards it, with our feminist comrades and other political forces.

There are no prescribed rules for giving birth, for appendectomies or for pulling teeth: there shouldn't be for abortion, either.

No woman needs a law to decide if and when she wants to be a mother.

That this is true can be seen by the fact that women have always aborted, despite laws, imprisonment and the risk of dying.

Liberalizing divorce is the only way of stamping out the profiteering which derives directly from the fact that abortions are done in secret.

For abortion that is to be not only on demand, but free, with medical assistance, all that's needed is that it be put on the list of operations to be carried out by the health services.

Free abortion doesn't mean compulsory abortion and we accept another person's conscience. In the same way we want other people to respect our wish to become mothers only when we want to.

Document, 1979 'Free abortion on demand', 'No law on our bodies', 'No penalties': the Women's Liberation Movement has been fighting on these principles for ten years, looking for backing from both public opinion and the institutions. We have used a number of different methods: demonstrations, pickets, rallies, sit-ins, leaflets, open challenges to the sanctions of the Penal Code, as when women publicly admitted having abortions. We also established self-help abortion groups, and organized public screenings of the first film on abortion using the suction method.

But all of our commitment, as well as that of the whole feminist movement, which counts on the support of tens of millions of women on this issue, hasn't been able to prevent the harshness of the party political game – coming from the alternative between referendum and the anticipated elections – forcing through the current Law 194.

This law is the result of a mixture of fake morality and political balancing acts: all it does is crush women, trampling on their dignity, their freedom to determine their own lives, not to mention their real needs.

But finding ourselves saddled with a law we didn't want has not meant giving up. Our first response, as soon as the law was passed, was to try to exploit the tiny space which the law offered us, denouncing whole gynaecological wards for not doing their job, becoming the plaintiffs in action against fake conscientious objectors.

Now after months of hard and humiliating procedures – the tragedies of under-age girls, the reality of thousands of women forced into backstreet abortions which have become even harder to come by, and much more expensive – daily we hear the statements of women's experiences, in the Women's House in Governo Vecchio Street. Once again, we refuse the sterile path of just saying that our worst fears have been realized, and we must once again choose direct intervention in the law.

One point of departure is the practice of our self-help groups, taking control of our own bodies and our own health, in order to demand full self-determination within the institutions, and the collective control of these institutions; that is, a collaborative management. In this sense, we won't accept the constrictions of the law; the requirement to prove that abortion is really needed, the discriminating casuistry, and the paternalistic way it is carried out. The absurd refusal of abortion for women under age, the punishment of women who are forced to have backstreet abortions, the fake conscientious objectors who institutionalize the self-interested obstructionism of the medical profession.

For each of these points we have formulated proposals, which we lay out below.

First, a few more words on the practice of self-help groups. These have been a continual thorn in the side of the institutions, working to make them listen and acknowledge our demands; they are also an example of a structure which is not part of the state, but which is public, collective, without being institutional. From the fusion of two different forms of structure, the state structure which is liable to the control and management of its users, and consequently loses its bureaucratic and centralist elements, and self-management, which operates from and for the collectivity, a new way of conceiving the public and the private emerges, and with it our own position on the recent polemic about 'state abortion' and 'private abortion'.

We are against both these positions as long as they define situations which are seen to be crystallized and unchangeable. We refuse to be party to the sinister profiteering of the abortion industry, and we similarly refuse to offer hostages to fortune in the form of a centralized and bureaucratic power.

In the current situation, in which the only real choice is the lesser of

position we take up is nothing more than a political
therefore from a political point of view that we have
orarily to suspend the practice of self-help abortions and
to hammer the state structure until it provides women
with at least the service required of it by law. Until this minimal
objective has been achieved, the so-called 'freedom of choice' can't be
seen as genuine self-determination, but is merely a 'false choice'
between two structures, the first of which does not work and does not
therefore constitute a choice.

Let's look at the proposals for changing the law.

Self-determination: we suggest that article 1 should be changed to
read: 'The state recognizes the right to motherhood as the woman's
free choice, without age limits. It recognizes the right of all women to
turn to state hospitals and consulting rooms to get a free termination
of pregnancy', and consequently the elimination of all the articles of
the law which oppose this principle.

Culpability of the woman: we suggest the elimination from article 19
of all subsections which deal with this issue. We believe that the
woman should never be punished, not even for backstreet abortions,
and we believe that the disparity of treatment which would come into
effect with regard to the doctor who acted outside the public structure
(who would remain culpable) is only a superficial one. To make this
perfectly clear we refer to the law on drugs, which punishes the pusher
but not the addict.

Minors: we think it is utterly absurd that this law discriminates
against women who are under age, when it is absolutely obvious that it
should favour whoever needs the abortion most. But just eliminating
article 12 would bring the law within the norms of the civil code,
which requires parental permission for any medical operation on
under-age women, who have no means of being made a ward of court,
as sanctioned by 194 in cases of abortion (thus making it easier for
under-age women to reach a decision). So we would like to have it
written in that there are no age limits on the availability of abortion,
thus differentiating it from other operations, given the psychological
political and social implications of this operation.

Conscientious objection: it is precisely this precept, together with the
exclusion of women who are minors, that is the real obstacle to
carrying out this law, not on paper but sanctioned by nine months of
enforcement.

We have examined the legal and political aspects of this precept,
and conclude that it is a clever device for crushing the wishes, the
needs and dignity of thousands of women under a mask of false
libertarianism.

Instead of encouraging the most obvious solution (that the objecting doctor should leave the public system because he is unwilling to provide the service he should to the consumer), the Italian state has set up an anomalous system to approve a law which is patently absurd. The state guarantees a service in principle, then allows the very person who should be carrying out the service, the doctor, to evade the law. In order to defend that institution they have recourse to a supposed conflict of conscience, like that of soldiers who are conscientious objectors. But given the absence of any compulsion (the doctor is perfectly free to leave the state system and practise privately), it is quite obvious that the personal conflict of every gynaecologist concerns only his own interests; the decision is whether or not to abandon a position of prestige and power in the hospital. As we can see, the comparisons to be made with military conscientious objectors are very few indeed.

These are the considerations which have led us to propose the abolition of the whole of article 9 except the last part, which, by obliging hospitals and clinics to make sure the service is available, constitutes some sort of guarantee for the woman.

But if we are to fight such a reactionary and profiteering class of people as the medical profession, it's not enough to scrap existing sections of the law without laying down new guidelines. We propose that the first part of article 9 be replaced with a section making it impossible for medical and paramedical personnel who declare themselves conscientious objectors to be employed in hospitals, surgeries or clinics.

This is a necessary corrective to the current situation in hospitals, where, as we know all too well, the majority of doctors have declared themselves conscientious objectors. These measures are also necessary to make sure that doctors who do practise abortion are not professionally confined to this simply because there are so few of them who are willing to do it.

A letter to the local government of Lazio *Coordinamento Consultori*, 1979

Just one month after the passing of Law 194 on abortion, all the contradictions and limitations which led the feminist movement to define it as a 'bad law' are already evident. The most gross consequence is that it has done nothing to stop backstreet abortion; if the current situation goes on much longer, these will not only increase in number but will become increasingly dangerous, expensive, sources of uncontrolled profiteering.

The reasons for all this lie in the fact that it is practically impossible to apply the law: on the one hand it legislates free abortion and assistance, but on the other it arms doctors and health structures with the most ambiguous and least controllable weapon that exists, that of being a conscientious objector.

Doctors have exploited this to the full, happily claiming it as guarantee of professionalism, career and stability. Welfare organizations declare themselves unwilling, and even preliminary procedures such as certificates, examinations and so on, which would in no way damage the doctor's 'honour', are denied to the woman from the height of article 9.

We are by definition in favour of free choice for the individual, but it's clear that here conscience has nothing to do with it. And yet that 'conscience' which subverts the rights and goes against the needs of half of the population is a source of great ambiguity.

As feminist comrades and as participants in Advisory Bureau meetings we therefore refuse to carry on paying the price of someone else's blunders, and we would ask the region to abandon reticence and ambiguity and speak out clearly on the following points:

1 The incompatibility of conscientious objection with the work of a clinic; not just because the clinic would stop carrying out the minimal service which is already so precarious, but because as women we reject the idea that any such an objector can be entrusted with the whole complex relationship of prevention, contraception and discussion envisaged by current legislation.
2 A full-time gynaecologist to be in the clinic, and the free contraceptive service to be fully carried out.
3 Public and licensed health services to be obliged to provide operations using the suction method in all cases where applicable. In order to achieve this there should be:

   (a) area distribution of hospitals and other structures so that demand can be regulated, thus not overworking some and allowing others to stand idle.
   (b) non-renewal of licences to centres and private clinics which refuse to practise abortion.
   (c) two-way mobility for objectors and non-objectors (if two willing doctors move into structure X, two objectors can move from these into structure Y, for example).
   (d) the doctor who says he's a conscientious objector must be

willing to participate in an educational health service.

(e) inclusions in the service of terminating pregnancies, of medical and paramedical staff in general medicine and general surgery who have followed appropriate courses, so that the woman doesn't just undergo the abortion, but consciously participates in the operation.

(f) revision of the organs and structures dealing with all the above and future measures.

4 Equipping Surgeries in the various districts for terminating pregnancies.

5 The organization of separate courses, to be run by supervised bodies, so that medical personnel can acquire techniques and instruments which will make the service of terminating pregnancy the least traumatic and least painful possible for the woman.

6 An obligation for hospital structures to guarantee a number of abortions to suit the demand.

7 The service of terminating pregnancy always to be on offer, even during holiday periods.

8 Severe penalties not only for doctors who pretend to be conscientious objectors, but also for private clinics which continue to practise abortion for money: this is clandestine abortion, and illegal.

9 Having set out all the foregoing points, if there is not an immediate and public response from the region, women reassert their commitment to fight to achieve all these objectives.

Final statement from the conference 'For a new culture of sexuality' *Coordinamento Consultori*, 1984

The National Coordinating Women's Movement for Advice Bureaux is a coordinating body for those women who – in various ways – take part in the life and problems of the advice bureaux.

Public advice bureaux have been the result of a long battle which was begun to achieve a national law, then the various regional laws and, finally, the actual ways in which Municipalities and Local Health Centres (USL) should put these laws into practice. The experiences in legislation, management and participation have been rich and sometimes different in the various regional situations. Thence originated the need for a research of data and a confrontation of experiences which may help to make the quality of the service better and make it more suitable to the users' needs.

Our commitment and our goal is to achieve a better use of laws, and to make advice bureaux become – through a larger participation – one of the instruments of cultural, social and sanitarian transformation. The possibility for women to tackle in this service – with the people involved and among themselves – a new way of understanding and living sexuality as an emotional and physical expression of the human being is still nowdays a qualifying moment of the advice bureaux' activity.

In these recent years there has been much discussion in our country about the social roles of men and women, but the discussion is not over yet: modifying those predetermined social roles means changing the concept of sexuality they imply, and this is an essential condition for a transformation and humanization of life.

Our conference in Rome is meant to be the first great national moment of research of a new culture of sexuality.

In the lively and painful discussion, it has turned out that the title of the congress itself is outdated in comparison with the individual elaborations women are making in our loneliness. It has been very important to achieve a level of communication which allowed each one of us to introduce and compare her own research, her achievement, in a political and therefore collective place.

The congress has been an important moment of retrieval of the method of making politics 'starting from ourselves' which, by upsetting all the classic standards of politics, allows all women to have a reference for problems which have long been undervalued by society.

It is not therefore a search for a new sexuality, but rather a great and passionate search for a new female personal and collective identity. Only the proposal of a new role, rather than the one imposed by male stereotypes, can make women overcome anxiety and uneasiness, which are often misunderstood for pathology, but actually are the explosion of a great contradiction existing between women's new consciousness and the modes which have traditionally been proposed by our current culture.

In order to make confrontation and discussion easier during the congress, we divided ourselves into four working groups (concerned respectively with sex and sexuality, sexuality–reproduction and production, sexuality and contraception, sexuality and uneasiness), but the basic common idea, which has acted as the thread of the whole debate, has been the relationship between sex and sexuality. The division of the two themes, sex and sexuality, with the consequent considerations, seemed to us essential, starting from the realization of the fact that the superficiality and confusion that exist still nowadays lead sexuality to be superficially identified with sexual intercourse. We women, through confrontations – in different ways and moments (motherhood, contraception, abortion, couple relationship, and so on) – expressed the need to face the central knot of sexuality, without however managing to give an univocal definition of it. The only way to overcome this problem is the collective search for our identity, through a larger confrontation among women and a reflection on how each of us has experienced and understood sexual liberation.

Thanks to the recognized value of the diversity of our experiences and routes, we managed to avoid an ideologization of the canons of sexual liberation: the debate showed how much women want to escape a crystallization in formulae of the various stages of the achievement of their own sexual reality and what already constitutes the 'new culture of sexuality'. This includes the affirmation, coexistence, confrontation and communication of a plurality of experiences.

It seems to us important to underline the positive outcome of the meeting, because of the multiplicity and variety of the attendances, the level of communication and tension, the desire to transfer and study this research in depth in the various regional areas.

SEXUAL VIOLENCE: THE 1979–1980 DEBATE

Today, a movement of 'democratic' women *Lidia Campagnano*

Today, a movement of 'democratic' women choose to draft a law about sexual violence. Perhaps it is time to rediscuss the use of law by women.

At the end of last Saturday's debate in Milan on the draft of a law against sexual violence, some of the organizers of the debate turned down the request made by a woman there to suspend the collection of signatures in order to discuss the whole subject more fully, asking for respect and understanding for the 'effort and suffering they had put into formulating the draft'. Respect means understanding why, I think; so the first question that springs to my mind is, how come it's so much effort for women to work out the draft of a new law together? And also, where is the motivation to do it, the energy and pleasure in doing it? On Saturday this wasn't much talked about. The women promoting the bill have made it clear that it should be the women's movement, here understood as a whole series of recognizable organizations, who make the law. In the past, when we were talking about abortion laws, a lot of us maintained that the movement shouldn't present its *own* laws, because no legislative form would ever be able to take on board and resolve the irreducible sexual contradiction that shows up even in abortion, even in the woman's self-determined choice in the matter.

So the whole business was ideologically hijacked, and one woman from MLD put it quite clearly. The women who do things now, who *exist* as the woman's movement, are the organizations which can be identified by name or initials, whose presence everybody recognizes; the movement is no longer small groups which are 'getting fewer all the time', which think about things 'over a coffee' and basically dabble aristocratically in 'the practice of the unconscious, *autocoscienza* and the analysis of writing'. Organizations don't do this sort of thing (or do they?), they act, they make laws, and they don't waste time wondering why they are doing it.

This is the classic mode of political thought sneaking back in among us who had refused it, and I'm not saying this to insult anybody but to try and get to the bottom of the whole issue. Those who choose the path of organizations and initials can never forget that they are a part of *women*, and not just of feminists, in exactly the same way as are those who work in small and more or less anonymous groups. The problem for all of us is the same problem we have always had, of broadening the channels of communication between different women as well as between women who just go about their consciousness-raising in different ways.

How do we do this? How do we find enough points in common between our different positions and our different ways of talking? On Saturday this was passed over very quickly, and again according to a praxis familiar in politics, that of mediation and compromise: 'Everybody had to give up something, for example the women of Pompeo Magno, a collective in Rome, had to give up their wish for a stiffer punishment for rapists.' At this point one feels allowed to add that this law will perhaps attract the support of other women who are willing to 'give up' about the death penalty for rapists, who will compromise with regard to this fantasy of theirs, because after all the only thing they will be asked for is a signature, and with that signature they will join together, they will communicate, they will become the 'people', since we are talking about a law by popular initiative.

What kind of 'people' is this? Democratic, reply some supporters of the law, for whom those who don't want the law are undemocratic, unconcerned that rape isn't defined as a crime against the person, which would automatically bring about prosecution by the state. It seems to be a blindingly obvious example of the fact that certain definitions – a democratic woman, an undemocratic woman – don't even work as well as they work for men, and that is saying little enough. What's democratic about thinking that prison will stem the flood of rapes? Can the fact that women would no longer be the accomplice of their rapist husband or son, and the call for the death penalty, really be called a gain for democracy? Or when faced with such a political choice, where we must take sides – say yes or no to this bill – is it of so little importance to us to know of the intentions, the fantasies, the paths taken by the women who are doing the choosing? This means skipping over women's politics in order to take up sides: a 'democratic' practice in the oldest sense of the word. To spell it out, it is a bourgeois practice. In other countries a part of the women's movement has been integrated into this path of accepting the rules of politics and democracy; yet this does not seem to bother those who have always reproved us, the *autocoscienza* ones, I mean, for failing to take 'class factors' into account. I don't know any way of escaping submissiveness to this political language other than continuing to put in common what comes up from the depths and makes us do what we do. This is why I think it is so important to ask what leads women to construct a law together. And since nobody has told me, I'll try to imagine what might have happened in this case.

I want to imagine 'good' and interesting fantasies, not punishing ones. For example, the fantasy that we are no longer represented in state law or in the public mind in terms of 'honour', 'morality', 'family name'. The law in itself tends to represent itself as the vital and privileged place where these changes in thought 'happen' at a serious level, become the norm of thought for everybody. (Actually, I don't agree.) But perhaps suffering begins when these fantasies are articulated into articles of law.

So if, for example, woman becomes a person 'by law', and so therefore does her new-born child, and if the mother kills that child, there will be no more mitigating circumstances. It will be called murder and the punishment, the years in prison, will increase. Is that what we want? We know very well that no law will succeed in reducing the mother–child relationship to an 'elementary' relationship between two 'persons', and we know that it is simply appalling to lock up a woman who has gone this far not for twenty years but for one. On Saturday I was told that these crimes can be prevented through collectives, clinics, contraceptives and so on. But if we are so optimistic about the progress of the female condition in this society, I wonder why it is necessary to make even more harsh the penalties for those who remain outside this 'progress', thus making it virtually impossible for them ever to get back onto the path of change.

Is this what is meant by struggling for women to become 'persons'? Or does woman become more of a 'person' because she is forced by the law, *forced* mind you, to make public her rape in the form of a trial, a form set up to identify a crime, a criminal and a punishment, and certainly not to reconstruct a damaged sexual identity? Perhaps we are thinking of the exemplary value for men of crimes and punishments, but I have no faith at all in this kind of crime prevention, because I feel sure that the person of the rapist constructs itself through the complicity of a number of forms of blindness, deafness, misery and sexual violence which are impossible to codify as crimes, unless we are all to become judges and policemen.

I give these examples because, while I would be very happy to see removed from the code everything which swathes us in a cloud of morality, honour and family name, and while I am certainly not against research in the sense of women confronting legislative language with their new desires and the changes that have happened to them in order to find ways to defend themselves, it does seem to me that this law goes way beyond these desires, that it hopes to wipe out, contain or abolish all the violence of sexual contradiction through the use of the courts.

This law wants to impose – and to punish – too much. Why? I can't get out of my mind what was said on Saturday about who the 'movement' was, and who it wasn't. I can also imagine that in the women behind this law there is a desire to make their presence felt, to show a strong hand, and to express these with the instruments of the dominant power because they do not acknowledge the strength and power for change of our own strategies, of what we have done over these past few years. It's a way of asserting our value which actually helps the campaign of devaluation and political annihilation which others have been carrying out for a long time now. And these others are not just the rapists themselves.

Women assembling as in the golden days *Vania Chiurlotto*

Women assembling as in the golden days; but to discuss not the law but the movement

In the debate that has opened up it seems clear to me that we are talking about the law now in order to talk about the movement, and so I have decided to go firmly down this second path. There will be other times and other places – including the manifesto, I hope – to go into the various articles and the bill as a whole. This seems to me just as useful for what we are trying to do: if the law is an instrument, so is the movement. The goal is the same: our liberation, the liberation of women. Let's leave to the side for the moment the question of whether it's emancipation *and*, *or*, liberation, with a dash separating the and–or, or with a bar, *and/or*, putting them in a dialectic relationship. The point is the definition and very conception of the movement, and this has been shown by the various articles which have appeared in this newspaper and in *Lotta Continua* and *Quotidiano Donna*. It is also demonstrated, if in a different way, by the confusion being created, fuelled even, between those who support the initiative and those who belong to the steering committee.

Some women are bitter because the bill has been put forward by the MLD, the UDI, the Pompeo Magno feminist collective, well-known women's groups that have not really consulted the movement about it, with the result that the debate is now running along the lines of a text which has already been fixed and which cannot now be changed. Others are concerned above all that the movement should never put forward its *own* laws, because our contradictions could never be enclosed within them. Other women again declare themselves to be totally estranged from any logic or form of institution, from parliament to the courts.

Through all the articles 'against' there runs a kind of 'how dare you', which I don't, however, want to lay too much stress on. Our practice over the last few years has gradually taught us that as long as we keep in mind that behind the signature lies the person of the companion communicating her dissent, and behind the initials indicating a group are concrete women struggling to achieve a particular goal, it is still possible to discuss and perhaps work together. For the sake of clarity rather than arrogance I think it right to note the fact that, if the movement as a whole is again asserting its political nature (women assembling as in the golden days, they have written in Milan), it is because a part of it has taken on the responsibility of creating a precedent. Some will say this is arbitrary, a claim to speak in the name of the whole movement by those who put no trust in the more hidden but genuinely more alternative paths of real communication between women.

And yet we should remember one thing: that this very discussion about the movement gradually produces and will produce political clarity, precisely because it starts with the concrete.

Is this just the efficiency mania of organizations who have thus always had an element of the 'masculine'; undervaluing the theoretical work of those who for years have been developing something else, weaving other webs (innocent and friendly, it goes without saying)? No. It is simply that in the relationship that has grown up between those of us who have taken this law in hand to make it *one* of the instruments of the movement, we have discovered that, making use of our respective characteristics as a source of wealth to be shared rather than as grounds for discriminating against each other, we felt good and we felt useful. This doesn't mean exchanging construction of unity in the movement for a federation of more or less homogeneous chunks; rather it means putting into practice a new way of doing things which requires clarity on all sides.

We formed a steering committee not because we wanted to be exclusive or to exclude, but to make it clear that this initiative comes from the movement, from its *specificity* and its *autonomy*, and it is under this flag that we must fight all the way. This is why we accept all expressions of solidarity, and all concrete collaborations from non-specific organizations, and all declarations of help and consensus from political groups, as long as they are not trying to use us, and as long as they accept working for the initiative itself.

The speed with which the press – and the *Nazione* in Florence gets a special mention here – jumped on the 'splits' in the movement over *female commissions* in political parties is significant. It's clear to us that *female commissions* are the political party with all its consequences. While it is possible for individual militant women, where they want and are able to, to create the conditions for debate and collecting signatures, it is neither possible nor desirable for them to take part in local initiative committees in the form of *female commissions*. And this holds for all the other, different ways of acting of which our country is fortunate to have so many. They are all useful, all democratic, but they are neither specific nor autonomous. This is only natural, since each has its own area of interest.

Many women object that the failure to discuss the project before-hand with all the groups in the women's movement – for whom specificity at least is not in question – prevented adequate reflection and a wider unity. It would be both simplistic and mocking to reply: (1) to those who don't want to become legislators that any discussion would have been useless from the start, given their own principles; and (2) to those who defend their right of protest as an instance of self-determination, that there are bills based wholly or partly on this principle, they have been put forward by the PCI and the PSI, and they can recognize themselves in those.

We want to say rather that the concept of denunciation and the concept of protest are hedged by two forms of logic which need to be confronted by as many women as possible, even before the institutions. By now the terms are clear. They should be confronted first of all because the discussion itself will give a lot of women the confidence that change is possible, that there is within us an overall image of passivity which needs to be defeated; and then because it will take the whole movement away from the recurring temptation to take a census amongst us – who after all are still few – rather than setting up processes that we can see through to the end.

Rape is a hideous crime   *Rossana Rossanda*

Rape is a hideous crime. Women have suffered it too long. Women have the right and the duty to defend themselves. But doesn't the law by popular initiative against violence simply relegitimize the old idea of punishment and blame?

There's a debate going on in the women's movement about the law by popular initiative against violence, put forward by the MLD. The debate has centred on a few aspects in particular: whether or not the case can be taken to court through the evidence of any person, or only through that of the injured party. In the first case society takes upon itself the direct representation of the injured woman, in some ways violating her decision to appear or not to appear at the trial; and in the second case a woman who has already been cruelly hurt is also burdened with a responsibility which, in a number of cases, can prove too much for her.

But this is not the point that I would like to address in particular. Having recourse to instruments of law inevitably shifts the social ground and opens up problematic areas like this one. But there is a bigger question behind it, which is how we conceive crime, deviance and punishment. What is a crime? And should it be 'punished'? Whom by? In what way?

We all remember that one of the fundamental characteristics of movements between the sixties and the seventies was their criticism of the law and state apparatuses, especially the judiciary and repressive ones, as partial and non-neutral. Who can forget the denunciations made of the prison system, the battles for 'ordinary' as well as for 'political' prisoners (in a sense they were all 'political prisoners'), the doubt as to whether or not society should be able to 'discipline and punish', to quote the title of Michel Foucault's famous book.

This wave of protest had solid foundations, starting with the way it put into question the whole concept of blame and guilt. Not only is blame, it was said, a historical and relative judgement, it actually comprises all deviation from an order which sanctions it and attacks anything which violates it. This order always corresponds to a model of power held by the dominant class or groups; the figure of the deviant expresses individual or group 'non-integration' with regard to this model. The abomination heaped on the guilty person is nothing but the protection of the ideology of power. This was the first argument, which it is difficult to argue with other than to say that 'deviance' does not occur only with regard to the order of constituted power. If someone crosses the road and knifes me, it might well be possible to trace his action back to complex reasons and motivations, which the common sense of order can disavow and degrade in the idea of 'delinquency'; but there can also be no doubt that 'my' reasons, no less complex, and the inviolability of my own person are also disavowed at the same time.

So in the ferment of ideas in 1968 the question of 'deviance' became a question of a 'collective' principle of freedom, in other words a norm, a law, a limit imposed on individual liberty and a social organization which both limits and defends that liberty. In the discussions of these new movements this point, which lies at the heart of all social regulation and is the basis of all law, either remained an open problem, or was simply avoided. At a later stage it was linked to social mechanisms, not necessarily state or legal ones, which might function as guarantees of collective liberty and freedom, and which at the same time might encompass the person of the deviant, liberating him/her from both the abstraction of public sanction and moral execration, by recuperating and rehabilitating him/her. This was a liberating, non-repressive cultural moment; we might almost say enlightened. True, its limit was not knowing how to think of a different 'form of society', not underpinned by state or legal intervention, a 'popular community', a 'defence of all' which could also be the 'defence of each one's differences'; but it's also true that the criticism of the abstraction and the repressive non-neutrality of judiciary power was correct, and to my mind irrefutable.

So 1968 went back to the fundamental problem: whether rules, and which ones, could or should be made for a collectivity of 'equals' – and what kind of practice could be devised in the meantime by a movement for equality and liberty in society as it was. This is a problem which is probably destined not to be resolved until it is inserted into a movement of deep social change. In the meantime, however, the criticism of the new left tackled it and, I think, resolved what it took on. Indeed, if it is difficult to think of a society without rules, it is possible to think of a society without punishment; and it is even more possible to think of a society without prisons, which are a particular type of punishment.

Even now we can in fact separate deviancy from punishment: the punishment inflicted is either a barbarous compensation, as if so many years in prison could make up for so much damage inflicted, and all calculated on the basis of some bizarre exchange system, or a senseless and vengeful hypothesis of 're-education through punishment'. Even if we admit that a society always produces some people who are dangerous to others, the system of grading or defence or deterrent should not necessarily be left to punishment. Leaving aside the underlying argument – that is, that a different organization and different values would prevent a large number of 'crimes' – there is no doubt that even today society can consider 'crime' as an injury received rather than to be avenged, and stop thinking of crime as something 'to be paid for', other than in the case of attacks against the inheritance of all or the poorest. Society can alter its relationship with the deviant, so that it no longer takes revenge on him but leads him back to the acceptance of a sort of collective contract. The principle of punishment implies that this would happen through a prison sentence, while it is clear that this is *not* the way. If it is difficult to imagine a different path, it's easy to see that this one is radically flawed. Thus the struggle of the new left against the 'vengeful' elements, with regard to deviancy, specifically imprisonment and more generally the 'exchange' between injury done and reparation, is to my mind still totally valid and could lead the way to practicable forms of social organization.

This having been said, there's no denying the fact that this same new left which called so loudly for these changes has never itself put them into practice. I'm not talking for the moment about the current resurgence of a cult for the formalism of law, which has led some of our magistrate friends to conceive of history as a series of sudden moves between 'breaks in the law' and the 'institution of the next law' as 'formal guarantee': we will be coming back to this debate at another point. Much more simply, the new left has thundered against prisons yet has itself invoked them, as in the case of right-wing groups such as Ordine Nuovo; it has reviled bourgeois justice yet had recourse to it; claimed to be against the 'discipline and punish' approach and yet shown itself in favour of it. Discipline and punish whom? The enemies of the people, of course, the people to be understood as the oppressed, the defenceless, children, women, comrades picked on by the palace.

There's nothing new about this; the new left has just rehearsed the scenario of the 'dictatorship of the proletariat' without being able to wield its power; for the moment, until we are all communists, repression is a useful tool. So is the state. But every time it did this there is no question but that it contradicted its initial position by returning value to the state, as a repressive apparatus at that, while on the whole it continued to avoid the knotty question of which 'transitional state' should be put forward by a revolutionary formation in a society as complex as ours.

This is a contradiction which today weighs particularly heavily on women. Of all the new movements, that of women has been the most resolutely anti-institutional, the most hostile to the 'abstraction' of the law, the most forceful proclaimer of the inalienable value of the person's *difference*. The relationship between women and politics is difficult; between women and the state it is hostile, between women and justice practically non-existent. Or, rather, bizarre; men's justice criminalizes relatively few women, as if 'deviancy' is thought of within masculine frames of reference for men only. But women are also the weakest socially. Theirs is a particular kind of weakness, and so they are relatively (very relatively) protected on the level of general social violence: they are not soldiers, they don't go to war, there is legislation which keeps them away from particularly dangerous or harmful functions. But they are exposed like nobody else to the violence of the male–female relationship as it is today. This is a relationship of *unequal power*: on a physical, social and economic level, the woman is (or is brought up to be weaker). She can be raped, or anyway beaten, she is poorer and less organized. Of these three inequalities which act against her, the first is the most savage (the least internalized), and women are beginning to resist. In order to resist they have to overcome an infinite number of social taboos. And when they have overcome the social taboos which would have them suffer in silence, women have to deal with a man–made justice which listens to them little, understands them less and exposes them utterly.

So this recourse to the law is more difficult for women than for anyone else. It's the same for all the oppressed, who know they should be wary of the courts and keep well clear of them. And yet women think they have no other choice if they want to defend themselves. They run to the law, conquering the hostility of others and their own deeply held beliefs at the same time. All of a sudden they acknowledge the law, they want it 'applied'. With this law by popular initiative they also accept the idea that the state apparatus can be the arbiter of their rights, and they noisily make the principle of compensation through punishment their own. The most 'anti-institutional' part of the new left becomes hyper-institutional.

Hence the debate. It's no accident that while the other patent contradictions of the new left on this subject are passed over in silence, this contradiction for women has produced a stormy debate both amongst them and in other quarters too. Is it possible to find a way out of the pure contemplation of what is irreconcilable, between the weakness of victims and the oppression of apparatuses? Perhaps it is. Perhaps a less unilateral reflection is possible in 'reformist' and 'revolutionary' quarters on the form of a law-bound society and the state. On how to use the law in order to destroy it – *rendering it useless through differential social functions and responses*.

Perhaps the time is also ripe for more courageous thinking on the relationship between male sexual deviancy and its prevention and repression. Is it really possible that the deterrent of prison has any effect in this area governed by the most obscure psychic mechanisms?

Is it possible that as in the days of Gortyna's tables women want 'compensation' for their violated sexual freedom? By means of prison? Is there no other way? Couldn't we even begin to imagine another way? In the symbolic 'lira' asked as damages by Tina Lagostena at the Latina trial, can we not see the principle of declaring null and void the idea of an 'exchange' between injury and punishment, the overarching need to state a value, a cultural principle, a free use of the law? And can't we go beyond this too? Women might object: but why should we be the ones who have to start? We can only say with due humility that at *Il manifesto* this is the path we have always tried to stick to, although we have not always succeeded. It would be totally hypocritical to ask women what we do not ask of others, if we didn't think that they had in them the germ of a different idea about possible collective relationships, even if at this stage it is still embryonic and obscure in form.

An important advance　*Lea Melandri*

An important advance made by our political practice is the impossibility of drawing a clear dividing line between love and violence, consensus and force, happiness and unhappiness.

I'm glad the question of love has been brought up, because otherwise it would have been difficult for me to speak at a meeting which is so 'orderly' and politically disciplined. If there's one thing which worries me about this law, and which makes me laugh a bit too, it's the underlying assumption that you can make a clear distinction between physical violence (beatings, rape and so on) and love.

I come from a large, peasant family in Romagna who are very much ruled by their passions, and beatings were the order of the day. Everybody hit everybody else (daughters-in-law, sisters-in-law, husband, wife, grandparents and so on), and since we all slept more or less together I can tell you that they went about their love-making with the same persistence. It didn't occur to me at the time to wonder whether the women consented or not. In the dark, and a bit confused by it all, I didn't understand very much of what was going on. I certainly thought they agreed to it. Perhaps the only one who didn't agree was me, who watched helplessly, with the same sense of anguish whether they were belting each other or making love. An important and original advance to come out of our political practice is that we have begun to analyse the man–woman relationship in all its complexity, and thus to recognize that it is essentially impossible to draw a clear dividing line between love and violence, consensus and force, happiness and unhappiness: as long as love is as we know it now, anyway.

Yet this law claims amongst other things to be able to tell precisely when a wife consents to sexual relations with her husband and when she doesn't. Rather than consent, I would prefer to speak of *availability*. Nobody can deny that women have made themselves *available* to men, and the whole business can't be reduced to the imposition of external pressure or an act of violence. The man–woman relationship in all its manifestations (mother–son, husband–wife or whatever) contains within it this availability of women, and it often reaches the point where they become completely drained.

If we think about rape, the violent use of the woman's body and absence of consent is obvious, but we should also think that enormous loss of self and exhaustion of energies can go hand in hand with what appears sweet and desirable, such as the relationship a mother has with her son: the endless waits, the hours spent waiting for the family to come home. I'm not just talking about *other* women here. I protest against the violence in the lives of woman who live this way, concentrating all their energies on the survival of others in order to guarantee their own in their imagination, but I also sometimes miss something which I haven't had, the tenderness of people in the house, children for example. It's clear to me that we can't talk about violent appropriation of women's bodies without bearing in mind the whole complex issue of relations between the two sexes, which has shaped itself historically in the mother–son relationship, where the woman's availability has circumscribed the conditions of her survival: always identifying her own life with that of her son, believing that she gets her strength and her capacity for relating to the world only through a son or a man.

The fear of loneliness, the sense of death, misery and human frailty which we experience when we are no longer loved: this is the form which women's consent has taken historically and which this law is now trying to quantify (one night yes, another night no).

Living only to let others live: women don't seem to have any other way of symbolically legitimizing their existence. To my mind this is the most dramatic and difficult condition which we have to change. Not even the political practices of the last few years have managed to produce any profound changes in this sense. A number of women today have constant and daily relationships with other women, including sexual ones, and yet the fact that they hold on to a man, a son or a father as a place of survival is not even up for discussion. This separation means that the axis they lean on to escape solitude, to survive, is still the same: the area of feelings is often separated from the area of sexuality. But I would also like to understand why we and the relationships we have between us are continually dogged by *man's law*, here in the very specific sense of *prescribing by law*. This would seem to be the case of approving a penal procedure which clearly works against us and against that section of men, the killers and rapists, who – and I know this will create a scandal – are of all men the ones who have the most trouble integrating themselves into the law of the father. We don't need psychoanalysis to explain this to us. Every mother or woman who has some experience of teaching knows this. When we have at school a boy who is 'maladjusted' or a 'delinquent', we bend over backwards to protect him from disciplinary rules which would have him expelled, and try to dig out the underlying causes of his behaviour.

Then we come across him again when he is eighteen years old, a rapist who beats up his father and his sisters, and we brand him as our enemy. I have no sympathy for murderers or rapists, but I realize that their history touches me more deeply than does the history of men who have apparently done nothing wrong. So why do women feel so strongly this need for legislation?

I've read that this proposed bill stems in part from the experience of rape crisis centres. I suppose the women who have participated in them have found themselves in the usual difficulties, in being women listening to other women, helping and advising them, and so on. But it's easy to guess what might have happened in those centres, because I teach a 150-hour course for women, and so every day I hear similar stories of suffering and abuse. So I wonder: faced with the complex problem of women's submissiveness, why do some women think they can bring about any real change by means of a law, while I think that what we need, if anything, is a political practice which weakens this need for dependency at a deep level?

The confusion between pleasure and self-destruction, happiness and dependence – because death is also the absence of mobility, the impossibility of developing one's own abilities – is a condition which is so dramatically rooted in our lives that there are no words for it. It's a fact of life and there's no need to go looking for it amongst housewives or beaten women. We have seen in our groups how difficult it is to change this attitude, even though we tried to pay the closest attention to the workings of the unconscious mind.

Only when women begin to express themselves, to go out, when they realize that they have their own energies, does the chain of dependency begin to get unbearable. Recourse to the law not only does not produce this change, it can only spring from the sense of helplessness and annoyance that we feel when faced with the fact that women, as somebody said before, don't know how to 'take control of their own lives'.

There is a clause in the law which offers the possibility of legal intervention in the sexual life of a married couple, when consent is wrenched from the woman by 'authority' or 'deceit'. But isn't 'deceit' a part of falling in love, when love becomes total devotion to the other, loss of energy and so on, and doesn't 'authority' already lie with the man, who has been delegated the task of protecting us and defending us from loneliness? Even if we can document rape, there's no way that submission achieved through 'deceit' or 'authority' can be measured by any law.

Forcing a woman to denounce a man she's tied to in such a contradictory fashion is just the same as saying 'But of course, if women are masochists and enjoy pain, the law will set about liberating them from their oppressors, automatically, making them autonomous.' We know this is nonsense and that women themselves will reject this solution.

Moving on from personal authority   *Luisa Muraro*

Moving on from personal authority to public authority: is this what we really want? Going from our almost official non-existence to being citizens on a par with men?

I want to tell you what's been going though my mind the last few days. The whole business of this law, which has been put together by some women on behalf of all and will be put to parliament with the support of all those who will sign it, seems to me to pose some questions which reach down to the depths of our history. I don't just mean as a political movement, but the real history of women. I think we can, indeed should, make specific criticisms of this law, but without losing sight of what it means for all of us that there are now female organizations which take the initiative to regulate our condition with laws.

In both past and present, women have been disciplined by the personal authority of men. It's well known that the female prison population is very small compared to that of men, and this shows that women rarely clash with public power to assert their own rights and interests. We are more likely to clash with particular authorities and it is in these encounters that we learn to submit. Only during the witch hunt did it happen that some women were released from personal judgement and exposed en masse to the judgement of public authorities: but we certainly cannot say that the episode bridged the abyss between women and public power. Quite the opposite; it only made that abyss all the more clear. After that, society went back to its normal regime, with women being disciplined by men, whether father, brother, husband, companion, doctor, director or whatever. Women don't think about the law in general, but they do think about the wishes and interests of the people they are in contact with, and they feel more bound by that than by any more general rules.

This is the situation even today. I have the feeling that with this initiative we are trying to push women into the sphere of public discipline. This is a great historical change: women begin to be disciplined directly by the law, by the state. The transition is supposed to be made easier by the fact that to start with it's a law thought out and put forward by women, and that should win us over.

My problem is this: is a change from personal authority to public authority what we really want? Do we really want to go from our marginalization, from our almost official non-existence, to become citizens on a par with men? Or from this marginalized position do we want to start a process which will change both our own condition and that of all society? In other words, are we to put right our marginalization by saying that we too can appear before a judge, be plaintiff or accused, do what the law prescribes and commands, become if necessary protagonists on the public stage and so also write laws? In that case it would be like saying that we want nothing to do with our marginalization, and just want to cancel it out, that we refuse to read it as an element of criticism and modification of society. There's no way round it, we're inferior to men in so many ways, we're less able politically, for example, we're not as good at writing laws (and this proposed law leaves no room for doubt on the matter). Well then, this inferiority, which is so humiliating, do we want to be rid of it at whatever the cost? Do we want to be told that women can do it too, or do we want to recognize this inferiority as estrangement and so as a point of strength for an alternative way of looking at society and changing it?

We're at something of a turning point. Over the last few years we have engaged in a political practice which was unlike men's. *Autocoscienza*, for example, is something which men totally exclude from their politics. Has the time arrived for us to use this political wealth of

ours to integrate ourselves on a level with men in society? Ten years
ago a law thought out by women would have been greeted by other
women with contempt and mistrust precisely for that reason. Not
now, because ten years of our political movement have helped us
overcome our lack of confidence and self-esteem. This is political
wealth. Do we want to spend it all in overcoming social disparity?
Isn't it perhaps better to continue down our road of a different kind of
politics?

I'd like to add one last thing. The most wrong-headed thing we
could do here now would be to set up a movement and counter-
movement, to say 'I'm in favour of the law' or 'I'm against it.' It would
be really banal to take sides in that way. I've noticed in meetings over
the past weeks that there are very deep differences amongst those who
support the law, as well as among those who are critical of it. When we
were talking about that wretched clause, for example, which abolishes
mitigating circumstances for infanticide, one woman said, 'Infanticide
is women's political crime', and another woman, who wasn't at all in
favour of the initiative, gave quite a start.

Another example. One woman who was a passionate supporter of
the law was left with her mouth hanging open when she realized that,
if this went through, women victims of violence would be obliged by
law to accuse their attackers publicly; she had been convinced that
making a statement meant that women could step aside and leave the
whole thing to the court. If we obey the logic of taking sides, all
arguments, doubts, problems and questions would be wiped out at a
stroke. So let every woman say what she has decided, if she has, but
she should come to her decision from her own experience and in
accord with the reasons inscribed in her own subjectivity.

You will say to me: you start, with the reasons inscribed in your
subjectivity. I'm a woman who in some way has attempted integration
on a par with men. Not for nothing do I get asked to make the opening
speeches in debates, and they are always the most embarrassing ones.
The attempt at integration, at being successful on a par with men, has
always cost me an enormous effort, and every move to get women to
learn to insert themselves into society as it is today, to be bright and
capable, seems to me to lead to total exhaustion. This time too I felt
the strain of speaking first and breaking the ice, even though it wasn't
really ice but diffuse chat . . .

I feel that the liberation we are struggling for is not to continue to
insist and push for women to place themselves in society on a par with
men. Few succeed, and then only by dint of great effort. The others
remain in their passivity. Liberation comes from a change by which I,

for example, can exist in society and speak without being forced to make such a huge effort, or to say to myself, 'You have to make it, you have to' while others are saying to themselves 'It's useless, I'll never make it, never.' This is a discriminating factor determined by a prescribed model outside and above us, according to which being a woman is an inferior state to be overcome.

This is my personal attitude to a law which says to women: you have to learn to get justice from the courts, learn to take on the law, the courts, the judges ... I don't believe that this sort of pressure is liberating for women. I don't believe it is because I think that, for me, it would mean greater slavery.

We have supported the drafting of this law *Collettivo COM-Tempi Nuovi*

We have supported the drafting of this law against sexual violence. We know its limits and its contradictions. But in the meantime the richness of the debate it has provoked shows that the women's movement is still alive and well.

What decided us as a group to support the initiative for the law against sexual violence was certainly not the vain hope that we could improve women's lot in the social context by means of laws. Even though it approached the whole subject differently, and emphasized different aspects, we have already seen this sort of debate on the usefulness and legitimacy of a law which seeks to enter into the 'lives' of women and codify them, during the battle for the abortion law; and the debate served then to bring to light how contradictory and out of step collective norms were with personal problems. But in spite of this contradiction it became clear, at the same time, that we couldn't ignore the concrete historical conditions in which only by accepting a high level of risk could women decide to terminate an unwanted pregnancy.

There is no doubt that in the case of the law against sexual violence we find the same contradiction, between the content of the law and the real needs of women with regard to protection of their sexual freedom. But in this case it's made worse by the fact that it is women who are putting forward the bill: women who, it seems, want to entrust the protection of their rights to a legislative body, and ask for justice from a state apparatus whose inability to enforce in practice the theoretical parity of men and women is well known.

R. Rossanda is right to remind us in more general terms that one of the clearest gains of 1968 had to do precisely with the recognition of the fact that the law is not neutral, that punishment has a negative effect, in that it does not rehabilitate the deviant but becomes rather a request for compensation. She also encourages women to value the cultural significance, in the context of the struggle for liberation, of the fact that women become active in formulating norms and asking for compensation.

But there is still a large question mark. In the current situation can women, as historical objects and as a movement, do without the law?

It's the very same question we were asking when we discussed abortion, even before giving our verdict on the quality of the law under discussion. What paths, what real, concrete initiatives visible to all women (and not just the few privileged ones who can count on a feminist collective or a UDI group) can we take to say we've had enough of a violence which has always been tolerated in the same way that an endemic disease is tolerated; tolerated even when it explodes in ways which would deny life? Aren't we always being told, 'Nothing would have happened to you if you had stayed at home'?

The abstract body of society, the material body of women For us the debate which has opened up since this law was first put forward has had two equally important consequences. The first is that within the women's movement there is a renewed collective examination of the conditions under which we live and of the relationship of the individual woman as a social subject to the social context as a whole.

We have always known that the object of sexual violence is the woman's body. But beyond that, the fact that the current code of law includes sexual violence not in crimes against the person but in crimes against public morality spotlights the ideological conception which serves as cultural background to the law. It shows that some values (the concept of scandal, family, honour . . .) are adopted ahistorically and that the abstract body of society is substituted for the material body of the woman, for her person, for her sensibility.

To realize this is to understand what we women can expect from law and justice; and to understand that a battle must be fought to change a power relationship which has historically seen women in the subordinate position; and it's a useful reminder to us not to be fooled into thinking that this society is capable of altering a relationship based on violence and internalized as such. It's to understand how it is that one can say, and believe, that 'If the woman won't have it, violence isn't possible'; it's to understand that even if its objective is to safeguard personal liberties, the fact that the present law requires the woman to be plaintiff for an investigation to start shows that it is surrounding the violence with silence, protecting the rapists every time the injured party doesn't make a statement; and again, it's to understand that unlike other kinds of criminals in this society, rapists have the right to a clean record.

The 'personal' as a collective dimension   These questions, together with others which women have debated, have helped the movement go beyond a stage which seemed close to exhaustion, the stage of 'the personal is political', because not only does this 'personal' now have an individual connotation (my body, my sexuality . . .), it also takes on a collective dimension, because the subject we are talking about is the woman in her relationship to society.

The second consequence is a matter of political forces being involved in a sphere which is exquisitely political.

The point in question is the possibility for groups and women's associations to support the plaintiff in that they represent interests with a collective dimension. Once such a rule, which radically affects the criminal process, was established, the consequences could not be limited to women's groups or associations, but would open the way to similar requests from groups and informal associations, groups which, while they are not always organized, nonetheless represent particular collective interests – from unions to local groups to ecological associations.

We didn't have to wait long for the reaction of the political forces. The biggest political parties, PCI, PSI, DC, speak as with one voice; they have all presented their own bills on the matter. But as well as official bodies the debate has led others to speak out, critics of this women's bill, and of these it's particularly interesting to look at the response of the Catholics. In *Avvenire* and *Discussione*, lengthy articles on the law linger over the fact that this law would throw into some doubt the principle of the woman's control over her own life, because of the intervention by the state in the prosecution.

We certainly can't accept from such a pulpit sermons on this 'value' which women have 'invented' in order to make more sense of their right to decide about their own lives. Clerical forces railed against women's control over their lives when it was a question of terminating pregnancy. Today, with a cunning that doesn't surprise us, they are deliberately and clearly twisting this point of the law in order to claim that feminists, blinded by their anti-male ideology, are capable of forgetting their own interests and the *conquests* of women themselves!

The duty of sexuality Conservative Catholic forces pose another question too, and as believers this affects us more closely. It's the possibility of taking your husband to court if he forces sexual relations on you without your free consent. For those who follow the official teaching of the church, to acknowledge that violence can occur within the marriage relationship means casting doubt on the doctrinal lines which would have the woman obedient (first to the father, then to the husband), ready to sacrifice herself, always prepared to satisfy the needs of others before her own. Sexuality has always been presented to women in the twisted and twisting light of 'duty' – the duty to be a mother, or to accede to the husband's requests. A whole cheap morality has been built up on this 'conjugal duty', a morality which totally leaves out of account female sexuality and, at a cultural level, has expanded beyond the bounds of 'practising Catholics' to become the value or criterion of the whole of society.

In the context of Italian society, a change of perspective on this point would imply a change for the whole of society at a cultural level. It leads us to wonder what might be the total effect of this law on the most backward and conservative situations, and so to reflect on the capacity of the women's movement to set in train processes of transformation which go even further than the initial objective.

As well as making a point-by-point analysis which would help us within the movement to discuss our line, we think this is also a good opportunity to evaluate the extent to which women can put valid and innovative proposals to the rest of the world, precisely because of their marginalized position. And with reference to this condition of being marginalized, which has sparked off a heated debate within the movement, we would invite you to think about one thing. Adopting marginalization as an immutable value, as the condition without which women lose their own character as an 'other' force set against organized political forces, means essentially to make it absolute, to make it ideology and to abstract it; and this would be to adopt a type of reason and politics which as women we have always rejected.

If our historically marginalized condition is today an instrument for raising consciousness and for struggle, it doesn't mean that tomorrow, from another position and a different power relationship in the social and political picture, we can't decide on other ways of making our demands and other levels of confrontation. But starting from today we can't give up trying to reduce the extent of our marginalization, provided that we are aware of the contradictions that open up, and that we balance out the price to be paid. The opportunity this law seems to us to offer is the opportunity to make a leap in quality in our work as women. The richness and articulateness of the themes brought up in the debate, the very power to mobilize, show today too that there is a real vitality in the movement.

Non-violability in the sexual domain *Maria Luisa Boccia*

Non-violability in the sexual domain shouldn't just be recognized in itself, it needs to be made to be recognized, but without transforming the body into state property.

Even if I think it right for the movement to put forward a law, I don't think it helps anything to simplify difficulties, or to pretend that some don't even exist, for the sake of the side we are on. Let me say straight away that many of the things Lea Melandri said were quite right, even if I don't share her conclusions. I don't say this through any love of submissiveness, but we can't deny that the dividing line between love and violence is a very thin one, that there is an element of shared 'passion' in sexuality even when it expresses itself in violence or even in rape; but this does not necessarily mean complicity, imply consent or require solidarity. In the same way it is profoundly true that our personal or collective relationship with power and with the law is conditioned primarily by the principle of family authority, and this is often our basis when we choose what to do or not to do in our social behaviour. If somebody doesn't agree with this perhaps they can explain to me why so many laws having to do with women have been defined as 'protective'?

If we forget all this when we propose to appropriate for ourselves an instrument of authority such as the law, we are following a political praxis which denies years of our work and, what is worse, we risk not being able to control how and why we adopt it. I think this has happened in part with regard to the current bill, and this is the source of the difficulty in avoiding dissent and preventing many women, even militant ones, feeling estranged. Many divisions today are perhaps inevitable. But we all still have the problem of calculating the implications of what we do, not only with regard to the choice in itself, but as to how far it allows us to find positive solutions.

So I wonder if those who want the law shouldn't indicate more clearly its outcome. It has been said that it is a question of dealing with the reality of rape, of removing the woman from the violence she is currently exposed to. If this is what it is about, it is a 'defensive' battle which will never win over women who want to cross other frontiers.

Personally I don't think I can ever turn down a weapon of defence, especially if by my refusal I help deny it to other women. But I think there is another possible answer. A law is destined to weigh – and the point is whether we want to do this, and what is the most effective law to achieve it – on certain forms of behaviour which develop in a society. If it can't do this, it is a very feeble instrument of defence. But with regard to the argument put forward by our comrades, beginning with the identification of its subject, it should be said that this law neither resolves nor modifies the complex dynamic of sexual violence, but introduces a hiatus between the act, the consciousness of the person committing the act and the way it is inscribed into the social order.

I don't believe that a law inhibits first of all because it punishes, but mainly because it modifies the interiorization of the norm, because it makes it more complex for the person to recognize her/his individual or social being. We don't reduce politics to struggling for particular laws; we know this is not enough, and indeed it might produce new kinds of violence, if it doesn't go hand in hand with other, deeper forms of change. But the law cannot deal with that kind of change, nor do I think it should.

Once we intervene in this dimension, and I think it's important that we do, it is important to do it well. This is why a number of points in the current proposal about sexual violence do not convince me. For a start, how is it possible to sanction every form of violence as if it were just one type of behaviour, without taking account of the relationship in which it occurs? There is a generalizing confusion here which hinders the law's efficiency; not just because many forms of violence, including rape, are more difficult to ascertain in a couple, but because to lump 'guilty men' together because of what they have done, rather than their relationship, is to go in a different direction from the one I was speaking of just now. On the contrary, I agree that it is important to put together acts of lust and carnal violence, because female sexuality doesn't respond to the primacy of coitus, and so is not more violated by this than by any other act. Also, the offence is undeniably to the person. Perhaps this innovation abolishing 'honour' is the one which has caused most misunderstandings, because of the way it has been adopted.

I don't believe it is right to make state prosecution dependent on this. I would say that there is a fundamental ambiguity in this clause, which is also the one which has met with most opposition. And so I come to the questions raised by Rosanna Rossanda. What position do we adopt with regard to *penal* law? I think it's clear to everybody that it's not the same thing to affirm our rights and to affirm our own being by sanctioning the possibility of punishing – in other words imprisoning – another person. I too am unwilling to take on for myself, just because I am potentially the 'injured party', the current dominant concepts of crime, blame, sentence and possibly damages.

There is doubtless a contradiction here. How are we to translate into a rule the condemnation of a social behaviour, and affirm the value of sexuality for the integrity of the person? In a society which distinguishes in this way between normality and deviance I have no hopes of a utopia. But can I use the law in another way? Perhaps I can, and perhaps, in the light of everything that has been said and attempted over the last few years, it is time for us to look again at the problem of punishment. It's certainly possible to refuse damages. And to my mind it is essential to avoid state prosecutions. For a start I'm not convinced by the call to value the 'good' to be defended; I see in this, rather, an uncritical embracing of the principles of current penal legislation.

I think that every woman who has recourse to the law because her sexuality has been abused should do it with full responsibility towards herself and towards the guilty man. It's not a matter of always and hastily waving the flag of self-determination. But I'm worried by the ease with which state authority, the power of the judiciary and the collective good are restored. Is society abused in my body? Does it carry more weight to call on the collective *value* of sexuality, by which in every woman all women are abused? Do we want to be defended as victims; is it the old need for protection rearing its head again? Why does the fear of our traditional weakness lead us to transcribe our *own* proposal in terms no different from the law of the father? Because this is what we are saying, if my body becomes a 'good', and the state deprives me of the right to denounce the fact that it has been abused. I also think there is an aspect of irreducible individuality which will not consent to this expropriation. And I *want* the woman to be the protagonist of the process, because this is also an indirect way, based, that is, on our conscience of not automatically accepting the concepts of blame and punishment.

For this same reason I don't think this law should be used to fill the prisons with rapists; frankly I don't have much time for facile simplifications about victims and persecutors. It should be used to have 'political' trials, to use the courts to involve institutional powers, the press and public opinion. Why do we have to do all this just to get the law into some sort of shape, even before carrying it out? It wasn't the same with abortion. In this case it's important that women participate in the trial by taking their place together with the plaintiff. But the first consequence is that the movement must look at its own organizing forms, the way it institutionalizes itself, we might say. We cannot make a choice like this, which is so important and has so many implications, without being able to guarantee that we can carry it through at the decisive moment of the trial.

Parliamentary report on the proposal for a law by popular initiative *Angela Bottari, MP*

Honourable members – In these past six months a huge debate has exploded around our proposed bill, a debate which has drawn in thousands of women.

This was our main aim, in accordance with the practice of our movement which chooses and privileges women as those to whom we address ourselves.

We could have come here and reported all the stages of this debate, documenting all the situations of violence which each of us goes through every day in this sexist and patriarchal society, but we didn't choose to do that.

We contend that anyone who is called upon to enact laws on this subject should already be sufficiently well informed. Our accumulation of exposition and experience will constitute an inheritance to be used by the women's movement for its own political practice.

Today more than ever we women are convinced that sexual violence is a crime against the person and not, as it is considered at the moment, against morality (article 1); it's incredible that if as a woman I am beaten, molested, kidnapped or raped, it is not me but morality that is the injured party.

If we rightly affirm that rape is a serious crime against the person, it follows that prosecution should automatically be brought by the state and not just the result of a suit brought by the injured party. The stated aim of the lawsuit is to safeguard the women's sense of dignity and honour, but as it works out it tends to protect both the man who is her 'guardian', who 'possesses' her, and her attackers, thus giving men licence to attack. We believe on the contrary that sexual violence in whatever form is a serious matter which is perilous to society, and for this reason it is inconceivable that the burden of bringing charges or not should be left to the injured party alone.

We strongly reject the argument which declares state prosecution to be an expropriation of our right to self-determination. We refuse to accept that there can be any self-determination in a crime committed by a third party, and we hold this to be yet another element of discrimination and false concern which comes into play only when the victim is a woman and the crime committed a sexual one. Certainly in the case of a state prosecution we women need a lot of courage, but then the need for courage goes hand in hand with the fact that we are women. So we think the argument that says that with state prosecution women will be dragged into the courtroom against their will is a false one, both because, in the overwhelmingly majority of cases, we are the only ones who know about the acts of violence we have suffered and so the whole legal process can be started off only by us, and also because, when the facts are in the public domain, for this very reason the action no longer serves the purpose of guarding our 'dignity'.

We believe it to be of the utmost importance that, in order for these state prosecutions to take place, the structure of the legal process as it exists today should be modified with regard to the questions and forms of interrogation, the publicity given to the trial and also to the speed of the procedure, which we believe should be as rapid as possible (articles, 3, 4 and 5).

In particular, we thought it indispensable to insert the part of the plaintiff in our proposed bill, even though we realize that this is a more general problem which should be resolved in all its complexity; too often our request to act as plaintiff in a rape trial has been rejected by the judges, while they commonly accept analogous requests by other organizations representing collective interests. The significance of taking on the role of plaintiff in a sexual violence trial is not so much the aim of being awarded damages as being able to intervene where things get out of balance or should be corrected, and there is no doubt that a group taking part in the trial with the injured woman serves to control the operations of the judges, as well as make the woman feel less alone. In this way we also intend to drive home the point that an offence to the sexual liberty of one woman is an offence perpetrated against all women, who have always been considered sexual objects and are all therefore potential rape victims.

We women firmly refuse to be considered just as bodies to be used, and for this reason we reject the logic of the current code of law, which differentiates between the acts of carnal violence and acts of lust. Our proposal affirms, on the contrary, that there is just one crime, that of sexual violence (article 8), given that we do not want to be divided into bits on which are carried out one time an act of lust, another an act of carnal violence, one time an abduction for purposes of lust, another time an abduction for purposes of matrimony.

What counts is the violence done to our bodies against our will, the humiliation, the annihilation as people that we have suffered. We believe this to be applicable also in cases where the person who offends against this right of ours, to live our sexuality when and how we want, is the husband.

We also deemed it necessary to introduce a new offence, that of group violence (article 9), in which the man's attack against the woman is plainly organized.

As for the 'cause of honour', it seems to us a waste of time even to explain our reasons for abolishing it, since we believe it to be a hangover from ways of thinking which we have long gone beyond.

However, we are aware that the abolition of the cause of honour will open up enormous problems in cases of infanticide.

What we are keen to assert is that the cause of honour (which is not that of the woman, as we have said, but that of the man) should be abolished as an extenuating circumstance in particularly serious cases.

We should like to affirm that those of us who are forced into such a serious act are themselves the first victims of violence and force.

Given the extreme importance of the problem, the women's movement will find ways and places to speak about the issue.

We also think that the crime of incest, punished by current law not in itself but insofar as it causes 'public scandal', should be abolished; we reject the hypocrisy which lies behind this formulation and believe that where an incestuous relationship is imposed it should be included with cases of sexual violence.

Any thinking on violence cannot ignore the violence perpetrated on children in families. The current code punishes abuse, thereby presupposing as permissible the use of methods of correction.

We believe that the use of violence is not a valid educational method and so we would modify the laws governing it (article 23). We would also contemplate the possibility of state prosecution for wounds inflicted less than ten days previously (article 24), in order to break the connivance and silence which surround all the daily small acts of violence which, put together, become one single, enormous violence.

12

Women at Home: Salaries for Housewives

For Italian feminists, increasing stress on the exposure of the middle-class ideology of the family was reinforced in the early seventies by the campaign in defence of the newly approved divorce law, and by the growing mobilization for the legalization of abortion. The debate concerning salaries for housewives was a further indication of how the rejection of the family implied a total questioning of the organization of society, as well as the rejection of the dominant images of women.

Thus the discussion of this issue was concerned with the division of labour, and therefore with practical problems such as child care and with the particular implications of mothering; but it also took into consideration the theoretical implications of family structures, often with a Marxist approach, albeit in a perspective very critical of Marxian theory with regard to women and their work.

This debate was particularly important in the first half of the seventies, but was resumed at intervals during the eighties. Lotta Femminista of Padua – which later joined with other groups from the same area to found the Triveneto Committee on salaries for house-wives – assumed this issue as central to its reflection and action, and organized several meetings and conferences to discuss it with other feminist groups.

We have included here a short extract from one of their documents, a statement of the MRF (Pompeo Magno) at a 1973 conference in Naples, and a selection from the journal *Orsaminore*, where the question was taken up again in 1982. Together, these pieces give some idea of the scope of the debate. The arguments are dangerously ambiguous. On the one hand is the problem of ascribing theoretical value to the confinement and subordination of women; and on the other is the significance of the domestic sphere as an affirmation of power and expression. The questions raised extend beyond the immediate debate to crucial issues like the tricky accommodation of the public and the private; aspects of action, alienation and identity in paid and unpaid jobs; the different 'roles' adopted by men and women, and so on.

Ultimately the demand for salaries for housewives seems to have become not a goal, but a moment in the struggle for a new and different sphere of existence for women.

INTRODUCTION TO THE DEBATE   *LOTTA FEMMINISTA*,
                                1973

For us women, Marx has never been a myth. 'Our' Marx didn't waste too many words on women and on their work, domestic work. It's also true that at the time he was writing, women workers scarcely had the time to reproduce themselves and their children. But if he was a theoretician of a whole period, he must have perceived the centrality of domestic work. So if we feminists quote some of his work, it is to make our comrades who refer to him all the time go back and re-read more carefully the passages where we can perhaps see him approaching the problem.

Let us begin where he approaches the problem but does not touch it:

> the worker ... gives himself means of subsistence to keep up his working strength, just as a steam engine is given water and coal, and a wheel is given oil. So the worker's means of consumption are pure and simple means of consumption of a means of production, and the *individual consumption of the worker is a directly productive consumption.*

Except that, and our man does not see this, this consumption presupposes work of some kind.

This work is housework.

Housework is done by women.

This work has never been seen, precisely because it is not paid.

It seems to us no accident that theoretical obsession with productive work has never even touched on the problem of the productivity of housework. If Marx at least came close to the problem, his followers have always carefully kept their distance.

As for the *workers*, we acknowledge their hard struggle over pay, at the moment of production in the factory.

But the workers' struggle has always failed to include the reproduction of working strength and the absence of pay which mystified that reproduction.

The workers have never turned their attention to that part of the productive cycle which has always been carried out without pay.

This is no accident. This was women's work, the other half of the class which, as a class, has been denied by all.

One part of the class with a salary, the other without. This discrimination has been the basis of a stratification of power between the paid and the non-paid, the root of the class weakness which movement of the left have only increased. Just to quote some of their commonplace accusations, we are 'interclassist', 'corporative', we 'split the class', and so on, and so on.

Even today more than half of the world's population *works without remuneration*.

So women's demand for pay for housework is today the most revolutionary and strategic demand for the whole class.

STATEMENT AT A MEETING WITH LOTTA
FEMMINISTA   *MOVIMENTO FEMMINISTA ROMANO*,
1973

Giving housewives a salary means transforming a mass of enslaved individuals, who work without pay or organized hours, into a salaried workforce.

But what will this salary consist of?

The members of Lotta Femminista rightly compare the demand for salaries for housewives to social security (the so-called 'welfare' of Ango-Saxon countries); and it would in fact be nothing but a concession, a charity on the part of the government. This is because housewives, given the private character of housework and emotional implications connected with it, do not possess any contractual power. By what means could they obtain a salary rise? Would they leave children and husbands, the elderly and the sick, and so on, in order to take part in demonstrations? Would they fold their arms and refuse to do the housework, knowing that, afterwards, they would have to slave twice as hard in order to regain lost time? And, finally, who would pay the social cost of this salary if not the women themselves, through price increases and salary cuts elsewhere in the workforce? Nevertheless, even a small income concession may appear to be an achievement to women who have always worked for free, and without recognition, and who have been forced to be totally dependent on their husbands or fathers. In our opinion the demand for salaried housewives conceals elements which are not only reformist, but also dangerous, because:

1 it confines women to their traditional role.
2 it endorses their social function as private, though it grants it some social, economic and symbolic value.
3 it stands in antithesis to the demand for social services and to the involvement of men in them.
4 it defines as work an activity which cannot be considered as such, because it does not have time limits or precise methods.
5 it presents itself as an obstacle to the inclusion of women in the world of active production, because it will facilitate redundancies and self-exclusions.
6 it recognizes the scientific organization of work based on the division of labour (manual/intellectual, master/servant), and the specific division based on sexual difference, which, as Engels says, is the foundation of all other divisions.

It is, in the end, a dangerous struggle. At this point, we'd like to remind you of the fact that the female section of the Francoist party in Spain is currently trying to introduce salaried housework as its national policy. This demand is based on the principle that it will strengthen the family and, consequently, the state. We should bear in mind that Franco and his party are so conscious of the fundamental role of women in the family as the pillar of the present regime that they have created a special law which forbids writing or saying anything against the family. Our slavery has continued for thousands of years, and we can understand the impatience to find immediate tactical goals to galvanize women into action. In this respect, though, and in order to become politically aware of our exploitation and oppression, the salary demand appears restricting, because it does not question the real power-relations of men and women, and the whole ideological basis on which this power rests, but simply makes of it a question of economic discrimination and unpaid work. We then ask ourselves: what is the actual meaning of a struggle for salary? If it is about a mobilization for its own sake, then we must bear in mind that that would not really be an autonomous fight, in that it would require men as intermediaries, because they are in direct contact with the production of exchange value. They are also possible supporters of this struggle, since it does not question their role in profiting from a series of privileges connected with it.

We think that the fight against the patriarchal and the middle-class ideology of the family is fundamental for the liberation of women and of the whole society. Women must be able to refuse marriage in order to achieve full independence.

A massive request for jobs for all women who are currently housewives would go against the system, which cannot renounce gratuitous housework.

The right to manage our own bodies, the collectivization by the state of all the social services (canteens, local laundries and so on) currently provided for free by housewives, collective education of small children, equality of work with no sex discrimination – these are our objectives. But to achieve them women must come to realize their objective condition. It is impossible to say today how this will happen or how long it will take, but women's struggle has only just begun. The fact that it is spreading throughout the world shows that it responds to needs so real that it could put a bomb under all the contradictions of bourgeois, patriarchal and male society.

A PRICELESS ROLE   *CARLA CASALINI*, 1982

Salaried housework was a key issue in the feminist movement even in the early days; for example, in the groups in Padua, as well as in the publications of the Autonomia femminista of 1975. It indicated the denunciation of, and the demand for, a quantitative answer to the way the state was swindling women, by resting its budget on the gratuitous labour exploited in the name of the allegedly 'primary natural' function of women.

Nowadays, this theme has been taken up again by Catholic women as a possible new ideal. The ANDIC (Association of Italian Catholic Women) relaunched the issue at a conference. Whilst speaking of a job that is literally invaluable, the association intends to set as its first task not so much a salary as the juridical recognition of the figure of the 'housewife'. Elsewhere, as the bills introduced by several parties (from the PSDI to MSI to the Christian Democrats down to the radical party), the price of the job is explicitly stated because of the woman's 'right' to a salary. This is simply a revision of family allowances, which nowdays ought to be cashed by women, rather than by the head of the family. The mixture of public and private in this act of compensation is significant: if the husband has a good income, then he can give money to the 'housewife', otherwise the state backs the husband up. The actual result is a sort of subsidy for the poor; that is, for marginal categories who have no other chance of 'appearing' on the stage of the world and of the market.

Perhaps it would have been more interesting if the discussion about housework – now revived – had originated not only among house-wives, but rather between them and the thousands of women who do the same job in public places; namely in service, in bringing up children, in health assistance. These women receive a salary, and yet they have been speaking of an extra share, a sort of surplus value which goes beyond the codified exchange, and which allegedly expresses their natural female attributes.

This would have been interesting, because the whole sphere of reproduction, in its private and public aspects, would have come into the discussion; and, consequently, into the discussion of the position of women. Perhaps some ideas concerning the possible organization of these services and needs would also have emerged. In the absence of this contact, women stay isolated in their roles as 'housewives', and they speak of making a salary contract. But what kind of salary?

Over and above the reorganization of family allowance, of subsidy, can they really be paid for housework? In order to be recompensed, a job has to be recognized and codified as a set of tasks. How do you break up and reciprocate the housewife's activity? You have the food preparation, the bringing up of the children, being 'receptive' to the needs of the whole family, and – in between – the relationship with a man. There would be queues in public offices, because of the detailed bureaucratic work, but also because of the task of converting family needs into a code comprehensible to its *terminus ad quem*, which means in an abstract, impersonal and quantitive fashion. The housewife's job is a complex combination of socializing and giving love; and the above are only some possible examples. What is the equivalent in terms of money? Certainly not just some hundred thousand liras. If we want to be optimistic, if money is a sign of social representativeness, then the lack of correspondence between service and compensation reduces the answer to a mere subsidy.

It is precisely this incongruity, this impossibility of breaking down the various tasks, translating them into quantitative terms, which reveals the problem. The activity of the 'housewife' – that is, of the woman who stays at home – cannot, in my opinion, be defined as work. 'Housewife' – if we think about it – is not equal to 'worker', but rather to her male counterpart, the 'producer'. It is not work, but a 'role', as it was once called.

Now, at the moment when the primary male role has been so much shaken, men try to react by strengthening its possible competitive value. Women, on the other hand, instead of bringing the discussion back to the intertwining of all the various spheres of life, production and reproduction, accept this old division, which is – furthermore – codified at a lower price. In the meantime they are thrown out of the public places belonging to the 'producers', and the state announces further cuts in the budget of local governments; that is, in financing services. If you intend to ask for a subsidy, you must bear in mind that it is nothing but a survival income, which outcasts receive without questioning the reasons for their own status.

What interpretation do we give, then, to juridical recognition? Women went to work outside the home, realizing it was necessary, but could not fulfil themselves in these jobs. But nor were they satisfied by housework. Women have a whole tangle of relationships in daily life, sexuality, children, giving birth, future generations, immortality, people, power, solitude, material and spiritual nourishment. I do not think you can solve these difficulties by asking the state to act as a mediator in this tangle of relationships. I don't think that this would make women's private and public lives easier. How can you reduce 'women' to housewives?

It is peculiar and interesting that women – in general – appear more and more as the class which is bargaining for its own needs in bits and pieces. The meaning of 'partiality' used to be different; it was like an external point of view, from which you could have a total, exhaustive and eternal vision of the world. Little by little, women have realized that they are within that vision rather than being pure, external observers. Consequently, they have had to create their own defensive techniques, without, however, simply pretending to leave the game, or pretending not to know its rules. It is one thing to know the rules, and another to recognize them more and more as your own.

Is it really useful to abandon that 'partiality' rather than having it play a part in all fields? Then we would find ourselves with an unstable identity, and be forced to accept being catalogued as a collection of bits and pieces of life and segments of persons, pains and needs, and all this only in order to acquire recognition. Is it really possible to assign the state the task of giving us an identity? Is it to be hoped that the state will identify us as 'victims of rape' or 'housewives' according to the occasion?

WITHOUT POLEMICS: REASONS FOR A DEBATE   *CARLA CONSEMI*, 1982

There have been many contrasting comments on the essay 'And what if all housework were not real work', by Ritanna Armeni and Paola Piva, which was published in *Orsaminore* (no. 2). This essay has frequently been taken as a pretext to criticize our magazine . . .

In *Effe* (no. 4), Silvana Cichi maintains that not defining housework as work only means 'starting from where we began', calling it once again 'the mission and gift of love'. 'Work seems – to the women-writers' eyes – to be nothing but a robot's movement, a lifeless assembly-line, a lack of emotional interaction.' Whereas if 'more and more women ask for an outside job and then fall back on housework, their disillusioned return is not a free choice. Rather, it is a form of submission caused by powerful discrimination and by a work routine which is unsuitable for women. It is the fear of a difficult clash with a society which is still not adapted to female presence, which makes one choose withdrawal, rather than insisting on change.'

Giuseppina Santilli too, still in *Effe*, critizes Armeni and Piva:

> When has work ever been defined as only those particularly sad and repellent activities, which used to be exclusively determined by an external constraint, perhaps by the jailer's whip hitting the unfortunate worker every ten seconds? If this were true we would live in a world of idle people. On the contrary, every employer knows perfectly well that it is convenient to leave the employee a certain amount of freedom, creativity and responsibility. In the same way every employee tends to look for a minimum of satisfaction and personal realization in his job.

This essay, therefore, has been discussed at length by the editorial staff of *Orsaminore* as well.

However, at least two observations induced us to publish it. Firstly, the fact that the essay was the result of the thought of two women who were not only emancipated but also strongly committed to a trade union activity, and who, consequently, knew better than anyone else the character of paid work with its thin margin of – limited – 'non-alienation': in other words, two women who have no intention of going back to being housewives. What is driving them, we were wondering, to think of housework in its specificity, unless – perhaps – a drastic reduction of housework itself to reproductive, invisible and unpaid work, a reduction made from the 'pure' feminist point of view? The necessity – we answered ourselves – of looking closely at paid and unpaid jobs in order to find their dimensions/aspects of action, alienation and identity. This research needn't be exorcised by ortho-dox Marxists or feminists.

Secondly, we found a theoretical reason, which we think went unnoticed by Marxist criticism; namely the fact that housework, besides having the nature of a peculiar service (a service whose beneficiaries are known, and which is therefore tied up with a form of interpersonal communication) produces use values rather than exchange values. It does not produce 'goods', it will not be transformed into money – unless in a very indirect, incalculable way (which is still to be examined), in the sense that the 'pure' housewife is compensated by having a roof, food, clothes and all the rest, paid for by the man, or by social security. Otherwise, she could not exist as such any longer.

It is certainly true that both women and men (if they have started to take part in domestic activities) can find a peculiar gratification in the production of values of domestic exchange. These activities can be tiresome, but they will still be more various and free – in time and choice – than in the most articulated section in the most advanced firm. Cooking for strangers in a canteen or restaurant is different from cooking for friends or children at home, even though the menu could be theoretically the same. It is probably 'more different' for somebody who is not a cook by profession; but that is not necessarily the case. This is also true of the production of values which do not have a domestic use. Do-it-yourself, for example, is chosen by those who want to escape from the pure model of industrial consumerism, as by those who, while normally obliged to consume industrial products, want to create their own domain of creative activity. This can even happen inside a factory; the evidence of the Hungarian Haraszti about the activity workmen 'steal' in a factory is indicative in this regard. The worker works on the same machine with the habitual material (scrap), but for himself; it is a 'different' work, not only because of the emotional involvement, but also in the material sense, because he is not producing goods.

This said, the fact remains that housework is mostly a hard, daily, tiresome and normally unpaid activity which is entrusted to women, in an invisible chain of the reproduction of the labour force and the 'lubrication' of services. It is useful to study its function of 'excluding' women from other jobs and spheres of power, as well as the specific relationship with the housewife herself. Let us do this without rows, even though – perhaps – we do not agree among ourselves. Because, once we put the 'geneology' back in order, the question is still there; and it is a huge question, worth facing without the fear of losing, antagonism or difference. The debate is open.

WHAT IF THERE WERE ONLY THORNS? *ANNA CIAPERONI*, 1982

We cannot say that the openly provocative intention of the essay by Armeni and Piva on 'housework' (*Orsaminore*, no. 2) did not hit the mark. The impression left by the text is a mixture of incredulity and ironic disheartenment. You wonder whether we have been getting it all wrong these last ten years, whether we have done everything for nothing, and have suffered so much only to end up back where we started from, namely in the traditional division of roles. This would mean confining women to their homes/houses, with the extra understanding of feminist criticism and the definition of non-work. What are the two authors saying, in short?

The main argument is the following: since women working outside the home – whether workwomen brutalized by menial jobs or emancipated intellectuals – are still anchored to 'housework', then housework not only possesses value, but even a 'logic of its own', a principle of value which does not come from the market! Women cannot get used to the world of male work, 'which is incompatible with the female way of being'. As a result we participate in the 'rediscovery of a strong tie, of a revaluation and reassessment of the domestic sphere'.

We come to this through the belief/assumption that there are areas in domestic life where 'it is hard to draw the line between working for others and experiencing for yourself.' Therefore the motivations behind working women cleaning the house on a Saturday morning are not – according to the authors – determined by need or habit (they refuse part-time domestic help) but rather by the 'culture and choices of women themselves'. Thence, the individuation of the domestic sphere as 'a new affirmation of a moment of power and expression of women'.

But there is more to it. According to the authors, housework is untouched by capitalist production (but they contradict themselves here because they admit a relation between productive work and housework, to deny it later on). In fact, they ask themselves how to explain this attachment of women to something which is subordinate to capitalist production. Consequently, a dangerous and arbitrary distinction is made: housework becomes synonymous with 'the principle of value', whereas productive work equals alienation. The sphere of housework thus turns out to be a neutral place, which is unmarked by capitalist laws, and is therefore alienated from the world of social

relations. To sum up, a sort of 'reign of freedom'! Following on from
this is the suggestion that all the values of 'housework' should be
transferred into extra-domestic work.

One could raise more than one objection to these hypotheses. I will
outline/comment on just a few:

It is undoubtedly true, for example, that – in the domestic sphere –
it is difficult to draw the line between 'doing' and 'living'. But is this
not true of any other activity as well, including outside work?

And, again, how can you deny that any woman intending to remain
such obviously does not identify herself in male working patterns?
However, I think it hasty to proceed from this to the affirmation that
the domestic sphere offers self-fulfilment. In fact, more and more
women nowadays do not find themselves, whether in outside jobs or in
housework only. Are we not going backwards in this respect too, in
comparison with the theories and struggles of women against the
present organization of work – which is certainly not suitable to
women – as against the whole social organization, which is as surely
dictated by the sexual division of roles as is the existence of the real
housewife?

Secondly, why the inclusion in the definition 'housework' of all
feelings, as well as psychological wellbeing? Is it not perhaps possible
to look for feelings and psychophysical health as well, for example, in
a socially rich life, or even – why not? – in an extra-domestic job?

I think the authors are creating some confusion: namely between
actual housework, and between motherhood charged with housekeep-
ing: between some factual data – such as the recognition of reassuring
features surviving in the domestic sphere – and their own valorization,
up to their being proposed as 'models'.

However, leaving aside these easily recognizable objections, the
arguments put forward by Armeni and Piva appear dangerously
ambiguous for other reasons.

In my opinion, it is insidious to try to re-establish – even through
filters from feminist experiences – a theoretical value for the agelong
confinement of women to domestic activities, though unconstrained,
because how many women actually choose housework? In this way
one risks erasing ten years of feminist struggle and practice, for the
destruction of the ideological basis of female subordination. The latter
was identified – as everybody knows – in its reproductive function,
which was arbitrarily charged with negative virtues and consequently
caused a division of roles.

The authors propose here – let us be clear – not the legitimacy of the
ambivalences and contradictions which every woman experiences in

the spheres of productive work as well as of the family and affections. Rather, they present us with the one dimension; namely, the family, the domestic dimension. So much so that the hard, daily oscillations between house and work, the continuous mediations which women have to make, are not interpreted as the practical results of women being still charged with the family organization and child care. Instead, they are almost proposed as ways of achieving self-fulfilment.

Besides, although I am not motivated by the ideology of work, I am, rather, convinced of the necessity to change our concept of work. I think that it is impossible to cut out such an important aspect of any individual life – be it the life of a man or a woman – nor, even more so, to accept Manichean divisions between black and white. In my view, both alienation and chances of self-fulfilment coexist in housework as much as in any job. On the other hand, it would be worth enquiring about the ambivalence which women experience in both spheres. Housework is experienced as a refuge, a reassurance, an exercise of power, but also as a means of oppression and discrimination. In the same way, extra-domestic work is experienced with many contradictions. One finds in it the possibility of economic independence, professional self-fulfilment and social recognition. But one also feels, at the same time, the impossibility of adapting oneself to peculiarly male patterns (total identification, competition, rhythms, timetables). Now I think that one cannot deny, hide or remove this ambivalence, by choosing – time after time – univocal solutions. On the contrary, I believe one should refuse to regard productive work as an exhaustive element, as a filter through which all the rest – feelings, emotions, creativity – are mediated and subordinated. This view is typically male, and it would imply a refusal of living up to the principle of a female way of life, as alternative and contrary to productive work and its social dimension.

Solutions are certainly difficult to put into practice: those women who want or try to live in the dimension of ambivalence doubtless pay high prices. But the point is – in my opinion – to practise and use ambivalence, contradictions and diversity in order to transform housework, productive work and the social organization. I think, therefore, that it is important to study in depth the female way of life, the values we have internalized and project onto every sphere of our life, starting from the family and continuing down to housework and extra-domestic work. It seems to me that an understanding of the (historical-cultural-social) origins, features and expressions of female diversity, and research on the nature, ambivalences and contradictions inside our consciousnesses, our minds and bodies – in order to assume

Changing the Context

Changing the ContextChanging the Context

Changing the Context page 272272   Changing the Context272   Changing the Context

and experience them afterwards – are the fundamental means of liberating and transforming our lives.

In their essay, Armeni and Piva also indicate the limits of change in the productive sphere, since for them production should be transformed through the acquisition of 'housework' values. In this way they exclude a process of general transformation of all the spheres of individual and social life: from housework to interpersonal relationships, from the family to the whole social organization, from culture to politics. Finally, they exclude the social dimension and the time women have for themselves in their lives, since they are supposed to live only between home and work, rather than among work, family and social relationships, with time for themselves. Why then do they choose only these two poles, neglecting all that is neither house nor work?

Besides, their aim seems even more dangerous when we think that they are proclaiming – or would like to proclaim – the death of feminism, whereas we are witnessing a new concentric attack on female employment on the part of consistent, Catholic forces, now accompanied by widespread housewives' organizations everywhere. Not to mention the fact that a disturbing process of technological reorganization is being directed by a recessive economic policy, causing mass redundancies. All this certainly does not bode well for female employment.

The argument that Armeni and Piva present is therefore ambiguous and reductive in comparison with the degree of knowledge and of difference now open in the lives and movements of women. Indeed, even the positive aspects of the essay, as for example the necessity for men to discover personal values, are made vain by the regressive message which – consciously or unconsciously – prevails.

To sum up, the attempt to give theoretical value to the difficulties – sometimes equal to real forms of existential uneasiness – which women experience in trying to combine – out of a schizophrenic dimension – professional fulfilment and emotional satisfaction, is certainly noble, but cannot prefigure univocal solutions, which have already been outdated by women's experience.

13

Women at Work: Trade Unions

A SURVEY   *ALESSANDRA MECOZZI*, 1989

In reflecting upon the question of Italian women workers and feminism, I shall take into consideration the period from the early seventies to the present day. For it is through an examination of this period, that the unanswered questions which will be carried on into the nineties can also be set.

As for the geographical boundaries of our argument, this essay will have a national perspective, but with particular focus on the central-northern belt, where my personal experience has taken place.

When I talk of the relationship between feminism and trade unionism, I intend to address the question of the many and diverse forms of representation and self-organization which exist for women within the unions: forms which derive from a collective choice in favour of self-representation and mutual trust, based on a feminist culture born in Italy in the period between the end of the sixties and the first half of the seventies. This culture, coming into contact with traditional union values and with the analysis of women's work, has produced a new analysis, and new forms of organization and trade union activities. In a first phase, these activities had to do with the struggle against sex discrimination (which was found to exist at the very heart of class discrimination); in a second phase, the affirmation of sexual difference and of an autonomous female subject has become the goal of this process.

It is also important to remember that the period outlined here represents a critical stage in the unity of the unions – a process of instability, begun in the mid-seventies which was ultimately to lead in 1984 to the scission of the three principal organizations (CGIL, CISC,

UIL). This also has some influence on the position and activities of women in the unions. In the seventies, in fact, the organizations set up by women trade unionists share a unitarian feature (for example, the National Coordinating Committee of FLM (iron workers) women, or the Piedmont *intercategoriale* group, which included many categories of women workers from the CGIL, CISL and UIL). In contrast, after 1984 there are only organizations from the single union (CGIL or CISL or UIL) although the effort to collaborate persists.

However, I shall not go into this problem in detail, for my major concern here is to underline the kind of autonomy which exists for women both within and outside the unions: that is to say, the dynamics pertinent to subjectivity rather than to external factors, even if such elements have had and continue to have a not insubstantial significance.

In this sense, even the dynamics which underpin women's employment (good attendance and increase in the workforce), and the changes at the demographic level (the gradual decrease in the birth rate), though telling indicators of the evolution which has taken place as regards women and employment and women and maternity, won't be given much importance. It is useful, however, to keep these facts in mind, since they are the most informative indexes, at the statistical level too, of an aspect of the process of women's self-affirmation, of the changes in women's roles and identity. Despite having taken place outside the unions and traditional political structures, this is a process which establishes the necessity of constructing forms of social as well as political representation, and forces the unions to confront such a necessity: that is, the need to defend women's interests and to find the means of enforcing their validity. It is a struggle which goes beyond the old struggle against discrimination.

In this respect, the definition of feminism as a political movement, which activates sexual difference in the fight for social equality between the sexes, is particularly apt. So is an older, more subjective definition employed in the early eighties, which saw feminism in terms of the identity crisis of the emancipated woman. For when the new Italian feminism was born in the early seventies, the emancipation of women had for the most part taken place.

From the outset of the seventies, women have in fact sought to disassociate themselves from a well-established tradition which is also an integral factor in the very structure of the workers' movement; that is the habit of viewing women as a specific category, and as a result of this only in a position to contribute to the general policies decided by others; or to see them only as a unified force in the struggle for equality with man. Thus in this period, women broke with tradition, in order to articulate their desire for active participation and for change – in the trade unions as they stood, but also in all established power structures and power-relations; a desire which in the last two decades has touched women of both the southern and northern hemispheres, although their feminism is expressed in different forms.

The nineties will bring new problems and issues from the eastern countries: but this is an area which remains as yet unexplored.

The seventies

It is in these years that we witness a great change in the traditional interrelations between women and the unions, by virtue of an originally non-European feminism, which spread rapidly this side of the ocean as well. In order to understand the significance of this change in an Italian context, it is revealing to consider a number of publications by women trade unionists which describe their experiences as feminists. *L'acqua in gabbia* (Milan, 1978), *La spina all'occhiello* (Turin, 1979), *Spezzare il cerchio* (Naples, 1979) all serve to demonstrate a dissatisfaction with and impatience towards union organizations, soon to take the form of open conflict; but they also articulate the more positive sense of belonging to the growing number of women's movements.

For these years are to be remembered as those which heralded many campaigns for the women's issues: the campaign for divorce which took place in 1974, the movement against clandestine abortion and in favour of a woman's right to take responsibility for her own life (this legislation was passed in 1978), the setting up of a new jurisdiction of the family which broke with the patriarchal tradition. As regards of the union movement, those are years of important struggles: for salary increases of an equal percentage for all (1969–74); to dismantle rigid categorization of labour as either manual or intellectual; for the right to further education, without loss of salary (the iron workers drew up a contract in 1973 which stipulated 150 hours for such activities).

For women workers and trade unionists, new forms of organization came into being, by virtue too of the 150-hour courses for women, which were a great chance to meet and discuss together. The first group of this kind was founded in Turin in 1974 and included women from the three unions, CGIL, CISL and UIL; this group of women held their weekly Thursday meetings at the headquarters of the CISL until 1985, when the trade union federation dissolved it, justifying this decision by claiming that within divided unions unitary groups cannot subsist. These new kinds of organization, based on a feminist analysis of employment and society, were to obtain a national influence, particularly in industrialized areas.

In comparison with the past, when the issue of women and employment was relegated to being a minor issue on the agenda of both national and federal offices, and when direct participation of the workers was scarcely taken into account, these organizations were characterized by a greater involvement of the rank and file, by subjective criteria of formation not decided by the organization's leaders, by their appeal to all women without limitations imposed by their own organization, by a common feminist analysis and by a new relationship with the unions on what could be termed a contractual basis. This means that the coordinating committees or the groups of women delegates, with the participation of those few women who hold positions of responsibility in the unions' structures, formulate their own proposals and decide the necessary measures to be taken, which they subsequently discuss with the unions.

Another factor of particular importance is the relationship with feminist groups, which often leads to common activities and to an exchange of experience and opinions, be it on most decidedly feminist themes like sexuality, health, abortion, or, later on, on the question of women's work.

A significant, though by no means exceptional example of this cooperation between women trade unionists and feminist groups, is the 150-hour course for women planned and coordinated by both groups. This course on women's health and medicine, which took place in Turin in 1978, was attended by 1,300 women factory workers, office workers, housewives, students, women with posts in the union and with the participation of women gynaecologists whose thought was moulded within the feminist movement. The seventies are years when feminist trade unionists fought against discrimination, for a woman's right to employment and for new contractual clauses such as paid leave-of-absence for both parents to bring up small children. In reality, this goal was achieved only in few cases, facing severe opposition on the part of large industrial corporations such as Fiat. However, it is worth underlining for its drive to bring to the negotiating table the traditional ordering of 'male' and 'female' roles and to review their practical implications.

This campaign against discrimination also assumed an institutional form: in fact the sex discrimination act (passed at the end of 1977), which in deference to international changes, prohibits any form of discrimination towards women in the workplace, and its implementation between 1978 and 1979, were to bring new opportunities for thousands of women employed by Fiat, but also in many other factories.

I have no intention of eulogizing the seventies from the point of view of the new dialogue established between women and the unions; for even during these years the recalcitrance of the unions towards the feminist movement was considerable and our progress minimal. Only as regards the question of abortion did the women's movement bring about changes, overcoming opposition not only from expected quarters, namely the Catholics, but also from those who believed that the quest for negotiation on many other issues, in order to preserve the unity of the unions, could not be jeopardized by a policy which gave precedence to the interests and rights of women. Within the unions, the emergence of an autonomous female subject with its own ways and means of expression met with resistance and obstacles. This was true even in struggles of a traditional kind, such as the campaigns to defend women's jobs.

A good example is the campaign at Fiat in 1980 against redundancies, when an attempt was made to initiate a specific struggle and a political campaign for women. Fiat intended to make redundant many women workers; the majority of them had just recently been taken on, precisely on the basis of the new sex discrimination act. These female workers had brought with them new questions, and moreover, the urgent need to find solutions to the new problems which arose from the very presence of women in a traditionally male environment. For the sake of productivity and restructuring, Fiat wanted to get rid of them.

During the struggle, the very attitude of the unions demonstrated that it was not simply a matter of disagreement on concrete issues. The conflict arose from the refusal to recognize the existence of men and women as different subjects with different needs, or the right to be represented, which also differs for each sex. We were and are convinced that realization of this fact, in contradiction to accepted union logic, would have strengthened and not undermined the struggle for *all* workers.

After all these experiences, we arrived at the eighties with a greater strength and with a clearer vision of the question of autonomy. At the same time, the dynamics of social conflict and the drive of workers' struggles were on the wane; this coincided with the systematic breaking up of the Italian unions, the undermining of the sense of solidarity even between individuals. It was a time in which groups

with extremely different goals arose and the independence of the
political parties was in question. In such a context, the diversity of
women's progress and the autonomous character of their positions are
evident even from an objective point of view. But women were *within*
the unions, part of their structure; the very sense of belonging to the
organization, as well as their own weakness, made women unable to
impose their diversity.

In effect, in spite of the attempt to maintain a sense of unity as
women over and above the specific union membership, and to
establish the priority of solidarity among women and of their common
interests, in the end the rules of the organizations were stronger, and
led to the dismantling of women's unitarian organizations even among
iron workers or in those regions in which they had a longer tradition.

This imposed division resulted in an identity crisis and in a critical
re-examination of the relation with the unions; thence a period of
apparent silence and inactivity. In the meanwhile, all through the first
half of the eighties, the entire women's movement was seeking out
new and more significant forms of identity and activity, all underpinned by a new sense of independence. As a result of this, we see the
emergence of many women's centres, generally self-funding and at
times receiving grants from state institutions, namely municipal and
regional councils. In 1986, at their National Convention at Siena,
there were more than a hundred such centres. Not only was there a
search for new forms of organization; feminist thought grew in depth
and complexity as it searched for a theoretical basis in the formation of
an autonomous system, and the attempt to affirm the female subject.
Women's revision and deconstruction of established disciplines (history, sociology, anthropology, economics) also involved a new philosophical thought. The theory of sexual difference began to question
(and for this it is often accused of having theological aspirations) the
unity and neutrality of the universal. Feminist practices and struggles, in a continual quest for an individual and collective identity, had
resulted in the seventies in the recognition and affirmation of sexual
difference as a distinct value; the following decade was to theorize this
difference as the constitutional heart of the female subject. Also, the
question of differences between/among women took on a new significance, and is still central to a great deal of feminist thought.

When the universal is not one and neutral anymore, but is defined
in dual and sexed terms, women are no longer an anonymous,
amorphous mass in the eye of the other. On the contrary, they acquire
an identity entirely their own, be it individual or collective. The
theorizing of sexual difference has not failed to influence also women's

analysis and activities about women and employment, women and the unions. With the abandonment of a protective policy which considered women's difference as a reason for inferiority, the very concept of equality – as approval of male standards – comes into question. Indeed, equality was often used to justify a worsening of women's work conditions. Almost immediately, one notes that for women equality meant night-shifts or heavy labour, but not career prospects or more qualified posts, while in the domestic situation little seems to change as regards the redistribution of chores and the masculinization of domestic tasks. Women have accepted the challenge to take on all forms of work, even in posts considered male strongholds; but the sense of an imbalanced exchange is ever more manifest. And this unequal exchange is bound to a conception of work which considers and values only male labour, as being productive and as responding to the demands of the market.

From this emerges our first priority: to reformulate the criteria of definition in this area, to reconceptualize work by taking into account all of women's activities; that is activities of *production and reproduction*. The first convention of women from industrialized countries, which took place in Turin in 1983, bore exactly this title: there were about 600 women, from all over Europe, from the USA, Japan and Australia. The conference was promoted by women of the Turin *intercategoriale* (a group of women from many categories of women workers, members of CGIL, CISL and UIL), from the UDI, and by feminist groups from the women's centre in Turin.

It was a very important moment in the search for a new approach to the problem of women's work, and it marked a decisive stage for the formulation of subsequent analyses of women's role in politics and of the question of their political representation.

After a year of preliminary work carried out by various groups in different European countries, the conference gave expression to the characteristics of women's action in the unions and their modes of relating between/among themselves. To summarize, they are:

1   A criticism of the traditional trade union culture, marked by industrialist and productivist values. In its stead, the formulation of a new conception of work which values all forms of women's labour, in order to elaborate work policies which correspond more realistically to women's interests; this would also be a necessary step for overcoming the sexual division of labour.

2   A common project undertaken with women's groups outside the unions too, in order to gain a greater autonomy, both at the

political and at the representational level and a greater power in
dealing with both the unions and other institutions; a much wider
social and political dialogue. This has not been possible in all
situations to the same extent; now as in the past it depends on the
force of feminism in a given situation, and also on the greater or
lesser willingness on the part of women trade unionists to break
with traditional structures and to exercise more freedom in their
jobs in respect to well-established rules.

3 Acceptance of a separatist policy as women's own political expression to confirm even within mixed organizations (those composed of
   women and men) a collective identity, and to bring into them the
   values of women's culture.
4 Exchange of information with feminist groups of other countries.
5 The importance of women's cultural production and of its visibility; this is also to oppose the split between those who create culture
   and those who take action, between intellectual and practical
   labour.

This last characteristic of Italian feminism was to be in the forefront
of a conference, held in 1986 at the University of Modena. 'La Ricerca
dell Donne' ('Women's Research') was promoted and coordinated by
many women academics, who presented their research projects, all
inspired by feminist tenets, within different academic disciplines
(ranging from psychoanalysis to economics). This conference
attracted women trade unionists, whether simply rank and file or
elected union representatives, those obviously with first-hand experience of the feminist movement: but this shows the extent of social and
political dialogue produced by women's culture.

The propagation of the feminist viewpoint, or rather of a new
political standpoint for women, also stimulated discussion and change
within the Communist party. 1986 was marked by a most telling
occurrence, namely the publication of The Charter of Women Communists, with the subtitle Women's Stength Comes from Women.
This was a dense document, which is based upon the theoretical
concept of sexual difference with regard to all the most pressing
political issues (employment, peace and war, the relations between/
among women, women's relation with other movements), carrying the
debate on to women members of the PCI. Feminism enters the
Communist party, one could say; yet, at the time the movement had
formed no conclusions concerning the nature and the characteristics of
the party. The debate regarding the structure of the party itself was to
take place later on, and is still central to the more general questions

pertaining to the role, name and very identity of the Italian Communist party.

A critical issue for women in the Communist party, as well as in the unions, is the belief that it is sufficient to maintain or construct areas of autonomy within the existing mixed organization, without, on the one hand, attempting to overcome classic and traditional forms of discrimination against women (which means that very few of them ever reach a high post in the hierarchy) and – more importantly – without, on the other hand, assuming a critical stance as autonomous subjects.

The concept of sexual difference justifies and precipitates the synthesis of these two moments, which in turn creates the need for a radical review of old forms. And it is within this framework, even one could say riding on the wave of the achievements of women in other countries (Germany, for example), that the question of minimum quotas of women in positions of authority re-emerges: a question which the CGIL addressed, putting forward the figure of 25 per cent as a basic acceptable ratio.

The question of quotas and more generally of representation (and of the value and possibility of representation for women) has become in the last few years a central problem. This is true both for mixed organizations and for those institutions set up for women in these years, such as the equal rights committees (either at a regional, a provincial or a municipal level) intended to enforce the equal opportunities bill; or the advisers in this field, appointed by the Department of Employment in every region; or the committees outlined in some national work contracts, whose purpose is to examine forms of discrimination and to implement constructive measures to combat discrimination against women.

The question is neither straightforward nor homogenous, not even for those women involved in organizations such as the unions and the political parties; and these problematic issues became interwoven with the crisis which also besets these very same organizations, concerning their capacity actually to represent Italian society. The different standpoints can be summarized as follows:

1 Criticism of the way quotas are structured because they might result simply in the co-optation into organizations with a strong masculine tradition of a few women, who would have no real political force and would therefore be easily coopted; this would undermine and not reinforce their relation with other women, and it would not represent their interests. Women who hold this opinion believe that a

far more viable option is self-representation by means of groups with internal ties, breaking with traditional structures and policies. An example of this is Sindacato Donna – an association of women founded in 1987 *within* the Piedmont CGIL, but having its own statute and rules. The association was founded by full-time women trade unionists, from other unions too, and is open to all women, including non-members of the CGIL. This standpoint is in opposition to the following one.

2 Acceptance of the quotas system as a momentary tool to overcome discrimination against women in numerical terms, and as an occasion of collaboration between women in positions of authority to formulate an autonomous policy, although within the existing structures and rules.

3 Women should nominate their own representatives in the governing bodies. This is in opposition to the following view.

4 The idea that women should be nominated and elected by the governing bodies in so far as they are to be general delegates.

5 There are also some feminist trade unionists who maintain that it is essential that women strengthen their position on the basis of a strong mutual relationship, making dialogue with other women a priority; obviously, in this way, any value attributed to quotas is nullified.

As I have previously stated, however, the line between these positions is not rigidly drawn; indeed they are often found to coexist within same groups. Certainly they all exist within the unions; it is a work in progress, the search for common goals and common methods. The aim is more power for women and the affirmation of sexual difference, in order to criticize and strike to the very heart of the dominant, long-established power centres which are still founded on a male social pact. This pact can only be opposed successfully by a social and political pact by women.

There is no clear awareness of all this within the unions, accustomed at most to consider women as one of those many and diverse social minorities (such as immigrants, the young, the handicapped); a perspective which results in a deeply flawed yet politically significant strategy.

Firstly, there is some confusion between women as a political group, which is in reality a minority, and women as a social group, which on the contrary is decidedly a majority (51 per cent). Thus, women's rights are undervalued as though they were those of a minority, whereas they are rights which are relevant to one half of the population. It was with the same logic that the first few women who campaigned in the suffrage movement were attacked.

A second error is in equating women with other social minorities. But sexual difference is an originary and structural difference; other groups are marked only by fleeting or well-defined or professional differences.

It is possibly in an attempt to combat such interpretations that women have been compelled, in the initial stages, to identify themselves as a unified group having male oppression as its defining characteristic; only after having overcome this domination on many issues has it become possible to face and recognize the differences between/among women themselves. The internal differences within the 49 per cent of the population made up by men have been called history (by political parties, nations and unions, also through their internecine conflicts). The claim that women are a minority carries considerable political resonance since it suggests a quest for specific rights instead of universal rights; rights which therefore have no bearing on the rest of the population. This happens because women have no collective rights.

I think that today we are at a stage in the progress of the women's movement when the most telling issues to be faced, by the unions too, in the course of the nineties can be summarized in three words: power, rights, freedom: what sort of power, what sort of rights, what sort of freedom – how to rebuild a pact between women which creates a new social and political pact in which women are a forceful and autonomous subject.

14

Keeping Silent, Speaking Out – Some Instances

Though remarkably 'political', the Italian feminist movement has also been wary of politics. It has been very averse to an involvement in terms of the already given categories of political action, and very careful not to become a tool for someone else's purposes. The Italian feminist movement has indeed stood up for certain aims, agreeing to enter the institutional game, but without totally adhering to its rules, and without much trust or conviction. On events and themes of 'general import', that is, not directly and specifically concerning women, its aversion to involvement has been even greater.

In this section we offer four instances of events/themes of great political relevance, nationally and internationally, outlining the different attitudes taken by the feminist movement towards them.

The Moro affair

Silence, in the case of the Moro affair Aldo Moro was kidnapped by the Red Brigades in 1978; after months of fruitless searches and of heated debate among the parties on the advisability and rightness of negotiating with the kidnappers, he was found dead in a car boot, parked in the centre of Rome, within walking distance of the Christian Democratic and the Communist parties' headquarters.

Moro's 'execution', as the Brigadeers called it, came at the height of years of political terrorism in Italy, which had seen an escalation of violence on all sides – the extreme right, the extreme left *and* the police – with bombings, kidnappings, ambushes. It is a story of the illegal involvements of the secret service, of idealism gone awry, of blood and of repressive measures which bordered upon the denial of the rights of the accused.

Women – and even more, feminists – did not take part in the political discussion which this event provoked: a voluntary silence which perhaps expressed their feeling of not-belonging in the arena of male politics, and their distance from the interpretive categories used in such discussion. In the piece reproduced here, which was the introduction to a series of interviews on this subject with women in the media, in politics and in the feminist movement, Anna Maria Mori attempts an analysis of this opting for silence.

Terrorism: the 1979 debate

Unwilling but passionate discussion about terrorism, and more precisely about women terrorists There were women among the terrorists, including those who kidnapped Moro. Their choice posed a problem for the feminist movement, who debated it in connection with an attack by an all-women commando unit against a woman jail warden in 1979. The first six pieces in this section come from that debate. In the same year, the need to understand also led to the publication of a collection of writings by women involved in political violence – of these, 'Pushed by the violence of our desires . . .' is included here. Finally, we have chosen a general reflection about the problem, which also appeared in 1979.

Military service for women

A rehearsal of the equality/difference opposition concerning the issue of military service for women The idea of instituting compulsory military service for women as well as for men has been discussed more than once by the political parties, and might soon be on the agenda again.

It has generally evinced opposition from the feminist movement, as the pieces by Edda Billi, Marlena Fabris and Lidia Menapace illustrate. But in connection with the draft of a law presented in 1986, and included here, some women in the parties, such as the Socialist MP Elena Marinucci, argued in its favour in the name of complete equality between the sexes. Such equality, most feminists would claim, is founded on the acceptance of the male as model; eventually, equality could be better attained by abolishing military service altogether.

Chernobyl, 1986

*The decision to speak out as women (though by no means a decision shared
by all) on the Chernobyl disaster, viewed with a transforming gaze as a
concretely and symbolically significant event for women, who ought to
offer their own interpretation of it and take upon themselves the right and
the responsibility of speech and action* The pieces in this section
partially re-create the discussion about this issue, also hinting at the
subsequent connected debate in feminism on science, which Chernobyl triggered off in the feminist movement in Italy.

THE MORO AFFAIR

Preface from *Il silenzio delle donne e il caso Moro* Anna
Maria Mori, 1978

'To negotiate or not'? 'With the State and against the Red Brigades' or
'with neither the State nor the Red Brigades'? And again 'Press silence
or not'?

These are essentially the questions and the choices which had to be
made by the political world and the press (objectively not so much its
opponent in dialectic or even dialogue, but its corollary and appendix)
during the fifty-five days from the kidnapping to the assassination of
Aldo Moro. Indeed, for the sake of correct reporting and 'objectivity',
it should be said that the press even beat the politicians (and the
degenerate offshoot of politics, the Red Brigades), in outlining and
putting to the country the first and most dramatic of these questions
and choices: 'to negotiate or not?'.

The men who make the news interpreted and even anticipated the
thoughts (and the letters) of the Red Brigades. They announced the
reasons for the Moro kidnapping to the Italian people, and declared
that what would be demanded was a deal by which the prisoner Moro
would be an object of exchange for the freedom of the prisoner Curcio
and his comrades.

This interpretation was put forward with such conviction that as
soon as the question/choice ('to negotiate or not') had been put an
answer was found ('no deals'), and it was even attributed to the most
authoritative voice in the whole affair, that of Moro's wife Eleonora.
Facts were later to show that she was far from wanting to make such a
decision, but within a few hours of the shoot-out in Via Fani the press

agencies and hence the newspapers attributed this choice to her: 'My husband's life is not something to be bargained with.' This choice and statement were immediately denied by Eleonora Moro through her official spokes*men*, Rana and Freato.

The men of the Red Brigades . . . politicians: men . . . newspaper-*men* . . . 'opinion-makers': men . . . and what about women?

The Moro affair is even today, and who knows for how much longer, a dramatic question mark. Who knows, perhaps history sooner or later will deliver a just verdict on these events. But in the meantime, just a few months on, what we can try to do is to rethink the story itself. This is just one of the many critical rethinkings possible, and it is the one which informs this book: from Mrs Moro down, what was the role (not) played in the fifty-five days from the kidnapping to the assassination of the president of the Christian Democrats by Italian women?

We want to question the role of women in the tragedy not only of Aldo Moro and his family but of the whole country: why?

The answer is in the premise which underlies this work: implicitly or explicitly the desire, the hope, the utopia of a society without violence, without blood and without 'necessary victims' are there in the history of all women who have thought, written, believed, struggled: the mothers and grandmothers of feminism today. Woman's historical memory of herself is of a scream and resigned tears, which are *against*: against a logic of violence (not just sexual, clearly, even if the male sexual will to power is the premise of all other forms of violence) of which woman is both witness and victim, and against which she has no redress. She is and always has been excluded (according to anthropologist Ida Magli, matriarchies never existed) from the processes of decision making, unable to impose her logic of life and peace and so defeat the male law which has dominated and clearly continues to dominate history, and which is a law of war and death. It's the same law that we find operating in the Moro affair. Today we feel the presence of women: a few, still very few, take part in the processes of decision making, but there are still many, many women out in the streets trying to get their point across. But during the Moro affair all these women stayed silent. Why?

Apart from Eleonora Moro, who are the women in question here? Since the panorama which we have to consider here, in a case like that of the fifty-five days between Via Fani and Via Caetani in Rome, is the political one together with its voice, the information systems, the women we refer to will be mainly the ones who are part of the world of politics or the media. There is, for example, an association of women journalists. Did they address themselves at all to the question of how the press behaved towards Eleonora Moro?

In the world of politics or the media, the woman (even more than in sexual relationships or in the cinema, and I hope the women's movement won't hold this against me) is far from enjoying the role of subject of opinion. Is her role, then, to be the instrument of assent or consent towards one or other current of ideas put forward by men involved in politics or information?

We looked through the back numbers of some Italian dailies throughout those fifty-five days in order to find evidence for this hypothesis, through *La Repubblica, Il Corriere della Sera, La Stampa, Il Giorno, Il Giornale Nuovo, Il Messaggero, Paese Sera, Il Tempo, L'Unità* and *L'Avanti*. (We didn't examine *Il Manifesto*, since it is the only press outlet for a political group and a cultural-political area where in this case, indeed as always, woman is present as subject of both political and cultural opinion.

We looked for female signatures beneath the headlines, for female characters in the articles, to see if and when they were taken into account in the course of the affair. We posed one question, which was this: with regard to the important issues on which the political world and the whole country was invited to choose, to take up positions (as we said right at the start, 'to negotiate or not', 'with the state and against the Red Brigades', or 'with neither state nor the Red Brigades', not to mention the other possibility, 'with the Red Brigades against the state'), what about women, what role did they play?

Leaving aside for the moment what their answers would have been on these issues, our question stops a little before that: were women called on to express an opinion at all, an opinion shared with or even perhaps opposed to that of men? We were in a state of war. And we all know that wars are the concern of absolutely everybody, since we are all asked individually or collectively to pay the price, whatever it may be. But at that time, when hostilities were declared, were women consulted?

The answer is 'no'. In those fifty-five days women did not speak. They couldn't, didn't want to or didn't know how to express their opinion on these matters, over which the whole country was called on not so much to choose as to endorse choices made in their name or on their behalf by political parties, by individual politicians and by individual representatives of the cultural world. Some women (but few) signed this or that appeal, thought out and put forward by men: once again they silently endorsed, for whatever side, plans and proposals which were still, as ever, of male origin.

'Alternative' socialist thought made itself heard during those days. It lost the battle for negotiations, and probably knew it would lose. But this didn't stop it raising its voice to defend a choice and an opinion, even if it was in a lonely minority.

And what about the female or feminist 'alternative'? If we take into consideration these same fifty-five days we would have to come to the conclusion either that it doesn't exist or at least that it has nothing to do with wider political choices. It may well be something to do with 'control of one's own life', but only our 'private' lives: women's health, sexuality, abortion, birth. As if to underline this there was an international feminist conference held in Rome in the middle of these fifty-five days (on 24, 25 and 26 March), where (feminist) women emphasized the fact that the whole affair was nothing to do with them, and as a 'provocation' they decided to take into consideration only questions of violence done to and by women. The communist press, led by *L'Unità*, gave an angry response, condemning their aloofness and estrangement. But this condemnation was on the basis of the usual presupposition, that women should be an 'organic' part of a wider plan, a political plan which comes from the (male) top. In other words women shouldn't stay outside in the cold, they should come in, make themselves heard, but all this in order to support our ideas, the ideas of the party executive and leader, so that they will achieve greater support on the streets and in people's homes. Or else (look at the initiative taken by the UDI the day after the slaughter in Via Fani: laying a flower in honour of the victims) to continue in the cultural and historical vein which characterized 'femininity', which is complementary to the 'harshness' of war and politics, filling both of them (after it's all over, of course), with all the 'human' qualities (faith, hope and charity?) with which the woman is 'naturally' endowed. So men provide the (necessarily harsh) decisions and women move in to give voice to pity. As long as these two things, decisions and pity, don't occur at the same time we can acknowledge that they both exist.

And as for the social battle in favour of negotiations for Aldo Moro's release, it must be said that the Socialist party leader doesn't seem to have consulted any female representative (thin on the ground for that matter) of his party, nor did he seek to enter into dialogue with these depositories of those 'human feelings' on the basis of which he said he came to his decisions. Their counter-argument is ready: it's hardly an exclusively female privilege, is it, surely men can embody humanitarian moments too? Certainly they can, but if they take this line they should remember and respect the fact that for thousands of years it has been the woman's historical privilege, or rather the reason for her marginalization from history: for woman has always chosen 'feelings' as against or independently from 'necessity' (which in this and in many other cases means reasons of state). If woman is for man the other side of the moon, it is also because she has never been able, been willing or known how to take part in the male politics of the 'end which justifies and cannot but justify the means'. And so when once humanitarian principles like this one are invoked, how is it that women are not called upon to have their say?

The situation at the moment seems to be the following. The 'Palace of Power' ignores women; the women's movement ignores Power. This raises a question, which is to wonder whether in this way these two, who loudly and officially proclaim themselves antagonists, don't finish up in reality by becoming accomplices in a common design, one consciously and the other not. This design would be the continuing exclusion of women and that 'alternative which woman historically carries with her as her culture' from political decisions. And all this still as always on the basis of a historical division of roles: power manages the 'public' while women deal with the 'private'.

This is more or less what they say. We will check this against the real situation with the material available, the material which makes up the reflections of this book. In the fifty-five days of the Moro affair, other than the questions 'to negotiate or not' and so on, which we have already mentioned, there were also others: for example the whole argument about the authenticity or otherwise of the prisoner's letters, the need or otherwise to push through harsher laws for public order and even the odd voice calling for the reinstatement of capital punishment. In this book we will look in all this, in all the political and cultural decisions and arguments, for the role or non-role which women played, and try to evaluate the reasons for the significance of it.

Let's start with Eleonora Moro. We've already spoken about the attempt to 'appropriate' her, turning her into one of the major weapons of those who had decided that the best or the only way had to be to say 'no' to any negotiations right from the start. And we should also speak about what happened after, when it became clear that the wife of the Christian Democrat president was of a very different mind, that in her opinion no stone should be left unturned in the attempt to get her husband back alive.

When she said this she and her children were treated to a mixture of reproof and paternalistic understanding, and were defined as the 'party of the family'. And in a society where Catholics and historical left-wing movements, but more generally men (or males, as feminists would say), have always been in the habit of making a dichotomy between the 'private' (the family) and the 'political', it's clear that only with some irony could the family be called and considered a 'party'. And only in the end because there was some other group, which really was a party, which made the thesis of Mrs Moro and her children its own.

But it should also be said that what Eleonora Moro constantly held against the political class in the fifty-five days of her family's tragedy (and after, when she refused a state funeral for her murdered husband) was in part also the result of a logic of which she made herself the living symbol, not only throughout those fifty-five days but throughout the whole of her life at the side of one of our very foremost and most outstanding politicians. That is, the split between private and political (it's not by chance that on 2 April, in *Paese Sera*, the headline of an article about her and her marriage to Aldo Moro read 'Barrier between public and private'), the stubborn insistence of both her and her family that the private is private and should never be 'contaminated' by the political.

The Catholic Eleonora Moro herself paid the price of this (Catholic) ideology. Throughout the fifty-five days her appeals and those of her children, her interventions in an attempt to save her husband's life, her protests against the political class, were taken and reported by the press as the protest of the 'private', of the 'family', of feelings: of the 'non-political'. And of this, of course, the 'public' cannot take account. The 'political' decides, without her and even against her, for Eleonora Moro. And she, Eleonora Moro, at the tragedy's epilogue, opposes the 'political' with her 'no', her refusal of the 'political'. Now that he is dead her husband belongs only to her, the family, the 'private'. Hers was a whole series of 'nos' which earned her right from the beginning, from Indro Montanelli, the extraordinary interpreter of the collective historical unconscious, the 'honorific' title of 'Thoroughbred' (*Il Giornale Nuovo*, 21 March).

And after Eleonora Moro another woman, Tina Anselmi, had a protagonist's role in the fifty-five days of the Moro affair: she was the Christian Democrats' messenger to the Moro household, and back again. Apart from the obviousness of giving a woman this role, the historically female role of mediator and intermediary, another question occurs to us here which the newspapers never publicly asked. In those fifty-five days, what did Tina Anselmi think as she carried out this role? And more than what she thought, privately and in her heart, what was her opinion about the whole business?

At that time Tina Anselmi was employment minister; now she is minister of health. When she was chosen for the role of messenger between the Moro family and the Christian Democrat party, was she chosen as a woman or as a political representative? Because if Tina Anselmi was chosen in her role as politician she should have had an opinion, a political one, on the whole business, and logic requires that she should have been called upon to express it.

The fact is that if minister Anselmi had or has an opinion about the Moro affair, whether it is the same as Zaccagnini's ('Don't give in to the Red Brigades' blackmail') or the opposite one of Mrs Moro ('Look for another way to come to some agreement'), it is an opinion which has never been made known. And nobody seems ever to have felt the need to encourage her to express it. Just as we never knew the opinion of another eminent woman in and of the Christian Democrats, Maria Eletta Martini, who also played a great part in the whole tragic business of Aldo Moro, to whom she was very close personally and politically.

However, it was only to the first of these women, Tina Anselmi, that the newspapers granted a small amount of space. But it was an exclusively photographic space. The image of Anselmi frequently appeared, like that of Mrs Moro, at silent prayer in church, or crying in her car. And we all know that crying and praying are activities belonging to the sphere of women; not thinking or deciding.

At another level of these events we find women journalists who were dealing professionally with the Moro case: Lietta Tornabuoni for the *Corriere della Sera*, Sandra Bonsanti and Laura Laurenzi for the *Giorno*, Silvana Mazzocchi and Liliana Madeo for the *Stampa*, Miriam Mafai and Vanna Barenghi for the *Repubblica*, Orietta Bongarzoni and Bimba de Maria for *Paese Sera*, Flora Antonioni and Evelina Tarroni for the *Tempo*, Luisa Melograni and Vanja Feretti for *L'Unità*. The *Messaggero* published just one article by Vanna Bellugi, which approaches the matter very indirectly, through an interview with Rudi Dutschke. Just one female journalist, the American Sari Gilbert, appears in the *Giornale* in connection with the Curcio trial, and in *Avanti* we find the signatures of Rita Bisestile, Marcella Andreoli and Paola Cacianti. As for the *Repubblica*, the daily paper with the largest number of women writing for it, we should say that other women journalists intervened in the Moro case too, even if indirectly: Daniela Pasti, for example, myself, Natalia Aspesi (her interview with the supposed terrorist Brunilde Pertramer) and Vittoria Sivo, who also gave occasional reports on the position the unions took on the affair. And again in the *Repubblica*, on 17 April, we finally find a woman, a representative of 'female' culture, addressing one of the questions which had produced the greatest number of cultural interventions during those fifty-five days; that is, with the state and against the Red Brigades, or neither with the state nor with the Red Brigades. This was Ida Magli, explaining the reasons for the intellectual's alienation from the world of politics and from the state.

Of the huge number of articles which appeared in the whole of the Italian press during the fifty-five days, we have paid particular attention to the ones written by women. What comes out of all this is that Italian women, whether in journalism or in politics, are not called upon to make or to express opinions in their own name.

Opinions, some of which then became decisions, were given not only by male politicians – Zaccagnini, Andreotti, Berlinguer, Craxi, Fanfani and La Malfa – but also by the male 'opinion makers' of the press such as Eugenio Scalfari, Indro Montanelli, Giorgio Bocca, Enzo Forcella, Gianni Baget Bozzo, Leonardo Sciascia, Alberto Moravia, Gaspare Barbiellini Amidei, Gianfranco Piazzesi, Raniero La Valle, Marshall McLuhan, Umberto Eco, Aldo Sandulli and so on.

It was these men, and others with them, who entered into the debate, asking questions and answering them themselves: to negotiate or not? With the state and against the Red Brigades? Is it possible to be with this state? Should Moro's letters be considered authentic and should they be acted on or not? Are current measures for public order sufficient, or should they be strengthened? Might this not be the moment to think about reintroducing the death penalty?

Faced with these questions which they never themselves asked, women were 'dumb'. Women politicians, led by Tina Anselmi, were dumb. So were women journalists. Throughout the fifty-five days in question their role was that of reporters, whose job it is to relate the facts and the opinions of others: it might have been better if in their role as reporters they had at least been free to choose which facts to relate. For the most part they were deployed on the 'party of the family' front. These are two helplessnesses which finished up by merging together, two 'private worlds' which as such do not form an opinion or a political gesture.

We have excluded from this analysis female weeklies, for these would need a whole separate investigation. Political 'power', and with it political-journalistic power in a narrow sense, continues to ignore women when it does not exclude them altogether. Or if it does admit them, it's only after an explicit or implicit oath of fidelity: thus we have silent women politicians (and as we know silence is a form of consent) and the women journalists, the 'faithful reporters'.

It's clear that in this analysis the Moro affair in a sense transcends itself. It is a political moment in the life of our country, one of the most highly dramatic moments, from a human point of view as well as a narrowly political one. And as well as the infinite number of other analyses it lends itself to, it seemed to us an opportune moment to draw up a balance sheet as to the real weight the women's movement and individual women have acquired in terms of political bargaining and cultural dialectics, with regard to concrete political and cultural power in Italy. These are fifty-five days which can, indeed should, make women reflect. It calls for the umpteenth examination of our own consciousness, to consider the significance of our recent battles, the possible emergence from these battles to political victory which might finally have some real effect on the renewal of political life, under the sign of the primacy of the 'human'. Sexuality, the fight against rape, abortion, all these things are fine. But the fact that women have made their own slogan 'the private is political' should or at least can mean something else: the will and the capacity for autonomous and alternative choices to traditional, male cultural and political power, in all areas of our political and cultural life.

Over these last few years women of the movement have fought against the so-called 'emancipated' women, women who themselves enter into political life, the very few women who have managed to become authoritative in neutral cultural fields, in other words those not strictly and declaredly feminist, the few women called on to be a part, even if only in a minor or marginal way, of masculine institutions. They are accused of being just the same as men, of being 'white blacks'. And what has this struggle achieved? 'Emancipated' women have only become even further isolated within institutions and in the eyes of public opinion. Not only do they continue to suffer the age-old lack of respect and support of the 'males', they also now have to contend with the parallel lack of solidarity from feminism. All this has probably detracted from their power, their credibility, their right to express themselves 'as women' both within and outside the institutions. If nothing else it has pushed them, simply to survive, into identifying themselves if anything even more closely than before with the institutions in which they work, since they lack the support and solidarity of militant feminism, and that crumb of power which the movement has won, given its ability to mobilize women in the streets.

All this goes for women (politicians, journalists etc.) present in institutions. Other women, those in the movement, refuse to take part in what affects our country. In the field of economics, for example (about the clash between private and public economy to name just one), in the struggle for control of means of mass communication, in the politics of sport, and so on. They even theorize this lack of interest, just as they theorized it with regard to the political and cultural debate about the Moro affair. They come up again with a 1968-type choice: refusal; without getting at the very heart of these various problems by putting forward a positive suggestion of their own, which it might by then be impossible to dismiss out of hand. The problem is that in a society like ours the principle of 'silence means consent' is still clearly in operation. But what is it that women consent to? What did they consent to by their silence during the fifty-five days from the kidnapping to the assassination of Aldo Moro?

TERRORISM: THE 1979 DEBATE

Broadsheet *Prima Linea*

The communiqué which the agencies didn't pass on. *We want to know everything, and then we'll judge.*

This morning an attack group of the communist organization Prima Linea [Front Line] made up exclusively of women comrades struck down a woman guard in the female section of the prison Nuove Rossella Napolitano. She had particularly distinguished herself by her diligence and industriousness in carrying out her filthy job of spy and jailer, and is a part of the staff who are not directly linked to the military and who don't soil their hands with tortures and beatings; these are passed on to the usual people such as Cotugno and Lorusso, even in the female sections, whenever the guards' and the sisters' blackmail is no longer enough to maintain normality.

The function of the staff who run the female section is exclusively one of control, of soothing tensions and offering the proletarian women imprisoned there models which have always ensured the subjection of women: housework, prayer, obedience to hierarchies, passivity. These bigoted and reformist 'ladies of charity' like Mrs Cabrini are, in the minds of power, our examples of virtue. The guards, the sisters, the social workers who form part of a whole network to run the female sections as an instance of extortion and division and as a weak link in the process of socialization and organization of the imprisoned proletariat, should be more careful from now on. The struggle inside the prisons has identified their role and pointed them out as targets for the proletariat and its organized wings . . .

Combat Organization
Front Line
February 1979

We have read and re-read that broadsheet *A comrade,* Women's Movement in Turin

Turin – When the document written by the women of Prima Linea appeared in Turin, I heard someone comment, 'Right analysis, wrong conclusions'. But I felt as I have always felt, that mistaken choices are always underpinned by forced, false and ideological analyses of reality. I was also extremely irritated to find in the document statements which have been made too often by men or by those such as the Christian Democrats and the PCI, who have always done their best in words and deeds to denigrate the feminist movement ('the movement is generic but contradictory', 'a false unity between women which hides diverse material conditions').

I will never get tired of saying that the feminist movement in Italy has never been and is not ambiguous or petit bourgeois in its practice. I myself am unemployed with two children, and I came to the movement through my activity in the unions and in local women's collectives, a practice which reached me in the same way as it reached so many other proletarian women. I found a movement which, like all movements and the workers' movement itself, certainly has its differences, but because of the type of mobilization through which it has grown (abortion) and the practice it has chosen (local and factory collectives) has ended up attracting a whole mass of women. If we are not fooled by the media's image of feminists, it will be seen that these women have little indeed in common with the petite bourgeoisie.

In the Prima Linea document I read that 'whoever tries to suggest a separatist practice today . . . places herself outside the revolutionary movement'. It seems to me that the feminist movement in Italy, the one on which I have gambled my whole existence and all of my political practice, has always *in fact* used separatist practice to gather together its stength, anger, awareness and clarity, and has never pulled back from clashing with the institutions, even when to do so has cost us suffering, division and so on. I'm thinking of the 6 December demonstrations in Rome, the government we brought down, the struggles with the local authorities to get our clinics, the occupations of the hospitals, the struggles during difficult years in which traditional movements were already partially paralysed by the Christian Democrat-PCI vice. It seems to me that by doing all that we entered into the real live class struggle in Italy, changing in a revolutionary direction some of the games which the political (male) bigwigs thought they had sewn up. All this meant that we lived as political subjects within a revolutionary programme which couldn't be just this or that political party, but was the wider and more valid one of the class struggle of the proletarian masses for their liberation. In Italy this struggle does not always slavishly follow the plans and objectives of this or that party.

The women of Prima Linea then tell us that the law for freeing abortion was the institutional response to women's just demands, and that hospitals and clinics are today the state's network to control the proletarian body, and they they spit in our faces saying that this operation was made possible by the ambiguity of the feminist movement. We can't have this.

This is the logic of self-destruction, projecting the enemy onto ourselves and then destroying ourselves in order to destroy the enemy.

I will carry on saying that backstreet abortions had to be and still need to be brought to an end, and that if today state abortion is card-indexing the proletarian body, backstreet abortions were and are the death of the proletarian woman's body. And another thing, you Prima Linea women: where do you go to have your abortions when you need them? Where do you go when you need contraceptives? Can you afford a private doctor, or like us do you use the spaces, restricted as they may be, won by the mass women's struggle?

If the state has taken advantage of my struggle to give me something and distort other issues, the enemy is not me or my struggle but the state and its institutions.

My weapon is separatism   *Margherita, Movimento Femminista Romano*

The personal and collective analysis I made with the women of my collective and of my small group of *autocoscienza* has led me to a point which, according to me, is one of the most problematic for women: namely, the need for power. Here comes the difficulty: what kind of power? Male power perhaps, which is based on oppression, abuse and institutions? Or women's power? Which one? Has it ever existed? And what are the means to achieve it? I do not really know what it is and whether I really and absolutely want it, but I know it is for me a contractual means to live better and better in a male world which is completely indifferent to what is not to its advantage. In order to exist in a capitalist patriarchy based on power-relationships, I must have – in any case – instruments which allow me to use my strength, women's strength, and to transform it into a collective means of power. Practising women gave me assurance on this point: this force of mine has been so far undervalued, first of all by me. I used to see only one real power, male power, and I did not realize that male power existed only because my force, which could have been used for myself and other women, was building up and supporting man's castle of power. At this point – and it is not so paradoxical – I vindicate the fact that, if there has been – and there still is – power, this is a female power, which has been enslaved and stolen by men. However, I know it is difficult to see this clearly if you do not have a separatist practice of relationships with women.

There is often desperation for other women, as well as generical and dispersive anger, lack of self-esteem and self-consciousness, blindness about their own needs and desires. These motives come into play in the choices those women make, choices which are actually against themselves and myself. In this sense, I may be interested in talking about 'women terrorists'; judgements of merit, acquittal and blaming certainly do not either help or enrich me.

The problem of women shooting is similar to that of women identifying their needs with those of men. It is an old story, not the present story of twenty women of the Red Brigades. There have always been women supporting men, but we have continued our action. Furthermore, the conviction of separatism as my only revolutionary weapon for victory is more and more strongly rooted. I know that my force lies in a clear separation from the violent male, and in a strengthened relationship with women. This is the only way to achieve more female power. Afterwards, we shall decide together what to do with this power.

Non-violent, but for how long? *Filo*

To speak clearly, in principle and for my political convictions I am against both political and physical violence. Now, after the events in Turin, I have been called in question as a feminist. Sincerely, I did not feel up to condemning the women comrades who made the precise choice of armed struggle. Too often, after the death of too many comrades and the attack on the radio station Radio Città Futura, have I felt an uncontrollable anger. I do not know whether I would have managed to dominate my 'violent' impulses if I had had a weapon in my hands. I wondered anxiously for how long I would be able to sustain my non-violent practice. My daily life is a continuous violence. It is a violence not to have my space, a physical space, living with three other people in one room, not to have a moment for myself, because I cannot find a place in this horrible city to live my own life, find myself, things and people. It is a violence to live by makeshift, degrading myself in menial jobs in order to survive, when I need very little to go on living. It is a violence to wish something and not be able to buy it because that would mean renouncing lunch and dinner.

It is useless to give more examples. Many comrades have lived these same situations: I could go on for ever. Every gesture we make is a more or less evident consequence of a series of acts of violence of the present system.

How many of us have been living – unlawfully – in a students' residence hall, the ghetto *par excellence* of many comrades coming from different places? Well, I live in this situation. I fall asleep at night anguished in case the police arrive to throw me out, or worse, because I cannot live there. It is not simple fear; it has already happened that I woke up at 5 a.m. when armed policemen arrived, bursting doors and wardrobes open and throwing everything up in the air in search of God knows what! Perhaps something accusing you of being on the other side of the barricade, because – according to the police – all comrades living in the students' residence hall are either supporters of the Red Brigades or delinquents. Not to speak of the squalid relationships among students themselves, many of whom are members of the Communist party, or sympathizers with it, who make your life impossible even in the smallest details, like turning the radio on at full volume at six in the morning. What can you do? Go away? Yes, but where, and how? I still come back to the harassing question: for how long shall I react to violence with non-violence?

A great love is needed in order to understand   *Maria and other comrades*

'We wrote these lines putting together our experiences, our emotions, our struggles, because we wanted to explain and to communicate them', said the women who wrote this piece as they gave it to us.

Only a great love can push you into making decisions which bring into play your whole life, and a great love is needed in order to understand. A lot of love and a real effort of participation. If you feel distant from all the monstrous crimes, tortures and barbarities, if you can't bear to see them, if you think you can hide away in your own sheltered places where you feel safe and protected and where you don't feel involved, then you will never be able to understand how a woman can reach the point of shooting another woman who 'was only doing her job'. The people who planned and constructed the ovens in the Nazi camps were only doing their job.

Reaching the decision to shoot is the result of a situation where power in all its forms has for years shown that it can act with impunity in the most illegal way, with no denunciation, petition, peaceful demonstration or election able to put an end to its bloody policy. There are so many horrors to remember, so many massacres: from Vajont to Piazza Fontana, so many robberies, from Belice to Friuli, Italcasse, Lockheed, the thousands who died at work in Seveso and at Icma, the children in Naples . . . and who will pay for all this? Who is paying for all this blood? Magistrates, doctors, policemen, jailers, bosses and their underlings, all of them have tried as hard as they can to make a profit, to make a name for themselves, to get rich; and they succeeded, they have succeeded for thirty years, sure that they would not be punished. Now things have changed and they know that 'nothing will go unpunished.'

Women's participation in this new form of political action can certainly not be put down to a sense of competition, or the need to show that they have courage too. A woman who decides to have a backstreet abortion or to do it herself with a knitting needle because she hasn't got the money for the 'golden spoon' is far braver than our General Della Chiesa, who goes around in his armoured car with his armed escort. Cretins, idiots, some in bad faith and others who are just plain stupid, drag out their ridiculous pseudo-psychoanalytical crap and start going on about penis envy, which makes us take to the gun; or they go on about the world of reptiles and mammals and females as bearers of life; then they draw pictures of angelic women who are always ready to understand, to comfort and to put up with everything because that is our natural function . . .

Maria: 'When I was a child they were always saying to me "You're a little girl, there are things you mustn't do," If a little boy thumped me and all I did was cry, everybody would pet me and try to make me feel better, but if I got thumped and got my own back by giving him a good thrashing, then I suddenly became a little monster to be told off and punished: "Shame on you, you're acting just like a little boy!"' As we grow up we always have to respect these roles. *Roberta*: 'As an adolescent I had to pretend to be afraid when I wasn't, so the boys could feel big and tough and could "protect" me. If I ever strayed from this role they looked at me really suspiciously.' *Manuela*: 'It was the same thing at demonstrations: all those "cocktails" we carried but never threw! "Hold this . . . go down that road and wait for us at the corner . . ." They set off to attack the armoured cars or the Christian Democrat headquarters and there you were with your "nice" dress on and your plastic bag full of molotov cocktails, going through the police with a shy, stupid smile, and you even had to put up with their comments on your arse, and then you went round the corner to wait for your companions who needed fresh supplies.'

And then the 'orders of the day' meetings, men only of course, and when there were posters to be put up in fascist areas it was 'the women don't come tonight', and when there was someone to keep tabs on you were used to make 'the flirting couple', but any action was carried out only by the men. Bit by bit we managed to take part in some action too, but with the men there you feel like a hanger-on. They are in control of things, they decide, even if more than once they showed they couldn't keep their nerve as well as we could, and they didn't have their wits about them as much.

The fact is that for centuries we have been used to dealing daily with pain, blood and death. Giving birth the way they make you do it even today often means hours of torture, which not even the most refined followers of Videla would inflict on you. Bringing up a child takes constant courage and watchfulness. We've all had the experience of snatching him back as he leans too far out of the window, or having to decide what to do in two seconds flat when he swallows something that's choking him. These are the exceptional gifts we women have, which inspire so much fear and which after the action in Turin led to the front-page headline in the *Corriere della Sera*: 'If women start shooting it's the end.' Yes, it's the end, the end of their disgusting world of violence and exploitation.

We have always walked along different paths   *A comrade, Women's Movement in Turin*

Turin – As I was reading the Prima Linea communiqué, and then the rest of the page about armed women published by *Quotidiano Donna*, I realized that the people I should be talking to are the militants of the armed party, who it seems to me are urgently wanting to know who is with them and who isn't. But there's also a more 'political' reason. This is a knotty old problem which we drag about with us, and it seems to me it's time to talk about it.

The Prima Linea militants are asking us to put an end to long years' experience, to take up arms, to finish off and dismember the 'class enemy'. But who is the most dangerous enemy? One is Professor Grio [head of the gynaecological ward at the hospital of St Anna in Turin], whom we were trying to get into the defendant's dock, and whom the armed party decided to shoot. Another is Professor Grio, back in St Anna to receive an open-armed and jubilant welcome from his medical colleagues, all his sins forgiven. A strange mechanism is set up whereby punishment eliminates the crime, indeed restores the guilty party to a state of virginity. But let's go on, to the prisons, and let's look at the results of the 'policy' of dismemberment. After the last wounding, of Raffaella Napolitano, scores of letters of resignation and transfer requests began flooding out of the Nuove. A great result, apparently. For terrorism, which strikes at symbols, what greater victory than to inspire your adversary with fear?

The problem is that ordinary people are a thousand times more frightened than they were before. Indeed some strange things are beginning to be said and heard about the relationship between prisoners and their relatives; they are trying to convince people that contacts between imprisoned terrorists and those outside are relayed through these relatives. Before long, helpless as usual, we'll see prison life deteriorating even further, while the screws who have 'given up' will simply be replaced. Faced with a power which maintains and strengthens itself by the mass support which it is now managing to create, how many drops of 'proletarian counter-power' has the armed party managed to produce? After the shooting at St Anna, have women been better treated at all, have more abortions been done, has the power of the doctors been dented in the slightest?

You might ask what good it does to say all this. It helps me, it helps my comrades in Turin. For years a doubt had been nagging at us, which was to wonder how it was that women who had experienced common struggle and growth had turned down such antagonistic roads?

I've been trying to sort this out for some time now, looking at my relationship with violence, the fear of life with no security. I've examined my relationship with the masculine, even with that male which is a party, and the need a lot of us feel for it. In reality women can easily get to the point of armed militancy, even more easily than men. As for violence my impression is that we never did come to a dividing fork in the road, but that the divisions were already there, underneath it all. By 'political practice' we understand quite opposite things. We ask if and where efforts have been made to articulate a discourse on emancipation or a plan of liberation which would reach out to women who are different from us. This discourse is by no means over, and that includes the militant women of the armed party.

Pushed by the violence of our desires . . . *Anonymous*

You're asking me about woman today as a militant in fighting units. I can't tell you anything based on personal experience, because I have never belonged to any armed organizations. But I can tell you about some of the things I've thought about over the past few years, starting with my work in prison, relationships I developed inside, my knowledge of some fighting units right from their very beginnings, and my being a little more aware as a woman.

Are men and women driven differently to take up arms in order to change the world? Put like that the question is ridiculous. It depends what level of motivation we are talking about. The conscious motives are the same, obviously, the political analysis, revolutionary perspective and so on. The individual motives of character and personal history are infinite, and naturally have nothing to do with the sex of the person. And yet a collective female unconscious exists, and so perhaps there are profound motivations specific to the fact of our being women, which can become channelled into the armed struggle.

Perhaps it's our relationship with reality. We have a relationship with reality that is simultaneously concrete and fantastic. Men have a relationship which is abstract and rational. I'm not speaking about any man or any woman in particular, but things which have settled into our unconscious down the ages and which we have to get to grips with, even if to rebel against them. Man organizes reality into rational patterns, and superimposes a whole lot of other ideal patterns by which he can modify reality. So he chooses a strategy for struggle based on abstract but precise political considerations. Women on the other hand have always been used to being practical and, the other side of the coin, to creating fantasies. We are used to small, daily, concrete acts which visibly and immediately modify reality. At home we wash, iron, clean up, cook. But even in areas of work which are traditionally our preserve we are not the ones to produce ideas or plans; rather, we carry them out, we translate male plans into concrete terms. It is precisely this ant-like concreteness which brings into being our grasshopper-like imagination, our dimension of fantasy. It's a reaction, a secret and private revenge, proof of our own worth. We don't think the transformation of the world comes about by synthesis, by rational analysis of forces or whatever. We actually imagine the new world in a fundamentally analytical way, and we start with the particular: it means not being afraid to go out at night, it means discovering a new dignity, it means being able to contemplate the future of our handicapped child without terror . . . We are talking here about a different mental process.

The duality of our relationship with reality can also carry us towards armed struggle, especially after so many years of disorientation. We want to see practical results, we think it's possible to go beyond the abstraction of round-table politics, we want to see some concrete action. The urge to construct forms of action for ourselves is sometimes very strong, since we've had to put up with so many years of empty speeches. And imagination? It helps us to bear the clash with reality; in this case it helps us to avoid seeing what we don't want to see. Certainly it slips into and supports fanaticism. But men become fanatical under the yoke of their ideological schemas while we, more often than not, are driven by the violence of our dreams.

Assuming that everything I've said so far hasn't been completely wide of the mark, perhaps we can begin to see why it is that when there is an armed struggle going on women, both past and present, have always proved such good material to work with, have been so invaluable as organizers, providing an irreplaceable, concrete network of support.

I'll say it again; I'm not talking about individual choices or circumstances, but about something inside us which sooner or later, in one way or another, will always come out; it is something very ancient which comes from way back, even beyond our lives, something that you feel as a memory, even as a child.

I remember when I worked a number of years ago in a support group for the Algerian National Liberation Front. I remember feeling useful and important because I worked as driver, interpreter, secretary to the comrades, or because they sent me to buy a car or pick up a cache of rifles. I was satisfied because I was *doing* things, even if it was never me who took decisions, even if I barely knew what was going on. The Algerian revolution was round the corner, and that was enough for me. I just imagined the revolution, when it would happen, and I thought of it as a big party, a little sad maybe but wonderful, and at the end of it the comrades would invite me too, because after all I too ... and I would go to Algeria with all its red flags and music, the hugs and the frenzy to begin building up again, and love which would find its place there ... how often did I lovingly imagine the scene ... and instead what happened? After the revolution, which found itself somewhat betrayed, our comrades all went off to Cabilia to wage a bit of civil war; all in the nick or killed; no party. I never got to Algeria and who knows what is left inside me from that period of my life; something is left, certainly, but not what I imagined then.

Certainly, I saw the birth of the NAP [Nuclei Armati Proletari; Proletarian Armed Nuclei]. Since I took part in the prisoners' movement, I could see it coming. A long time ago it was possible to talk to some comrades from NAP. I was desperately opposed to their plans, and I did everything I could to convince them. What a ridiculous word, 'convince'! Many of them are dead and live on in my memory like brothers. They were men, I don't recall any women coming in at the start of NAP from the prisoners' movement; any that there were – and I never met any of them – came from abroad.

Now it's common knowledge that the embryonic political movement of the detainees found a detonator in 1968 and the following years, when so many comrades were coming and going from jail; from that ferment of activity sprang the Rome prison collective, the prison commission Lotta Continua and other groups dotted around.

What was not clear at the time to those of us who worked on the outside was why comrades in jail felt the need to join together even over objectives which were 'modest', or 'reductive' as Lotta Continua liked to put it: the right to vote, for example, the right to one's sexuality in prison, the abolition of censorship of the post and the newspapers, the abolition of criminal records, compulsory call-ups and so on. Too many of us thought the revolution was going to happen the next day; for people who had to get through on average ten years inside, these issues raised a lot of hopes destined to be brutally disappointed when finally they got out, with no job, no arms and perhaps repatriation papers in their hand. Then Lotta Continua went in for some self-criticism, changed its political strategy and finished up dissolving the prison commission. But in the meantime the repression inside had got very heavy, and the growth of the movement had a logic of its own, which allowed it to ignore the directives of the organizations; it was easy to foresee a bit of a reaction, a bit of adventurism.

I remember Sergio, who got out of prison when he was 17 and turned up at my house. He had always been a thief and when he was of an age to be convicted he'd been put inside. He was a street-kid from Naples who at the time only spoke dialect. His eyes were shy and watchful, as he tried to work out quickly and infallibly whether he could love and trust people or not. He wanted to make spaghetti, he was kind to my parents, he greedily read everything he could lay his hands on, he listened, he asked questions, he was always in a hurry, a damnable but very understandable hurry. Once I told him the famous sentence 'The fundamental qualities of a revolutionary are irony and patience', and he smiled: 'Must have been a bourgeois, that one.' He went to work as a bodyguard for Sofri: 'I'd die for him', he used to tell me. Instead he got himself killed with the NAP, together with Luca Mantini, in the shooting at Piazza Alberti, Florence, in 1974.

There are several reasons for the late birth of the female protest movement, which is still very sporadic if you don't count the women in the fighting units. The first might seem banal, but in 1969 there were no female comrades going into prison, and so it was difficult to make contacts. Who with? How could we be at all sure of them? Another reason is women's passivity, what I call our 'inner prison', the need for chains, the desire for expiation which all of us have inside us in one way or another, because sacrifice is ingrained in our existence, ingrained in our history over the centuries. This need to give without sparing ourselves, and to pay for it at the same time, to pay a very high price, almost religiously, is not an illness; it's a way, however twisted it might be, of somehow legitimizing ourselves, as if only by expiating both our sins and those of others can we win, I don't know, the right to be loved, liked, considered, in other words some kind of reflected identity. Women are extraordinarily resigned to the organization of prison correction. Sometimes I've even heard them taking pleasure in it, like some kind of self-flagellation: 'It serves me right, it's right like this, I have to pay for my mistakes . . .' and so on. This never happens among men. All us women have within us a sense of sacrifice as normality, which has taken root within us. Besides, this prison masochism is not really any worse than the other kinds of masochism of the women 'outside', who excel in building themselves horrific cages in which they can suffer and which it takes them a lifetime, if ever, to get out of. And all this goes for me too, for example.

In prison there are women detained for crimes which their men committed. Unlike their male comrades, women don't get together on the basis of politics, or games, or gangs. Instead they go to mass, they take communion, each of them believes she is a case apart, and that her fate may be very unfortunate, but it is hers alone. They don't think of breaking the rules collectively, on the whole they accept their sentences, deep down they are on the side of those who punish them.

They are in a state of monstrous insecurity. This is something of what I mean by an 'inner prison'.

When the prisoners' movement was born, we tried to establish contacts with the women detainees. The first link in the chain was a woman who had been a prostitute and who had had enormous difficulties, but was not altogether unaware of the political implications of her condition. Through her we began the usual contacts: books, letters, discussion of the news, the search for a possible future platform for struggle ... but we found ourselves in the role of patronesses, which they made us play, asking us for money, recommendations, information on the private life of someone or other. We never got away from just two main tracks, one of which was spending a huge and frustrating amount of energy only to feel like a Lady of San Vicenzo, the other becoming indoctrinators, following a political line such as 'Come here, dear comrade, you don't know anything and I'll explain everything to you.'

Those women had no major part to play in their lives, and they were especially impervious to what we thought should have been their 'logical' rebellion. Yet if we had thought about it a little more instead of just giving up, we would have understood something not only about them but about ourselves.

It's very difficult to uncover the real source of rebellion in a woman, and it's true that when you find it you have no need to nourish it; it's like a fire which is more violent the deeper it goes. It doesn't need to be nourished, as we naively thought following the models which the male prisons had imposed on us, by reasoning, short programmes to follow, righteous indignation over the speculation on the cost of food. The questions which we should have been asking both them and ourselves were much older than that: why am I writing to you? Why am I your sister? Who are you? What do you still want to do with your life? What can you still do with it? Is it right to experience love the way you (or I) have experienced it? Perhaps there is some other way ... there has to be some other way ... and what is this love anyway? What are you sure of in your life? Is there a free zone or have you too never managed to say 'Now, that's it'? Or perhaps you were too scared and so you lived in the dim shadow of received truths, then you found yourself here and you marked out your monstrous little refuge with its curtains and Saint Theresa on the wall and the doll lying on the straw? So many other questions and missed opportunities! It seems to me now that this was the way not only to release energy and radical feeling in women inside, but also to recognize them in us, which we always need to do.

As for the other women, the ones in the armed struggle, it's a completely different matter, and they should talk about it for themselves. I believe that all differences disappear: you are not there, you're neither a man nor a woman, you are the struggle, you are one with it. You become the task, the function, the signal. What counts is the integrity of the group, its material and affective cohesiveness. And this seems only right when you are tied together not only by faith, by complicity, by fear, but also by the monstrous sacrifice of having to watch your comrades die. I also believe that if you go down that road, it's the first step that decides everything; after that you are on a path with only one possible direction.

A look 'outside' the armed struggle   *Roberta Tatafiore*

It's often been said on the left that we can't form any judgement about the armed struggle without ourselves becoming judges and policemen. When Moro was kidnapped I often found myself wondering what was meant by the slogan 'neither with the Red Brigades nor with the state', which after all seemed to describe my position perfectly. It meant precisely not offering any judgement. But sometimes, in reality, the armed struggle induced in me a feeling of fear, the refuge of exorcism, the recognition of complicity. And these are all implicitly ways of judging.

I would like always to be able to say that I 'understand' someone involved in armed struggle, and when I see in the life of one of these people some personal anguish, the consciously calculated choice between the subjective and the objective, or else the confusing lack of liberating outlooks, I would like never to be called upon to pass judgement. Otherwise it would be like allowing other people to intrude into my life: it's a matter of self-love. But I know that making the individual responsible is only a luxury enabling me to find my way through the mesh of dominant values. It's no small thing, but I would also like to see an ethics of understanding social phenomena which made it possible *always* to defend individual choices against social responsibilities.

But the armed struggle also brings me face to face with the world of its victims. And the victims have often been people who are more or less in the service of this system, or who keep it going. To be able to say this seems to me a liberty which I would like to retain, because it's a liberty which a lot of people have got into their heads. Who would deny that most 'ordinary' people didn't even know what Aldo Moro's theory of 'parallel convergences' even meant? And when the kidnapping and murder happened, for a lot of people he was the famous victim of the detective story of the century. A bit like when I was a kid and my mother told me about Lindbergh, the first man to fly across the Atlantic, whose son was kidnapped and killed by a gang of criminals. The only 'social' thought in my mother's story and my imagination was that 'Well now! Famous people can come unstuck too!' But the victims were ordinary people too, they were left in frozen vans all night, and I felt a vague but helpless kind of pity. The only exception was the murder of Guido Rossa: working-class culture has tradition and roots in our country, and I saw this culture contorting itself in order to understand this business of the armed struggle: a participation expressed by the anger in the factories and the people at Guido Rossa's funeral.

So I realize that my only terms of reference are the values expressed by the mass politics and culture of the left. These values are traditional, with terms like 'class struggle', 'transition', 'insurrection', and each of these terms is a dictum made more and more meaningless by the reality of the personal and social transformations we are living through. So they are not much use to me. But as I live day by day with politics and my feelings, there are two values which I know I can't give up: the search for a different conception of justice and a passion for the truth. This still means understanding, clarifying and not judging, but on a different level: with regard not to the people involved in the armed struggle, but to the fact of the armed struggle itself.

There was a series of (irreversible) death sentences, all of them accompanied by communiqués – pure propaganda. Then, in the summer – thanks to the existence of a paper like *Lotta Continua* – came the 'looking inside the Red Brigades'; two sections of the armed struggle set themselves to tell us about their analyses, their motives, their strategies.

I don't understand why so many people seized on the 'Red Brigades rigid' document, and without a moment's hesitation defined them as 'fossils'. The 'soft' and the 'hard' elements both seem to me to be members of the same family, on edge because things are going badly; they can't stand each other any more, so decide to have a public squabble so as to drag other people in and fight over who supports whom. And it's only too clear that I could be one of these 'other people', as I pore over leaden column after column of two sets of analyses and deductions which both claim in their turn to be different but which are absolutely identical on one fundamental point: both choose to organize clandestinely.

But this word is not neutral for me, and I don't want to be scandalized by it. I'm only too well aware that it excludes subjects from which it derives its tortuous route, that the limit of the clandestine is aphasia, in its shaping of consciousness and its forms of organization. So the problem is not the clandestine in itself, but the choice of the clandestine as a precise instrument with which it is decided to maintain contact between those who want to form a society, and those who want to fight it. I don't believe that the instrument used to communicate can be different to the way one arrived at the choice to communicate. When the act is secret, calculated, it still needs to be thought 'elsewhere', somewhere other with regard to the consciousness of the person who lives, struggles, makes demands, achieves, changes and is changed, who doesn't make weighing up in advance the life of others, be it an enemy or even an army of enemies, the be-all and end-all of his militancy. To fight with a gun is like taking it upon oneself to think for others, not only the moment of rupture, of revolt, but holding to hostage an ideal of life which lay behind the rupture, bringing it about.

I would like always to 'see' people, but the dead bodies of the armed struggle have oppressed me, throwing back in my face any effort to find a different concept of justice. I am always alarmed when I glimpse in the writings or accounts of people involved in the armed struggle actions destined to corrupt or become corrupted, to demand solidarity, to impose silence. Actions by individuals so meticulous in expounding political praxis, actions rewarded with the careless indifference of an increasing number of people to the intrigues, the injustices carried out within these intrigues, the dazzling spectacle of provocation and repression. My passion for the truth, and for space in which to exercise it, has certainly stumbled at the threshold of the armed struggle.

MILITARY SERVICE FOR WOMEN

Long live utopia *Edda Billi*, 1982

At this point everything is clear, there is no doubt about it. The difference between emancipation and liberation is before our eyes, dear comrades. Emancipation: a survival on a par with man. Liberation: a life on a par with women. It is not clear through which 'sick' mechanism the male teaches and decides over death. His much-praised 'transcendence' (for this reason he would become distinct from the divine mothers, so the wise men say) is in his totality, addressed to destruction, to wars, to massacres. Wars that have been waged, cold wars, armed truces, balancing acts of terror, the strongest abusing the weakest. Everywhere, under every sky, in whatever economy. They would make us believe in a conquest of equality when they give us military service 'as a present'. Let us not be fooled. The armies, the weapons, the bombs, all dirty, to a greater or lesser extent, that are being prepared are destined to be used only for one thing. Do we really need to say which one? So, we want to suggest something: let us close down all the barracks, for men as well. And instead of this structure of death, we should build structures of life for life. Utopia? Fine. Long live utopia.

Moving out of a violent prehistory   *Marlena Fabris*, 1982

Reform? Revolution? Neither of these much discussed terms seem to fit the draft bill proposed by Accame, but innovation is for sure the feature that characterizes its full meaning. This is true especially on two fundamental counts.

Firstly, there is the establishment of an entirely autonomous civil element within the structure of national defence, conceived not only to act against any enemy, but also, and in my opinion most importantly, to preserve the territory and the environment. To create soldiers who work with shovels and pickaxes or with words and caring gestures is by definition to create an anti-army, to emerge from a violent prehistory that identifies strength with weapons.

Secondly, we have, in a situation where women are joining an army which has been so radically transformed, absolute equality with men in their offices and privileges. As a real 'citizen', at last, according to article 52 of the constitution, any woman will be able to find, in this totally new dimension, new areas and new situations in which she can put into practice in everyday life that right which the law offers and guarantees her.

Draft of a law on military service for women   *Ministry of Defence*, 1986

Article 1 Female citizens participate – on a voluntary basis – in national examinations and training courses for the recruitment of professional officers and regular army forces, and of military troops in voluntary service in the armed forces.

The aptitude and fitness requirements will be established on the basis of appropriate physical parameters and coefficients to be established by ministerial decision.

Article 2   The female military forces cannot be used in fighting activities and assignments.

The activities, assignments and units to which female military forces are appointed are established by a decree of the Ministry of Defence, on the proposal of the Chief of General Staff of Defence, having consulted the Chiefs of General Staff of the army, the navy and the air force.

Article 3   The legal status, disciplinary regulations, promotions and pay formulae governing female military forces are subject to the same rules as those in force for male military forces.

The rules in force in the civil service concerning the protection of the conditions of women are extended to the female military forces.

Within two years of the present law coming into force, the government of the republic, by presidential decree, and at the proposal of the Minister of Defence, is delegated to issue regulations about the legal, disciplinary and promotional status that may be necessary in order to render the body of legislation of the first subsection above compatible with the employment and service of the female military forces.

Article 4   The Minster of Defence, at the proposal of the Chiefs of General Staff of the army, of the navy and of the air force, is authorized to issue, annually, and in agreement with the Chancellor of the Exchequer, the decrees necessary to determine the quotas, the corps, the categories, the specialities and specializations of each Military Force in which the recruitment of female forces will take place, in relation also to the functional and employment requirements, on condition that the constituent parts of these organizations remain unchanged.

The aforesaid decrees will be issued from the second year after the date of the present law coming into force.

Article 5   The economic burden due to the application of the present law is estimated at a total of 9 billion lire, of which 1 billion lire per annum are allocated for 1987–9 and 2 billion lire per annum for 1990–2. The above economic burden will be at the expense of the budget on chapter 4005 of the Ministry of Defence forecast for the financial year 1987 and the corresponding chapters for the successive years.

The allocation for the above chapter 4005 cannot exceed, in the years 1988–9, the amount resulting from the budget approved by the government for the year 1987 and for the years 1987–9, exempt from the reductions in the above subsection and increased according to the anticipated rate of inflation.

It's only the first step towards real parity   *Elena Marinucci,* 1986

With the opening up again of the debate on the question of military service, fresh thought and initiatives also have to be given to and on the question of military service for women.

This is the situation in which Spadolini's draft law (*DDL Spadolini*) is inserted, retracing the steps of the previous draft, presented as a government initiative in 1981 by the then minister, Lelio Lagorio.

This is a draft law which aims to apply article 15 of the constitution, which guarantees to 'all citizens of either sex' the possibility of 'access to public offices'. Law 9 in February 1963, N.66, had applied this constitutional precept by opening to women the doors of the last professions which had up to that point been an exclusively male preserve: those of the bench and diplomacy. The same law announced measures which would follow, designed to provide the structures for 'the enrolment of women into the armed forces'.

That was twenty-three years ago and Italian women are still denied access to the academies; neither can they apply for positions in the military magistracy or the Forestry Corps, for this very reason: that a military career is still reserved exclusively for men.

This is why we can no longer accept a prejudiced and ideological refusal of a reform which cannot be put off any longer.

Spandolini's draft law, however, is unsatisfactory in its present form.

It is so first of all because, while article 3 states that the 'legal status, disciplinary regulations, promotions and pay formulae governing female military personnel are subject to the same rules as those in force for male military forces', the preceding article 2 excludes women from 'fighting activities and assignments', limiting placements for female personnel and so limiting their career. There's more too. Not only does it leave much of the delicate material in question to ministerial decree, it also gives the Ministry of Defence the responsibility of issuing year by year the decrees necessary to determine, according to its own requirements, the quotas, categories and specialities of each service into which female personnel will be recruited.

We don't know how far the willingness of Minister Spadolini, declared to the press, for a more equal law will be concretized into an amendment, which the Minister himself should present, to the government draft law.

In any case our position will remain the same. Nor should it enter into it that in nearly all European countries women are excluded from 'fighting activities and assignments'. These are all old laws, passed when these countries hadn't yet introduced legislation for equality in the field of work.

When we discuss today a law which opens the door of a military career to women, we have to remember Law 903 of 1967, and the cultural change brought about by the presence of women in every field of activity.

There is still the problem of the draft, in other words whether the 'duty' of military service should be extended to all women.

Indeed, while article 51 of the constitution guarantees the right of access to all professions, article 52 imposes the 'sacred duty' of defending our country. A reading of the prepared notes for the Constituent Council confirms that women were not meant to be excluded; indeed, an amendment aiming to clarify that this 'sacred duty' referred only to male citizens was rejected.

So access to a military career is a right and therefore a choice which will be made, once the draft approved today by the Council of Ministers becomes law, by the few or many women who will discover in themselves an aptitude for this kind of activity. We will need to continue to think about the question of duty.

Women have never claimed it for themselves. If it's true that men are dehumanized by the fact that they alone are 'called to arms' when they come of age, it's also true that women are burdened with more or less all of the duties tied to maternity, looking after the family and the house.

Besides, the extension of the draft to women can only be discussed in the context of a more far-reaching reform. This has already been anticipated by the proposals of the socialist Balzamo, which seek not only a reduction of military service for everyone but also the possibility for men and women alike to opt for civil service instead.

We don't like rose-tinted uniforms   *Lidia Menapace*, 1986

It's all very well being well mannered, tolerant, open to all forms of reasoning: but taking seriously idiotic ideas seems to me a sign not of civic virtue but of mutual stupidity. I'm referring to voluntary military service in the armed forces for women, 17–26 years old, unmarried or at least without children. Surely we only have to put it like that to realize it's something we should reject out of hand? Parity isn't a question of aping what's already there, it's a space for diversity. This is not even a formal sort of charity – come off it!

I'll give an example. If a 'green' biologist, one of those given over to 'nature', were to say (and there are such people around) that 'betrayal by the male is less serious than by the female, because at times the male has an impelling need to discharge his seed', would it occur to anyone to take any notice of such rubbish, perhaps trying to put forward the opposite argument that between one period and another women go through hormonal upheavals as a result of which they might behave like so many followers of Bacchus? No, any reasonable person would say that this way of doing biology smacks politically of Nazism, and that in the human species there is no such thing as 'objective betrayal': everything depends on what agreement the two partners have. In the human species instincts are culturally developed, not least because the species has developed a brain rather than claws, tusks or other tools.

However, if generals (American, for the most part) 'discover' on the basis of research and questionnaires that women are just as intellectually capable as men and perhaps more so, but they can carry lighter weights and can't manage the regulation step of 90 centimetres as long as men, instead of having everybody rolling around in the aisles laughing at them, the figures are quoted and discussed on precisely that basis. It's just as if I were to write that men are just as intellectually capable as women, but have a huge amount of difficulty with pregnancy: and then waited for the applause to start.

The request for women volunteers to go and do a bit of service in the barracks is a result of a fall in population and the growing alienation of young men from a service which has no sense, in the hope that, by 'mobilizing' the reserve army to go and be the reserve in the army, they might also make it a bit more appealing. Any reasonable person who wasn't also a general or minister of defence might begin to wonder about starting with more modest solutions, such as having civil structures carry out the services to the army. Is there really a need for military health care, for example? If you listen to the horror stories of boys who have been in military hospitals, they are more of a danger to health than to disease. Do we really need military cooks, military administrators, military judges? Couldn't we go to the market-place for some of these services, to civil justice to defend our rights? Apart from anything else, even these few ideas would have the effect of narrowing the gulf between the army and civil life, and this would have at least some benefit.

I shall go on, with the sort of arguments that even generals and ministers can understand. I won't even try to suggest pacifist, antimilitary and feminist 'utopias' which are against armies as a matter of principle, or which try to show how useless and even damaging they are in European national states. My point is this: if armies are having trouble for demographic reasons, instead of wanting fewer women who have children (17–26 is the most common period in which to have children), why don't they make motherhood a more attractive option? Not by giving subsidies, which have already failed in France, but with policies which make the world at least an acceptable place for anyone who happens to be born into it. But no: the generals 'reason' differently: they say that the fall in population reduces the male contingents genetically able to be soldiers, and for this reason women must take the place of some of them. And women, all of a sudden, suddenly become genetically disposed to be soldiers.

It's very strange, but the only other person I heard 'reason' like this was a well-known young professor at the polytechnic in Genova, who then put it in writing. So I can quote it, because when I heard it with my own ears I almost thought he was joking. In the middle of a debate the illustrious lecturer began: 'Up to a few years ago our Faculty was *immune* to female presence: but since the falling population restricted the pool of males genetically predisposed to study engineering, it was necessary also to admit a few women.' He still encouraged them to go into teaching or to study literature instead, because being so undisciplined ('they don't like drawing for eight hours, and they want all the formulae explained'), they show that they are not really suited to the polytechnic, 'an institution invented by Napoleon for military purposes'. The wonderful power of logic! Or rather, as a witty woman biologist from France puts it, the power of anthropology.

We've listened to enough of this rubbish, and it isn't even funny. There is a relationship with what we have always said and written about the army, about institutions of this type, and this proposal isn't the moment to draw conclusions from our thinking about the role of the army or other possible forms of defence. We also have some responsibility towards the girls who are interested in doing military service: they have the right to know that the whole thing has nothing to do with parity or equality, and they will be very much the second team. Besides, given that when they are asked about their choice they say that at least it's a job, it's clear that the answer lies in the creation of more jobs which are *useful* rather than *damaging*. If they want to run and shoot then we should make available to them, too, adequate sports facilities and games. If they want to be more independent of their families, raising levels of attainment at school, civil service and the possibility of work are healthier and more positive ways for them to reach autonomy, rather than unqualified, shoddy army service.

We should be talking rather about why even today girls have less access to work (employment and unemployment continue to increase at different paces, employment much more slowly than unemployment), less access to sports facilities and less personal autonomy in choosing and organizing holidays and trips, less knowledge of the world.

CHERNOBYL, 1986

Call for a demonstration *L'Unità*

Rome – Women and the 'Chernobyl aftermath'. A national demonstration will be held next Saturday in Rome, organized by this city's feminist movement. The procession will leave Piazza Esedra at 6 p.m. This is the text which appeals to women to join the demonstration.

The Chernobyl incident was not only the explosion of a nuclear power station, but yet another symptom of planetary contradictions which now affect not only the powers that be and the living standards of all, but also the very existence of mankind and its ability to reproduce.

This is not an accident or an error, but the foreseeable result of a deceitful concept of progress and of an abstract scientific practice forgetful of the material aspects of life. Nowadays it is particularly necessary to continue to clarify the distance which lies between ourselves and those who would have us be silent accomplices of choices which we do not share.

Women refute a way of thinking which, by pretending to be universal when in reality it expresses only the partiality of a single sex, pursues, in the name of everyone, an idea of false well-being which threatens to bring about the destruction of mankind and nature; they hold against it a way of thinking which cares about life and which has always been with women throughout the centuries of history.

With feminism women have brought this way of thinking into the construction of their very subjectivity and into a political practice able to produce different ways of life and knowledge.

We know that there are differences between women and that in these last few years we have continued to produce different strategies.

But there is, today more than ever, one awareness that unites us all: women want to and must have a say in things, and realize themselves as a sex/gender with relation to their history and thought. We know, too, that affirmation is possible only if we count on our own strength, if we become bound one to another, if we hold ourselves in debt one to the other for whatever good we succeed in achieving.

The demonstration on 24 May aims to be a visible gesture of this pact of conscience between women.

Supporters should inform Centro Separisto Femminista Romano,

Another demonstration about Chernobyl – composed solely of women   *Letizia Paolozzi*

One segment of the demonstration which took place on 11 May in Rome consisted only of women. An extremist group at the back (Autonomia) repeated incessantly: 'Nato bases out of Italy'. The women tried to shut them up. Then they let the group go ahead, and made the traditional gesture of feminism – thumbs joined and spread at the base, index fingers touching each other pointing upwards. The group passed by . . . and gave the middle-finger salute. It is not a nice language, but this is not the reason why the women will demonstrate, on their own, Saturday 24 May.

The discussion is about the reason for this demonstration. It is a tough and sharp discussion. Not only men raise objections about the reasons behind this 'separatism', and about the aims and the pass-words, about the danger of having a more subdued repetition of what they have already seen. They do not grasp a specific subject; precision is lacking. Will it be all right to turn up wearing skirts?

Accusations of a lack of (political) intelligence, of (emotional) naivety, of (theoretical) oversimplification all pour down. There is passion here, tensed in order to convince the impudent ones to give in. This passion alone would be enough to make people suspicious. If there are women joining in, if one woman, meeting with others of her sex, tries to understand – instead of repressing – what is actually crossing our minds, the advantage will be clear. Clear for everybody.

It is true that a demonstration is successful when it brings together, in the same protest, people with different opinions; people who believe that a blow has been dealt to their own rights. Other people join in because they declare a feeling of solidarity. There is a principle at stake which has been ridden over roughshod, a principle that must be reasserted. It is the principle of life, in its daily fabric, which is under threat. It is the future that becomes uncertain, unpredictable, uncontrollable. It is the relationship with one's own body, with its limitations, and at the same time with its completeness, that breaks down, almost as in an explosion.

All of this is part of the reflection/speculation that women, before anyone else, tried to express. The church, no doubt, has said great things, but, obviously, with strong religious overtones. Therefore it is fair that women should remember it, even if their thoughts were partly wasted . . . However, it was difficult to put into practice those thoughts, so new – real discoveries. It was difficult to apply them in the fields of economics and science. In all this there is a delay. To me, it looks as though women want to start to make up for lost time; they want to have their say.

There is an objection: in the demonstration there will be those women who accuse men of being ugly, dirty and bad; warmongers and violent; supporters of nuclear power, recruits of Dr Strangelove. And in the same demonstration, there will be those who promise: 'Only we women can save the world. Only we women can fight for peace. Only we ensnare the Comiso power station, spinning around it a web of fine thread.' There will also be those asking for a 'membership strike' from politics and parties. There will be those rejecting science and technology, even if they listen to music on record players and keep meat in the fridge; and, indeed, there will be those protesting because there is no salad. So what? The objection against the demonstration goes that, while on one hand we women have to create a new ethics for a generation that would link together the present and the future, on the other hand we still have the complaint about the salad. What do ethics have to do with salad?

Well, when a principle is under threat, it is best protected when starting from different viewpoints; this is to say by the richness expressed by different opinions. Otherwise we will be parading in vast groups, but not necessarily in the best groups.

Let us consider science as well. Of course, the relationship with salad seems to be nonexistent, unless one chews it up in pills.

Therefore, one cannot perceive the relationship between the two. This is precisely the problem; that is to say the invisibility: the step from concrete to abstract, indeed, the separation of man from the material world. We have a world divided between those who measure themselves against reality, those who dominate nature (to a certain extent), those who work on abstract numbers, those who look at vast amounts of data; and those who transform things with their own hands, those who know what reproduction is, those who have a kind of self-sufficiency (and who are happy with it). The problem is that the logic of probability does not consider the individual; that abstract numbers excluded the minimalism of everyday life; the feelings of security given by the fact that 'small is beautiful'. Everyone digs one's own shelter; in this way, we carry on as if we did not, even as individuals, have any responsibility towards the world, the community, or future generations.

Concrete against abstract: a broken bond, a bond we must reweave. Otherwise some people (especially women) will be only expressions of emotionalism, while others (especially men) will be only expressions of rationalism. It is not by chance that, during the days of the Chernobyl cloud, not only Gorbachev kept silent, but also France and Italy, and that the news coverage was confusing. People were not to know about it, because of the risk of panic.

This is the reason for the demonstration. There is another reason, in addition: to stand up against the two separatisms, the two static natures, taking the general together with the minimal, in a continuum. Such an enterprise cannot be carried out if women do not seize hold of their thoughts, in relationship with their sex. We know women who are important individuals, in economics, science and politics. Until now it does not seem that they have created an explicit bond, welded with their own sex. It is true that analysis is necessary, research on these subjects should continue even after the demonstration. This, too, is the promise of these women. Otherwise we would not understand their desire to be in the streets together, only women.

Why the demonstration will be women only   *Franca Chiaromonte*

There are already many supporters for the demonstration organized by women taking place in Rome, Saturday 24 May: well-known signatures as well as lesser known names, various groups and representatives of the feminist movement, have given their support to the demonstration organized in the wake of the Chernobyl disaster; but this demonstration is not meant to be just a demonstration against nuclear power. The meeting point is Piazza Esedra at 6 p.m. Women will parade along the streets of the centre and will end their protest with a sit in that might last until dawn.

During one of the meetings that have been held to discuss the national demonstration on 24 May, one woman said that, paradoxically, she would have preferred to have seen the face of a woman among the long line of faces on television speaking in defence of nuclear power, and that, among the people who had gradually made decisions concerning energy and ways of using science, there had been one or more women 'I would have known better whom to get angry with.' She added that women have experienced a double loss in relation to the Chernobyl tragedy: like men, they have felt the consequences of decisions which had been made on their behalf without any consultation; unlike men, women share a situation in which opinions, criticism and also protests are made even more difficult because of the fact that the important decisions are made by males. So this is a double defeat, a double feeling of alienation.

I believe that this statement has a lot to do with the decision to organize a separatist demonstration. The discussions among women on this choice have been far-reaching. For many women the starting-point has been the peculiar way in which women had experienced the radioactive cloud, connected to their relationship with everyday life, with the problems concerning food: it's women who go shopping; it was women who ran from one shop to another, chasing after milk with an expiry date from before the disaster. In addition, there is the reflection of the feminist movement: on the body, on the relationship between body and mind and, again, on daily life. For all, there is the necessity for a thorough theoretical and political investigation on the meaning we want to give to the critique of the conception (and of the model of development), of which the nuclear choice is a consequence, or, perhaps, a premise. The demonstration may be an opportunity for such research. It will not be a demonstration about nuclear power and nuclear power only. The Chernobyl tragedy is the starting point for a debate on the meaning that has been attributed to the words 'progress' and 'welfare', on the model of development which has been followed so far, on the relationship between that model and the real life of real individuals. However, women want to debate these things in a way which reinforces and gives political meaning to their mutual relationships, to the building up of a network which will be made more and more full of sense and visibility.

There are some things I would not like the demonstration of the 24th to end up as: first of all a demonstration in which women become, or feel like, symbols for something, peace for instance. I believe, in fact, that behind the sensation of being a symbol or a carrier of some value or other, there is a difficulty of self-legitimization, the desire and need to justify a life and a political belief which is otherwise experienced as meaningless. In addition, I would not like to bring into the demonstration women's innocence, for example, in relation to the nuclear choice. Speaking of innocence simplifies a relationship, that which exists between women and the world around them and of which they are part, a relationship that is far more complex and that should rather lead back to a search for the reasons behind what has been defined more aptly as female ex-traneousness. I think it is difficult to find some advantage for women which derives from the various simplifications of this relationship, even more so when the simplification is done in the name of neutral concepts like 'guilt' and 'innocence'. An example of this attitude is the presentation of women as those who put right what men break, when left on their own. I would not like to bring into the demonstration this need for 'mothering'. Also, I would not like a demonstration speaking the language of accusations and demands. For this reason, too, I am convinced by the choice of having women and only women as our point of reference in the demonstration. Finally, I think that we should not bring in the heroism of the female sex, the ability to deal with daily life and the thousands of troubles related to it. I do not believe in this strength, if it is not transformed into political and social strategies; in other words, into the will to win through.

On the other hand, the demonstration could well turn out to be the time when a force which has continued to gain momentum in the last few years finally asserts itself, to find its place, its meaning and its political strength: more and more women vote for other women; more and more women read articles and books written by women. This is to say that more and more women are referring to their own sex, which they choose as a bridge between themselves and the world. Valuing this force means taking up once again the critique of the apparent neutrality of social and political relationships. The demonstration is addressed to women, even to those who are active members of parties and institutions. To reinforce a binding force, a common world, a pact – says the statement – of conscience. I think it is important for women, and for communist women as well, to join this pact.

Whose job is it to clean the world?   *Alessandra Bocchetti*

I belong to that part of the human race that, in spite of having a meaning, does not give the same meaning to others. The reality of what I am saying is almost a joke: try to pronounce the sentence 'man has got two legs', and you will feel the presence of a sense which spreads itself over the whole human race like a big, white, reassuring parachute. The sentence 'women has got two legs' instead gives us a sense of apprehension at our incompleteness, it seems as though we have to complete the sentence with any kind of adjective as soon as possible, we should say 'woman has got two beautiful legs' to feel at ease. To my sex, therefore, belongs the consciousness of partiality.

The history of my sex is an obscure one. In the dramatic reports from Beirut that we often see on TV, if we withdraw our gaze from where the shooting takes place, from where a bomb has just exploded, and we direct it along the fronts of buildings, there is almost always a woman beating a carpet or shaking a cloth. This absurd, obstinate gesture fills me with rage and moves me to tears. Women have been kept busy in an everyday struggle to clean the world, trying to stop its deterioration. This, as Hannah Arendt says, has very little to do with heroic deeds. Making up, every day, for the damages of the day before, is not a sign of courage, but of patience. Nevertheless, this job has made history possible. Well, I speak from this standpoint: from a partiality I cannot escape, and from an attention which is aware of life in its daily materiality. These are, respectively, my philosophy and my history. I realize that I am using two important words to define those things that have always been considered women's faults, and I do not deny that, sometimes, I have thought the same. I am not doing this arbitrarily, out of arrogance, but because the present situation allows it, and indeed, imposes it. If today we are all forced to question ourselves about the survival of life on our planet, the faults of my own sex are miraculously transformed into values. I am not being presumptuous. The consciousness of my partiality stands out in opposition against a thought that, having no measure of itself, inevitably ends up losing the meaning of life: my attention to daily life stands in opposition to whosoever, in the name of a more and more wonderful future, destroys its potential.

What did I think in the wake of the Chernobyl incident? I thought the same as I imagine everybody else thought: it was an utter disgrace, it filled me with fear and made me impotent. But being a woman, for me there was something more, something that made me suffer even more, that at that moment made my rage and impotence greater than the rage and impotence that men, too, had to feel. It took me time to understand what that something was. I did not find peace until I understood this: that if men were feeling betrayed by their fellow men, their peers, who had made choices and decisions for them, on behalf of everyone, concerning the kind of energy necessary to guarantee the future, I as a woman was betrayed twice because none of my fellow women, of my peers, had ever chosen or decided this. And if men, confronted by the tragic limitations of a thought which was always directed towards overcoming itself, had to admit that this thought belonged to their history as men, my history, on the other hand, had not said a word, my thoughts did not produce choices. I, too, would have liked to have my own peers with whom to be angry.

My peers never appeared, not even in the long television programmes which dealt with the incident, where scientists and politicians took it in turns to argue with one another. Women appeared only during the traditional interviews with people in the markets, saying they did not know what the hell they had to do; at that time this was my problem, too. Among the worries Chernobyl gave me, there was also this feeling of being alone, more deceived than the deceived, more excluded than the excluded.

What is my peer? My peer is such when she gives voice to the history from which we both come. Now we all know that this does not always happen, and that a woman can act in a manner which does not seem like a woman acting towards a fellow woman. In a process of emancipation, for instance, if a woman succeeds in administrating even the smallest power, forgetting about the interest of her sex, she does not behave like a peer to the other women. We also know that the possibility of success for this woman is minimal, because nothing really meaningful or important or creative can be fulfilled by forgetting her own history. In a political party, this happens very often: in the presence of a strong sense of idealism, sexual difference disappears.

In the mirage of acting in the interests of everyone, acting in the interests of one's own sex can seem to be an evil gesture indeed, most of all for anyone who belongs to a devalued sex. That makes politics a field with little success for womem. I remember the long debate preceding the law which closed down asylums. It was a moment of great idealism: society as a whole was taking upon itself the responsibility for mad people, the abolition of segregation seemed to be a rightful gesture. Not even one female member of parliament on that occasion spoke for the interests of her own sex, none of them said that the weight of this liberation would fall back onto other women, mothers, wives, sisters and daughters of those wretched creatures. Of course, in a moment of such a high level of self-awareness, it would have seemed evil.

Nevertheless, if women had had the courage to do this, they would have not done a bad service to society. They would have forced everybody to realize that there were not yet alternative support structures, that it was necessary to create them as soon as possible, and in this way, maybe, we would not have reached the painful situation which we have today. One does not have to be ashamed of thinking like a woman; men have always thought like men; of course, they are sure that in doing so, they are thinking for everyone, but the damage caused by this illusion is great.

But let us go back to our problem. If today it is necessary and urgent to make the history of women speak, because in this history one can trace that measure and that attention which would give the possibility of building up a more decent and less idiotic world, where there is no risk of confusing life with death, and the research of welfare with collective suicide, *women have to construct their own peers*. This is the only way out.

This is what women think if today, when the more civilized ones think of nothing but dissent, they organize a demonstration not to disagree, not to denounce, but to sanction a pact of conscience between themselves, a precise pledge to carry forward their interests. The affirmation of their own interests is the biggest contribution that women can make to free themselves from an ethical and civil disaster of which Chernobyl is only an 'extreme' example, but which started some time ago.

To construct their own peers, they have understood that it is necessary to take account of their mutual debt: let those women in power acknowledge the debt they owe to other women for their power, let those women who have a right to speak acknowledge the debt to other women's speech. A debt is a bond which is not only ethical, but concrete, of immediate interest. Nothing else can guarantee women their own visibility. It is a very important turn in women's politics. The feminist movement that will demonstrate in Rome, Saturday 24, that has called women of the political parties, of unions, of culture together with all the others, is a more pessimistic form of feminism than that of the past, one that no longer considers it enough to ask and to denounce, because it does not believe in the possibility of a different audience if not that of women amongst women. This new form of women's politics, at a time when politics seem not to exist any more, is the sign of the vitality of a movement that was wrongly given up for dead. It is a political gesture, of great significance and great courage, that of bringing into the demonstration not our own hypothetical strength, but the conscience of our own weakness in order to be able to conquer it; not our own innocence of the tragic facts of the present, but the breaking out of a complicit partnership.

The fear of life   *Lidia Campagnano*

Look, look how the Chernobyl cloud brings back again the idea of the future, which has for some years now been so out of fashion. The idea of the future that involves the need for a project of the self, the awareness that every single project of the self ends with one's own death, the desire to leave something of oneself behind (and so leave 'children' to the world), something good which one will not see. The idea of a future deeply rooted in the present.

Do women have something to say about this connection between present and future?

I think that working out the idea of the future is very difficult for women, who for centuries have left it in the hands of men. This is because it was not obvious for women to be engaged in a project for herself, independently, there was no idea of the daughter as the future, and, at most, there was resignation in respect of the son's 'departure' towards a future which was unknown for the mother, an act of abandonment about which women have always complained under their breaths; and the fact that the daughter would not leave, would not take this departure towards the future, was the only reason why the mother could 'prefer' her. And there was a cyclic idea of time: day is followed by night and night by day, breakfast is followed by lunch, then dinner and then breakfast again, until death comes. Women delegated the future to men.

A story of the past? I do not believe so; I think it is still a problem which is deeply rooted in women, and not easy to solve, especially now that man's idea of the future, which goes by the name of progress, is Chernobyl.

Chernobyl means that the male consciousness no longer relates to the present, to the project of the self which each of us builds and achieves day by day and hour by hour (based for men not on lunch or dinner, but on moral values which must be followed), to his own death and to the future. Clearly, the future does not matter; what matters is to postpone, to postpone continually his own death, knowing that this is not possible for ever, but, nevertheless, doing it in a mad frenzy. All this is done in spite of all the possible 'children', those bad witnesses of old age. In this way women are effectively lacking any model of emancipation: this man is not a model, he is a stupid child, and the more he has distanced himself in order to become powerful, the more stupid he has become: the more he knows, the worse he is. What can we say of a mineral engineer who shamelessly tells us the exact number of extra cases of leukemia that we should expect to have after Chernobyl? Where has the tough and virile speech about the necessary specialization of knowledge and roles gone, where the compulsory selection of studies and careers; in a nutshell, that whole world of values and concepts that women believed they had to be a part of in order to emancipate themselves – where has it gone?

It is difficult to compare and differeniate with a pattern which seems to have no more representatives (supposing it ever had). Also, things do not get any easier if men, scared by this Old Father Time, so funereal, think they can raise up the flags of femininity from the mud, and fight hard for the vegetables, for lunch and dinner and for lunch the following day. This is the point: maybe that pattern was just a pattern, and women have always related to an idea of man (of future) which is really within them and which is deep-seated.

If this is true, we must start from there, in order to propose an idea of present and future, and to propose it in a different way. And why could and should women take this task upon themselves? For a very simple reason: because they are wounded in two parts which have been vital so far: the so-called 'female part' (historically), which is that of the conservation, minute by minute, of the human race, and the so called 'male part' (historically), that of their identity, of the individual adventure and of sociality. Two parts that have been split until now, and, what is more, which have been projected out from the woman's self: onto the mother and onto the man.

To recognize them, at last, in that mess that they have become inside of us. To know that we have never really been just conservative and creative, in love as well as in maternity, and never just 'progressive' in emancipated life, and if instead we have tried hard to be so, the discomforts of the split spoke for us without our ever having realized it. Sometimes we turned things upside down: masculine, 'progressive' towards love, children, especially towards daughters, towards women, and conservative in social life and so on, because each woman is completely different from any other woman.

In the speechless mess or in the split division, women do not acknowledge one another favourably. And the simple extraneousness in this world surrounding us seems to me to be the reflection of our own mess and split, more than the real result of our work towards self-recognition. At this moment – let us admit it – we recognize that we are terribly afraid, we even have the sensation that we women are more afraid than everybody else. This is an ancestral fear, like that of little girls suspecting someone has the right to choose whether we live or die, to stop our growth. Christa Wolf comes to my mind to mitigate this fear, when she asks herself, in *Introduction to Cassandra*, whether fear could be a good starting point to avoid a catastrophe and to find courage. A verse by Sylvia Plath comes to mind – how much we need mothers and sisters! – in order to understand this fear: 'The sexless child we were, cries out its fear of life in a male-female world.'

The 'feminine': singular and plural   *Lea Melandri*

It is not easy to justify a demonstration by women which denounces the disastrous turn that male history has taken.

Virginia Woolf's arguments (*Three Guineas*) look inappropriate and limited nowadays. This is not because many of the material conditions that are necessary for women's participation in public life have been obtained, but because it is precisely this process of emancipation which has revealed deep, unconscious roots of a different nature, that persuade women to be accomplices, lovingly dedicated to man's welfare and happiness. The 'society of outsiders' is still far away, and the 'indifference' in every single woman's history can only be a search which lasts one's whole life.

In my opinion, however, it is even less appropriate to suggest the line by Brecht: 'Who cooked the victory dinner?' (Alessandra Bocchetti, 'Whose job is it to clean the world?', *Il Manifesto*, 23 May 1986 [reprinted earlier in this chapter]), when it is known that many women who today write and speak about the sexual problems of their sex do very little cooking and even less dusting. And if the sense of rage and pain is so great in seeing a woman with a brush in her hand, then it is better to lock the door of our kitchen and not to look around the neighbourhood, because the vision of a population of 'housewives' (for money or for love) is enough to make anyone live their life in tears.

Even if the Middle East is far away, and the images on a televison screen pass rapidly by, the movements and gestures which go through a house remain the same and repeat themselves. They are the *everyday routine* on which it would be worth opening up a glimmer of understanding.

But ideology has an endless capacity to cover things up: one can use the grammatical ways which the 'I' thinks, says, believes, and drown in a resemblance, cried out by words, the multiple sexual, economic, cultural, imaginative differences that keep women divided within themselves and in their mutual relationships.

Whom should women who have gained social power 'look like', when it is so difficult 'to look like themselves', when prestige and authority go to cover up that very emptiness of respect and self-love which it is so annoying to bring to light?

In previous years, when the debate on the sexes was urgently needed, there was criticism of the simplification and superficiality of an idea which concerned only the quantity of power, as well as of the limitations of any definition of political and social 'justice' which does not take into account childish dreams and demands, insidious nostalgias, tied up with a pattern for survival that it seems to be possible to renounce.

Nowadays, one would like the disparity, inequality, dependence, attribution of power – changing sign, sex, place – to change their very substance as well, and we would prefer them no longer to provoke the jealousies, wounds, rejections and renunciations that we know they can.

Instead of measuring the huge distance between a female cook and a male scientist, it would be much more useful to see what ties them together in such a subtle and strong way, and makes them into two faces of the same coin. The men that destroyed the air, sowed the seeds of death in nature and in the lives of their own fellow men, grew up, without any doubt, next to a woman, kept her company, consoled her physical loneliness, valued her feelings. Tenderness and violence appear together, inseparable, inextricably linked, and it does not make any sense to keep our eyes and arms open wide in relation to one, but to close them in desolation to the other.

Yet women love freedom   *Libreria delle Donne di Milano*

To the women that have organized the demonstration on 24 May against nuclear power, Lea Melandri says that their reasons, the reasons they can give against the present use of technological power, are unfounded. Women, she says, cannot appeal to a female extraneousness with respect to this society, because they are accomplices of the male enterprises, even the most deadly ones; neither can they be confident about their common female sex, because the resemblance between women is destroyed by the differences which exist between them (*Il Manifesto* 24 May 1986 [reprinted here as the preceding item]).

Clearly this way of thinking does not only criticize the practice of female or feminist demonstrations, a practice with which we would agree. This way of thinking goes very close to the impossibility of women's politics; but this is not Lea Melandri's position. Therefore, we want to compare ourselves with her, pointing out the elements of her discourse which we believe are missing or wrong.

For a start, one very simple and fundamental thing comes to light: female complicity does not exclude extraneousness; the discovery of a female complicity does not invalidate what Virginia Woolf wrote in *Three Guineas*.

Lea Melandri makes an absolute statement about complicity so as to affirm that the 'woman cook' and the 'male scientist' are 'two faces of the same coin'. This is not true. It is not true objectively. The woman who, through need or love, or both together, ties her destiny to a man with social power does not have the same responsibilities as this man.

It is not true subjectively; first of all because the hidden face of male power is never reduced to being only the female support. We must not lose sight of male homosexuality, not that shown by gays, but the hidden homosexuality of men in power. And it is not true because even the more involved or more enslaved woman, when giving her energies to a man, wants for herself something she never gets back completely.

There is a female desire for freedom. If we recognize it inside us, let us not deny it in another woman.

When for the first time, through the practice of the unconscious, we shed light on female complicity, we never thought it was a definitive statement beyond which one cannot go, neither did we think that complicity said everything about all that a woman is, or all that she wants. We have always tried, together, to shed light on two more things: that part of a woman's desire which she tries to let through into the open even in a subordinate form; and that which women have always signified outside of their subordination and complicity, and which social representation has always tried to ridicule, deform or rub out.

Let us not forget the English spinsters, Barbara Pym's *Excellent Women*. Let us not forget either that women, the great majority of women, keep their distance from male politics, exactly as in Virginia

Woolf's times. The process of emancipation has revealed, as Lea Melandri notes, elements of complicity, but it has also revealed and more powerfully, the fact of a female extraneousness. When exterior barriers have fallen down, others have arisen, those of sexual difference, and we have seen that women do not take them lightly.

Finally, let us not forget the women's movement. Separatism means women's desire not to be accomplices. Of course, engaging in politics in separate places does not exclude the fact that, on other levels and in other places, women remain accomplices. But this second fact, if we really want to understand it, is not everything. There is something else. There is also the fact that the 'woman cook' interrupts her domestic chores to meet other women, amongst whom there are women who have never cooked for anyone.

The 'resemblance' that Lea Melandri finds empty, in comparison with the differences that divide women, may be stronger than the differences. After all, for years and years she has been the teacher of many housewives – she cannot ignore that. In the same way, she cannot ignore the symbolic and social strength which arises from this meeting of women who exchange, *through* their differences, an understanding of female difference.

Giving life to free social relationships between women, the movement has produced a modification which we consider to be essential, inasmuch as to say that belonging to the female sex can be for a woman a source and measure of her own social value.

So saying, we do not think we are pointing out a reality established within society. This is not the case. We refer to our own experience, to the experience of women who do not depend completely any more on male judgements and measures in order to regulate themselves, in order to know what they should think about themselves and the world. Because in the judgements and measures of other women they found a better understanding and, most of all, a guarantee of a freer comparison, the evaluation of themselves does not pass any more on or against being women.

'Nowadays, one would like' – writes Lea Melandra at one point – 'the disparity, inequality, dependence, attribution of power – by changing sign, sex, place – to change their very substance as well, and we would prefer them no longer to provoke the jealousies, wounds, rejections and renunciations that we know they can.' One would like? We want it. We want it and we say so because it is possible, provable and proved. The substance of power is not neutral, not indifferent to signs, sexes and places. The power mechanisms which seem unchangeable together with their negative effects, their mechanical repetitiveness and their negative consequences upon the female sex, have something to do with – do we really need to say it? – human sexed nature and with the history of relationships between the two sexes.

What is unchangeable when the woman finds herself compared and measured with relation to man becomes changeable when the woman finds herself compared with a female sexual yardstick.

But, let us be clear, this does not happen in a spontaneous or automatic way. In fact we are saying that a political practice of disparity between women is necessary. And when we affirm the capacity for change in some mechanisms, we base ourselves on this practice that we have been carrying out for a number of years. We are not speaking just for the sake of it, but in the light of facts. Female envy is a first-class human experience. If it is finally understood in its roots and reasons, if it is lived out in free social forms, as we are trying to do with the practice of disparity and entrustment, it can bring a woman a long way in the liberation of her human energies. But, we repeat, it is not a spontaneous process.

Freud, as we know, believed female envy to be anatomic envy of men. However, Klein understood that that envy has its origins in the relationship with the mother. Thus, changing sign and sex means entering the realms of possible modification. The practice of disparity and entrustment – a female *political* practice, because the road to female freedom is not given to us and we have to open it on our own and to want it – is this possible modification.

As will be clear to all, we who are writing these things believe in the efficacy of political change; in the same way we believe in the power of some traumatic events. Feminism, female separatism has been this event as far as the social specification of female difference is concerned. In the same way we think that the analysis of the unconscious is precious as long as it can be brought to an end.

The moment comes when we have to stop the inner search and draw some conclusions. The inner search could go on endlessly, promising to reach the bottom of things eventually, and thereby to possess their fundamental secret.

It is an illusion which is no less deceptive than the opposite one, by which men believed they would solve the problems of humanity by producing the maximum increase of technological power.

Therefore, it is not 'inside to the bottom' or 'outside to the maximum', but inside and outside, outside and inside, thereby modulating our difference and its free social existence.

In this modulation, it is important to return to that way of thinking which takes oneself as the starting point, and which has characterized the language of women's politics. It is not necessary to remain within the limits of personal experience, but to tie together subjective and objective. Without this link, as we know, female reality remains crushed under simplified representations that do not let anything appear of the female desire for freedom. And we ourselves run the risk of being crushed.

The woman's fear of loneliness is one of these representations which has no middle course and which is therefore crushing. Yet there are women, and we know them, some of them amongst us, who live alone out of a love for their own freedom. Lea Melandri is one of these women, but we could name others and also add our own names to the list. If we wish to argue about female complicity and the dependence of women on men, let us not draw conclusions without taking into account the social manifestations of women's love for freedom.

The same goes for the relationship between intellectual work and women's work. Arguing against the Brechtian reasoning of Alessandra Bocchetti, 'Whose job is it to clean the world?', Lea Melandri invites those women who write and speak of women's politics to open up 'a glimmer of understanding' on the repetitive, daily routine of women's housework. And she does not see that a glimmer, and not only a glimmer, has already appeared before her and our own eyes. As well as those women who, in order to devote themselves to political or intellectual work, never do housework and those who spend their lives doing this work, there are some who do both. There are women, we who are writing, maybe Lea Melandri and Alessandra Bocchetti themselves, who do not live at the mercy of daily needs.

There are many of these women, and their example is worth considering, if we want to think in concrete terms about female difference and about the roads which lead to women's social freedom.

Practising the inside/outside of female existence, seeing female difference in the steps which link, or can link, one woman to another, trying out the paths between childish pretences and adult fears, are all ways of expressing the necessity of a female sexual mediation.

The practice of disparity and entrustment between women responds, or would like to respond, to this necessity. The woman who faces the world in isolation, alone with her enormous pretensions and great fears, is crushed by it. But if she relates herself to the world, through that which her peers have said or done, and through that which other women expect her to be able to say or do, then it is different. Then she finds in her own sex, through her belonging to the female sex, the strength and the yardstick by which to be able to know herself and to face the world.

Piera Bosotti, Lia Cigarini, Luisa Muraro and others

Broadsheet   *Vivere Lesbica*

Busy for years in getting rid of the prejudice of male stupidity, once again we have been violently disturbed by an act of violence which has been repeated, accepted and codified into our daily life and which today finds its broadest and perhaps ultimate resonance in nuclear power.

The resistance of women in preserving and conserving living space for everyone has shown itself historically to be a lost cause. This resistance has been used against us to confine and confirm us in a passive, 'feminine' role which has made us dumb, powerless, spectators of a progressive process of destruction.

With political and existential separatism, lesbian and feminist women started, some time ago, to avoid these functions of support and, in a wider context, lots of women seem to be moving in this direction: they are stopping having children, they do not go to the male-dominated churches, they are looking for independence. In addition, this avoidance again implies a daily resistance to the social blackmail which varies from physical and verbal violence to persistent discrimination, to which is added a well-orchestrated cultural action, varying from the worried tones of a misogynistic pope to the falsely soft and free-and-easy tones of certain mass persuaders, who suggest that 'Feminism is now far too old', we are standing in front of 'the sunset of ideology', and who discover among Italians an incipient 'desire for capitalism' (and therefore for nuclear power) and among women 'a refound desire for femininity'.

We ask ourselves, then, what sort of connection exists between feminism and lesbianism and nuclear choices which involve problems and political realities which are apparently so diverse.

The answer is complex because it lies in the thousands of years of history of the two opposed sexes, of which one, ours, dedicated to the conservation of the species, is against war and violence. We women cannot become part of a hierarchical power system supporting itself upon war and violence, except in a marginal way which is based only on political consent.

Instead, we lesbian women want to refuse male society any kind of consent, and we believe that arriving at total destruction is written into the history of man, which yet is made of wars and partial destruction; so extraordinary that it would definitively mark man's dominance over nature and over that mother who generated him, and who has been identified with nature.

Slogans for the demonstration *Union of Italian Women*, 'La Goccia', *Rome*

A pact of conscience between women

The military secret
all can conceal
It's not just Chernobyl
but Polynesia, the Sahara
and the whole of Nevada!

We have cleaned bodies and houses
from dawn to dusk
You have reduced the world
to a pile of trash

Feeling alone
feeling deceived
in certain choices
we have not been consulted

Rape, rape
against nature
is another result
of your culture

Woman, woman, woman
Don't just stand and stare
fight with us
against nuclear war

We reject the needs
of which we have no need

If the body detaches itself
from the mind
it goes completely insane

May every woman with us unite
in a pact for life

Nuclear peace
nuclear war
thrown out of the world
for evermore

We still have time
We are not fatalistic
Our impotence
has never existed

We are fond of fields
of the sea and flowers
We are all
against nuclear power

Women together
in a pact of conscience
against nuclear power
violence and war

Sexual violence
nuclear violence
the same male logic

This mad male society
has raped nature, too

Oh sorcerer
oh scientist
you, patriarch, have tired us to death

Homo sapiens
you have become demented

I'll do without TV and food mixer
but don't take away from me
the luxury of utopia

With the knowledge of woman
a new science will be born

Power will pay dearly for
its arrogance
Science will pay dearly for
its ignorance

Women will change
the course of history
because of the body, too
they hold a memory

To affirm your essence
you destroy our existence

Scientists, politicians and cardinals
all you produce is evils

From the angel of the home
to nuclear death
how much bullshit you can produce

You are revered, even well paid
and this is what you have made

Women are afraid
but not of the fight
They want power
. . . and also their food rights

Down with radioactivity
We want more sentiment

I am willing to be thrifty
but try to use your loaf

How little you love life
if you are willing to give it up
just for another watt

15

The Issue of Political Representation

Another aspect of the problematic relationship of the feminist movement with the institutions concerns the possibility, and eventually the
desirability, of 'representing' sexual difference in the very sites of
political power (be they the governing bodies of political parties, or
the various local councils or the parliament itself). In other words, can
women as a gender achieve representation by sending other women as
their delegates and spokespersons to positions of responsibility? And,
in that case, what should the relationship between the electors and the
elected be?

Proposals for the creation of a 'women's party' had already been
advanced – and regularly defeated – in the seventies and again at the
beginning of the eighties; the general feeling then was against a direct
involvement of the feminist movement in the institutional arena. This
is, in a sense, still true, but the discussion has taken a different turn in
the last few years.

In 1986 the problem was raised again by the Communist Women's
Charter, in which the influence of feminism is clearly detectable, as we
hope the excerpts included here will illustrate. There is the recognition of gender, and of sexual difference, as a central category of
thought. There is the decision to make it act within the party, and
within society, as a positive 'obstacle' to neutral and therefore unjust
visions of politics; there is the proposition to turn this 'obstacle' into a
factor for change. There is also the will to bring the whole party to
accept and support these positions, and the concrete commitment to
achieving a fairer balance, in numerical terms, in the sexual composition of democratic institutions.

When a general election was held in 1987, the Communist Party did
in fact number many women among its candidates. It also gave space

to women – either members of the party or not – who openly stated their allegiance to feminism. The issue of representation was again discussed in crowded feminist meetings, stressing both the necessity for a greater presence of women in the institutions and the drawbacks of such a presence.

The items by Lia Cigarini (of the Libreria delle Donne in Milan) and by Maria Luisa Boccia (a communist always active in the feminist movement) look at the various facets of the problem. Women are neither a class nor a corporation, but a gender, and a gender cannot, as such, achieve political institutional representation. But women can value and give credit to projects assumed by women candidates, thus creating a link based on reciprocal recognition; the ambition of the single woman, and the adhesion to her project of other women who choose to uphold it, can find legitimation in a common assumption of belonging to the female gender.

Following the 1987 elections, when a larger than ever number of women entered parliament, mostly in the ranks of the Communist party, the reflection on this theme has not been abandoned. In this collection, it is present, though in an indirect form, in the DWF editorials about 'Political responsibility' and 'Forms of politics', as well as in the survey on the impact of feminism in trade unions by Alessandra Mecozzi.

EXCERPTS FROM THE COMMUNIST WOMEN'S CHARTER 1986

Introduction: from women to women

Over the last few years our lives as women have changed for the better. They bear the signs of our new identity, won by hard work interspersed with risks, defeats and gains. Our conditions of life have also changed for the better; but not for everyone. Reality is harsh towards many women, denying them fundamental rights such as work. And yet the strength of women does not have sufficient space in political institutions. Indeed, it's often the case that even those of us involved in politics feel that its language, its rules and the issues it addresses are distant from our daily lives. We know that this is no accident. It has to do with the processes of these last few years which have sought to impoverish politics, to concentrate the sites of decision-making power and separate them off from representation and popular participation.

It has to do with a fundamental fact which is far too complex to be synthesized here. Political institutions remain the area most closed and hostile to female identity, history and life experience. This is why we women communists want to suggest to women an alliance in order to win a challenge, to establish a new relationship between our lives and politics, to act so that our lives 'invade' the institutions of politics, the governments and parties which make them up, so that our lives become 'awkward' for them, and oblige them to take us on.

We want to construct in society and in political institutions 'women's strength', which can only derive from women themselves through a strategy of relations and communications amongst ourselves; women's strength which would express our contract with the political sphere and would carry weight in this phase of politics. So we are suggesting a 'women's charter', an 'itinerant' charter which seeks to encourage this communication and relations between women, which wants to enter into their lives and get to know their problems, encourage them to speak out. The charter contains only a hint of our value options, our ideal choices and our concrete objectives; it wants to enrich itself, modify itself, fill up its gaps through this relationship with women, through knowledge of their problems, and through listening to their suggestions.

We intend to meet with women in the parties and to involve women from the movements and feminism, women in associations, women in unions, intellectuals, and women working alone. But above all we want to involve 'ordinary women', the ones we meet all the time in our daily lives, the ones who suffer most the weight of this harsh reality, the ones who are weakest, most alone, most vulnerable. This is an undertaking requiring intelligence and initiative from all of us. Only if we are united and large numbers of us are engaged in politics can the charter get some results. It will have to activate a series of encounters and discussions, go more deeply into questions of struggle and agreement over concrete objectives such as work, health and education.

We began with a week of meetings and talks with women workers to discuss the issues connected with the battle over work; we have launched a mass petition over pensions; women in the south have become mobilized over work. We will continue with a conference on motherhood, on working hours, and . . . and so it goes on, up to our programmatic convention, a stage in the construction of the prog-rammatic convention of the party.

'From women, women's strength' does not mean us siding with the party nor does it mean separating ourselves from men. If anything it wants to translate into facts what has been recognized in the conference thesis: the value of transforming sexual contradiction. 'From women, women's strength' is the biggest contribution we can make to our party in this phase. And so we say to our comrades: we are talking to you, find a suitable space in your political agenda for the issues women put to you, because they are vital if we want to investigate, understand and resolve the general problems of society and win the fundamental battles.

The charter

We are communist women. We have chosen the PCI to put into practice our desire to be involved in politics, in order to change our condition and the world we live in. For us political involvement is a daily engagement which we want to see lived with intelligence and passion, concreteness and idealism. It is our intention to examine our choices, our battles and struggles in the positive changes we manage to achieve in people's lives. The day-by-day and the dimension of the future, the little things and the great problems of the world, these are the reasons for our interest, our engagement, our battles. To look far ahead and act within the everyday: this is how we understand our political activity.

Being active within our party does not lead us to forget that we belong to a sex with its own history and condition which urge particular needs, choices and priorities. We have learnt that in politics choices bear the mark of sex and class. Often the will to pursue something in the general interest, something worthwhile for everybody, forgets about the unnamed sex, the female one. We believe that a real effort to transform society means giving a name to the needs and purposes of men and women so that they can meet and engage with each other, communicate, define together real common interests. But for women to be named they first need to give voice and authority to their own needs and desires, which should then become political facts and proposals. And this is unthinkable unless women, in their thinking, planning and political activity, refer to other women, establish strong communication and relations with them. Only in this way is it possible to experience political allegiance as a strength and not as a weakness.

Constructing women's strength is a task which we owe both to ourselves and to the party in which we are active. With women's strength it is possible to construct a 'human society' in which women as women, and men as men, can fully recognize each other. This is why we want so many women to be actively involved in the PCI, so that we can recognize each other as women in every area or field of our activity. Choices and values expressed by women are today one of the foundations and one of the most profound raisons d'être *of the left and the PCI.*

Our life has changed over the last few years. Women plan their future and think of it as a future in society and no longer as simply private. Women work. Women want to work even when and where everything seems designed to discourage them from doing so. Work has become for women an important constituent part of their identity and their life. Women have asserted, and learned to live, their right to sexuality; they have put forward and put into practice the value of responsible freedom in sexuality and in procreation. They have measured, often bitterly, the complexity of this journey, and the social and cultural obstacles put in their way. Many women today live in a state of acute conflict between a new awareness of the self, their knowledge of the rights they have acquired and the opportunities which are in reality offered to them. For many the reality is harsh, emphasizing social inequalities. The condition of women living in the south, the poverty which afflicts many women, the situation of so many women who are alone and so many who are old, place a burden of responsibility on us.

In these last few years women, involved in politics and beginning with the oppression common to our sex, have acquired a consciousness of sexual difference.

We want today to look at the reality for women in all its complexity: the wretchedness and weakness of a socially disadvantaged condition, but also the wealth and strength of an undifferentiated female subjectivity, which shows itself in a plurality of expressions. We have recognized the disparities of situation and strength which exist between us. There is the unjust face of disparity which sanctions social and cultural inequalities. We denounce disparity when it is unjust. We say again that emancipation and liberation are the journey of every woman, in the interests of everybody. To define our common interest and project, however, we need to start with the experience of each of us, from that which unites us and that which divides us . . .

Women's wish to:

affirm themselves in their own eyes
work, all of them
construct a new sexual culture
affirm responsible freedom in procreation

value the work of their own intelligence
live naturally with both reason and feeling;

all these things express women's interests and also a great political
challenge to the ability of the left to govern the society of the future. It
is therefore necessary to start from our interests and our history to
construct women's strength, without which our party would be
incoherent in the face of its own project.

Starting with women's interests is a process experienced by whole
generations of communist women, an experience which has tied them
to Italian women, helping to give them a voice in politics. Today we
are grateful to these women, to whom we owe so much. Our strength
today is based on this experience.

*To build our strength we need great communication between women; we
must listen carefully to each other, be aware of what each needs from the
other. The strength of each one becomes an advantage and a resource for the
other. We must release this women's strength from women.*

A strength which we want to bring to bear within political institutions.

*A strength which we want to employ at this political juncture in
particular . . .*

*The everyday life of women with its cares and its small successes, its
questions and its needs, its hopes and disappointments, does not have
enough space in politics at the moment.*

*Today governments and the parties which form them speak a language
which increasingly ignores individual and social concrete existences.*

*In these last few years the forums of political decision-making have
become restricted and have tended to distance themselves from popular
representation and participation. There has been an attempt to reduce what
counts as politics, to impoverish it to the point of a clash between a few
interest groups. This is the crux of the political cycle which has operated in
the USA, Europe and also Italy: neo-liberalism. Striking out against gains
made by workers, the hopes for development of Third World countries, it
has aggravated social inequalities, marginalizing ever larger numbers of
women, and has encouraged a new male chauvinism.*

Our very sexual difference has been employed to reassert and
emphasize the sexual division of social roles. It is no coincidence that
in the USA as in Europe the meaning and value of important laws has
been attacked and obscured – laws regarding issues such as the
voluntary termination of pregnancy and sexual violence.

These neo-conservative politics are profoundly contradictory, partly because changes in female identity in work and procreation have
encouraged, and still encourage, precise innovative choices.

Neo-conservative politics can be turned around and beaten. To this end we need a new project of transformation. We believe our presence as women to be necessary in this struggle to give its development new impetus, and so that it is marked by our identity.

For this reason too we see the need and urgency of translating women's individual and social strength into political strength. We would say that women have some kind of contract, and that they are visible in society and in politics.

We want the daily life of women to *invade* government and the institutions, to become 'awkward' for them, obliging them to 'stumble' over it . . .

So we would like a detailed dialogue with women from the democratic parties. We want to compare notes constantly with women from the movements and associations, in meetings which, with respect for our reciprocal autonomies, would enrich all our ideas and initiatives; we feel it is indispensable to have a continuous and worthwhile relationship with the innumerable agencies of female intellectual activity.

We want to establish communication and relations with the women we meet every day in the workplace, in the course of our daily tasks, to get to know their difficulties and their opinions and to encourage them to speak out.

We think it is essential for all women to contribute to the definition of what politics is actually about.

The schematic points we have presented are a base for what we hope will be widespread discussion between women. We are not interested in empty encounters with no concrete consequences: on these points and others which will come out in the course of our meetings, we intend to monitor the difficulties and the successes, as well of course as fight to win.

So we look on this document as an itinerant charter, a platform which considers and constructs itself in its direct relationship with women, which examines and searches the lives of women, to understand the problems and the questions, to make all our ideas and initiatives that much richer.

This is how we see the programmes: a direct line to the daily life of women, encouraging them to speak out.

Our strength in the institutions of politics In our country 28 per cent of women work; 52 per cent of girls study; there are many businesswomen and managers; but *of those elected to parliament only 7 per cent are women, exactly the same as in 1946.*

Today there are women magistrates, lawyers, senior policewomen, prison governors; they work in the places where laws are put into action, but their contribution in determining and deciding them is little or nil.

Lack of female presence in the institutions of politics is much more noticeable and persistent than in other fields of social life. Women are for the most part excluded from moments and places of decision-making. And yet they know the seasons of politics, the practices of social mobilization, responsibility, ethical, cultural and civil passion. And, too, many have taken on the political institutions, trying to enrich their sphere of activity and bring them closer to people's lives.

We communist women want to bring the *contradiction of sex* into the political arena. Our last congress acknowledged this issue and its challenge to liberation. It makes for a renewal of politics in the sense of widening horizons, it enriches its scope by bringing to bear issues previously discounted, and it changes many of the ways in which politics has until now expressed itself.

Inscribing the contradiction of sex and affirming sexual difference in the institutions of politics leads to the critical examination of ways in which citizenship and political representation have historically been defined. Women want to enter fully into politics, and yet they cannot inhabit it in the same way as do men, who have constructed it and worked out its rules and codes.

Why do the institutions of politics remain the areas most resistant to female presence and identity?

More than ever this question requires an urgent response, given the growth and wealth of women's presence, in so many different forms, in society.

The question of power, and particularly political power, is the order of the day.

An extensive and varied network of female groups has sprung up, involved in anything from cultural production to assessment of professions, and in the course of their activity most of them come up against the people and rules of politics, and interact with them. These days we can see a consolidation and enrichment of the network of groups involved in experiences of solidarity and in issues such as peace and the environment: here we see the work and intelligence of large numbers of women. But we cannot remain silent about the critical state in which they are leaving important areas of social management and participation, areas which in the seventies were significant, and involved a great number of women: clinics and schools, for example.

We communist women are within the institutions of politics and we want other women to be there too, strong in their history and their experience,

actively engaged in winning a power whose rules and decisions are the ones
women need. For this reason it is important that women involved in the
institutions of politics and citizens, either as individuals or as groups,
should each act as a reference point for the other, and should never cease to
be in active relationship with each other.

How can we fill with significance, starting with the lives and
experience of women, words such as democracy, participation, state,
government, administration? This is the challenge which faces us: we
must take it up together, as women, with respect for our reciprocal
differences and roles, in order to assert ourselves. At the same time,
this is a great contribution towards the renewal of politics and a
process of transformation. It is a challenge made all the more difficult
by the degenerative processes which political institutions are going
through. We only need to think of the shifting of decision-making
from elective assemblies to centres of economic power, semi-legal and
illegal centres of hidden power. The slogan 'less state, more market',
which has significantly informed political processes over the last few
years, has knocked sideways the direction of economic policies among
other things, and has struck at more than just the public–state
dimension. More profoundly, neo-conservative forces have put under
their charge the whole culture and experience of socialization, of
articulated democracy, of the participation of ordinary citizens in the
choices and management of areas which are extremely relevant to their
own lives.

We are addressing women in the democratic parties: those of us who are
involved in politics and want to push forward the issue of emancipation and
female liberation should be alarmed by the degenerative processes which are
striking political institutions; we should feel the responsibility and the
ethical passion to fight together to assert a precise political conception;
inspired by values and referring to real people whose contribution it must be
able to draw on constantly.

It seems to us there are three dimensions in which to elaborate a
women's politics in order to build up women's strength.

Representation We pledge ourselves to win, through alliance with
women, full representation for our sex. If history marks power
differently for men and women, it is time this diversity no longer
worked against us.

To restore balance to rights and powers there is, amongst possible
choices, the practice of guaranteed quotas. This is being much
discussed within the European left, and affects us, even if it does not
exhaust the search for ways of making real women's rights present in

the places where decisions and fundamental choices are made.

To be visible in institutions, in political forums, also means equipping ourselves with the forms and instruments of autonomous groups. In parliament, some regions and councils have organized themselves as 'groups of elected deputies in the PCI lists'. Their experience could become a valuable source of common reflection, to examine what potential is expressed by an instance which makes representation and female initiative more visible. Consideration of this experience and of how to create real communication between elected women and women in society can also help us discover more effective proposals and solutions to difficulties.

Contractuality In order to obtain rights, to satisfy needs and interests, to realize one's own identity in society, it is no longer enough for women to fight for legal citizenship and parity. We see now a search for the best ways of giving contractual force to the many aspects of women's social existence, the most important of them being work.

It should be made possible for all these groups of women (cooperatives, cultural centres, professional organizations, and so on) to have access to available resources, to gain political citizenship, contractual spaces and force.

For this to happen we need new institutional instruments; we need to find new ways of contracting with public power or between social sectors.

Management Women work in the state apparatus, carrying out duties, applying laws. Women continually turn to the state in many aspects of their daily lives. We believe that a different idea and practice of social and public management can and should emerge from the meeting between women, workers and citizens, those who work the system and those who use it, to reform and humanize the relationship between citizens and state.

This also has to happen in order for us to be sure that everything we achieve or impose in the way of choices is not then distorted and betrayed at the very moment it is translated into the organization of daily life; in other words, when it penetrates our lives, our work, our families and the social sphere.

In all these issues we have only indicated the problems as they have been seen up to now. It is our intention to get together with women from the parties, with female intellectuals, with women from the movements, so that together we can work out more precise analyses and more effective proposals. We intend to organize shortly an occasion where we can consider these matters together.

FEMALE 'SEPARATENESS'   *LIA CIGARINI*, 1987

When, at the end of the Milan conference last December on the practice of sexual difference, I heard some people say that it was time to confront the political representation of difference, for a moment I felt acutely uncomfortable.

I wondered how it was that old word had cropped up, bringing in its wake a powerful institution which cancels or imprisons, wipes out at a stroke the search for women's words freed of the rules and expectations of masculine society (the father's), our search for original languages (languages of our origins).

Besides, on neither day of the conference was there the slightest doubt (how could there have been?) that women were a sex and not a homogeneous social group – while political representation presupposes common interests and needs. The meeting at Milan had been an effort to bring together women who speak from different positions, and declare these positions, with different, sometimes contrasting, individual and collective projects. This context made it impossible to conjecture any representation even of the women who were there. Absolutely impossible; in fact a good deal of our discussions were taken up with some insistently asking others: where are you speaking from, where are you coming from, how can you logically and politically remain in a party, in a parliament, and yet be here with us? The others would answer, 'We've come here, but part of me is on the bright stage of grand politics where our destinies are played out.' Or 'I'm here, but a part of me is with those whom everybody, men and women, forgets about, with the labourers from Puglia . . . And what's the point of your separatist politics?'

There was something else which made any discussion of representation out of the question, and that was the widely shared thought that the sense of sexual difference requires us to reason with the force of its inner necessity, and not with any force legitimized by neutral or male institutions.

The woman who put forward the idea of representation then explained that it was to be understood as an 'authorization by women of other women', and as a way of 'making present' the power of sexual difference. She also thought that, since classical democracy does not permit sexual difference as a subject of representation, by representing it we could really put the cat among the pigeons.

Apart from the authorization of women by women – which really has nothing to do with political representation – I have grave doubts that being a woman, which is something absolutely qualitative, can be represented in the numerical or quantitative manner of classical democracy. And I especially doubt that the presence of a number of women in parliament will weigh heavily on that institution or ruffle any feathers at all, creating an 'obstacle' to its neutral functioning.

First, because if you believe it's vital to be on the inside of parliament to make difference visible, you're saying that you value highly a place set up by men of a particular social class when that class had achieved a surplus in economic knowledge and power. And you show you don't believe in the feminine source of social authority that is beginning to take shape.

Who is to say anyway that women actually *want* to be in all the existing institutions, the parliament, the army, the church? Some do, but the woman who goes into the army or the church clearly goes into it for herself, while the woman who goes into parliament, the institution of representation, and goes into it with the idea of a possible female representation, overrides the wishes of those who keep out of it.

As for the possibility of being an 'obstacle', let's not forget that in terms of 'function' men and women are equal and sexual difference is regarded as a useless anachronism. People soon get used to seeing a woman in place of a man when she carries out the functions laid down by the social order thought up by men. Sexual difference cannot signify without transgression, without a subversion of the existing order. It can't simply be traced over the received symbolic order . . . not, that is, if we are struggling not just for equality with men, but for female liberty.

I think, then, that a greater female presence in parliament will not in itself upset anybody, because the representatives have to mediate their action with a number of powerful forces; the party which has them elected; the inevitable participation in and legitimization of male power which is expressed in it; all the intervention and compromise which the business of making laws implies. All of which is a far more drastic curtailing and censorship of female desires than the famous veils the male imagination had covered the female body with. In practice, then, all the deputies will be able to achieve is the right to veto laws concerning women. Or else they will function as a small lobby group, along the lines of American democracy.

I want to make it absolutely clear that I'm not referring here to women who openly go into parliament to fulfil their own desires, to exercise their abilities and achieve their own ambitions. What I'm criticizing is the idea of any possible female representation, and the women who use this idea to disguise their own desires.

When I was involved in mixed politics and met workers at meetings, I remember I was struck by the way their bodies signified their work, and by the precise and concrete way they described and analysed the reality of life in the factories. I was convinced that, as they took the floor from me and made me feel totally vacuous with their knowledge and the materiality of their contributions, in the same way they would make a formidable challenge to the people trying to bring about some kind of consensus in the institutions, be some kind of embarrassment, an 'obstacle' even. It didn't and doesn't happen. The system of representation deprived them of their knowing bodies, silencing them, making them themselves mediate the thing which they represented.

I'm convinced we can't do without these mediators. Indeed, I think that mediations can give strength to female presence, but only if they are faithful and responsive. If there are women who want to go into parliament, just as others have gone into the professions and the work market, they should be honest about the desires which motivate them, their political aims; they should say what sort of universality they are prepared to gamble upon, and they should say how they propose to put into practice their female partiality. This is what we need for a form of mediation which is faithful both as regards the institution and to women. This way they tie themselves to other women, to me, not through some notion of representation but through the declaration of their female desires. This way, too, we bypass the impotent two-stage politics, the first stage to acquire personal dignity, the second (which will never happen . . .) to inscribe our own indecent difference. We said our goodbyes at the Milan conference promising to carry on talking about all this. We realized that the question of representation of sexual difference, which had been brought up at the conference in order to be theoretically rigorous, could in practice tempt some women to put themselves forward as mediators between the women's movement and institutional politics.

We also need a deeper understanding of how the desire to succeed in society and the quality of otherness are linked, and how to deal with the tension arising from these two different parts of our being. And we have yet to begin analysing the overlap between the language of the mother (of feelings) and the social language transmitted by the father. We need to find a way of communicating simply what we mean by the body's silence, since evidently women speak men's language without any clear difference. We need to find a way of putting into the world all the knowledge, changes and desire to succeed that women's groups have produced, without our actions seeming to be a female reflection of men's actions.

Things have moved faster than we foresaw. The government crisis and the early elections have brought up the question of political representation as a useful concept, especially for communist women, to get the parties to put up more women candidates and, indeed, to get more elected.

THE GENDER OF REPRESENTATION   *MARIA LUISA BOCCIA*, 1987

The search for difference

(1)   The first hint of interest in women's presence in the political system occurred forty years after the birth of the Republic, A Rai 3 broadcast edited by Rossana Rossanda made visible and public a scandal which up to then had been accepted as normal, or simply forgotten. Only 7 per cent of those elected into representative institutions were women, and the percentage remained constant over those forty years. An article in *Il Manifesto*, also published to mark forty years of the Republic, set out to look at the reasons for this persistent exclusion.

At the end of that same year the matter was again highlighted by the Communist Women's Charter [reprinted in this chapter] ... In numerous debates during the course of those months feminists discussed the problem of the relationship between women's political practices and the sites and forms of power. The first elements of analysis began to emerge, which I will here indicate briefly.

First of all democracy is not seen just as an 'imperfect' democracy to be put right, by widening its constituency and the spheres of influence of its rules: rather, it is seen on the one hand as an *instrument* of men's historic domination, and on the other as a form of state and government built on a presupposed universalism which conceals the reality of its correspondence to male subjectivity. Female alienation is traced back to the very foundations of politics and the state, which exclude women and determine the social and political insignificance of relations between the sexes, even though this is a relationship marked by conflict of powers. The forms which society gives itself, and the content of the 'pact' which legitimizes them in order to regulate conflict, do not foresee regulation of the conflict between the sexes;

this conflict, and its subjects, tend to be denied the value and sense of a political conflict.

On the other hand, women's participation in politics has counted for something in the historical formation of the modern state. Right from its beginnings women have been familiar with forms of mobilization: either to claim equality of rights as free and independent individuals, 'subjects' in a way no different to the figure of the 'citizen' to which the liberal democratic state refers, or as a specific social group with common interests because marked out by their different social condition. What's more, despite the sanctioned, dismissive attitude of both state and politics to the relationship between the sexes and the sexed determination of individuals, in practice they turn to women and to areas of the relations between the sexes, such as the family, in order to create a few from marginal dynamic between women and the state.

With the vote and other civil and political rights, the question of women's consent opens up. Some research . . . has shown how little weight can be given to the thesis of the consent of passive women, directed by others (husband or priest), and problematizes the predominantly conservative female vote. More noted but less taken into account in recent analyses is female political participation in political movements and organizations, in ways which are not marked by women's sexual experience and identity. Just one question would be to ask how much the fracture we have seen in our historical memory, our collective conscience, has influenced forms of mobilization in recent history. What was the effect of the defeat of feminist positions, as opposed to those which regarded the 'woman question' as the 'social question', affirming that the overall emancipation of the oppressed, and especially the working class, would bring with it the emancipation of women? Why have women themselves forgotten for so long the warning of Annamaria Mozzoni, that '[the liberation of women] is the rock, the citadel where divine right, the power of force and the system of the exploitation of one individual by another, take refuge and for centuries yet can raise a challenge to all possible revolutions'?

In short, from the simple observation that politics is the most rigidly single-sex sphere and that this closure is all the more intolerable in a society whose increasing 'feminization' is now being underlined, we have gradually been coming to see the particular characteristics of the relationship between women and politics, between institutional forms and forms of sexed domination, between feminist theory and practice and the practice of women in politics and in the public sphere.

It would require too much space here to go back over all this ground and develop this argument fully. What I want to focus on here is forms of representation and female political subjectivity. This is a theme which is directly connected to developments within the theoretical and political debate of women. There are two aspects which highlight representation as the central issue: (1) discussion on the 'pact' between women, which for a considerable period of time has been the communicating thread between the practice and the theoretical reflections of women very much divided among themselves; (2) the development of feminist political practices, based on the relations between women and the recognition of sexual difference, within the political system; in particular political organizations such as the PCI, but also the Greens, the unions and representative institutions.

With regard to the first point, we should note that the question of the pact between women appears as the need to give shape to and work out forms for the relations between women, so separating it from the informality of social practice or the 'movement', and so defining in what ways it has made an impact on the public political scene. Indeed, the pact between women recalls the question of the democratic social pact, and the throwing into doubt of its legitimacy by and for women. Clearly representation is of the utmost importance here as the form which gives the pact shape, in that it guarantees the relationship between those who govern and those who are governed, between citizens and state. Can a pact between women be inserted into structures of representation, and what effect would it have on them? And the other side of the coin: in what way is the relationship between women (which forms the basis of this pact) changed in the market in which it becomes formalized and in which it seeks expression in political institutions?

With regard to the second aspect, representation is reconsidered both as the institution in which female political presence is most consistent, and as a form of different legitimization of that presence. If women who participate in the political system choose to locate the motivation for this presence in difference and not in being the same, privileging the relation between women over other political affiliations, this opens up the problem of sources and forms of political legitimization between women, and of political authority and responsibility within women's political practices.

It is from this perspective that the age-old question crops up again as to the motives which have until now determined the absence of a political preference of women for women candidates. In a purely proportional political system, with a significant weight being given to preferences for specific candidates, why is it that women don't choose to be represented by women? Even taking on board the thesis of a social group disadvantaged in the possession of resources which favour access to the political system; even taking into account the indirect handicap represented by women's predominant orientation towards social roles and functions, which require attitudes and qualities far removed from those predominant in politics; we still need to explain why female organizations themselves have not traditionally supported female candidates in elections, or why women politicians themselves have not enabled other women to enter into politics.

Phenomena such as these remain unexplained, and finish up by leading us back to stereotypes of female weakness or political conformism – the passive acceptance of already-existing rules. However, they acquire another meaning if they are read with a careful eye on the modality of a direct relationship between women and the tension between equality and difference which underlies female political participation. If we take as our starting point the hypothesis of exclusion of sex determination from politics and from the social pact, we can understand women's diffidence and sense of alienation from those of them who do go into politics without marking it with their sexed identity (and entry does not in itself guarantee any . . .); and on the other hand we can understand how it is that women politicians do not find themselves in a situation of privileged communication with their own sex, but on the contrary feel the need not to favour any calls made upon this allegiance, in order to lessen the weight of the disadvantages it brings with it.

Twenty years of feminism have widely celebrated how well-founded is most women's conviction that it will not be the institutions themselves that develop answers or the possibility of expression and recognition of their most profound need for freedom and social affirmation. I don't believe it is possible to think rigorously and *truly* about women's relationship to politics if we forget the radical critique with which feminism has addressed its own reason for being, the profile, which it encourages or brings out, of existence and being for individuals and groups.

This critique says that it is not in the political sphere that the solution to the domination of one sex by another will be found, nor will politics get to the root of the matter. This is because politics bases itself on a presupposition that the nature of the relationship between the sexes is not completely 'human', in that it is not social but natural. Assigning the whole matter to a sphere by definition removed from political action makes it possible to establish the efficacy of its means

and the legitimacy of its ends. As soon as what was seen to belong to
another order, what has been kept out, makes its presence felt on the
political scene, the very credibility of the ends and means of politics is
in shreds, as is the order which their correspondence puts into action.
For contemporary feminist thought, in other words, if modern forms
of politics and the state cannot be completely understood except by
highlighting their basis in the existence of domination between the
sexes, this domination cannot find a resolution in them. I will come
back to this point.

It is important to emphasize here that it is always highly problematic and never straightforward for women to enter the political scene.
This can in no way be attributed to female passivity, to a lack of
sensibility and passion for the collective dimension, to a facile
adaptation to codified roles. Alienation and mistrust come out of the
high moments of women's theorizing and subjectivity, and are
recurring traits through years of experience of strong mobilization and
participation. So why are women so soon *disappointed* by politics?
Why do we constantly see in female political experience a swinging
between an extreme form of conformity, denying sexed identity, and a
sense of rejection and incompatibility if this identity is referred to?

Is there a possible women's practice which could take this oscillation on board, which would recognize both what takes women into
politics and what alienates them, undermining this presence from
within, thus undoing the possibility that they use the resources of
politics to their advantage? Is it possible to unite in the one practice
and the one project the need to improve the position of women in the
social and political order as it is currently structured and organized,
and the need to construct in society a sexed order founded on the *free*
social existence of the two sexes? Is it possible, that is, to fight an
effective social and political battle, in which women finish up by being
aligned with the physiognomy of social groups, and at the same time
work for a radical transformation of what we call 'society' and 'state',
the whole bundle of rules, institutions and languages which structure
relations? How can this radical project be carried out, why and how is
it possible, necessary indeed? These are some of the problems which
feminism is thinking through.

(2)   The 1987 election campaign represented a political acceleration
of the debate, and in some way turned it into more of an issue *within*
politics. By this I mean that the decision of the PCI women to take
part in the electoral campaign through female candidates, developed
within a practice of women's relations strongly marked by the fact of

being female, ended up by concretizing the positions of those who were 'for' and those who were 'against', and so forcing the hand of debate and analysis. Many of the questions we asked above are destined to remain unexpressed, because they belong to a non-assertive value of truth which does not prescribe behaviour, which reveals ambivalences and contradictions at the level of the needs themselves ... The complex of plans, the fecundity which this represents, is to some extent sacrificed to the urgency of choice and of speaking out, on the part both of those who support the chance to be present in the elections and of those who are critical of this choice.

Before going into the pros and cons of these questions, which developed because of the approaching elections, I would like to underline one aspect which I feel very strongly about. For some time I have been convinced that feminist practice betrays a weakness each time it fails to affirm its *ambivalence* and, so to speak, resolves the factors which make it up into an articulation of feminist positions, which are sometimes veritable battlelines. By ambivalence I mean the determining of points of view and behaviour resulting from factors which would seem to be opposed or even irreconcilable.

If we stay with the problems we have already outlined, feminist ambivalence expresses itself, for example, in holding together aliena-tion and participation in politics; in wanting to enact a presence and achieve a result which both tackles and involves the political system, while holding onto and indeed making plainly visible its position of eccentricity, of not being inscribed in the political order, given its own subjectivity and the sex-contradictions to which it refers. Or we have ambivalence between the need/will to produce concrete changes in female existence; proceeding along a path of claims and rights with the awareness that female liberty does not belong to the order of civil and political freedoms and is not to be realized through a different social justice and a widening of citizenship. Finally there is ambivalence between the emancipation of women and even the struggle against sexual division of labour, and the realization of a sexed social order.

To speak of ambivalence is to assume awareness that levels distinct one from the other do not place themselves in logical and temporal succession, but present themselves as simultaneous, within the one theoretical achievement and the one political and social behaviour. It is this simultaneity which signifies the possibility of acting, holding *together* the efficacy of concreteness and the radicality of the project. It is always simultaneity which makes it possible to stay within all scenarios, without being imprisoned in the mask which they try to impose on us.

In the raw, allusive language of the seventies we spoke of 'inside and outside' to indicate that the movement's practice had to proceed assuming female/feminist both belonging to and in alienation from the entire world, from structures and languages. In the day-to-day business of the movement this translated itself into the construction of a practice which sought to be as incisive as possible on the external, and to interrelate as closely as possible with, and give maximum attention to, the internal; and while it is obvious what the 'external' indicates, by 'internal' we understand the practice of relations between women and reflection on what they produce as modification of female subjectivity and its perception of the 'external'. This was the only way the struggle for the abortion law could be fought, limiting the risk that feminist theorizing on the body, on sexuality, on the social control of women and on self-determination be reduced to the request for a more up-to-date codification of social behaviours.

It seemed worthwhile to make this digression because it helps clarify what is lost every time, in feminist practice, ambivalence gives way to the opposite need of 'fidelity' to the most radical kernel of the project, or to efficiency or incisiveness. The opposite needs can appear in many other pairings, and when they appear ambivalence is seen as ambiguity, as lack of determination or as confusion, and a simplifying drive prevails. The widespread prejudice contained in the formula *simplex sigillum veri* [simplicity is the sign of truth] shows itself to be obdurate even amongst women.

(3)   In the search for forms for female presence in political institutions, we soon see the tendency to solve the knot of problems which appear just by simplifying them.

One of the first simplifications occurs in the way the words 'representation' and 'sex' are used. On the one hand there are those who say that establishing a relationship inevitably makes for a reduction of sex to social category or group, thus reinserting women in the nomenclature of interests, distinct from those of other groups and common to themselves. On the other hand the decision to ask women to vote for women in order to correct a weighty discrimination, and to take the bodies, words and interests of women into the institutions, appears as 'representation of sex'. The way in which these arguments are posed in the political institutions helps to favour this simplifying contrast. In the debate of the communist women, formulated within the party, the call for political 'reform' which 'representation of sex' will bring with it comes up time and time again. These arguments underline the view that women bring with them values, behaviours and social functions which can only be innovative in the political sphere. More deeply, they underline the contradictions opened up by the decision to create a representative channel from woman to woman with regard to the way in which representation functions, both as access for social subjects to politics and as selection of elites. And there are also those who read the decision to favour the entry of a numerically consistent number of women into institutions as a shifting of the advantage of political resources to women, as an act of contractual force and substantial redistribution of power between the sexes.

These positions are articulated more interestingly at the level of principles, even if this articulation too is destined to leave no choice other than clear agreement or rejection. The argument of those who are against representation is substantially that to inscribe difference in forms which the male symbolic has elaborated as forms of equality (that is, women's insignificance) is to legitimize them again, and to deny that in society there exist and operate women's words and actions which carry any authority. This presence, they say, does not produce contradiction and is not 'awkward', because transgression, the subversion of the order in which this presence inserts itself, is unforeseen and unthinkable.

Those who look more favourably on the transposition of sexual difference into the institutions follow a line of reasoning in some ways opposite to this. They move from the *fact* that a *form of authorization* for the presence of women within institutions has developed in women's practice. This female source of choice is already a significant break with channels of representation, since it creates a *sexed* relationship between representatives and those represented. This is what makes it thinkable and possible to take the relations between women, which are the foundation of their subjectivity, into other places such as the institutions. Without this source such a transposition would make no sense. But is this act sufficient to determine a disruptive effect for sexed representation and to guarantee that it will not be assimilated into existing forms? . . .

I will here focus just on the dangers attached to the disruptive force of representation, of 'being present' and 'making visible' difference, creating *recognition* between the word of the representative and the represented woman, because the speaker draws on the experience of the woman who pronounces it, and so it is not a simple copy of that of men. The accent on this aspect of representation introduces into the argument the centrality of the symbolic order, and so confrontation is not so much with the function of the representative institution as with the cultural code of representation, with the symbolic mediation which it puts into effect. In this sense this aspect of representation should not be undervalued.

And yet I am not convinced that the possibility of offering a representation of difference remains attached to its direct signification in women's words. The symbolic force of the institution lies precisely in its ability to disembody itself, to abstract from 'experience' and then place itself in signs which are widely (universally) useful. It is in the almost intangible forms of the norm, the mediation between particularistic differentiation and uniformity, procedural and behavioural techniques, the codification of subjects and the substance of choices, that the single-sex character of representation remains hidden. Signifying difference means undoing this order and working out the elements which might go to making up a new one.

What doesn't convince is that this could happen by having recourse to the exclusive register of representation without dealing with the *function* of political representation, with the content of the social pact and with the concrete process which realizes them historically. This function concerns us both because representation operates for us *too*, and towards us – are we not then citizens, even if not female citizens? – and because it is the way it proceeds in indifference to the conflict between the sexes and female subjectivity that motivates the choice to 'be present', so that this situation will not perpetuate itself.

The oscillation between maximum fidelity to the project, founded on its being other, external and outside, and minimal realization returns in the hypothesis of signifying oneself in difference. Indeed it can easily happen that the great claim to signify difference on the symbolic level goes together with the difficulty of, and even resistance to, dealing with the *ties* of the process through which this symbolization is produced. It is not a recent phenomenon that omnipotence and misery are the two shores of female existence, and the growth of the female claim, which the very idea of sexual difference introduces into women's lives and women's plans for themselves, risks being easily perverted into a cynical calculation of possibilities and means, simply because this claim is so such removed from the need to deal with the ties which it encounters.

(4) The 'function' of representation seems to bring up again the problem of the 'representation of sex', both in terms of specific content and in its reference to 'all women'. In this way difference presents itself as one of the differentiations of the social body, an expression of social pluralism. We can see how this equivocation generates consensus or concern according to the value we place on

social pluralism and the neo-corporative versions of political representation. However, the mistake is frequently made of opposing models of representation for equality to those of representation for interests. As Adriana Cavarero rightly states, there is no contradiction or opposition between the two accepted meanings of representation; rather, one complements the other since 'the individual is double, naturally made up of both reason and passion', and if equality assures everybody of 'equal possibilities and resources', 'the ability and passion of the individual creates differences.' Differentiation of interests is in itself infinite, since we can regard as interests all the passions, needs and desires of individuals who ask for satisfaction and recognition in the public sphere.

The common good is, in fact, defined as 'common interest', the fruit of a complex work of bringing together the particular and the general, difference and equality. This system of regulation is glued together by the collective organizations which gather in homogeneous groups, giving them a collective identity, those who are drawn together by similar interests, who have a common and shared idea of what constitutes the general interest. Or to put it in terms much more in use today, individuals unite into groups in order to have greater power in competition, and to be able to determine to their own advantage the distribution of resources. Since the individual is, in his or her neutrality, the referent both of equality and of interests, representation is always enacted somewhere between differentiation and equality.

In this sense, classic theories of emancipation which assumed equality between men and women as a progressive realization of the project of modernity, and pluralist theories which assimilate women to interest groups, or to 'minorities', are not so far apart. For if we stay within the confines of modern politics, as liberal-democratic theories and the history of states have delineated them, it is clear that for women it's a question both of winning statutory equality and of their position as an interest group. Besides, as Anna Rossi-Doria states, the political history of rights and female liberty has developed by having recourse to both these principles, that of a 'specific' group and that of the universality of the human condition and subjectivity.

Yet in the most recent accepted meaning of 'representation of sex', in terms of an interest group, we see some differences, since it seems to move away from the problematical nature of equality, not unlike what happens on a more general level with the stressing of the corporative and particularistic character of interests. We should note above all that the delineation of the female interest tends to appear progressively uncoupled from the problems of social inequalities and the hierarchy of social roles and functions, and restrict itself to a mapping out of anti-female discrimination within equal social conditions. In some way the affirmation of emancipation seems to produce a request for 'additional emancipation' in terms of resources and of conditions for access to them, a request which supports a widening of female presence in political institutions. Women in the Socialist party seem to constitute the most exact point of reference for this request, but I believe that motivations of this sort are not foreign to other political forces too, which are experiencing a 'feminization' of militancy and the electorate, even if these motives are not spelt out because they clash with the prevailing ideology of those parties.

More risky in pluralist positions is that they take on the idea and practice of sexual difference, making it a form of differentiation of interests. This is why expressions such as 'representation of sex' become equivocal, because the call to solidarity of the 'female sex' allows sex to be assimilated to other determinations of interest or political issues. Terms such as 'representation of gender' or 'sexed representation' are less open to this kind of equivocation, because they realign the sexual determinant of representation with the quality of its form and the subject who enacts it, rather than with the configuration of a social body.

While the reduction of women to a social group with homogeneous interests, to a 'minority', does not satisfactorily express the originality of the female position with regard to the political and state order, we should not undervalue analyses of the dynamic between female action and institutional action carried out by political scientists and sociologists. They help us to understand which are the characteristics of homology and which those of the originality of those female and feminist practices which 'by definition' refuse to act within the logic of a pressure group. A model of this kind of work, for example, could be usefully applied to the study of the women PCI members' policies, and also to some feminist groups, which have found themselves acting in relation to the institutions.

It would be very interesting to see political scientists analysing female behaviour within the development of the representative function, showing in particular how much of this behaviour is determined by whether it is addressed to male interlocutors, who largely coincide with the subject institutions, or to female interlocutors: organizations, political partners, women members of the public, and so on. We could learn a lot that would be useful in defining the project of signifying difference, if we knew more about the effective presence women have in politics.

The question of quotas is usually brought up in connection with the perspective of an interest group: quotas are seen as safeguards, a guarantee for the minority. In reality the weight that 'numbers' have is more complex. Dahlerup has made two very interesting points about this. The first regards the fact that the woman or few women elected in the institutions take on the character of a 'symbol': symbol of formal equality, and symbol of women's lesser capacity to play that part, remaining above all 'female'. The second regards the 'critical mass' that a substantial minority can constitute. The hypothesis is that below a certain numerical threshold there is not even the possibility of giving one's own presence some autonomy and influence. In particular there is no possibility of constructing a transversality of women's relations and actions with regard to political allegiances and institutional rules. If it is correct that quantity does not in itself guarantee the leap to quality, in other words that not even parity of numerical presence would of itself produce forms of representation which were not homologous, nonetheless numbers are important, because where women are few and isolated, it is more difficult for them to find the strength or the chance to relate to each other, and so make for themselves an effective autonomy.

(5) We have up to this point referred to the principle of difference without worrying about defining it. Why does the theme of difference come out in contemporary feminism, what is its status and how does it constitute a key to the working out of a different political order, so allowing us to speak of a 'sexed representation'? This is the substance of a huge amount of feminist research, which here we can only allude to.

Let us stay with difference for the moment. The use of the term 'difference' is an indication that by 'sexual difference' reference is not being made to femininity; it is not 'female' character or identity which is being stated here. Femininity, like masculinity, is a symbolic production marked by the relationship of domination between the sexes. As such it cannot fail to concern every woman, for what woman is really free from this domination in a society in which her 'being a woman's body' continually projects it onto her? Yet clinging on to it is a gesture of existence, or an act of thought, which of itself places woman in a position of subordination. So the emergence of sexual difference marks in the first place the production of a *distance* between femininity and the perception which women have of themselves. It is in this space of not belonging to the 'feminine' that the principle of sexual difference appears.

If it is not obvious that to be a woman is to be 'female', what am I, a 'woman' – what is it to be a woman? In the modern age this question becomes a *social question*, and affects more than the individual in her search for self-definition. This distance from femininity appears in the form of a widespread *social alienation*, a growing sense of female unease or suffering. Here I cannot review even the titles of the stages and manifestations of this process. I will simply expound my thesis.

The modern age puts at the centre of society, politics and history the figure of the individual, and the dynamic between liberty and equality profoundly disturbs the balance of relations between the sexes and the social and political order. Each existence and each relationship is called on to measure itself against the paradigm of the free, independent, sovereign individual, and we all know that the possession of the self, of goods and even of other existences is the foundation of freedom, independence and sovereignty. Woman and man are both by definition 'individuals', but while man can recognize himself in the figure which embodies the individual, woman cannot. Even the oppressed and exploited man can recognize himself in it, and indeed he struggles to overthrow the conditions which make his freedom, independence and sovereignty imperfect. Woman too, struggling for her own emancipation, fights to be an individual amongst individuals, to rid herself of the determinations which make her 'different', unequal, deprived of the attributes and the 'rights' of individuality.

But while the other oppressed have nothing to lose but their chains – though is this really so? – woman, by continuing to affirm her emancipation, 'discovers' that it has a very high price, the progressive loss of correspondence – partial as it may be – between her own social being and the process of defining the 'I', this last being inevitably tied to sexuality. The more widespread and profound emancipation becomes, the more unbearable it is for women to have to reconcile the identity it produces with female identity. Woman becomes alienated from herself, because she is alien both to femaleness and to that strange, indefinite identity which is given her when she takes on masculine behaviour and characteristics in a woman's body.

The feminization of society which characterizes contemporary societies brings out this change in female subjectivity. Sexual difference appears not as backwardness, dissonance due to the survival of more archaic social forms, but as a ripe fruit of modernity, an effect of emancipation processes, of the redistribution of roles between the sexes, of the growing overlap of spheres and functions which were previously distinct.

If the reasons for this emergence lie in the fact that women's female being has become problematic for them, on the other hand the feminization of society disperses characters, abilities, functions and qualities which were held to belong to women. Not only are women more widespread in the social fabric, but the very connotations of femininity become available to both sexes. Yet despite this growing 'confusion' between the sexes, between male and female, the sexed structure of society remains, and can still be very rigid. And the relationship of power which marks it has barely been dented. Society becomes more feminized, but its code, and the subject able to attribute its historicity to himself, remains masculine. The principle of difference enunciates, unlike the female intention to put herself forward as subject who produces history, because it gives an account of itself. In this sense it responds to social alienation by trying to offer female existence a way of remaining close to itself, bringing together processes of social and political identification which affect it with processes of subjective identification. It is not by chance that feminism combines political and psychoanalytic thought.

In other words the question of sexual difference emerges in the earth ploughed by emancipation and the new contradictions which it has produced. If the perspective which it inaugurates is that of an autonomous female subjectivity, its definition is still attached to the nature of the relationship of domination between the sexes. The need to found female subjectivity on an assumption of difference from the male is the only way to make it progressively autonomous from femininity too, from a form of identity which has dependence inscribed in it.

If, on the contrary, women were to pursue a project of progressive indifferentiation, of definite 'confusion' between the sexes, femininity would remain a powerful attraction for them. For there is an area of strong resistance to indifferentiation, and that is sexuality. Even if it was thinkable, the idea of an androgyne to replace figures of the same and the different, which regulate the complex material and symbolic world of sexuality, seems to me highly undesirable.

On the other hand, the history of emancipation shows that it is impossible to come up with a solution to social and political relationships between the sexes without making the sexual order central. It is this need to liberate sexual difference from dependence on a masculine subject, which has thought of it only as a 'natural' determination, that makes of it the principle of political action and the foundation of female autonomous subjectivity. This action and this autonomy move from one point: that *women know themselves to be different*. In recent years they have circulated this knowledge, given it form. But it has still not acquired social credibility, or legitimization or recognition. It appears as a pretension, women's positive prejudice in favour of themselves as compensation for the consciousness of having historically been a minority. The task feminism has set itself is to produce both deeds and conceptualizations which affirm sexual difference in society. The very simultaneity of the two processes obviously makes them more precarious.

If the choice to introduce the principle of female authority in social and political areas is strong on the political level, the conceptualization of this experience is rather weaker. As Adriana Cavarero says: since it is the relationship between women that is 'the concrete ambit in which the principle functions and unfolds itself, the concreteness of the relation (which is always a relation of these women, with this experience, in this place) cannot immediately translate itself into a model of order valid for all women.' So the relation is always specific, and yet stands as a signifier of another 'order'. We cannot miss the clear affirmation expressed here of *will* and *decision* as sources of legitimization and even more so of the creation of a new dimension. Yet Cavarero herself warns us that the act of will remains tied to a *prejudice* which makes it possible, or to the conviction that the 'neutral-masculine order' is penetrable, that 'the political sphere, totally other and alien to sexual difference, should not be left to its perennial but burdensome otherness and alienation.' Putting difference this way as something 'thoroughly other', its being the origin, signifier and outcome of the project, hinders the possibility of a conceptualization of the forms in which it acts.

This conceptualization appears to be more possible if we take the following as reference points: (1) that women participate in both orders, the 'neutral-masculine' one and the sexed one; (2) that the order of sexual difference is not in practice 'parallel' to the 'neutral-masculine' one, but assumes visibility and form as it gradually replaces, conflicts and interacts with the existing order. While one part of feminism understands autonomy and the freedom of the female subject in terms of the constitution of a 'parallel' order, constructed in non-difference and separate from the 'neutral-masculine' or existing one, I would say that female autonomy and freedom construct themselves by introducing plenitude where there was a gap, the presence of a subject where there was an absence, without the possibility of suspending the level of relations between the sexes.

In this sense the production of a 'sexed' order, a social and political order which assumes the existence of two different subjects, masculine and feminine, if it presupposes the existence and autonomy of the female subject, cannot be realized autonomously by women, but will be the result of a conflict which sees men and women as opposites but simultaneously present. It is clear that without relations between women, without female authorization, without production of a knowing of difference by women, we will not see even the conditions which configure this kind of conflict. But the state in which female subjectivity will be located will be a complex and mobile one, which will see simultaneously relations between women and relations between women and men.

Table of Women's Centres

City/town	Name of Centre (and translation)	Year founded
Ancona	Biblioteca delle donne (Women's Library)	1983
Bergamo	Lastrea: Centro di documentazione delle donne (Lastrea: Women's Resources Centre)	1983
Bologna	Centro di documentazione, ricerca e iniziativa delle donne (Women's Resources, Research and Initiative Centre)	1981
Brescia	Centro della donna (Women's Centre)	1977
Cagliari	La Tarantola: Centro studi e comunicaz sulla condizione femminile, libreria delle donne (The Tarantula: Centre for the Study and Communication of the Female Condition, Women's Bookshop)[a]	1977
Caserta	Centro studi documentazione e ricerca sulla donna (Centre for Women's Studies and Research)	1984
Civitavecchia, Rome	Terradilei (Herland)	1980
Como	Centro culturale dimensione donna (Female Dimension Cultural Centre)	1979
Ferrara	Centro documentazione donna, associazione e biblioteca delle donne (Women's Resources Centre, Association and Library)	1980

City/town	Name of Centre (and translation)	Year founded
Florence	Libreria delle donne (Women's Bookshop)[a]	1980
Foggia	Centro documentazione e ricerca donne (Women's Resources and Research Centre)	1985
Genoa	Coordinamento donne lavoro cultura (Coordination for Women, Work and Culture)	1984
Genoa	Demetra: Associazione, gruppo culturale, centro di documentazione e libreria delle donne (Demetra: Association, Cultural Group, Resources Centre and Women's Bookshop)[a]	1983
Genoa	Gruppo communicazione visiva (Visual Communication Group)	1979
Grosseto	Centro donna (Women's Centre)	1985
L'Aquila	La biblioteca della donna (The Women's Library)	1983
Livorno	Centro donna (Women's Centre)	1984
Mestre	Centro donna del Commune di Venezia (Venice City Council Women's Centre)	1980
Milan	Centri di studi storici sul movimento di liberazione della donna in Italia (Centre for Historical Studies on the Women's Liberation Movement in Italy)	1979
Milan	Centro studi Sibilla Aleramo, centro di documentazione, associazione biblioteca delle donne, centro culturale (Sibilla Aleramo Studies Centre, Resources Centre, Association, Women's Library, Cultural Centre)	1980
Naples	Centro donna (Women's Centre)	1979
Padua	Centro documentazione donna Lidia Crepet (Lidia Crepet Women's Resources Centre)	1983
Pisa	Centro documentazione donna (Women's Resources Centre)	1982
Pordenone	Centro di documentazione l'acqua in gabbia (The Water in the Cage Resources Centre)	1983
Rome	Associazione centro studi	1977

Table of Women's Centres

City/town	Name of Centre (and translation)	Year founded
	DonnaWomanFemme – DWF (DonnaWomanFemme Study Centre and Association)	
Rome	Centro culturale Virginia Woolf (Virginia Woolf Cultural Centre)	1979
Rome	Centro documentazione e studi sul femminismo (Feminist Resources and Study Centre)	1978
Siena	Centro culturale Mara Meoni (Mara Meoni Cultural Centre	1980
Turin	Biblioteca delle donne sorrelle Benso (Benso Sisters' Women's Library	1976
Turin	Camera Woman (Camera Woman)	1983
Turin	Centro di documentazione sulla salute della donna Simonetta Tosi (Simonetta Tosi Resources Centre for Women's Health)	1985
Turin	Associazione Livia Laverani Donini (Livia Laverani Donini Association)	1983
Turin	Produrre e riprodurre (Produce and Reproduce)	1983
Verona	Il filo di Arianna (Ariadne's Web)	1984

[a] Women's bookshops are listed only if they are part of a Centre or are non-profit-making.

Chronology 1965–1986

This chronology does not – obviously – aim at exhaustiveness. As far as international events go, both in general and with regard to feminism, the few events listed here are meant to set the reader's memory in motion, rather than to give a detailed panorama. Italian politics, the Italian women's movement and Italian feminism are given more attention, as they are probably less familiar to the reader. But even there, omissions and simplifications are inevitable.

For example: the seventies were a decade of political violence in Italy, with many terrorist groups, both left- and right-wing, carrying out actions of different kinds (bombings, kidnappings, woundings etc.). Reporting them all would have made this chronology much too long; we have chosen to mention specifically only some of them, and to refer generically to the continuing terrorist activity every now and then.

Trying to report, let alone explain, all the political and financial scandals would also have been too much: brief references are made to the most important ones.

The foundation dates of the Centri Culturali are not registered here, as they can be found in the table of women's centres.

Finally: the dates are always correct with regard to the year, and have been carefully checked as far as possible with regard to the month. But in the latter case, some uncertainties remain, and we have shown this with a question mark put in parentheses before the indication of the event.

We chose the period 1965–86 in order to present as fully as possible the most recent and active phase of feminism.

	INTERNATIONAL	ITALY
1965		
Jan.	Great Britain: Death of Churchill	Saragati (PSDI: Democratic Socialist Party) first non-Christian-Democrat president of the Republic
Feb.	USA: Assassination of Malcolm X Bombings on North Vietnam begin	(?) Sicily: Franca Viola refuses to marry the man who abducted and raped her – marriage would absolve him of his crime
Apr.	Coup in Santo Domingo, with the support and intervention of the USA	
June	Coup in Algeria – Ben Bella ousted, Boumedienne in power	
Oct.	(?) USA: Betty Friedan founds the National Organization of Women (NOW)	
Dec.	France: De Gaulle re-elected president of the Republic	Milan: Demistificazione dell'Autoritarismo (DEMAU: Demystification of Authority) comes into being
1966		
Jan.	India: Indira Ghandi becomes prime minister	First, short, sporadic occupations of the universities occur all through the year in Trento, Naples, Rome
Mar.	France leaves NATO	
Apr.	China: Beginnings of the Cultural Revolution and the Red Guards movement, encouraged by Mao Ze Dong	
1967		
Jan.		Pisa: Occupation of the university
Feb.	(?) Great Britain: Abortion Act	Milan: Occupation of the Faculty of Architecture

	INTERNATIONAL	ITALY
Apr.	Greece: Military coup	Venice: Occupation of the Faculty of Architecture
		(?) Unione Donne Italiane (UDI) puts forward a law for the protection of work for women
June	Israeli–Arab war	(?) Bosco bill on protection of work for women
	Berlin: Demonstration against the visit of the Shah (Benno Ohnesorg, a student, is killed by the police) marks the beginning of widespread student protest in Germany	Turin: Six-day occupation of the university
Aug.	USA: Black riots in Newark	
Oct.	Death of Che Guevara	
Nov.	(?) Berlin: Frauenhouse opens for beaten women	Occupation of the universities in Naples and Milan
	Cyprus: Clashes between the Greek and Turk inhabitants	

1968

Jan.	Russian space module *Surveyor* reaches the moon	Occupation of universities in many Italian cities
	Spain: Strikes in the universities	Earthquake in Belice, Sicily
	Washington, D.C., and New York: Peace marches by women	In the Senate, the right obstructs the establishment of the regions
	Czechoslovakia: Confrontation in the Communist Party between Stalinists (Novotny) and reformers (Dubcek); Dubcek secretary of the party	
	Japan: Clashes between the police and left-wing students demonstrating against a USA military base.	
	Vietnam: Tet offensive	

	INTERNATIONAL	ITALY
Feb.	New York: Shulamith Firestone of the Red Stockings feminist group describes consciousness-raising techniques	Clashes all over Italy between students and the police; more occupations of universities
	USA: Antiracist demonstrations in Orangeburg, South Carolina: three killed and fifty wounded	Trial of Sifar (secret service) for involvement in illegal interferences in Italian politics
	Student demonstrations in France and Germany against Vietnam war	
	Palestinian guerrilla actions begin	
Mar.	Poland: Student demonstrations against censorship	Student protest spreads to schools
	Rhodesia: Five leaders of the nationalist movement condemned to death	
Apr.	Brazil: Student demonstrations	Turin: Strikes at Fiat factories
	USA: Riots in black ghettoes following the assassination in Memphis of Martin Luther King	Rome: Bomb at Boston Chemical Company, producer of napalm
	Berlin: Attempt on life of student leader Rudi Dutschke; demonstrations all over Germany	UDI invites women to vote for women candidates
		Student demonstrations against attempt on Dutschke
May	France: Student protest at its peak – occupation of universities, demonstrations, violent clashes with the police	General elections
	USA: Student demonstrations against Vietnam war	
	Paris: Negotiations begin between USA and North Vietnam	

	INTERNATIONAL	ITALY
June	France: Worker occupation of Renault factory, massive strikes all over the country	First Fortuna divorce bill
	USA: Robert Kennedy killed	
	Strikes and demonstrations in Israel on the anniversary of the Israeli–Arab war	
	Student protests in Brazil, Argentina, Uruguay; violent clashes in Rio de Janeiro	
July	France: Couve de Meurville prime minister	Encyclical *Humanae Vitae* published
	USA: Riots in black ghettoes	Strikes and occupations in many factories
	Mexico City: Student demonstrations, many killed and wounded in clashes with the police	
	PLO hijacks an Israeli plane; hostages exchanged for Palestinian prisoners	
Aug.	Warsaw Pact troops invade Czechoslovakia	The Communist Party condemns Soviet intervention in Czechoslovakia
Sep.	Iran: 20,000 killed in earthquake	Venice: National conference of students' movement
	Mexico City: Demonstrations and clashes continue	
	Biafra war at its end: reunification with Nigeria	
Oct.	Mexico City: Police shoot and kill in student demonstration	Student protest and occupation of universities resumed
	Mexico: At the Olympic Games USA black athlete winners salute with clenched fists	Many female students active in student protest from the start: some also begin to meet in women-only groups
	New York: Valerie Solanas writes *SCUM*	
	Portugal: Caetano replaces	

INTERNATIONAL	ITALY
Salazar as head of the government	
Northern Ireland: Beginnings of religious-political strife	

	INTERNATIONAL	ITALY
Nov.	Athens: Police charge at Papandreou funeral	Eighth congress of UDI
	Berlin: More clashes between students and police	Reaction of Catholic hierarchy against socially engaged Catholic groups: Cardinal
	Athens: Panagulis trial	Florit asks Don Enzo Mazzi to leave the commune in the Florentine parish of Isolotto
	Chicago: National Conference for Women's Liberation	
	USA: Nixon elected President	Rome: Trial for collapse of Vajont dam begins
Dec.		Constitutional court declares unconstitutional the inequality between the sexes with regard to the law on adultery

1969

	INTERNATIONAL	ITALY
Jan.	Paris: South Vietnamese government and the Liberation Front join the negotiations	
Feb.	(?) Israel: Golda Meir prime minister	Rome: Demonstrations against Nixon's visit
Apr.	France: De Gaulle resigns	
July	Man sets foot on the moon	
Aug.	USA: Woodstock rock concert	
Sep.	Death of Ho Chi Minh	'Hot Autumn': Workers' demonstrations all over Italy, which continue to the end of the year
	Germany: SPD victory at the elections, coalition government with the Liberals	
Nov.	(?) Berne: Women march for the vote	Constitutional court repeals law on concubinage
Dec.		Milan: Fascist bombs at the Bank of Agriculture in Piazza Fontana – sixteen dead and many wounded

	INTERNATIONAL	ITALY
1970		
Feb.		Milan and Rome: Rivolta Femminile groups come into being
		Milan: Anabasis group comes into being
Mar.		Padua and Rome: Birth of Lotta Femminista collectives
		Trento: Birth of Il Cerchio Spezzato collective
May	France: 343 women report themselves to the police for having abortions	Fortuna–Baslini law introducing divorce is placed on statute books
		Foundation of the Movimento di Liberazione della Donna (MLD), affiliated to the Radical Party
June	Great Britain: Conservative victory, Edward Heath prime minister	
July		Milan: Rivolta Femminile publish and post up on walls their *Manifesto*
Aug.	USA: Housewives strike	*Donne e politica*, journal of women in the Italian Communist Party, begins publication
Sept.	Death of Nasser	
Oct.	Chile: Salvator Allende president	
Dec.	Spain: Trial of Basque separatists in Burgos; six later given death penalty	
	Poland: Demonstrations in Gdansk; Gierek becomes leader of the Communist Party	

	INTERNATIONAL	ITALY
1971		
Feb.	Switzerland: Women granted right to vote in General Elections	Rome: First Congress of MLD
Mar.	France: Gisele Halimi founds Choisir, in favour of the legalization of abortion	Constitutional court repeals a law article which made the advertising of contraceptives illegal
May		MLD present a bill to regulate the termination of pregnancy, and begin campaign of women declaring they have had abortions
		Rome: Lotta Femminista organizes exhibition on violence against women in advertising
June		Fronte Italiano per la Liberazione Femminile (FILF) comes into being
		Milan: National meeting of feminist groups
		Rome: First bill to regulate abortion read in the Chamber
Nov.		Rome: International demonstration against the repression of abortion
Dec.	Kurt Waldheim UN general secretary	Passing of five-year plan to provide 3,800 council nurseries
1972		
Jan.	Los Angeles: Birth of Feminist Women's Health Centre	Milan: Birth of the Via Cherubini collective
	Great Britain, Ireland and Denmark in the EEC	Rome: The Movimento Femminista Romano (MFR), also known as Pompeo Magno, comes into being
Feb.	Nixon in China	

	INTERNATIONAL	ITALY
Mar.		Rome: Police charge against women of the MFR (Pompeo Magno) demonstrating on International Woman's Day (8 March)
May	Boston: First rape crisis centre founded East Germany: Law passed on termination of pregnancy	General elections
June	France: Mouvement de Libération des Femmes organizes a European conference in Vandea Germany: Ulrike Meinhof arrested	
July		Rome: Lotta Femminista from Padua organize a conference on women's work and salaries for housewives Trade unions CGIL, CISL and UIL form a federation
Sep.	Munich: At the Olympic Games, Israeli raid following PLO guerrilla action – many dead and wounded USA: Watergate scandal	Rome: MFR (Pompeo Magno) organize exhibitions in the popular district of San Lorenzo, asking for clinics to be opened
Oct.	France: Psychanalise et Politique (Psycho & Po) organize European conference at Chateau des Vieux Villes	Chamber passes law reforming jurisdiction on the family
Nov.	London: Conference of the English feminist movement USA: Nixon re-elected president	

	INTERNATIONAL	ITALY
Dec.	Further escalation of the Vietnam war; Hanoi and Haiphong bombed, demonstrations against USA in many countries	Turin: The daily newspaper *La Stampa* organizes a collection of signatures in support of a law by popular initiative to reform the Merlin law, which had closed brothels
		Rome: MFR (Pompeo Magno) campaign against moves to change the Merlin law
1973		
Jan.	Denmark: Law passed legalizing abortion	Rome: Feminist monthly *Effe* begins publication with experimental issue, no. 0
	USA: A supreme court judgement states women have the right to choose abortion	
	Paris: Peace treaty signed between North Vietnam and USA; South Vietnam continues war	
Feb.	USA: Law passed on equal pay for men and women	Rome: Meeting of feminist groups, on the right to abortion, with Gisele Halimi and Juliet Mitchell
		Rome: MFR (Pompeo Magno) organizes a meeting on female prostitution in Italy
		Reading of the abortion law in Parliament
		The Centro Italiano Sterilizzazione e Aborto (CISA: Italian Centre for Sterilization and Abortion) is set up in various cities
Mar.		Milan: *Sottosopra* appears, organ of Milan feminist groups
		Varigotti (Liguria): meeting between the Via Cherubini collective and Psych & Po

INTERNATIONAL	ITALY
	Padua: Opening of the trial of Gigliola Pierobon for abortion; feminist campaign against the trial
Apr. Miners' strike in Chile	Birth of self-help groups
May Argentina: Campora becomes president, Peron returns from exile	Milan: Conference on sexuality organized by the FUORI (Homosexual Front) and by FILF marks the break of lesbofeminists from other homosexual women
	The metalworkers contract establishes the 150-hour courses for workers without school qualifications
	Naples: Meetings of Lotta Femminista and MFR (Pompeo Magno) to discuss salaries for housewives
June Sydney: Leichhardt Women's Community Health Centre is set up	Padua: Lotta Femminista pamphlet on salaries for housewives appears
Spain: Franco leaves the post of prime minister to Carrero Blanco	
July Argentina: Campora resigns, Peron president	
Sep. Military coup in Chile; Allende killed, Pinochet in power	
Oct. Middle East: Kippur war	Padua: Foundation of the Triveneto Committee on salaries for housewives
Nov. Armistice between Egypt and Israel	Rome: Feminist theatre La Maddalena opens
	Rome: Feminist monthly *Effe* begins regular publication
	Ninth congress of UDI

	INTERNATIONAL	ITALY
Dec.	Spain: Carrero Blanco assassinated by ETA The OPEC conference raises the price of oil	Rome: Arab terrorists attack Pan Am plane at Fiumicino airport
1974		
Jan.	England: Rape crisis centres opened	Trento: 263 women charged with illegal abortion Milan: *Pratica dell'inconscio* (practice of the unconscious) groups are set up
Feb.	West Germany: Abortion legalized Frankfurt: Conference of feminists in Western Europe USA: Impeachement of Nixon	Rome: Feminist groups for women's health come into being
Mar.	Belgium: Foundation of the United Feminist Party	Rome: Feminist clinic set up in the popular district of San Lorenzo
Apr.	Portugal: Fall of the dictatorship	Naples: UDI conference on the struggle for emancipation in Southern Italy The Red Brigades kidnap judge Mario Sossi
May	France: Giscard d'Estaing president	Referendum on divorce The Radical Party collects signatures to repeal the law which makes abortion a crime Brescia: Massacre in Piazza della Loggia, when fascist bombs explode at a crowded workers' meeting
June		Rome: First international conference of home helps Decrees passed for self-governing of schools Pinarella di Cervia (Emilia Romagna): First national feminist congress

	INTERNATIONAL	ITALY
July	Argentina: Death of Peron: his widow Isabella president	
Aug.	France: Francoise Giroud appointed undersecretary for women	Bombs explode on the train *Italicus*
	USA: Nixon resigns, Ford president	
	Greece leaves NATO	
Oct.	Great Britain: Labour victory, Harold Wilson prime minister	
Nov.	Western European Communist Parties' conference on women	Rome: UDI demonstration for the reform of jurisdiction on the family
Dec.	Japan: Prime Minister Tanaka resigns, after his involvement in a financial scandal	
1975		
Jan.	Austria: Abortion legalized	Milan: the 150-hour courses for women workers begin
		Milan: Opening of Libreria delle Donne (Women's Bookshop) in Via Dogana
		Milan: Via Cherubini groups move to Via Col di Lana
		First publications of feminist publishing house Edizioni delle Donne come out
Feb.		Constitutional court repeals provisions in the penal code on the protection of the race
		Milan: Conference on sexuality, maternity, procreation and abortion
Mar.	France: Veil law legalizing abortion comes onto the statute books	San Vincenzo (Tuscany): Meeting of *pratica dell'inconscio* groups
	USA: National women's health network set up	

	INTERNATIONAL	ITALY
Apr.	Vietnam: National Liberation Front enters Saigon	Reform law on jurisdiction on the family passed
		Law setting up clinics passed
		Rome: National meeting of self-help groups
		First issue of the journal *DWF* (DonnaWomanFemme) appears
May	Leeds: Woman's health group produces a video on the technique of menstrual blood extraction	Turin: Joint trade union commission of women from national federations of trade unions CGIL, CISL and UIL
	Mexico City: World Congress for International Woman's Year	
June	Great Britain: Equal Pay Act and Sex Discrimination Act passed	Local government elections: formation of 'red' city councils (communists and socialists)
Sep.		Circeo (Lazio): Rosaria Lopez and Donatella raped and tortured in a villa – Rosaria Lopez dies
Oct.		Rome: Demonstration against sexual violence
Nov.		Pinarella di Cervia: Second national feminist congress
Dec.	Spain: Clandestine National Day for Women's Liberation	Rome: International demonstration for the right to abortion
		Rome: First feminist meeting on lesbianism, organized by the MFR
1976		
Jan.	Vatican City: Declaration on sexual ethics	Milan: Feminists enter en masse into the Duomo in symbolic protest against the Vatican declaration
	Spain: Birth of the Frente de la Liberacion de la Mujer (Women's Liberation Front)	Milan: Palace of Justice women's group set up

	INTERNATIONAL	ITALY
		Milan: Leader of Red Brigades, Renato Curcio, is arrested
Feb.	USA: Lockheed scandal of illegal payments, involving some Italian politicians	Milan: National conference on women and work
		Rome: Intercollectives house opened in Via Capo d'Africa
Mar.	Great Britain: Wilson resigns, Callaghan prime minister	
	Coup in Argentina: General Videla in power	
Apr.	EEC: Court of justice judgement on equal pay for men and women	Rome: National feminist march in favour of abortion joins up with UDI demonstration on the same topic – for the first time UDI women and feminist women march together
		Rome, and Milan: More actions of 'red' terrorists
May	West Germany: Ulrike Meinhof dies in prison at Stemmheim	Radio Donna begins broadcasting as an autonomous section within the private station Radio Città Futura
	Athens: Panagulis dies in a car accident	Earthquake in Friuli
June	Conference of European Communists parties	Genoa: General Attorney Francesco Coco and his bodyguards killed by terrorists
	Puerto Rico: Summit of seven most industrialized countries	General elections; advance of the traditional left-wing parties
	Hijacking of an Air France airbus by a Palestinian group	Rome: *Differenze*, organ of the feminist collectives in Rome, published
July	USA: Military academies opened up to women	Tina Anselmi (Christian Democrat) appointed Minister of Work
	Entebbe, Uganda: Airbus hostages are rescued by Israeli soldiers in a bloody and spectacular raid	Seveso (Lombardia): Escape of dyoxin at Icmesa company plant

	INTERNATIONAL	ITALY
	Portugal: Socialist leader Soares becomes prime minister	Rome: Deputy Attorney Vittorio Occorsio killed by fascist terrorists
Aug.	France: Prime Minister Jacques Chirac resigns; succeeded by Raymond Barre	
	South Africa: Soweto riots	
Sep.	Brussels: International tribunal on crimes against women is set up	MLD opens the first anti-violence centre
	Bejing: Mao Ze Dong dies	
Oct.	Bejing: Hua Kuo-feng succeeds Mao; Jiang Qijng arrested	Rome: MLD takes over the abandoned building of the old district court in Via del Governo Vecchio
		Naples: Le Nemesiache organizes a showing of feminist cinema in nearby Sorrento
Nov.	USA: Jimmy Carter elected president	Rome: 'Reclaim the Night' national demonstration against violence
Dec.	Chile and USSR exchange Soviet dissenter Vladimir Bukovsky for Communist Chilean leader Luis Corvalan	Paestum (Campania): Third national feminist congress
		More dead, both terrorists and police, in ambushes and raids
1977		
Jan.		Rome: Eighty-one feminist collectives join the MLD in the occupation of Via del Governo Vecchio
		Milan: National conference on violence
		Bill legalizing and regulating abortion passed in the Chamber
Feb.		Rome: Occupation of the university and student demonstration

	INTERNATIONAL	ITALY
Mar.	India: Indira Ghandi's party defeated in the elections Kamal Jumblatt, leader of Lebanese left, killed	More student demonstrations, violent clashes with the police, episodes of urban guerrilla activity Terrorist actions and police repression continue Anti-terrorist measures passed, limiting the rights of the accused
Apr.	Israel: Premier Rabin resigns	Rome: All demonstrations banned for a month Rome: Regardless of the ban, women stage a peaceful national demonstration against rape
May	Paris: International Conference on Women's Health Israel: The right-wing party Likud wins the elections; Begin appointed prime minister	Rome: Sit-in organized by the radicals against the ban on demonstrations; Giorgiana Masi killed Rome: Again ignoring the ban, feminists gather in small groups at the site of the murder of Giorgiana Masi.
June	New Zealand: Conference of women united against sexual oppression	Bill legalizing and regulating abortion blocked in Senate by the right and the Christian Democrats Rome: National demonstration against the Senate's vote on abortion Series of Red Brigades actions MLD puts forward a proposal for setting aside 50 per cent of jobs for women Bologna: National meeting of extraparliamentary groups

INTERNATIONAL	ITALY
Sep. Germany: Hans-Martin Schleyer, president of German industrialists, kidnapped; release of Baader-Meinhof group members requested for his liberation	Opening of the women's bookshop *Al tempo ritrovato* RAI-TV begins broadcasting *Si dice donna*, a TV programme by Tilde Capomazza, with a decided feminist slant
Oct. Stuttgart: Andreas Baader, Gudrun Ensslin, Jan Carl Raspe die in jail France: Schleyer found dead in an abandoned car	
Nov. Israel: visit of Egyptian leader Sadat, first Arab leader to visit Israel in thirty years	Florence: National conference on women and madness
Dec. Egypt breaks with other Arab countries Ismailia: Sadat–Begin meeting	Rome: In the national demonstration of metalworkers, women march together Law on equality at work for men and women passed Debates and divisions between separatist feminists and feminists linked to extraparliamentary groups
1978 **Jan.**	Tenth congress of UDI discusses autonomy and separatism MLD splits from Radical Party Rome: National conference on separatism
Feb.	Life Movement against abortion active
Mar. Paris: International conference against sexual violence France: Centre-right coalition advance in elections; Barre again appointed prime minister	Rome: Kidnap of Aldo Moro and massacre of his bodyguards Rome: Lesbian groups Artemis and Identità Negata (Denied Identity) come into being

INTERNATIONAL	ITALY
	For the first time the Communist Party votes in favour of the newly formed government and is acknowledged as 'external' partner by the ruling coalition
Apr.	Rome: Opening of Zanzibar, women-only bar
	Rome: MLD and feminist magazine *Effe* organize national meeting against violence
May Czechoslovakia: Charter 77 dissenters arrested in view of Soviet leader Brezhnev's visit	Rome: Moro found dead in boot of abandoned car
Paris: Les bombeuses à chapeau destroy the Women's Bookshop	Rome: UDI and *Effe* join environmentalist demonstration against nuclear power
	Rome: Weekly *Quotidiano Donna* appears; national conference on information organized by its editorial board
	Rome: National demonstration of women textile workers against black-market labour
	Rome: National demonstration in memory of Giorgiana Masi
	Mobilization of feminist groups in a rape trial in Latina (Lazio)
June Spain: Decriminalization of adultery	Referendums against law on public financing of political parties and against anti-terrorist measures limiting the rights of the accused; both are confirmed
London: International meeting to decide on international day in defence of abortion	
Vietnamese troops invade Cambodia	Law 194, legalizing and regulating abortion, into the statute books

INTERNATIONAL	ITALY
	Rome: Feminist occupation of gynaecology ward of Policlinico
	Modena (Emilia-Romagna): National conference on violence against women
July	Socialist Sandro Pertini elected president of the Republic
	Montecatini (Tuscany): Meeting on women's cinema
Aug. Pope Paul VI dies; Albino Luciana elected pope, assumes the name of John Paul I	
Sep. Pope John Paul I dies	
Iran: Huge demonstrations against the Shah, violent clashes between demonstrators and army, curfew	
USA: Camp David summit ends with Israel–Egypt agreement	
Amsterdam: International Festival of Women	
Oct. Belgrade: International congress on women of socialist countries	Florence: Court case against CISA and its director Dr Conciani for propaganda on sterilization and abortion
Karol Woytila elected pope, assumes the name of John Paul II	Naples: Month-long occupation by feminist collectives of the CAP offices (Centre for Professional Training)
Sadat and Begin receive the Nobel Prize for peace	Catania: Sixth MLD congress sanctions the choice of separatism

	INTERNATIONAL	ITALY
Nov.	Guyana: Mass suicide of 409 members of the People's Temple religious sect, after the assassination of USA congressman Leo Ryan, two journalists and a photographer all involved in an investigation on the sect's activities London: *The Times* interrupts publication after 193 years	Red Brigades action continue Rome: In a press conference Kate Millett denounces the Iranian revolution's violence against women Milan: National conference on abortion and information
Dec.	Paris: Meeting of the international coordinating committee for abortion Iran: Hundreds killed in demonstrations against the Shah, repressed by the army	Rome: CEI (Conferenza Episcopale Italiana: Italian Bishops' Conference) threatens to excommunicate women who have abortions Rome: *Quotidiano Donna* charges the CEI with private violence, threats and abuse of the credulity of the people Rome: Ines Boffardi (Christian Democrat) appointed undersecretary for women, directly answerable to the prime minister
1979		
Jan.	Iran: Mohammed Reza Palhevi and his family leave Berlin: Molotov cocktails against the Women's House France: Demonstration in support of the Weil law on abortion Cambodia: Defeat of Red Khmers; Vietnamese-supported government formed	Rome: Attack of the fascist NAR (Nuclei Armati Rivoluzionari) on housewives' collective at Radio Donna; four women shot and wounded Rome: National demonstration against the attack on Radio Donna Genoa: Red Brigades kill a Communist Party member, trade unionist metalworker Guido Rossa

INTERNATIONAL	ITALY
	Florence: National demonstration for self-determination and right to abortion for under-age women
	Milan: First issue of journal *Grattacielo* appears
Feb. Iran: Ayatollah Khomeini returns from exile; trials and executions of persons linked to the Shah's regime	Genoa: National conference against nuclear power programme
Chinese troops attack Vietnam	
Mar. Paris and Brussels: Demonstrations of solidarity with Iranian women	Rome: Demonstration of solidarity with Iranian women
Great Britain: Callaghan's Labour government defeated in the Commons	Rome: Law 194 Defence Committee organize a national conference on abortion
USA: Incident at Three Miles Island nuclear power station, Pennsylvania	Rome: Conference on women and political violence
Washington, D.C.: Peace treaty between Egypt and Israel	
New York: Italian financier Sindona, linked to many Italian politicians, indicted for crack of Franklin National Bank	
Apr. Paris: Gisele Halimi and the group Choisir suggest the formation of a European Parliament centre for women	Padua: The 7 April case flares up; intellectuals of the extraparliamentary left charged with incitement of terrorism
	Rome: National conference on the European elections organized by the group Donne e Istituzioni (Women and Institutions)
	Rome: MLD, joined by UDI and MFR (Pompeo Magno),

INTERNATIONAL	ITALY
	puts forward a draft of a law on sexual violence
	Genoa: Congress on women and work organized by women delegates from FLM (metalworkers union)
	Modena: National conference on women and writing
May Great Britain: General elections won by Conservative party; Margaret Thatcher prime minister	Rome: March against nuclear power
	Forlì: (Emilia-Romagna): National conference on 'the crisis of feminism'
	Piacenza: National demonstration against Caorso nuclear power station
	Rome: Radio Lilith launched, broadcasting from the occupied premises of Via del Governo Vecchio
June Tudela (Spain): Antinuclear demonstration; Gladis de Estal killed by the police	Rome: National demonstration of metalworkers – for the first time women head the procession
First European elections	General elections; European elections
Tokyo: Summit of industrialized countries on the problem of energy, following the increases in the price of oil	
Vienna: Carter and Brezhnev sign the SALT 2 Treaty	
Pope John Paul II in Poland	
July Bonn: Housewives' union organized	Padua and Rome: Feminists charged under the anti-terrorist measures
	Italian feminist collectives protest at charges of terrorism against feminist activists

	INTERNATIONAL	ITALY
		Milan: Assassination of lawyer Giorgio Ambrosoli, in charge of investigating and winding up the affairs of Sindona's private bank
Sep.	New York: Feminist congress against pornography Philadelphia: March against violence to women	Rome: *Quotidiano Donna* starts a page dedicated to lesbians MLD, UDI, MFR (Pompeo Magno) and other feminist groups form a committee to collect signatures for the law by popular initiative about sexual violence
Oct.	Paris: March in defence of abortion London: March in defence of abortion New Delhi: *Manushi* appears, the first feminist journal in India	Milan: Conference organized by the Libreria delle Donne to debate the proposed law on sexual violence ENI-Petronim scandal
Nov.	Paris: National demonstration in defence of abortion Teheran: USA Embassy occupied by Khomeini supporters, who hold all the personnel and their families as hostages	Rome: Opening of the courses organized by the Virginia Woolf Cultural Centre Trial in appeal for Circeo rapes and murder
Dec.	Leningrad: Almanac *Women and Russia* appears Afghanistan: Coup – the new government is supported by the USSR, who help put down the resistance of the Islamic opposition	Rome: Zanzibar searched by police, five women arrested Law on introduction of Euromissiles passed Rome: National conference on sexuality and money organized by MFR (Pompeo Magno)

	INTERNATIONAL	ITALY
1980		
Jan.	Carter announces boycott of Olympic Games in Moscow, due to Soviet involvement in Afghanistan	Special legislation against terrorism put through by parliament
		General strike against the government's economic policies
		Birth of MIT (Movimento Transessuali Italiani, Italian Transsexual Movement)
		FUORI–Donna Conference (lesbians organized with homosexuals)
Feb.		Red Brigades kill Vittorio Bachelet, vice-president of the High Magistrates' Council
		First session of the Tribunale 8 Marzo (8 March Tribunal) which collects evidence of violence against women
Mar.	Salvador: Right-wing extremists assassinate Archbishop Oscar Arnulfo Romero in the cathedral; riots and clashes, with many dead and wounded, take place during his funeral	Turin: City Council gives feminist groups premises for a Women's House
		Rome: Feminist publishing house Felina is founded
	Teheran: Committee for Women's Solidarity comes into being	300,000 signatures collected for the law by popular initiative on sexual violence are presented to parliament
		Genoa: Police raid a Red Brigades base, four terrorists are killed
		The Italcasse (association of eighty-nine banks) scandal explodes, about illegal financing of political parties

	INTERNATIONAL	ITALY
Apr.	France: Law passed against sexual violence Iran: USA attempt at freeing the Teheran Embassy hostages fails	Assisi: Peace march Rome: Demonstration in support of a law subsidizing small cultural publications, which would favour the feminist press
May	Yugoslavia: Tito dies EEC Commission organized for women's rights Lisbon: First women's movement congress Tel Aviv: Israeli feminist movement opens centre for rape victims	Law 180 abolishing insane asylums passed Rome: Election of first woman magistrate to Court of Appeal Milan: Journalist Walter Tobagi killed by Red Brigades Rome: Fascist terrorists kill a policeman
June		An Itavia DC-9 explodes in flight near Ustica: all passengers (seventy-seven) and crew (four) die Rome: Tribunal for the Rights of Patients is founded Turin: UDI conference on women and work Assisi: UDI national assembly on autonomy, organization and liberation
July	Moscow: Olympic Games, boycotted by many countries Copenhagen: World conference of women, backed by United Nations; also First International Women Artists' Festival	
Aug.	Poland: Workers' strikes obtain legalization of independent workers' organizations	Bologna: Massacre at the railway station when bombs, probably fascist, explode; protest demonstrations all over Italy

	INTERNATIONAL	ITALY
Sep.	Former dictator of Nicaragua, Somoza, assassinated Iran–Iraq war breaks out	
Oct.		Milan: Killers of Tobagi arrested Rome: Feminist sit-in against RAI-TV for disinformation on the abortion referendum
Nov.	USA: Reagan elected president	Earthquake in Lucania and Campania
Dec.	Amsterdam: First international lesbian conference, organized by International Gay Association	UDI organizes women volunteers to help earthquake victims Rome: More Red Brigades attacks
1981		
Jan.	Teheran: USA Embassy hostages released	Milan: Birth of lesbian group Phoenix Florence: Birth of Linea Lesbica Milan: First national conference of transsexuals San Gimignano (Florence): Gianni Guida, one of the Circeo rapist-murderers, escapes from prison
Feb.	Madrid: Attempted coup China: Jing Qijng condemned to death Poland: Strikes – Prime Minister Pinkowski resigns and is succeeded by General Jaruzelski	Feminist protest against Guido's escape
Mar.	Kuwait: First conference of women of the Arab Emirates USA: Attempted assassination of Reagan	Lagorio bill on military service for women Rome: International conference of Brazilian women

INTERNATIONAL	ITALY
	Rome: Women of the joint trade union commission organize a conference on women and employment
	Memoria, a journal of women's history, begins publication
	Florence: International meeting on women's cinema
Apr.	France: Women's movement supports Mitterand for president	Milan: Red Brigades leader Mario Moretti arrested
		Turin: International conference on lesbianism
		Rome: National conference of CGIL women workers
May	France: Mitterand elected president	Turin: Trial of members of terrorist groups Prima Linea and Red Brigades
	Bonn: Birth of Fraueninitiative	
	Barcelona: United Nations Conference on condition of women in Uruguay	Referendum on repealing abortion law confirms the law
	New York: Conference on women's movement in Italy and USA	Investigations on the Sindona affair lead to discovery of secret masonic lodge P2, occult power centre involving many politicians, high-up army officers, industrialists, etc.
		Assassination attempt on pope
June	Geneva: Third international conference on women's health; Third World women attend for the first time	Turin: Waldesian community Agape organizes a conference on Christian faith and lesbianism
	Amsterdam: International meeting on feminist cinema and video	Red Brigades kidnap Roberto Peci, brother of repentant terrorist Patrizio (who decided to help the police)
		Parliamentary commission established to inquire into P2 lodge affair

INTERNATIONAL	ITALY
	Rome: First national conference of feminist lesbians
	Journal *Orsa Minore* comes out
July Bogotà: First feminist centre of Latin-American and Caribbean women	Stock exchange crisis
Tunisia: First centre for women's studies	Rome: Coordinating committee of women against the arms race comes into being
	Bologna: European meeting on violence and women's culture
Aug. 9 August is United Nations Day of Solidarity with Women of South Africa and Namibia	Scoglitti: Waldesian community Adelphia organizes a women's group on communicating as women
	Roberto Peci found dead
	Installation of Cruise missiles base in Comiso, Sicily, decided by the Cabinet
Sep. Beirut: Car packed with TNT explodes in Palestinian part of town – fifty dead, seventy wounded	
Oct. Beirut: Car explodes at the Moslim university – eight-five dead, 300 wounded	Agrigento: Two women charged with kissing in public; feminist groups stage a protest in Rome
Athens: Pasok wins the elections	Venice: Margaret Von Trotta wins the Golden Lion
Egypt: Sadar assassinated	CLI (Coordinamento Lesbiche Italiane, Union of Italian Lesbians) is created
Bonn: Peace march	
Paris: Demonstration against the installation of Pershing missiles	Rome: Feminists occupy *L'Avanti* (official newspaper of the Socialist Party) which censors women's communiqués
London: Demonstrations by CND (Campaign for Nuclear Disarmament)	
Poland: General Jaruzelski becomes secretary of the Communist Party too	Rome: Peace march
	Pescara: European congress on world hunger

	INTERNATIONAL	ITALY
		Bologna: Opening of the women's bookshop La Librellula
Nov.	The Hague: March by women's international peace movement	Brindisi: Palmira Martinelli (14 years old) burnt alive by prostitution mafia
	Poland: Government is granted full powers	
Dec.		Verona: Red Brigades kidnap Nato General James Lee Dozier
		Rome: Second national conference of feminist lesbians
1982		
Jan.	Belgium: Lesbian teacher Eliane Morissens sacked	Padua: Special police forces raid frees Dozier and arrests five Red Brigades members
	Poland: Riots in Gdansk	
Feb.	Poland: Court-martial for Gdansk demonstrators	Rome: Debate on Eliane Morissens case and criminalization of lesbians
Mar.	Bogotà: Women's House opened	Florence: Opening of Ciadamaré, women-only club
	San Paulo: Berta Lutz Tribunal for women's rights founded	Rome: Separatist feminist groups begin negotiations with city council for alternative premises to Governo Vecchio
Apr.	Falklands/Malvinas war between Great Britain and Argentina breaks out	Modena: Conference organized by coordinating committee of women historians on feminism and women's history
		Palermo: Mafia kill Pio La Torre, Communist leader and MP
May		Eleventh Congress of UDI; UDI chooses separatism and dissolves hierarchical organization

	INTERNATIONAL	ITALY
June	Israeli troops invade Lebanon Great Britain wins war with Argentina Great Britain: Calvi is found dead under the Blackfriars bridge, London	Scandal of the Banco Ambrosiano: its president, Roberto Calvi, disappears; Calvi's secretary commits suicide
Aug.		Parliamentary justice commission approves integral text of law by popular initiative on sexual violence Death of Carla Lonzi
Sep.	Aix-en-Provence: International conference on women's oral history Lebanon: Massacre in Palestinian refugee camps of Sabra and Chatila USA, France and Italy, send 'peace forces' to Lebanon	Law passed permitting transsexuals to change civic status Palermo: Assassination of General Dalla Chiesa, in charge of fight against mafia and terrorism
Oct.	West Germany: Kohl becomes chancellor	
Nov.	Moscow: Brezhnev dies, Andropov secretary of Communist Party	
Dec.		Comiso (Sicily): Women's sit-in at gates of NATO missile base Sicily: Feminist collectives organize demonstrations for peace and against Nato bases
1983		
Jan.	San Paulo: Festival of Women in the Arts	Comiso: Women's camp La Ragnatela founded Trial for Moro assassination ends with thirty life-sentences Bologna: Third national conference of lesbian feminists

INTERNATIONAL	ITALY
	The Chamber passes Casini amendment which declares rape a crime against morality
Feb. Israel: Sharon, held responsible for Sabra and Chatila massacre, leaves Ministry of Defence	Rome: National demonstration against Casini amendment
	Pordenone: First Italian conference on prostitution, organized by the Committee for Civil Rights of Prostitutes
Mar.	Birth of Coordinating Committee of Women's Cultural Centres
Apr. Beirut: Van packed with explosives at USA Embassy; tens die, a hundred wounded	Rome: Conference on a project for maternity centres proposed by DORIS (Documentazione Ricerca Salute; Health Research and Documentation)
Argentina: Plaze de Majo mothers continue their campaign (begun six years earlier) on behalf of *desaparecidos*	Comiso: Greenham Common women arrested demonstrating with Italian women against NATO base
May Chile: Trade unions organize demonstrations against Pinochet regime	Law passed allowing Italian women citizens to convey citizenship to non-Italian husbands
June Great Britain: Conservative victory in general elections; Thatcher prime minister again	General elections: increased number of women elected to parliament
	Rome: National meeting of Coordinating Committee of Women's Cultural Centres
July Barcelona: First conference of Spanish Feminist Party	
Aug. Great Britain: Women pacifists block Greenham Common military zone	Rome: City council votes to give part of Buon Pastore (an old building in the city centre) to separatist feminist groups

	INTERNATIONAL	ITALY
	Manila: Security services members assassinate opposition leader Benito Aquino	First issue of *Lucciola*, journal of Committee for Civil Rights of Prostitutes
		Bettino Craxi prime minister; for the first time a socialist head of government
Sep.	South Korean civilian plane felled by USSR	Uccellina (Florence): Women-only campsite organized by CLI
Oct.	Lech Walesa awarded Nobel Prize for peace	Rome: National conference 'Separatism Today' organized by MFR (Pompeo Magno)
	Bogotà: Meeting of Latin-American and Caribbean feminists	
	Beirut: Terrorist attacks against USA and French barracks	
	USA marines invade Grenada	
	Argentina: Alfonsin elected president in first free elections after seven-year military dictatorship	
Nov.	Chile: Protest against Pinochet continues	Milan: Conference on women and Third World organized by international voluntary services organizations
Dec.	South African bombings in Angola	Sicily: 10,000 demonstrate against Cruise missiles
	West Germany: Pershing missiles installed	Parma: National conference for civil rights of prostitutes and transsexuals

1984

Jan.	European Parliament vote recommending parity of treatment between men and women	

	INTERNATIONAL	ITALY
Feb.	European Parliament passes resolution against discrimination against homosexuals Moscow: Death of Andropov, succeeded by Cernenko; Gorbachov number two at the Kremlin	Agreement between state and Catholic church on new concordat Cut of index-linked pay increases decided by the government
Mar.	Salvador: Presidential elections, amid guerrilla actions and military repression	Reformulation of law on sexual violence entrusted to small parliamentary committee Rome: National demonstration (around 700,000 people) against cut of index-linked pay increases
Apr.	London: Policewoman killed in front of Libyan Embassy when fire is opened from the Embassy on exiled Libyans demonstrating against Gaddafi	Rome: Feminist protest at city council's failure to give promised premises to separatist feminist groups
May	USSR announce non-participation in Los Angeles Olympic Games	Rome: Conference on separatism, with the motto 'Women with women can'
June	European elections in France, West Germany, Greece, Belgium and Luxemburg	Death of Communist Party Secretary Enrico Berlinguer European elections
July	USA: Geraldine Ferraro (Democratic Party) is first woman candidate to vice-presidency	
Aug.	Great Britain: Greenham Common pacifist meeting of women against the arms race Drought in Africa, especially serious in Mali; situation difficult in Europe as well	National Equal Opportunities Committee set up
Oct.	Poland: Father Popieluszko kidnapped and killed by police	New bill on sexual violence discussed in the Chamber

	INTERNATIONAL	ITALY
	India: Indira Ghandi killed by Sikh bodyguards Gorbachov in Great Britain	Rome: Demonstrations against the new bill on sexual violence and in favour of the law by popular initiative
Nov.	USA: Reagan re-elected	
Dec.	Bhopal: 2,000 die, tens of thousands poisoned, by gas leak at Union Carbide	Bomb explodes on a train between Florence and Bologna; fifteen dead, a hundred wounded

1985

	INTERNATIONAL	ITALY
Mar.	USSR: In Moscow, Gorbachov elected general secretary of the Soviet Communist Party	Rome: Red Brigades kill economist Ezio Tarantelli Ferrara: Exhibition of feminist cartoons 'Women smile too'
Apr.	Famine in Sudan	
May	Bhopal: Malformed children born after Union Carbide gas leak South Africa: Massive black miners' strikes Brussels: Heysel stadium tragedy	Rome: Separatist feminist centre opens in Buon Pastore building, finally given by city council Rome: Conference on sexuality organized by the committee for the law by popular initiative on sexual violence
June		Referendum on abolishing the cut of index-linked pay increases confirms the cut
July	South Africa: State of emergency declared	
Aug.	Nairobi: UN International Conference of Women South Africa: Clashes in Natal between Indians and Zulus; violent repression in Capetown of demonstrations for Mandela's liberation	

INTERNATIONAL	ITALY
Sept. Earthquake in Mexico	The Coordinamento Nazionale delle Donne per i Consultori (National Coordinating Committee of Women for Clinics) is created by UDI women
	Milan: Lesbian group S'ignora comes into being
Oct. Israeli raid against PLO headquarters in Tunisia	
Palestinian guerrillas take over the Italian ship *Achille Lauro*	
Nov. Geneva: Gorbachov and Reagan meet	In many Italian cities students stage peaceful protests and demonstrations for better schools
	Rome: Fourth national conference of lesbian feminists
Dec. Vienna: Palestinian guerrilla attack	Rome: Palestinian guerrilla attack in Fiumicino airport
1986	Bologna: Conference, 'From parity to equal opportunities'
Jan. Great Britain: Minister of Defence Heseltine resigns in connection with Westland affair	
The *Challenger* space shuttle explodes; for the first time a civilian, Christa McAuliffe, was one of the astronauts	
Feb. Haiti: Revolt against Baby Doc Duvalier, who leaves the country	More Red Brigades attacks
Philippines: Cory Aquino wins the elections; Marcos disclaims the validity of the vote, but is finally obliged to flee	
Sweden: Prime Minister Olof Palme assassinated	

INTERNATIONAL	ITALY
Mar. Spain enters NATO France: Victory of the right in the general elections, Chirac prime minister Battle in the Sirte gulf; USA attacks Libya	Life sentence for Sindona; he dies in prison, killed by a poisoned cup of coffee Casa Balena (Spoleto): Seminar on the financing of women's projects
Apr. Jerusalem: International conference on sexual violence Oil price goes down Los Angeles: International conference on salary for housework France: Simone de Beauvoir dies USA bombings on Libya Chernobyl nuclear station burns	Conference of positive action backed by women from CGIL, CISL and UIL Genoa: Conference on women and new technologies organized by the committee on women, work and culture Modena: UDI organizes a conference on women and information Rome: National women's demonstration against war
May Fear all over Europe of the consequences of the nuclear cloud	Ministry of Health takes measures against effects of Chernobyl Rome: 100,000 people demonstrate against Chernobyl and nuclear energy Rome: Women-only demonstration against Chernobyl New bill on sexual violence discussed in the Senate
June Austria: Kurt Waldheim, suspected of past Nazi activities, elected president; international protest South Africa: Tension on Soweto anniversary; state of emergency; Prime Minister Botha meets Archbishop Tutu; demonstrations and repression	Lampedusa (island off the coast of Sicily): Libyan missile launched against island Rome: Conference on 'Pornography: a project against sexuality', organized by committee for law by popular initiative on sexual violence

	INTERNATIONAL	ITALY
July		Livia Turco first woman elected to PCI secretariat
		Umbria: Opening of women's campsite Terradilei (Herland)
Aug.	Gorbachov continues his 'peace offensive', proposing more disamament measures	
Sep.	Paris: Repeated Arab terrorist attacks	Siena: National conference of Women's Cultural Centres
Oct.	Brussels: International conference of prostitutes	Perugia: International conference of nuclear-free local councils
	Palma de Majorca: International conference on artificial reproduction	
	Reykjavik: Reagan–Gorbachov summit	
Nov.	Irangate affair	The Communist Women's Charter published
Dec.	France: Student demonstrations against Devaquet plan for university reform; a student is killed; Devaquet resigns	Student demonstrations against Ministry of Education policy
	China: Students march for freedom and democracy	Rome: First international conference on women's studies in Italian universities

Italian Feminist Periodicals

EFFE, MONTHLY, BARI THEN ROME

I, 1, November 1973–VI, 12, December 1978. New Series: I, 1–2, January–February 1979–IV, 7–8, July–August 1982

A monthly magazine, autonomously published by a group of feminists. *Effe* had a pioneering role in feminist information in Italy. *Effe* was not linked to a specific tendency of Italian feminism: the product of a collective whose feminist identity coincided with the production of the magazine itself, it reflected the evolution, difficulties, contradictions and advances of the movement. Sold on newspaper stands all over Italy, *Effe* greatly contributed to the diffusion of feminist ideas among women who would not otherwise have come into contact with the movement's view – undistorted by the sensationalism of the media – of questions such as abortion, violence (from rape to the subtle exploitation of advertisements), the role of the church in the oppression of women.

QUOTIDIANO DONNA, WEEKLY, ROME

6 May–16 December 1978, supplement to the daily *Quotidiano dei Lavoratori*. Then published autonomously as an 'irregular' weekly until December 1981.

Sold nationwide in bookshops and (from 1980) newsagencies, *Quotidiano Donna* (*QD*), like *Effe*, aimed at giving women autonomous, non-mediated information. Not as elegant in design as *Effe* and often more radical in outlook, *QD* provided a more 'in depth' treatment of themes central to the debate and political action of the movement; they were presented, as it were, more from an insider's point of view than having in mind a larger and heterogeneous audience. It also gave space to documents or *ad hoc* articles by different groups, either self-presentations of the group's rationale and position, or comments and proposals regarding specific issues. Besides reporting facts of direct relevance for the feminist movement, such as the story of the law against sexual violence. *QD* devoted space to general political issues, trying to analyse them from a feminist point of view.

DIFFERENZE, ROME

1, June 1976–12, May 1982.

Differenze was the voice of the Rome-based part of the feminist movement, with a rotating editorial board. Each issue was the product of a different group, thus acting as a site of expression and confrontation of these diverse viewpoints. To take a few examples: no. 2 was edited by the Roman Pratico dell'Inconscio (Practice of the Unconscious) collective; no. 4 by the Movimento Femminista Romano (Roman Feminist Movement: Via Pompeo Magno); nos, 6–7 by the Feminist Group for Women's Health. Of particular interest is no. 10, 'Sexuality and Money', published in preparation for a conference on the same theme held in December 1979. At a time when the feminist movement was being cornered between marginalization and normalization, it treated the question of women's political presence and action from a dual perspective: the foundation of new modes of relation among women and the individuation of ways to approach, use, change the institutions. The title points to the interpretive key adopted for the conference, that is, an analysis of the economic rules in the light of their sexually connotated basis.

ORSA MINORE, MONTHLY, ROME

1, June 1981–10, March 1983.

Orsa Minore (*OM*) was founded by seven women, hence the title, Orsa Minore being the Italian name of the seven-star Ursa Minor constellation. They were seven intellectuals of different backgrounds, bonded by friendship and by a habit of discussing and analysing together the life of each and its context, all politically on the left and all involved in/intrigued by the feminist experience. An 'irregular' monthly, *OM* presented and debated feminist themes, often in a broadly Marxist perspective (that is, not tied to any orthodoxy), privileging a theoretical approach which would transcend a mere commentary on current affairs, though not forgetting the concreteness of the problems at stake.

MANIFESTA, QUARTERLY, NAPLES

1, October 1988–date.

Manifesta is produced by a group of women well known for their lively and often provocative cultural activity, aimed at a re-viewing and re-founding of interpretive and expressive modes. Language, and in particular the language of the cinema, is therefore a privileged issue, as a site of formation and expression of the complex relationship which women entertain with the 'images' of femininity. But any other themes are given space in *Manifesta*'s project to render manifest the richness and complexity of the female universe, and also, perhaps more, its strength and resilience. Significantly, the opening feature of the first two issues was devoted to a reappraisal of the mythical figure of the Amazon.

ASPIRINA, BI-MONTHLY, MILAN

1, November 1987–5, July 1988 (plus an unnumbered issue, July 1989).

Produced by the Milan *Libreria delle Donne*, the satirical journal *Aspirina* (subtitle: 'Rivista per donne di sesso femminile'. 'A journal for women whose sex is female') published jokes, comic strips and short parodic texts, reflecting and commenting, in an ironic and self-ironic manner, on the issues currently at stake in and for the feminist movement in Italy. The capacity for synthesis which often characterizes the comic mode of expression and the pungent wit of the journal's collaborators combined in making *Aspirina* not only enjoyable and lively fun, but also a valuable though extravagant commentary on and critique of the ongoing debates about (to cite only a few) sexual difference, relations among women, Irigaray's writings, feminist politics, the link with the symbolic mother. The skilful choice of targets witnessed a partisan, caustic view of the patriarchal order (obviously!), of the feminist movement as a whole (not so common) and of the very positions the journal tendentially endorsed (almost unique).

RETI, BI-MONTHLY, ROME

I, 1, January–February 1988–date.

This might seem a slightly eccentric inclusion in a panorama of feminist journals, in view of its links with a political party. It replaces *Donne e Politica* (also bi-monthly, I, 1, January–February 1970–XVII, 6, November–December 1987) as the journal of communist women, it is financially supported by the Communist party and published by the party-controlled Editori Riuniti. Yet it must be included, for it reflects and illustrates the way in which feminist thought has seeped through and come to influence not 'politics' at large (though that has also happened in various forms) but *women* of a specific political allegiance, reshaping their awareness of themselves as women and therefore their self-positioning inside the party to which they belong. *Reti* (subtitle: 'Pratiche e saperi di donne', 'Women's practices and knowledges') is a result and aims to be a motor of this process. It invites contributions by women outside the party, actually defining itself as a journal 'promoted by communist women, created together with women of different political and experiential backgrounds'. Focused mainly on the areas of culture/politics/economics, it debates the possible autonomous modes of action for women with regard to, for example, bio-ethics, the labour-market, parliamentary representation, the bi-sexualization of culture.

FLUTTUARIA, BI-MONTHLY, MILAN

1, January–February 1987–date. Previously, two xeroxed issues, informally circulated among feminists in several Italian cities and towns.

Produced by an already existing group of women associated for cultural and recreational purposes, who have been in the past and still are a pole of interest in Italian feminism, the journal (subtitle: 'Segni di autonomia nell'esperienza delle donne', 'Signs of autonomy, in women's experiences') seeks to provide a forum for the expression and confrontation of all women engaged in the construction of an autonomous interpretation and experience of reality. It features articles and notices about cinema, theatre, literature, politics, science, work, sport, medicine, always in the perspective of a female eye looking at and reshaping the world. The attempt is to give voice to sexual difference as an active principle at work in the perception/creation of reality, at the same time stressing the multiplicity of points of view present in the feminist community regarding such a process and its practical forms: differences inside difference, to be acknowledged and accepted.

LAPIS, QUARTERLY, MILAN

I, 1, 1987–date.

Subtitled 'Percorsi della riflessione femminile' ('Itineraries of female thought'), *Lapis* originated out of a split in *Fluttuaria*'s editorial board. It testifies to the richness and diversity of such itineraries, but also to the truth of that old proverb 'There's many a slip 'twixt cup and lip'; or: acknowledging differences might be easy, accepting them and being able to live with them is quite another matter. To outsiders, the subtle political and emotional reasons for the split are not easily apparent or explicable. In endorsing the wish for the exploration of a wide and varied range of positions, and the necessity of an unprejudiced confrontation and exchange, *Lapis* underlines the importance of the experiential dimension of knowledge, the need to take into account the uniqueness of the individual subject and the weight of affective processes, their relevance for and correlation to social and political action.

NOI DONNE, MONTHLY, ROME

I, 1, July 1944–date.

Noi Donne (*ND*) has undergone a number of transformations since it was founded in 1944 – when Italy was still occupied by the German army – as a clandestine leaflet of partisan women. When the war ended it become, at first as a bi-weekly, then as a weekly from 1948, the magazine of the UDI (Unione Donne Italiane, Union of Italian Women), an association of left-wing women, mostly belonging to the Communist and the Socialist parties. The reasons for its inclusion here are similar to those given for *Reti*: feminism is contagious, and the UDI – after strong and at times bitter disagreements with the movement – has in some ways become part of it, severing completely its links with 'the father', that is, the political parties. The magazine has changed accordingly, going through an especially radical phase in 1982–4. From 1983 it has again become a monthly; a typical issue (80–100 pages) includes comments and surveys on current affairs, a dossier on a specific theme prepared autonomously by a group which arranges to take over that space from the editorial board, features on cultural events, books/cinema/theatre reviews – all with a feminist slant. Since 1987 *ND* also features a quarterly supplement of book reviews, *Legendaria*.

SOTTOSOPRA, MILAN

1, 1973–date.

Sottosopra (*Ss*) was initially created by women of various feminist groups in Milan as a space open to the experiences and elaborations of the movement in all its viewpoints and expressions, in order to foster communication and debate. Thus its first five issues (1973–6) collect documents, reflections, discussions in/by different collectives. Two issues are particularly worth noting, devoted each to an important nationwide meeting – one about abortion in 1975, the other about 'the state of the movement' in 1976. A long silence followed, until in January 1983 *Ss* reappeared as the voice of one of the most interesting and influential groups in Italian feminism, the 'Libreria delle Donne in Milan' (see chapter 5, pp. 109–38). Its irregularity is linked to the modes and rhythms of reflection of the group, who publish a new issue whenever (and only if) they feel they have come to articulate satisfactorily a position they wish to circulate and discuss. To date the issues have been concerned with the rethinking of the relationships between/among women and the need for a bisexualization of the world which will allow women to live in it 'at their ease' *qua* women, instead of having to assume male parameters (green Sottosopra, 'Più donne che uomini', 'More women than men', January 1983), the question of political representation and of its pitfalls (blue

Sottosopra, 'Sulla rappresentanza politica femminile, sull'arte di polemizzare tra donne e sulla rivoluzione scientifica in corso', 'On female political representation, on the art of arguing polemically among women, and on the present scientific revolution', June 1987), the concept of a female freedom (gold *Sottosopra*, 'Un filo di felicità', 'A thread of happiness', January 1989).

DWF, QUARTERLY, ROME

1, 1975–2, 1975. Then *Nuova dwf*, quarterly, Rome: 4, 1975–25/6, 1985. Then *DWF*, quarterly, Rome: 1, 1986–date.

For general information, see chapter 10. Themes of the monographic issues of *Nuova dwf* are: 1, Donna e ricerca scientifica (Women and scientific research); 2, Donna e trazmissione della cultura (Women and cultural transmission); 3, Donna e ricerca storica (Women and historical research); 4, Donna e istituzioni (Women and institutions); 5, Donna e letteratura (Women and Literature); 6/7, Maternità e imperialismo (Maternity and imperialism); 8, La donna dello schermo (Women on the screen); 9, Il corpo della donna: ideologia a realtà (Woman's body: ideology and reality); 10/11, Solidaristà, amicizia, amore (Solidarity, friendship, love); 12/13, Lavoro, non lavoro (Work and non-work); 14, Femminismo/socialismo – partiti/movimento (Feminism/Socialism – Parties/Movement); 15, Il luogo delle ipotesi. Femminismo e conoscenza (The site of hypotheses. Feminism and knowledge); 16, In hoc signo . . . ideologia a politica della Chiesa (In hoc signo, ideology and politics of the Church); 17, Per legge di natura. Donne e scienza (According to the laws of nature. Women and science); 18, Cieli divisi. Le scrittrici della Germania Orentale (Divided sky. Women Writers of East Germany); 19/20, Casa dolce casa (Home sweet home); 21, La piccola fronda. Politics e cultura nella stampa emancipazionista, 1861–1924 (The little Fronde. Politics and culture in the emancipationist press, 1861–1924); 22, Islam, tra un mondo e l'altro (Islam, between two worlds); 23/4, Amore priobito. Ricerche americane sull'esiste lesbica (Forbidden love. American texts on the lesbian experience); 25/6, Sulla scrittura. Percorsi critici in testi letterari del XVI secolo (On writing. Critical itineraries on literary texts of the 16th century). Themes of the monographic issues of *DWF* are: 1, Mi piace, non mi piace (I like it, I don't like it); 2, Progetti progettualità (Projects projectuality); 3, Biografie: effetti di ritorno (Biographies, rebounding); 4, Appartenenza (Belonging); 5/6, Responsabilità politica (Political responsibility); 7, Forme della politica (Forms of politics); 8, Sgwardi e immagini (Looks and images); 9, Il negoziato (Bargaining); 10/11, Donne ritrovate (Rediscovered women); 12, Pesi e misure (Weights and measures).

LEGGERE DONNA, BI-MONTHLY, FERRARA

1, 1990–date.

As the title ('Reading Woman') signals, *Leggere Donna (LD)* is basically a reviews journal, a sort of Italian *Women's Review of Books*. It also includes information and comments about the cultural activities of individual women and women's groups throughout Italy: exhibitions, shows, cycles of lectures, conferences and seminars. Besides, there are feature articles on political issues such as equal opportunities for women, or the case of Silvia Baraldini, imprisoned for 'conspiracy' in the USA following a trial of whose legality there are serious doubts. *LD* regularly publishes interviews with women – architects, film directors, scientists – actively and successfully engaged in the professions. Initially a quarterly (1980), after a short spell as a monthly in 1985–6, it became a bi-monthly in 1987.

MEMORIA, QUARTERLY, ROME

1, 1981–date.

Subtiled 'Rivista di Storia delle donne' ('A journal of women's history'), *Memoria* was founded by a group of women, most of them academics, engaged in the fields of history, literary criticism, psychoanalysis and the social sciences, as a contribution to that re-vision of culture fostered, in Italy as elsewhere, by the feminist movement. Acknowledging the differences of approach and with a view to their potential value for a richer understanding of reality, the editorial board's effort has been that of presenting in each issue a varied range of articles, trying to create a dialogue of positions and therefore a/many potential reading/s which would go beyond the sum of the parts. Themes of the monographic issues: 1, Regione e sentimenti (Reason and feelings); 2, Piccole e grandi diversità (Differences great and small); 3, I corpi possibili (Possible bodies); 4, Politiche (Politics); 5, Sacro e profano (Sacred and profane); 6, Gli anni Cinquanta (The Fifties); 7, Madri e non madri (Mothers and non-mothers); 8, Raccontare, raccontarsi (Narration, narrating the self); 9, Sulla storia delle donne (On women's history); 10, La solitudine (Loneliness); 11/12, Vestire (Clothes); 13, Donna insieme, i gruppi degli anni ottanta (Women together, the groups of the Eighties); 14, Soggetto donna. Dalla bibliografia nazionale italiana 1975–84 (Books on/by women. From the national Italian bibliography 1975–84); 15, Culture del femminismo (Feminist cultures); 16, L'eta e gli anni. Riflessioni null-invecchiare (Time and the years. On aging); 17, Prostituzione (Prostitution); 18, Donna senza womini (Women without men); 19/20, Il movimento femminista negli anni settanta (The feminist movement in the Seventies); 21, L'uso del potere (The use of power); 22, Giovane donne (Young women); 23, Il bel matrimonio (The good marriage); 24, Sesso differenza e simbiosi (Sex difference and symbiosis); 25, Genere e soggetto. Strategie del femminismo tra Europa e America (Gender and subject, Strategies of feminism in Europe and America); 26, Questioni di etica (Questions of ethics).

VIA DOGANA, QUARTERLY, MILAN

0, 1983–4, 1984.

A journal of book reviews produced by the Milan Libreria delle donne, it included both reviews of new books and of older texts, grouped around a theme, as follows: 0, Qualcuna lo ha detto per me, prima di me (Some said it for me, before me); 1, Disparità affidamento generazione (Disparity, entrustment, generation); 2, Il terreno dell'inconscio e il suolo della politica (The land of the unconscious and the grounds of politics); 3, La natura che tessa, la politica che trama (Nature weaving, politics plotting); 4, Inizio di discorso sulla guerra e sulle donne (Beginnings of a discourse on war and on women).

GRATTACIELO, MONTHLY, MILAN

0, December 1980, then I, 1, May 1981–I, 6, December 1981.

An illustrated 'irregular' monthly of culture and politics, it purported to look at the world 'with the eyes of a woman', as its subtitle, 'Occhi di donna sul mondo', stated. Its opening editorial claimed that it was 'neither a women's magazine, nor a magazine for women, but a magazine written by women; women who do not belong to a collective movement, but individual women', who wanted to write not so much on women's issues but more in general on what happens in the world at large.

MADRIGALE, QUARTERLY, NAPLES

1, 1989–date.

This basically theoretical quarterly devoted to feminist politics and culture is published by the association 'Lo specchio di Alice (Alice's Mirror), which in 1987 and 1988 was in charge of a few autonomously edited pages of the Neapolitan cultural journal *NdR*. It sets out to investigate a series of concepts identified as peculiarly relevant to feminist speculation in the present context: generosity, illness and pain, strength. Women's strength and women's power only arise out of a *plural action*; with reference to Hannah Arendt's thought, '*agere*' (beginning, promoting an action) and '*gerere*' (bringing it to completion) are seen as possible and coexisting only when women entertain amongst themselves a privileged relationship which is the source of their mutual strength.

D/D (*DONNE E DIRITTO*), QUARTERLY, BOLOGNA

1, 1988–date.
Published by the Equal Opportunities Committee of Emilia-Romagna, this journal is devoted to an enquiry into the complex relationship between women and the law, in all its manifold aspects.

MEDITERRANEA, QUARTERLY, COSENZA

1, 1990–date.
Subtitled 'l'osservatorio delle donne' (women's observatory), this new journal aims at becoming 'a medium of information and communication for women who want to exchange projects, experiences, or desires; with the simple ease of an established trust in women and in themselves as women, but without any undue certainty in being the possessors of truth and knowledge'. Published in a southern city, it also aims to give choice to the specific reality of that area of Italy.

SQUADERNO, ROME

1, 1989–date.
A lesbian journal of 'culture, politics, delights and crimes', with no fixed periodicity, *Squaderno* is not afraid of polemics, irony, eroticism. It means to question all the extant cultural and political conceptions, calling to task feminism too for its tendency to silence lesbianism in order to be more acceptable to a larger number of women.

IL PAESE DELLE DONNE, WEEKLY, ROME

Two trial issues in 1987, then regularly from January 1988.
Run by an editorial board of women, journalists professionally engaged in other projects as well, *Il paese delle donne* was at first a weekly page in the Roman daily *Paese Sera* (from April 1985 to September 1986). Not surprisingly, that page was the first to go when the newspaper ran into the financial difficulties which were eventually to result in its demise. But the women in the group started anew and autonomously, and this lively newsbulletin, which also features a commentary on political and theoretical questions, has now established itself as a respected means of information and debate within the Italian feminist community. The first trial issue of an international edition appeared in the USA in May 1990.

For a more exhaustive information on the feminist press in Italy, periodical and otherwise, see *Le donne delle donne ficono. Il femminismo attraverso la stampa delle donne*, Roma, Centro Documentazione Studi sul Femminismo, 1988.

Bibliography

1963

Gaiotti De Biase, P., *Le origini del movimento cattolico femminile*, Brescia, Morcelliana.

Harrison, 'l., *Le svergognate*, Roma, Edizioni di Nouvissima.

Pieroni Bortolotti, F., *Alle origini del movimento femminile in Italia, 1848–1892*, Turin, Eiaudi (rptd. 1975).

1964

Cappezzuoli, L. and Cappabianca, G., *Storia dell'emancipazione femminile*, Rome, Editori Riuniti.

Caruso, L. and Tomasi, B., *I padri della fallocultura* Milano, SugarCo.

Parca, G., *Le italiane si confessano*, Milan, Feltrinelli (1st edn 1959).

Pastorino, M., *Controllo all'italiana. Le interruzioni di maternità*, Milan, Edizioni Avanti.

1968

Travers, J., *Dieci donne anticonformiste*, Bari, Laterza.

1969

Ravaioli, C., *La donna contro se stessa*, Bari, Laterza.

Zardi De Marchie, M.L., *Inumane Vite*, Milan, SugarCo.

1971

Banotti, E., *La sfida femminile. Maternità e aborto*, Bari, De Donato.

Conti, L., *Sesso e educazione*, Rome, Editori Riuniti.

Lonzi, C., *Sputiamo su Hegel – La donna clitoridea e la donna vaginale, e altri scritti*, privately circulated.

Saraceno, C., *Dalla parte della donna. Le questione femminile nelle società industriali avanzate*, Bari, De Donato.

Spagnoletti, R. (ed.), *I movimenti femministi, in Italia*, Rome, Samonà e Savelli.

1972

Abba, L. et al., *La coscienza di sfruttata*, Milan, Mazzotta.

Accardi, C., *Superiore e inferiore. Conversazioni fra le ragazzine delle scuole medie*, Milan, Scritti di Rovolta Femminile.

Anabasi, *Donne è bello, Milan, Anabasi.*

Dalla Costa, M., Potere femminile e sovversione sociale, Padua, Marsilio.

Foletti, L, and Boesi, C., *Par il diritto di aborto. Con un'appendice sulle tecniche contraccettive*, Rome La nuova sinistra.

Harrison, l., *La donna sposata. Mille mogli accusano*, Milan, Feltrinelli.

Lotta Femminista, *L'offensiva*, Quaderni di Lotta Femminista 1, Turin, Musolini.

Menapace, L. (ed.), *Per un movimento politico di liberazione della donna*, Verona, Bertani.

Spano, M. and Camarlinghi, F., *La questione femminile nella politica del PCI*, Rome, Edizioni Donne e Politica.

1973

Frabotta, B.M. (ed.), *Femminismo e lotta di classe in Italia (1970–73)*, Rome, Savelli.

Gianini Belotti, E., *Dalla parte delle bambine*, Milan, Feltrinelli.

Lotta femminista, *Il personale è politico*, Quaderni di Lotta Femminista 2, Turin, Musolini.

Nozzoli, S., *Donne si diventa*, Milan, Vangelista.

Parca, G., *Voci dal carcere femminile*, Rome, Editori Riuniti.

Ravaioli, C., *Maschio per obbligo. Oltre il femminismo per l'abolizione dei ruoli*, Milan, Bompiani.

Ravera, C., *Diario di trent-anni, 1913–1943*, Rome, Editori Riuniti.

Tarina, T., *Una ragazza timida*, Milan, Scritti di Rivolta Femminile.

UDI, Dimensione Donna, Proceedings of the Ninth National Conference of the UDI, Rome.

1974

Fusini, N. and Gramaglia, M. (eds), *Antologia di testi poetici del Movement*, Rome, Savelli.

Grasso, L., *Compagno padrone: Relazioni interpersonali nelle famiglie operaie della sinistra tradizionale e extraparlamentare*, Florence, Guaraldi.

Guerricchio, R., *Storia di Sibilla*, Pisa, Nistri-Lischi.

Lonzi, C., *Sputiamo su Hegel – La donna clitoridea e la donna vaginale, e altri scritti*, Milan, Scritti di Rivolta Femminile.

Maglie, I., *La donna un problema aperto*, Florence, Vallecchi.

Noce, T., *Rivoluzionaria professionale*, Milan, Bompiani.

Pieroni Bortolotte, F., *Socialismo e questione femminile in Italia*, Milan, Mazzotta.

Ricciardi Ruocco, M., *La donna tra utopia e realtà*, Florence, Bulgarini.

1975

Buonanno, M., *Naturale come sei. Indagine sulla stampa femminile in Italia*, Florence, Guaraldi.

Collettivo Internazionale Femminista, *Le operaie della casa*, Venice–Padua, Marsilio.

Collettivo Internazionale Femminista, *8 marzo 1974. Giornata Internazionale di lotta delle donne*, Venice, Marsilio.

Cutrufelli, M., *L'invenzione della donna. Miti e tecniche di uno sfruttamento*, Milan, Massotta.

Emmy, E. *L'arte cambia sesso*, Vatania, Tringale.

Faccio, A., *Il reato di masse. La donna è una persona con diritto di scelta. Perché l'aborto linero, gratuito e assistito*, Milan, SugarCo.

Faccio, A., *Le mie ragioni. Conversazioni con 70 donne*, Milan, Feltrinelli.

Franzinetti, G., *I figli della scelta. Tecniche e metodi contraccettivi per una procreazione responsabile*, Turin, Gribaudi.

La moglie e la prostituta. Due rouli, una condizione, Florence, Guaraldi.

Maraini, Y., *Siamo in tante. La condizione della donna nelle canzoni popolari e femministe*, Rome, Savelli.

Martinelli, A., *Autocoscienza*, Milan, Scritti di Rivolta Femminile.

MLD–Partito Radicale, *Contro l'aborto di classe* (ed. M. A. Teodori), Rome, Savelli.

Montini, I., *La bambola rotta. Famiglia, Chiesa, scuola nella formazione della identità maschile e femminile*, Verona, Bertani.

Mozzoni, A.M., *La liberazione della donna* (ed. F. Pieroni Bortolotti), Milan, Mazzotta.

Nobili, D., *La mamma cattiva. Fenomenologia e antropologia del figlicidio*, Florence, Guaraldi.

Porta, C., *Senza distinzione di sesso. Guida pratica al nuovo diritto d famiglia*, Milan, Sonzogno.

Saraceno, C., *La famiglia nella società contemporanea*, Turin, Loescher.

'Speciale donna', special issue of *Inchiesta*, 18.

UDI, *Consultori di maternità: caratteristiche, finalità, proposte dell'UDI*, Rome, SETI.

1976

Ascoli, G. et al., *La parola elettorale. Viaggio nell'universo politico maschile*, Rome, Edizioni delle Donne.

Bacchetti, M., *Nella donna c'era un sogno . . . Canzoniere femminista*, Milan, Moizzi.

Badaracco, E., Dambrosio, F. and Buscaglia, M., *Maternità cosciente, contraccezione e aborto*, Milan, Mazzotta.

Balbo, L., *Stato di famiglia. Bisogni, privato, collettivo*, Milan, Etas Libri.

Barbero Beerwald, I. (ed.), *Donna e società industriale*, Turin, Editoriale Valentino.

Bernardi, S. et al., *La casalinga di Cristo. Inchiesta sulle suore in Italia*, Rome, Edizioni delle Donne.

Bruzzichelli, P. and Algini, M.L. (eds), *Donna, cultura, tradizione*, Milan, Mazzotta.

Bruzzone, A.M. and Farina, R. (eds), *La Resistenza taciuta. Dodici vite di partigiane piemontesi*, Milan, La Pietra.

Chinese, M.G., *La strada più lunga*, Milan, Scritti di Rivolta Femminile.

Collettivo Internazionale Femminista (ed.), *Aborto di stato: strage degli innocenti*, Venice, Marsilic.

Cutrufelli, M., *Disoccupata con onore. Lavoro e condizione della donna*, Milan, Mazzotta.

Cutrufelli, M., *Donna perchè piangi? Imperialismo e condizione femminile nell'Africa nera*, Milan, Mazzotta.

Di Nola, L. (ed.), *Da donna a donna. Poesie d'amore e d'amicizia*, Rome. Edizioni delle Donne.

Movimento Femminista Romano, *Donnità. Cronache del Movimento Femminista Romano*, Rome, Centro di Documentazione del Movimento Femminista Romano (Via Pompeo Magno).

Frabotta, B. (ed.), *Donne in poesia. Antologia della poesia femminile in Italia dal dopoguerra ad oggi*, Rome, Savelli.

Frabotta, B. (ed.), *La politica del femminismo*, Rome, Savelli.

Franco Lao, M., *Muscia strega. Per la ricerca di una dimensione femminile nella musica*, Rome, Edizioni delle Donne.

Gatto Trocchi, C., *Le giumente degli dei. Analisi antropologica del'ruolo economico della donna nelle società patriarcali*, Rome. Bulzoni.

Guippo Femminista per una Medicina della Donna (ed.), *Aborto libero? Il metodo Karman e la sperimentazione sulle donne*, Milan, La Salamandra.

Harrison, L., *Donne, povere matte. Inchiesta nell'Ospedale Psichiatrico di Roma*, Rome, Edizioni delle Donne.

Lussu, J., *Padre Padrone Padreterno*, Milan, Mazzota.

Macciocchi, M.A., *La donna nera. Consenso femminile e fascismo*, Milan, Feltrinelli.

Muraro, L., *La signora del gioco. Episodi della caccia alle streghe*, Milan, Feltrinelli.

Paggio, L., *Avanti un'altra. Donne e ginecologi a confronto*, Milan, La Salamandra.

Parca, G., *L'avventurosa storia del femminismo*, Milan, Mondadori.

Pezzuoli, G., *La stampa femminile come ideologia*, Milan, Il Formichiere.

Ravaioli, C., *La questione femminile. Intervista col PCI*, Milan, Bompiani.

Remiddi, L., *I nostri diritti. Manuale giuridico per le donne*, Milan, Feltrinelli.

Saraceno, C., *Anatomia della famiglia. Strutture sociali e forme familiari*, Bari, De Donato.

Tedesco, G., *Il diritto di famiglia. Conosciamo la nuova legge*, Rome, UDI.

Tiso, A., *I comunisti e la questione femminile*, Rome, Editori Riuniti.

Weller, S., *Il complesso di Michelangelo. Ricerca sul contributo data dalla donna all'arte italiana del Novecento*, Pollenzo, Il Nuovo Foglio.

1977

Ascoli, G. et al., *La questione femminile in Italia dal 900 ad oggi*, Milan, Angeli.

Bimbi, F. (ed.), *Dentro lo specchio. Lavoro domestico, riproduzione del ruolo e autonomia delle donne*, Milan, Mazzotta.

Caldirola, M.G., *Io canto la differenza. Canzoni di donne sulle donne*, Milan, Mazzotta.

Carrano, P., *Malafemmina. La donna nel cinema italiano*, Florence, Guaraldi.

Cecchini, F. et al., *Sesso amaro. Trentamila donne rispondono su maternità, sessualità, aborto*, Rome, Editori Riuniti.

Cutrufelli, M., *Operaie senza fabbrica. Inchiesta sul lavoro a domicilio*, Rome, Editori Riuniti.

Dalla Costa, M., *Potere femminile e sovversione sociale*, Venice, Marsilio.

Dalla Costa, M. and Fortunati, L., *Brutto ciao. Direzione di marcia delle donne négli ultimi 30 anni*, Rome, Edizioni delle Donne.

Emmy, E., *Donna, Arte, Marxismo*, Rome, Bulzoni.

Fossati, R., *E Dio creò la donna. Chiesa, religione e condizione femminile*, Milan, Mazzotta.

Grasso, L., *Madre amore donna. Per un'analisi del rapporto madre–figlia*, Florence, Guaraldi.

Guidetti Serra, B., *Compagne. Testimonianze di partecipazione politica femminile*, Turin, Einaudi.

Guiducci, A., *La donna non è gente. L'esistenza emarginata delle più oppresse*, Milano, Rizzoli.

Lonzi, C., Lonzi, M. and Jaquinta, A., *E' già politica*, Milan, Scritti di Rivolta Femminile.

Melandri, L., *L'infamia originaria. Facciamola finita col cuore e con la politica*, Milan, L'Erba Voglio.

Monteforschi, S., *L'uno e l'altro*, Milan, Feltrinelli.

Morandini, S., *. . . e allora mi hanno rinchiusa. Testimonianze dal manicomio femminile*, Milan, Bompiani.

Padoa Schioppa, F., *La forza lavoro femminile*, Bologna, Il Mulino.

Scrivere contro. Esperienze, riflessioni, analisi delle giornaliste presentate al convegno Donna Informazione 1977. Rome, Edizioni delle Donne.

Seroni, A., *La questione femminile in Italia 1970–77*, Rome, Editori Riuniti.

Tufani, L., *Bibliografia sulla condizione femminile*, Ferrara, Bovolenta.

UDI of Ferrara (ed.), *Perché la stampa femminile*, Ferrara, Bovolenta.

Visca, D., *Il sesso infecondo. Contraccezione, aborto e infanticidio nelle società tradizionali*, Rome, Bulzoni.

Vitas, E., *Io sono mia. La condizione femminile*, Bologna, Zanichelli.

1978

Aleramo, S., *La donna e il femminismo. Scritti 1897–1910* (ed. B. Conti), Rome, Edition Riuniti.

Alloisio, M. and Ajò, M., *La donna nel socialismo. Italia tra cronaca e storia 1892–1978*, Rome, Lerici.

Angelini, V. et al., *Sinfonia pateriale. Storia antologica del pensiero maschile sulla donna*, Rome, Savelli.

Banissoni, M., *Bibliografia sulla condizione femminile. Articoli, Saggi, ricerche psicologico-sociali*, Rome, Bulzoni.

Bettarini, M., *Felice de essere. Scritti sulla condizione della donna e sulla sessualità*, Milan, Gamma Libri.

Bompiani, G., *Lo spazio narrante*, Milan, La Tartaruga.

Buonanno, M., *La donna nella stampa. Giornaliste, lettrici e modelli di femminilità*, Rome, Editori Riuniti.

Cambria, A., *In principio era Marx*, Milan, SugarCo.

Camparini, A., *Questione femminile e Terza Internazionale*, Bari, De Donato.

Cavallo, Boggi, P., *Immagine de sé e ruolo sessuale. Analisi psicologica della condizione femminile*, Naples, Guida.

Castaldi, S., *Femminile pateriale. Vicende del femminismo fra matriarcato e patriarcato*, Milan, Vangelista.

Comitato Femminile Antifascista per il XXX Resistenza e della Liberazione (ed.), *Donne e Resistenza in Toscana*, Florence.

Coordinamento Nazionale Femminile CGIL, *Questione femminile e sindacato*, Rome, Nuove Edizioni Operaie.

Cutrufelli, M. (ed.), *Le donne protagoniste del movimento cooperativo. La questione femminile in un'organizzazione produttiva democratica*, Milan, Feltrinelli.

Dalla Costa, G.F., *Un lavoro d'amore. La violenza fisica componente essenziale del 'trattamento maschile' nei confronti delle donne*, Rome, Edizioni delle Donne.

Di Nola, L. (ed.), *Poesia femminista italiana*, Rome, Savelli.

Di Nola, L., *Il gioco delle riappropriazioni. Il femminismo si riappropria della psicolanalisi*, Milan, Moizzi.

Donne e Resistenza in Emilia Romagna, Proceedings of the Conference held in Bologna, 1977, 3 vols, Milan, Vangelista.

Forni, E. et al., *Essere donna oggi: ricerche sulla formazione dell'identità femminile*, Tento, Unicoop.

Fraire, M., Spagnoletti, R. and Virdis, M. (eds), *L'almanacco. Luoghi, nomi, incontri, fatti, lavori in corse del movimento femminista italiano dal 1972*, Rome, Edizioni delle Donne.

Franceschi, L. et al., *L'altra metà della Resistenza*, Milan, Mazzotta.

Gagliardo, G., *Maternale*, Milan, Edizioni delle Donne.

Gaiotti De Biase, P., *Sulla questione femminile*, Rome, CEDIS.

Garaguso, P. and Renzetti, E., *La mercificazione dell'immagine femminile nel cinema italiano*, Trento, Unicopli.

Garutti Bellenzie, M.T., *Idea a realtà della donna*, Rome, Città Nuova.

Gruppo 150 Ore, *Scuola media Gabbro Milano*, Milan, La Traversata.

Gruppo del Catalogo/Libreria delle Donne di Milano, *Catalogo. Testi di teoria e pratica politica. Sulle servitù della scrittura e sulle sue grandi possibilità*, Milan, Libreria della Donne.

Gruppo della Scrittura/Libreria delle Donne di Milano, *A zig zag. Non Scritti, Scritti*, Milan, Libreria della Donna.

Gruppo Donne del Palazzo di Giustizia di Milano, *Aborto quando, dove e come*, Milan, Teti.

Gruppo Femminista per il Salario al Lavoro Domestico di Ferrara, *Dietro la normalità del parto. Lotta all'ospedale di Ferrara*, Venice, Marsilio.

Gruppo Femminista per la Salute della Donna, *Gli anticoncezionali*, Rome, Gruppo famminista per la salute della donna.

Lessico politico delle donne. 1. Le donne e il diritto, (series editor: M. Fraire), Milan, Gulliver.

Lessico politico delle donne. 2. Donne e medicina, Series editor: M. Fraire), Milan, Gulliver.

Lessico politico delle donne. 3. Teorie del femminismo, (series editor: M. Fraire), Milan, Gulliver.

Lonzi, C., *Taci, anzi parla. Diario di una femminista*, Milan, Scritti di Rivolta Femminile.

Lonzi, M., Jaquinta, A. and Lonzi, C., *La presenza dell'uomo nel femminismo*, Milan, Scritti di Rivolta Femminile.

Lussu, J. et al., *'L'erba delle donne. Maghe, streghe, guaritrici: la riscoperta di un'altra medicina*, Rome, Napoleone.

Magli I. (eds), *Matriarcato e potere delle donne*, Milan, Feltrinelli.

Marinucci, E. and Remiddi, L., *Guida all'aborto legale. Come applicare e gestire la legge sull'interruzione di gravidanza*, Venice, Marsilio.

Mori, A.M., *Il Silenzio delle donne e il caso Moro*, Consenza, Lerici.

Noce, T., *Vivere in piedi*, Milan, Mazzotta.

Noi Donne 1944–1945 (photographic reprint), Rome, Cooperative Libera Stampa.

Non è detto che. Pagine di donne, Milan.

Nozzoli, A., *Tabù e coscienza. La condizione femminile nella letteratura italiana del Novecento*, Florence, La Nuova Italia.

Occhio, F. and Torchi A. (eds), *L'acqua in gabbia. Voci di donne dentro il sindacato*, Milan, La Salamandra.

Paggio, C.L., *Donna e . . . Piccolo manuale pratico di contraccezione, aborto, sessualità, gravidanza*, Milan, Emmes.

Parca, G., *Il plusvalore femminile*, Milan, Mondadori.

Pieroni Bortolotte. F., *Le donne nella resistenza antifascista e la questione femminile in Emilia e Romagna, 1943–1945*, Milan, Vangelists.

Pieroni Bortolotte, F., *Femminismo e partiti politici in Italia. 1919–1926*, Rome, Editori Riuniti.

Pizzoli, R., *Sessismo in casa e a scuola*, Milan Balla Parte delle Bambine.

Rasy, E., *La lingua della nutrice. Percorsi e tracce dell'espressione femminile*, Rome, Edizioni delle Donne.

Ravera, L., *Breve storia del movimento femminile in Italia*, Rome, Editori Riuniti.

Rossi, R., *Le parole delle donne*, Rome, Editori Riuniti.

Tomasi, T., *L'educazione infantile tra Stato e Chiesa*, Florence, Vallecchi.

1979

Ballestrero, M.V., *Della tutela alla parità. La legislizione italiana sul lavoro delle donne*, Bologne, Il Mulino.

Baruffi, L. (ed.), *Il desiderio di maternità*, Turin, Boringhieri.

Bechi, E. et al., *Tempo pieno e scuola elementare*, Milan, Angeli.

Bianchini, E., *Voce donna. Momenti strutturali dell'emancipazione femminile*, Milan, Bompiani.

Brawer, A., *Con Sylvia (nata Plath)*, Milan, La Salamandra.

Callari Galli, M., *Il tempo delle donne*, Bologna, Cappelli.

Cattaneo, A. and Pisa, G., *L'altra mamma. La maternità nel movimento delle donne. Fantasie, desideri, domande, inquietudini*, Rome, Savelli.

Cinato, A. et al. (ed.), *La spina all'occhiello. L'esperienza dell'Intercategoriale Donne CGIL–CISL–UIL* attraverso i documenti 1975–78, Turin, Musolino.

Chisté, L, Del Re, A. and Forti, R., *Oltre il lavoro domestico. Il lavoro delle donne tra produzione e riproduzione*, Milan, Feltrinelli.

Conti Odorisio, G., *Donne e società nel Seicento*, Rome, Bulzoni.

Coordinamente Donne FLM of Naples (ed.), *Spezzare il cerchio. Il rapporto difficile tra casa e fabbrica nelle esperienze di alcune donne*, Salerno, Coop. Sintesi.

De Cristofaro, M.L., *Tutela e/o parità? La legislazione italiana sul lavoro delle donne*, Bologna, Il Mulino.

Foletti, L and Tentini, A., *La bruca. Sillabario della sotterraneità*, Rome, Mjrine.

Francescato, D. and Prezza, M., *Le condizioni della sessualità femminile*, Bari, De Donato.

Gaiotti De Biase, P., *Questione femminile e femminismo nella storia della Repubblica*, Brescia, Marcelliana.

Gianini Belotti, E., *Che razza di ragazza: verso una nuova coscienza delle donne*, Rome, Savelli.

Grasso, L., *Madri e figlie, specchio contro specchio*, Florence, Nuova Guaraldi.

Gruppo Femminista per la Salute della Donna, *Infezioni vaginali*, Rome, Gruppo feminista per la salute della donne.

Gruppo Feminista per la Salute della Donna, *L'autovisita*, Rome, Gruppo femminista per la salute delle donna.

Gruppo Femminista per la Salute della Donna, *La Visita ginecologica*, Rome, Gruppo femminista per la salute della donna.

Lessico politico delle donne. 4/5. Sociologia della famiglia. Sull'emancipazione femminile, (series editor: M. Fraire), Milan, Gulliver.

Lessico politico delle donne. 6. Cinema, letteratura, arti visive, (series editor: M. Fraire), Milan, Gulliver.

Lilli, L and Valentini, C. (eds), *Care compagne. Il femminismo nel PCI e nelle organizzazioni di massa*, Rome, Editori Riuniti.

Lo Cascio, G., *Occupate e casalinghe*, Rome, Editori Riuniti.

Macrelli, R., *Ridiamo su Proudhon. Alle origini della teoria neo-patriarcale*, Rome, Edizioni del Movimento Femminista Romano (Via Pompeo Magno).

Mafai, M., *L'apprendistato della politica. Le donne italiane nel dopoguerra*, Rome, Editori Riuniti.

Micela, R. (ed.), *Oppressione della donna e ricerca antropologica*, Rome, Savelli.

Mizzau, M., *Eco e Narciso. Parole e silenzi nel conflitto uomo–donna*, Turin, Boringhieri.

Moretti, V. and Pivetta, M. (eds), *Il mio segno, la mia parola. Rabbia, amore, confessioni, appuntamenti, disegni, nella Casa della Donna in Via del Governo Vecchio*, Rome, Quotidiano Donna.

Paolozzi, L., *Viaggio nell'isola*, Rome, Edizioni delle Donne.

Piccone Stella, S., *Ragazze del Sud. Famiglie, figlie, studentesse in una città meridionale*, Rome, Editori Riuniti.

Pomata, G., *In scienza e coscienza, donne e potere nella società borghese*, Florence, La Nuova Italia.

Ravera, C., *Lettere al partito e alla famiglia*, Rome, Editori Riuniti.

Rossanda, R., *Le altre*, Milan, Bompiani.

Schiavo, M., *Macellum. Storia violenta e romanzata di donne e di mercato*, Milan, La Tartaruga.

Scroppo, E., *Donna, privato e politico. Storie personali di 21 donne del PCI*, Milan, Mazzotta.

1980

Barina, E., *La Sirena nella mitologia. La negazione del sesso femminile*, Padua, Mastrogiacomo.

Barile, P. and Zanuso, L., *Lavoro femminile e condizione familiare*, Milan, Angeli.

Bassanese, N. and Buzzati, G. (eds), *La mascherata. La sessualità femminile nella nuova psicoanalisi*, Rome, Savelli.

Bassanesi, D., *Donne di picche. Riflessioni sulla violenza e sulle possibilità del negativo*, Milan, La Salamandra.

Belmonti, M.G. et al., *Un processo per stupro*, Turin, Einaudi.

Cagidemetrio, A., *Una strada nel bosco. Scrittura e coscienza in Djuna Barnes*, Vicenza, Neri Pozza.

Chiaretti, G. (ed.), *Doppia presenza: lavoro intellettuale e lavoro per sé*, Milan, Angeli.

Conti Odorision, G., *Storia dell'idea femminista in Italia*, Turin, ERI.

Cutrufelli, M., *Economia e politica dei sentimenti*, Rome, Editori Riuniti.

Del Miglio, C. and Fedeli, L. (eds), *Il problema donna. Soggettività psico-sociale e identità sessuale*, Rome, Città Nuova.

Di Febo, G., *L'altra metà della Spagna. Dalla lotta antifranchista al femminismo: 1939–1977*, Naples, Liguori.

Finocchi M., Froncillo R., Valentini A. (eds), *. . . E la madre, tra l'altro è una pittrice . . . Dialoghi tra lesbiche*, Rome, Felina.

Federzoni, M., Pezzini, I. and Pozzato, M.P., *Sibilla Aleramo*, Florence, La Nuova Italia.

Finalmente sole! La donna nell'Ottocento attraverso i periodici della Braidense, Catalogue of the Exhibition, Milan, Centro Grafico IS.

Frabotta, B., *Letteratura al femminile. Itinerari di lettura*, Bari, De Donato.

Galoppini, A., *Il lungo viaggio verso la parità*, Bologna, Zanichelli.

Gruppo per l'Informazione nei Consultori (ed.), *Guida pratica agli anticoncezionali*, Milan, La Salamandra.

Lonzi, C., *Vai pure. Dialogo con Pietro Consagra*, Milan, Scritti di Rivolta Femminile.

Macrelli, R., *L'indegna schiavitù. Anna Maria Mozzoni e la lotta contro la prostituzione di Stato*, Rome, Editori Riuniti.

Manfredini, M.G., *Alle origini del diritto femminile*, Bari, Dedalo.

Mangiacapre, L., *Cinema al femminile*, Padua, Mastrogiacomo.

Miscuglio, A. and Daopoulo, R., *Kinomata. La donna nel cinema*, Bari, Dedalo.

Morandini, G., *La voce che è in lei. Antologia della narrativa femminile italiana tra 800 e 900*, Milan, Bompiani.

Saraceno, C. (ed.), *Il lavoro maldiviso. Ricerca sulla distribuzione dei cariche di lavoro nelle famiglie*, Bari, De Donato.

Saraceno, C., *Uguali e diverse. Le trasformazioni dell'identità femminile: percorsi di storia sociale nelle conversazioni a Radiotre*, Bari, De Donato.

Tribunale Otto Marzo, *Cosa loro. E' tutto vero, verissimo e non è tutto. Testimonianze-denunce*, Rome, Bulzoni.

Vergine, L. (ed.), *L'altra metà dell-avanguardia 1910–1980*, Milan, Mazzotta.

1981

Astaldi, M.L., Bompiani, G. and Fusini, N., *Virginia Woolf*, Rome, Edizioni Centro Culturale, Virginia Woolf.

Belmonti, M.G. et al., *La vera storia di AAA Offresi, scritta dalla protagonista*, Milan, Sperling & Kupfer.

Bocchetti, A., *L'ambiguo materno*, 'Programma 1981–82', Rome, Edizioni Centro Culturale Virginia Woolf.

Cacciari, C., Cavicchioni, V. and Mizzau, M., *Il caso Sofija Tolstoi*, Verona, Essedue.

Cambria, A., *Il Lenin delle donne*, Padua, Mastrogiacomo.

Cantarella, E., *L'ambiguo malanno. Condizione e immagine della donna nell'antichità greca e romana*, Rome, Editori Riuniti.

CGIL–CISL–IUL Peimonte (ed.), *Il sindacato di Eva. L'attività dell'intercategoriale donne CGIL–CISL–UIL e dei coordinamenti donne di diverse categorie, documenti 1978–1981*, Turin, Centrostampa FLM-Piemonte.

Colaiacomo, P. et al., *Come nello specchio. Saggi sulla figurazione del femminile*, Turin, La Rosa.

Conti, C., *Il tormento e lo scudo. Un compresso contro le donne*, Milan, Mazzotta.

Conti, B. and Morino, A., *Sibilla Aleramo e il suo tempo. Vita raccontata e illustrata*, Milan, Feltrinelli.

Cutrufelli, M., *Il cliente. Inchiesta sulla domanda di prostituzione*, Rome, Editori Riuniti.

De Tassis, P. and Griffagnini, G. *Sequenza segreta. Le donne e il cinema*, Milan, Feltrinelli.

Donne della Malpensata, *Storie di panni stesi. Emozioni e chiacchere di un collettivo femminista*, Bergamo, Donna della Malpensata.

Fantoni, F. et al., *Donne a scuola. Bisogno di conoscenza e ricerca di identità*, Bologna, Il Mulino.

Finzi Ghisi V. (ed.), *Forme di sapere e forme di vita*, Bari, Dedalo.

Gentileschi, A. and Tassi A., *Atti di un processo per stupro* (ed. E. Mezio), Rome, Edizioni delle Donne.

Faccio, A., *Una strega da bruciare*, Rome, Lanfranchi.

Fiori, G., *Simone Weil, Biografia di un pensiero*, Milan, Garzanti.

Luna e l'altro. Rappresentazione e autor appresentazione del femminile, suppl. to no. 16 of *Nuova dwf*, Rome, Utopia.

Mancina, C., *La famiglia. Teoria, storia e funzioni della comuità familiare. Crisi e ricerca di nuovi equilibri*, Rome, Editori Riuniti.

Morreale, M.T., *Nate per leggere. Annotazioni sulla cultura tedesca del Settecento*, Palermo, Libreria Dante.

Muraro, L., *Maglia e uncinetto. Racconto linguistico politico sulla inimicizia tra metafora e metonimia*, Milan, Feltrinelli.

Damiani C. et al., *Oltre l'aborto. Posizioni e documenti del movimento delle donne*, Rome, Cooperative Editrice Ottanta – Quotidiano dei Lavoratori.

Pereira. M., *Né Eva né Maria. Condizione femminile e immagine della donna nel Medioevo*, Bologna, Zanichelli.

Pizzini, F., *Sulla scena del parto: luoghi, figure, pratiche*, Milan, Angeli.

Pontecorvo, C. (ed.), *Intelligenza e diversità*, Turin, Loescher.

Riva, A., *La rabbia femminista*, Rome, Janua.

Zaccaria, P., *Virginia Woolf. Trama e ordito di una scrittura*, Bari, Dedalo.

1982

Balbo, L. and Bianchi, M. (eds), *Ricomposizioni. Il lavoro di servizio nella società della crisi*, Milan, Angeli.

Banti, A., *Quando anche le donne si misero a dipingere*, Milan, La Tartaruga.

Basaglia Ongaro, F., *Una voce. Riflessioni sulla donna*, Milan, Il Saggiatore.

Bocchetti, A., *L'indecente differenza*, 'Programma 1983', Rome, Edizioni Centro Culturale Virginia Woolf.

Bonato, I. et al., *Punto a capo*, Rome, Edizioni Centro Culturale Virginia Woolf.

Catalucci, E. and Sarinelli, R., *Donna e lavoro. Bibliografia 1970–1981: ricerche, saggi, articoli*, Rome, Bulzoni.

Chiaretti, G. and Piazza, M., *Educazione permanente: il caso dei corsi 150 ore sulla condizione delle donne*, Milan, Regione Lombardia.

Comerci, M., *I profili della luna. Riflessioni sulla creatività femminile*, Rome, Bulzoni.

Coop. Il Taccuino d'Oro, *Maria Medea e le altre, il materno nelle parole delle donne*, Rassegna stampa, Rome, Lerici.

Craveri, B., *Madame Du Deffand e il suo mondo*, Milan, Adelphi.

De Matteis, M.C. (ed.), *Idee sulla donna nel Medioevo: fonti e aspetti giuridici, antropologici, religiosi, sociali e letterari della condizione femminile*, Bologna, Patron.

Gaiotti De Biase, P., *Sulla questione femminile*, Florence, Le Monnier (enlarged edn).

Guiducci, A., *A colpi di silenzio*, Milan, Lanfranchi.

Gruppo del Catalogo/Libreria delle Donne di Milano and Biblioteca delle Donne di Parma, *Catalogo no. 2. Romanzi. Le madri di tutte noi*, Milan, Libraria delle Donne.

Gruppo Elle, *Le riviste femministe dal 1970 ad oggi. Catalogo*, Florence, Libreria delle Donne.

Longo, G. et al. (eds), *Donne e medicina: Documenti e testimonianze del Tribunale 8 marzo*, Rome, Bulzoni.

Lonzi, M., *L'architetto fuori di sé*, Milan, scritti di Rivolta Femminile.

Lussu, J., Moriconi, V. and Lenzi, M.L., *Donne, guerra e società*, Ancona, Il Lavoro Editoriale.

Miscuglio, A., Bonifacio, E. and Mandolfo, P., *L'immagine riflessa. La produzione delle donne tra cinema e televisione*, Catania, Litostampa Idonea.

Montefoschi, S., *Al de là del tabù dell'incesto*, Milan, Feltrinelli.

Percorsi del femminismo e storia delle donne, Proceedings of the Conference held in Modena, 2–4 April 1982, suppl. to no. 22 of *Nuova Dwf*, Rome, Utopia.

Orletti, F. (ed.), *Comunicare nella vita quotidiana*, Bologna, Zanichelli.

Ravaioli, C., *Il quanto e il quale. La cultura del mutamento*, Bari, Laterza.

Reale, E., Sardelli, V. and Castellano, A., *Malattia mentale e ruolo della donna. Dall'esperienza pratica ad una nuova toeria del disagio*, Rome, Il Pensiero Scientifico.

Riprendiamoci la storia! Momenti e biografia del femminismo in Italia, Unione Donne Italiane of Catanzaro (ed.), Catanzaro, UDI.

Salaris, C., *Le futuriste. Donne e letteratura d'avanguardia in Italia 1909–1944*, Rome, Edizioni delle Donne.

Secci, L., *Dal salotto al partito. Scrittrici tedesche tra rivoluzione borghese e diritto di voto*, Rome, Savelli.

Vergine, L., *L'arte ritrovata. Alla ricerca dell'altra metà dell'avanguardia*, Milan, Rizzoli.

1983

Ballestrero, M.V. and Livraghi, T., *Lavoro femminile, formazione e parità uomo–donna*, Milan, Angeli.

Bassanese, N. and Buzzatti, G. (eds), *Il vuoto e il pieno*, Florence Centro Documentazione Donna.

Buonanno, M., *Cultura di massa e identità femminile. L'immagine della donna in televisione*, Turin, ERI.

Casa, dolce casa. Modi e qualità dell-abitare, Proceedings of the conference organized and edited by the Commissione Femminile del PCI, 7 May 1983, Parma.

Cavallo Boggi, P., *La costruzione sociale del sé: divisione tra i sessi e identità di ruolo*, Naples, Guida.

CLI (Coordinamemto Lesbiche Italiane), *Il nostro mondo comune*, Rome, Felina.

Coppola Pignatelli, P., *Spazio e immaginario. Maschile e femminile in architettura*, Rome, Officina.

10 anni del Movimento delle Donne: innovazioni sul piano legislativo e presa di coscienza individuale e collettiva, Proceedings of the seminar organized and edited by the Centro Culturale Mara Meoni, Siena.

Farina, R. (ed.), *Esistere come donna*, Catalogue of the Exhibition, Milan, Mazzotta.

Fonti orali e politica delle donne: storia, ricerca, racconto, materiali dell'incontro svoltosi a Bologna l'8–9 ottobre 1982, Bologna, Centro di Documentazione, Ricerca e Iniziativa delle Donne.

Francescato, D., *Verso una prevenzione dell'aborto. Contributi di ricerca sugli aspetti psicosociali dell'aborto procurato*, Rome, Casa del libro.

Francescato, D. et al., *Personalità e questione femminile: famiglie tradizionali e a doppia carriera*, Rome, Bulzoni.

Gianini Belotti, G., *Non di sola madre*, Milan, Rizzoli.

Nappi, A., *L'alternativa. Esperienze di autonomia, identità femminile e nuovi rapporti sociali*, Milan, Unicopli.

Pomata, G., 'La storia delle donne. Una questione di confine', in N. Tranfaglia (ed.), *Il mondo contemporaneo*, vol. X, *Gli strumenti della ricerca*, , t. II: *Questioni di metodo*, Florence, La Nuova Italia.

Rossi, R., *Teresa de Jesùs. Biografia di una scrittrice*, Rome, Editori Riuniti.

Villa, N., *La piccola grande signora del PCI: Camilla Ravera*, Milan, Rizzoli.

Zancan, M. (ed.), *Nel cerchio della luna*, Venice, Marsilio.

1984

Bocchetti, A., *Discorso sulla guerra e sulle donne*, Rome, Edizioni Centro Culturale Virginia Woolf.

Cambria, A., *L'Italia segreta delle donne*, Rome, Newton Compton.

Cammarota, R., *Donna, identità, lavoro: il movimento femminista di fronte alla complessità sociale*, Milan, Giuffrè.

Campese, S., Manuli, P. and Sissa, G., *Madre materia: sociologia e biologia della donna greca*, Turin, Boringhieri.

Carbonetto, M.G. and Filingeri, L., *Il dialogo nascosto. Interazione madre-bambino durante la gravidanza*, Milan, La Salamandra.

Collettivo Le Papesse, *Maternità e lesbismo*, Catania, Collettivo le Papesse.

Comerci, M. et al., *Desiderio d'impresa. Azienda e cooperative al femminile*, Bari, Dedalo.

Coordinamento Nazionale Consultori/Gruppo Romano (ed.), *Per una nuova cultura della sessualità*, Proceedings of the conference held in Rome, 23–25 September 1983, Rome.

Coordinamento Nazionale Donne ARCI (ed.), *Maschile e femminile. Dell'identità e del confondersi*, Bari, Dedalo.

Fabbri Montesano, D. and Munari, A., *Strategie del sapere*, Bari, Dedalo.

Melucci, A. (ed.), *Altri codici*, Bologna, Il Mulino.

Michetti, M., Repetto, M. and Viviani L. (eds), *UDI. Laboratorio di politica delle donne*, Rome, Libera Stampa.

Mizzau, M., *L'ironia, contraddizione consentita*, Milan, Feltrinelli.

Produrre e riprodurre – Cambiamenti nel rapporto tra donne e lavoro, Proceedings of the First International Conference of Women from Industrialized Countries organized by the women's movement of Turin, held in Turin, 1983, Rome, Coop. Manifesto Anni '80.

Rasy, E., *Le donne e la letteratura*, Rome, Editori Riuniti.

Rossi Doria, A., *L'eccesso femminile*, 'Programma 1984', Rome, Edizioni Centro Culturale, Virginia Woolf.

Sarasini, B., *Sul limite,*, 'Programma 1985', Rome, Edizioni Centro Culturale Virginia Woolf.

Sbisà, M., *La mamma di carta. Per una critica dello stereotipo materno*, Milan, Emme.

Tilche, G., *La scienziala santa del Settecento*, Milan, Rizzoli.

1985

Addis Saba, M., *Io donna io persona*, Rome, Felina.

Associazione Culturale Livia Laverani Donini. *La donna e il corpo*, Proceedings of the seminars held in Turin, Jan.–April 1984, Turin.

Associazione Culturale Livia Laverani Donini, *Raccontare e riflettere*, Proceedings of the seminars held in Turin, Feb.–March 1985, Turin.

Bimbi, F. and Pristinger, F. (eds), *Profili sovrapposti. La doppia presenza delle donne in un'area ad economia diffusa*, Milan, Angeli.

Bocchetti, A. and Sarasini, B., *Il soggetto inaudito. Breve dialogo sulla differenza sessuale*, 'Programma 1986', Rome, Edizioni Centro Culturale, Virginia Woolf.

Bocchi, G. and Ceruti, M (eds), *La sfida della complessità*, Milan, Feltrinelli.

Buonanno, M., *Matrimonio e famiglia*, Milan, ERI.

Buttafuoco, A., *Le Mariuccine. Storia di un'istituzione laica*, Milan, Angeli.

Calabrò, A. and Grasso, L., (eds), *Dal movimento femminista al femminismo diffuso*, Milan, Angeli.

Cambia il modo di vivere perché cambia il modo di lavorare, 'UDI' of Catanzaro (ed.), Catanzaro, UDI.

Camboni, M. (ed.), *Come la tela del ragno. Poesie e saggi di/su Adrienne Rich*, Rome, La Goliardica.

Cantarella, E., *Tacita muta. La donna nella città antica*, Rome, Editori Riuniti.

Cappiello, A. A. et al. (eds), *Codice Donna. Norme interne e atti internazionali*, Rome, Commissione nazionale per la realizzazione della parità tra uomo e donna.

Centri di Studi storici sul Movimento di Liberazione delle Donne in Italia (ed.), *Luoghi e forme di aggregazione delle donne oggi in Lombardia*, Milan, Regione Lombardia.

Colombo, G., Pizzini, F. and Regalia, A., *Mettere al mondo. La produzione sociale del parto*, Milan, Angeli.

Costa, P.M., *Guglielma la boema: l'eretica di Chiaravalle*, Milan, NED.

Ferraro, F. and Nunziante-Cesaro, A., *Lo spazio cavo e il corpo saturato*, Milan, Angeli.

Le culture del parto, Proceedings of the conference held in Milan, Jan. 1985, Milan, Feltrinelli.

Libreria delle Donne di Firenze and Centro Documentazione Donna Firenze (eds), *I Labirinti dell'Eros*, Proceedings of the seminar held in Florence, 27–8 October 1984, Florence.

Longo, G. (ed.), *Modelli di donna emergenti nei mezzi di comunicazione di massa*, Rome, Commissione nazionale per la realizzazione della parità tra uomo e donna.

Magli, P. (ed.), *Le donne e i segni. Scrittura, linguaggio, identità nel segno della figura femminile*, Ancona, Il Lavoro Editoriale.

Manacorda, P. and Piva, P. (eds), *Terminale donna. Il movimento delle donne di fronte al lavoro informatizzato*, Rome, Edizioni Lavoro.

Merelli, M (et al., *Giochi di equilibrio. Tra lavoro e famiglia: le donne nella cooperazione*, Milan, Angeli.

Muraro, L., *Guglielma e Maifreda. Storia di un'eresia femminista*, Milan, La Tartaruga.

Pieroni Bortolotti, F., *La donna, la pace, l'Europa. L'associazione internazionale delle donne dalle origini alla prima guerra mondiale*, Milan, Angeli.

Centro Studi Donnawomanfemme, *Progetto Virginia Woolf. Parole. Immagini*, Rome, Quaderni del Centro Studi Donnawomanfemme.

Remiddi, L. (ed.), *120 anni di cammino verso la parità*, Rome, Commissione nazionale per la realizzazione della parità tra uomo e donna.

Rossetti, G., *Una vita degna di essere narrata. Autobiografie di donne nell'Inghilterra puritana*, Milan, La Salamandra.

Sbisà, M., *I figli della scienza. Riflessioni sulla riproduzione artificiale*, Milan, Emme.

1986

Addis, Saba M., Conti Odorisio, G. and Pisa, B., *Storia delle donne, una scienza possibile*, Rome, Felina.

Alberti, P. et al., *Maestre d'amore. Eroine e scrittrici nell'impero del rosa inglese*, Bari, Dedalo.

Archivio della Libreria delle Donne, *Rassegna Stampa. Politica dell'affidamento*, Milan, Libreria delle Donne.

Associazione Culturale Livia Laverani Donini, *L'eccezionale e il quotidiano*, Proceedings of the seminars held in Turin, March–May 1986, Turin.

Belforte, F. Lemmi, G. and Meucci, A. (eds), *Dal dovere all'amore*, Leghorn, Belforte.

Babini, V. et al., *Le donne nella scienza dell'uomo*, Milan, Angeli.

Barina, A. et al., *Melusina. Mito e leggenda di una donna serpente*, Rome, Utopia.

Bimbi, F. and Capecchi, V. (eds), *Strutture e strategie della vita quotidiana*, Milan, Angeli.

Bocchetti, A. and Muraro, L., *Vincere cosa, vincere cosa. La nostra questione con il potere. Dialogo* 'Programma 1987', Rome. Edizioni Centro Culturale, Virginia Woolf.

Borrello, G. and Fiorillo, C., *Il pensiero parallelo. Analisi dello stereotipo femminile nella cultura filo sofice e utopica*, Naples, Liguori.

Dalle donne la forza delle donne. Carta itinerante. Idee proposte interrogativi, Document of the Sezione Femminile della Direzione del PCI, Rome.

Del Bo Boffino, A. (ed.), *I nostri anni '70*, Rome, Coop. Libera Stampa.

De Leo, M. (ed.), *Autrici italiane. Catalogo ragionato di libri di narrativa, poesia, saggistica 1945–1985*, Rome, Commissione nazionale per la realizzazione della parità tra uomo e donna.

De Longis, R. (ed.), *La stampa periodica delle donne in Italia, catalogo 1861–1985*, Rome. Commissione nazionale per la realizzazione della parità tra uomo e donna.

Ergas, Y., *Nelle maglie della politica. Femminismo, istituzioni e politiche sociali nell'Italia degli anni '70*, Milan, Angeli.

Gruppo di Lettura La Luna, *Letture di Marguerite Yourcenar*, Turin, Rosenberg & Sellier.

Gruppo di Lettura La Luna, *Letture di Ingeborg Bachmann*, Turin, Rosenberg & Sellier.

Leonardi, G. (ed.), *Scienza, potere, coscienza del limite. Dopo Chernobyl: oltre l'estraneità*, Proceedings of the seminar organized by the Sezione femminile del PCI, held in Rome, 4 July 1986, Rome, Editori Riuniti.

Libreria delle Donne di Firenze and Centro Documentazione Donna Firenze (eds), *Tra nostalgia e trasformazione*, Proceedings of the seminars held in Florence, March/May 1986, Florence.

Melchiorri, P. (ed.), *Verifica d'identità. Materiali, esperienze, riflessioni sul fare cultura tra donne*, Rome, Utopia.

Nava, P., *La fabbrica dell'emancipazione. Le operaie della Manifattura Tabacchi di Modena: storie di vita e di lavoro*, Rome, Utopia.

Patrignani, S. (ed.), *Una donna un secolo*, Rome, Il Ventaglio.

Piazza, M. (ed.), *L'esperienza della vita adulta delle donne*, Milan, CITE, Regione Lombardia.

Sabatini, A. (ed.), *Raccomandazioni per un uso non sessista della lingua*, Rome, Commissione nazionale per la realizzazione della parità tra uomo e donna.

Sono l'unica lesbica al mondo! Ricerca lesbica: realtà, etica e politica dei rapporti tra donne, Proceedings of the conference held in Rome, 1–3 Nov. 1985, Rome.

Tassinato, M., *L'occhio del silenzio (Encomio della lettura)*, Venice, Arsenale.

Vessilli, C. (ed.), *Filosofesse e Papesse. La donna e la narrativa inglese femminile alla fine del Settecento*, Pordenone, Edizioni Studio Tesi.

Violi, P., *L'infinito singolare. Considerazioni sulle differenze sessuali nel linguaggio*, Verona, Essedue.

1987

Associazione Culturale Livia Laverani Donini, *Creare e procreare*, Proceedings of the seminars held in Turin, March–May 1987, Turin.

Beseghi, E. (ed.), *Le bambine tra libri, fumetti e altri media*, Teramo, Giunti e Lisciani.

Bimbi, F. et al., *Il filo di Arianna. Letture della differenza sessuale*, Rome, Utopia.

Camparini, A., *Donna, donne e femminismo. Il dibattito politico internazionale*, Milan, Angeli.

Capomazza, T. and Ombra, M., *8 marzo. Storie miti e riti della giornata internazionale della donna*, Rome, Utopia.

Centro Regionale Documentazione Donne e Diritto, (ed.), *Il servizio militare femminile volontario. Rassegna stampa*, Bologna.

Comerci, M., *La carriera inesistente. I lavori delle donne nelle pubbliche amministrazioni*, Milan, Angeli.

Diotima (Cavarero, A. et al.), *Il pensiero della differenza sessuale*, Milan, La Tartaruga.

Fusini, N., *Nomi. Il suono della vita di Karen Blixen, Emily Dickinson,*

Virginia Woolf, Gertrude Stein, Charlotte e Emily Bronte, Mary Shelley, Marguerite Yourcenar, Milan, Feltrinelli.

Giallongo, A., *Il Galateo e le donne nel Medioevo*, Rimini, Maggioli.

Gruppo di Lettura La Luna, *Letture di Elsa Morante*, Turin, Rosenberg & Sellier.

Irigaray, L. (ed.), 'Sessi e generi linguistici', special issue of *Inchiesta*, 17:77.

Libreria delle Donne di Milano, *Non credere di avere dei diritti*, Turin, Rosenberg & Sellier.

Marcuzzo, C. and Rossi Doria, A., (eds), *La ricerca delle donne*, Proceedings of the Conference on Feminist Studies held in Modena, 1986, Turin, Rosenberg & Sellier.

Mondello, E., *La nuova italiana. La donna nella stampa e nella cultura del ventennio*, Rome, Editori Riuniti.

Pieroni Bortolotti, F., *Sul movimento politico delle donne. Scritti inediti* (ed. A. Buttafuoco), Rome, Utopia.

Rossanda, R. *Anche per me*, Milan, Feltrinelli.

Sabatini, A., *Il sessismo nella lingua italiana*, Rome, Commissione nazionale per la realizzazione della parità tra uomo e donna.

Saraceno, C., *Pluralità e mutamento – Riflessioni sull'identità femminile*, Milan, Angeli.

1988

Alicchio, R. and Pezzoli, C. (eds), *Donne di scienza: esperienze e riflessioni*, Turin, Rosenberg & Sellier.

Archivio della Libreria delle Donne, *Rassegna Stampa. Educazione sessuale*, Milan, Libreria delle Donne.

Boccia, M.J. and Peretti, I. (eds), *Il genere della rappresentanza*, suppl. to no. 1 of *Democrazia e diritto*, Rome.

Buttafuoco, A. and Zancan, M. (eds), *Svelamento. Sibilla Aleramo: Una biografia intellettuale*, Milan, Feltrinelli.

Borghi, L., Livi Bacci, N. and Truder, N. (eds), *Viaggio e scrittura. Le straniere nell'Italia dell'Ottocento*, Florence, Libreria delle Donne.

Covato, C. and Leuzzi, M.C. (eds), *E l'uomo educò la donna*, Rome, Editori Riuniti.

Conti Odorisio, S. (ed.), *Gli studi sulle donne nelle Università: ricerca e trasformazione del sapere*, Proceedings of the First International Conference on Women's Studies in Italian Universities held in Rome, Dec. 1986, Rome, Edizioni Scientifiche Italiane.

Crisafulli Jones, L.M. and Fortunati, V. (eds), *Ritratto dell'artista come donna. Saggi sull'avanguardia del novecento*, Urbino, Quattroventi.

Cutrufelli, M. (ed.), *Scritture, scrittrici*, Milan, Longanesi.

Crispin, M.A. (ed.), *Esperienza storica femminile nell'età moderna e contemporanea*, vol. 1, Rome, UDI–Circolo 'La Goccia'.

Ferrante, L., Palazzi, M. and Pomata, G. (eds), *Ragnatele di rapporti. Patronage e reti di relazioni tra donne*, Proceedings of the conference organized by the Centro di Documentazione, Ricerca e Iniziativa delle Donne, held in Bologna, Nov. 1986, Turin, Rosenberg & Sellier.

Associazione Orlando, *Generare, trasmettere cultura delle donne. Progetto e programma dell'Associazione 'Orlando'*, Centro di Documentazione, Ricerca, Iniziativa delle Donne di Bologna.

Gruppo di Lettura La Luna, *Letture di Christa Wolf*, Turin, Rosenberg & Sellier.

Ipazia, *Quattro giovedì e un venerdì per la filosofia*, Milan, Libreria delle Donne.

Lanzarini, L., *Il linguaggio sessista*, Milan, Gruppo per la Promozione della Donna.

Le donne al centro. Politica e cultura dei Centri delle donne negli anni '80, Proceedings of the First National Conference of Women's Centres held in Siena, Sept. 1986, Rome, Utopia.

Centro Documentazione Studi sul Femminismo, *Le donne dell donne dicono. Il femminismo attraverso la stampa delle donne*, Rome, Centro Documentazione Studi sul Femminismo.

Marotta, G. (ed.), *La criminalità femminile in Italia*, Rome. Commissione nazionale per la realizzazione della parità tra uomo e donna.

Melandri, L., *Come nasce il sogno d'amore*, Milan, Rizzoli.

Passerini, L., *Autoritratto di gruppo*, Florence, Giunti.

Piazza, R., *Adamo Eva e il serpente*, Palermo, La Luna.

Vivere e pensare la differenza, Proceedings of the seminar held in Florence, 23–4 Jan. 1988, Florence, Centro Documentazione Donna.

1989

Archivio della Libreria delle Donne, *Rassegna Stampa. A proposito dell'aborto (1971–1989)*, Milan, Libreria delle Donne.

Archivio della Libreria delle Donne, *Rassegna Stampa. Lavoro-Sindacato*, Milan, Libreria delle Donne.

Artom, S. and Calabro, A.R. *Sorelle d'Italia*, Milan, Rizzoli.

Associazione Cultural Livia Laverani Donini, *Donne e trascendenza*, Proceedings of the seminars held in Turin, Feb.–May 1988, Turin.

Associazione Culturale Melusine, *Vivere e pensare la relazione madre–figlia*, Proceedings of the seminar held in Milan, April 1989, Milan.

Bocchetti, A., *Fare leva*, 'Programma 1989, Gruppo B', Rome, Edizioni Centro Culturale, Virginia Woolf.

Centro Problemi Donna, *Presenze. Giorni – attività, incontri, richerche*, Milan, Ediwoman.

Centro Simonetta Tosi, *Donna e salute*, Proceedings of the seminar held in Rome, 15 May 1989, Rome.

Che cosa vuol dire la libertà femminile, Proceedings of the conference held in Rome, 10–11 June 1989, Rome, Edizioni Centro Culturale Virginia Woolf.

Centro Culturale Mara Meoni, *Con voce di donna: pensiero, linguaggio, comunicazione*, Siena, Centro Culturale Mara Meoni.

Cotti, C. and Molfino, F. (eds), *L'apprendimento dell'incertezza*, Rome, Edizioni Centro Culturale Virginia Woolf.

Da desiderio a desiderio. Donne, sessualità, progettualità lesbica, Proceedings of the conference held at L'Impruneta, Florence, 5–7 Dec. 1987, Florence, L'Amandorla.

Del Bo Boffino, A. (ed.), *Donne e scienza*, Milan, Guerini Studio.

Cruppo per la promozione della Donna, *Donna e sacerdozio ministeriale: contributo alla riflessione*, Milan, Gruppo per la Promozione della Donna.

Calciati, G. et al., *Donne a Gerusalemme. Dialoghi tra italiane, palestinesi e israeliane*, Turin, Rosenberg & Sellier.

Calciati, G. et al., '(donne genere differenza)', special issue of *Passaggi*, 3:1.

Calciati G. et al., '(donne lògos ekklesia)', special issue of *Passaggi*, 3:2.

Crispino, A.M. (ed.), *Esperienza storica femminile nell'età moderna e contemporanea*, vol. 2, Rome, UDI–Circolo 'La Goccia'.

Fusco, M. and Piano, M.G. (eds), *Femminile plurale: relazioni e saperi per una scuola 'differente'*, Proceedings of the conference held in Cagliari, 1–4 March 1989, Cagliari IFOLD.

Giacobazzi D. et al., *I percorsi del cambiamento. Ricerca sui comportamenti contraccettivi in Emilia Romagna*, Turin, Rosenberg & Sellier.

Giani Gallino, T. (ed.), *Le Grandi Madri*, Milan, Feltrinelli.

Giorgi, S. and Tatafiore, R., *Le nuove amanti*, Como, Lyra.

Guadagnin, L. and Pasquon, V., *Parola, mater-materia*, Venice, Arsenale.

Guiducci, A., *Perdute nella storia. Storia delle donne dal I al VII secolo d.C.*, Florence, Sansoni.

Le donne ridono. Disegnatrici satiriche italiane, Ferrara, Leggere Donna.

Magli, I., *La sessualità maschile*, Milan, Mondadori.

Mazzucco, C., *'E fui fatta uomo', La donna nel Cristianesimo primitivo*, Florence, Le Lettere.

Merlin, L., *La mia vita* (ed. E. Marinucci), Florence, Giunti.

Perrotta Rabissi, A. and Perucci, M.B. (eds), *Perleparole. Le iniziative a favore dell'informazione e della documentazione delle donne europee*, Rome, Utopia.

Piussi, A. (ed.), *Educare nella differenza*, Milan, Rosenberg & Sellier.

Quintavalle, E. and Raimondi, E. (eds), *Aborto, perché?*, Milan, Feltrinelli.

Ricci, C. et al., *Se a parlare di Maria sono le donne*, Milan, Cooperativa In Dialogo.

Russo, V. (ed.), *Lo specchio infantro. Territori della differenza*, Florence, Istituto Gramsci Toscano.

Xodo Cegolon, C., *Lo specchio di Margherita*, Padua, Cleup.

1990

Boccia, M.L., *L'io in rivolta. Vissuto e pensiero di Carla Lonzi*, Milan, La Tartaruga.

Del Bo Boffino, A. (ed.), *Donne e pensiero*, Milan, Guerini Studio.

Diotima (Assolini, P. et al.), *Mettere al mondo il mondo. Oggetto e oggettività alla luce della differenza sessuale*, Milan, La Tartaruga.

Disagio, solitudine, pensiero della differenza, Proceedings of the seminar organized by the UDI group 'Differenza Maternità, held in April 1989, Ferrara, Rome, Cooperativa Libera Stampa.

'Donna-differenza', special issue of *Scuola notizie*, 2/3.

Filosofare. Interventi dal corso 'L'immagine del femminile in alcuni momenti del pensiero filosofico' tenuto da Rosella Pezzo, Milan, Università delle Donne.

Fusini, N., *La luminosa. Genealogia di Fedra*, Milan, Feltrinelli.

Longobardi, G. et al., *Simone Weil. La provocazione della verità*, (with an introduction by Gabriella Fiori), Naples, Liguori.

Minarelli, M.L., *Donne di denari*, Milan, Olivares.

Tatafiore, R. (ed.), *A prova di donna. Interviste sulla svolta del PCI*, Rome, Cooperativa Libera Stampa.

Index